GROWING UP UNDER THE MANGO TREE

Growing Up
Under the
Mango
Tree

LILY FORBES

SilverWood

Published in 2014 by SilverWood Books

SilverWood Books
30 Queen Charlotte Street, Bristol, BS1 4HJ
www.silverwoodbooks.co.uk

ISBN 978-1-78132-227-7 (paperback)
ISBN 978-1-78132-238-3 (hardback)
ISBN 978-1-78132-228-4 (ebook)

British Library Cataloguing in Publication Data
A CIP catalogue record for this book is available from the British Library

Set in Sabon by SilverWood Books
Printed on responsibly sourced paper

To my beloved parents, who had very little themselves, but provided me with their love and inspiration, throughout my growing years and beyond.

Introduction

The book is centred on the early part of my life, based largely in Malaysia but partly in India, before I left for England at the age of twenty-two. I was born into a life without electricity or running water.

Malaya during British rule had a population mix of Malay, Chinese and Indians with a mixture of cultures and religions. I was one of nine children raised in some poverty, growing up in a rural village, and a suburb of Kuala Lumpur. My mother's talents as a seamstress supplemented my Dad's wages as a railway worker. The grounds surrounding the house provided essential fruit and vegetables. Houses were mainly built of wood. Wells provided water. One thing we did not go short of was warmth; there was no need to worry about paying bills for central heating with an average daily temperature above thirty degrees. Warmth was created too in the form of a loving family.

I was the first in my family to fly the nest, to live away from the continent of Asia and experience a completely new way of life. I left Malaysia to come to England to obtain a qualification in nursing with the full intention of returning, but I met my future husband, broke from the Indian tradition of marrying within the caste, and in the process made it easier for the next generation to follow their hearts. We are now a multi-ethnic and multi-national family, embracing Americans, Australians and Europeans.

The life of the children in my family living in Malaysia today bears little resemblance to my life and the conditions of my formative years. One of the main reasons for writing this book is to show this and future generations a glimpse into the way their roots were formed.

For all my descendants, both the current generation and those of the future, I would like to think that there is something in this book that will appeal to you. To anyone else reading this book with whom I have no connection, I would like to share with you my experience of being born into a country that was war-torn by occupying Japanese forces during the Second World War and subsequently reclaimed by the British as part of their Empire. But Britain's influence and power was then on the wane as Malaya worked towards gaining full independence, achieving this in August 1957. Six years later what is now known as Malaysia was formed with Singapore (for a period between 1963-1965), Sarawak and Sabah. As I am learning to deal with life's challenges, so too is Malaysia, a young and independent country that is still learning to make its own decisions after so many years of British rule.

1

'Cheese sandwiches and dancing clowns...'

My First Journey

My conscious life sprang into being amid belching smoke, sticky bodies and ethnic diversity. Considering where my future was to take me, it seems quite a coincidence that my earliest memories involve travel – and an Englishman.

We hurried through the portals of Kuala Lumpur's main railway station, with Dad's dry, calloused right hand enclosing my moist left one in a firm grip. The tropical heat was rank with the odour of the steam chugged out by the giant metal engines, which showered grey particles and a cloying grease over the heaving crowds. I craned my neck awkwardly as I scuttled along, gazing in awe at this ornate palace with its high, horseshoe-shaped arches and tall, cylindrical pillars encircled by a series of smaller arches, all topped with domed pavilions. The bright white building dazzled my eyes and I shaded them against the strong reflected sunlight with my free hand. Behind my small fingers, my eyes were the size of saucers, hardly able to take in all of this grandeur.

The chubby Indian ticket collector doffed his hat at Dad, acknowledging a fellow worker, then winked at me and waved us on towards the platforms. The high, galvanised ceiling thundered with the echo of a thousand footsteps: heavy, light, casual, and frenzied. Wheels appeared in every direction and laden trolleys loomed over me. The air was being torn apart by the vibrations of noise.

Our train trundled into the station, the high-pitched screech of its wheels vying with the guard's insistent whistle and the raucous clamour of the crowds, as some alighted from the train whilst others pushed forward eagerly to claim the freshly vacated seats. The enormous green and black engine crouched at the head of the carriages, panting heavily as it took advantage of a short rest. Meanwhile I dodged swinging suitcases, heavily laden baskets and grown-up feet as Dad swung me up on to the steps of the coach.

Our destination was Gemas: a small town situated between Kuala Lumpur and Malaya's southernmost town of Johor Baru. Dad paid no train fare, while mine was heavily discounted – a perk for railway employees. Our journey of around 100 miles would take us almost a full day to complete.

The steam locomotive jolted forwards then slowly chugged into life, gathering pace as it pulled out of the station, groaning under the weight of the carriages. Couplings clanged into place. My chest tightened – we were off!

My curious gaze scanned our carriage, which held a hotchpotch of different nationalities – Chinese, Indian and Malay – all of whom scurried to seat themselves in family groups, brushing past each other unceremoniously as they negotiated the narrow corridor between the double rows of faded chocolate brown seats. Each of these could hold two adults side by side, or a mother and two little ones. Clutching the back of my Dad's trousers, I was squashed against the five-feet-eleven-inch frame of this lean, handsome man with sharp, bright eyes, as he beat us a safe path to an empty row. His right hand still gripped one of mine, whilst his left was swinging a bulging green cloth bag and a battered suitcase that knocked dully together.

The discomfort of the wooden seats, minimally padded and covered in cracked vinyl, barely registered with four-year-old me, but the adults were constantly changing their positions, shifting weight from one cheek to the other. Opposite us, a well-endowed Indian lady fanned herself briskly with the end of her scarlet and gold *sari*, the rolls of flesh between her *sari* waist and her blouse glistening with sweat. Her spindly husband, squashed against the side of the train in quiet resignation, stared straight ahead, mopping his brow at regular intervals with a handkerchief.

But it was the other, less familiar passengers who caught my curious eye: for example the bronze-skinned Malays, several shades lighter in colour than the Indians but possessing a smidgen of the flatness of feature of the even paler-skinned Chinese. I'd met few Malays up until now, and here they were surrounding me, vibrant in colourful outfits. The men sported conical hats at jaunty angles on their heads, whilst the women wore elaborately embroidered see-through cotton blouses with golden filigree brooches attached to a thin gold chain that hooked under every individual clasp to secure their buttonholes. The brooches flashed brightly in the slanting sun. Multi-coloured batik *sarongs* swung around their ankles. My eyes scanned my own pale pink, knee-length cotton dress, which stood out as plain and homely in contrast.

Further up the carriage, a group of Chinese ladies fluttered their hand-painted bamboo fans like frantic butterflies. Only the children seemed oblivious to the humidity. Two rows away, I spied a couple of Chinese boys threading rubber bands through their fingers, creating intricate star shapes. I stared and smiled in appreciation; but, annoyed at their privacy being invaded, the boys poked their pink tongues out at me simultaneously. Hurt and humiliated, I turned away – only to catch the eye of a most unusual-looking man who was sitting diagonally opposite me. His eyes twinkled and deep dimples appeared on both his cheeks as he gave a smile that instantly captivated me. I caught my breath and looked away momentarily in shyness, only to be irresistibly drawn back to his strange features. An overwhelming urge grew within me to touch his shiny pink cheeks and peer into those bright blue eyes more closely. How handsome he was! His hair and eyelashes were the colour of the Malay ladies' glittering brooches. Was he magic? I could hear the thud of my heart as my breath quickened and I squirmed in my seat.

Sensing my excitable state, Dad looked up from his newspaper and responded to the stranger's friendly smile with a nod and a wave of his forefinger.

'So, Lily, you are seeing an English uncle for the first time, eh? He does look like a nice man, doesn't he?' Dad smiled. Turning over the page he resumed reading his paper.

I nestled up to his warm, safe bulk, my sandaled feet kicking air, but my eyes were drawn back. The English uncle started a game of peek-a-boo, keeping me transfixed and giggling for some time. I noticed the Chinese boys staring and pointedly ignored them. My tiny stature swelled with importance as only I had been singled out for the attentions of this fascinating man.

Gusts of grey smoke blew in through the open windows as the train negotiated the bends on the tracks. A fine film of black dust settled over us, clinging to our sweaty skins. I relaxed and leaned back against the seat, lulled by the rhythmic melody of the train as it clattered over the jointed metal tracks, echoing like a song going round and round in my head. *Ta-ta-ta-tan, ta-ta-ta-tan, ta-ta-ta-tan.*

The scene on the outside changed constantly. One moment identical rows of rubber trees stood sentinel in vast plantations, the next minute wide expanses of lush vegetation rushed past. Birds, who were feasting on berries, rose simultaneously in rainbow-coloured flocks from the forest's canopy, as though pursued.

Mothers walked along dirt tracks, bent forward as they carried babies in lengths of cotton slung hammock-like over their shoulders.

Schoolchildren danced at their sides, grinning widely and waving joyfully at the toot-tooting train. Spindly legs ran alongside, trying in vain to keep up with the speed of the carriages. A few enjoyed pillion rides on their fathers' bicycles, weaving about amongst dusty cars and lorries. All waited patiently at the level crossings for the train to go past.

The snaking rails periodically allowed the hot sun to stream mercilessly into the carriage, forcing me to push myself back into the seat's recess, pushing my arms behind me to shield them. The light shimmered on both the ladies' oiled, coiled and ornamented hair and the men's sleek, brilliantined and parted styles.

About halfway through the journey, Dad lowered his paper.

'Are you hungry, *ma*? *Ammah* has packed us some *meehoon*.'

Nodding eagerly, I sat up in anticipation. The pangs of hunger having been fanned, everyone else seemed to bring out their lunches almost in unison. Some dismantled light blue enamel tiffin carriers, others unravelled brown paper packages lined with banana leaves, from which wonderful smells leaked out, making my mouth water. Many of our fellow passengers tucked into *nasi lemak*, rice cooked in coconut milk accompanied by a rich, chilli-hot sambal made with dried anchovies, crunchy fried peanuts and cooling slices of cucumber. Dad's long fingers delved into our green cloth bag and retrieved some newspaper-wrapped packages. He and I set to work on our slender, stir-fried rice noodles, flattened into brown rectangles, glistening with soy sauce. Strips of greens and crunchy bean sprouts worked into the mass on the banana leaf. Satisfied slurps and burps soon echoed round the carriage.

My mouth full of my Mum's savoury noodles, I watched with undisguised curiosity as the English uncle brought out his own parcel. Mopping tiny beads of sweat off his brow, he tucked into a mysterious, flat, white and yellow object with obvious relish, washing it down with some fizzy liquid from a brown glass bottle. Not until a few years later, when Dad brought home some cheese sandwiches from his English friend's house, was the nature of this mysterious food revealed to me – and it was many more years before I was introduced to a bottle of beer.

We finished off our lunch with a hard-boiled egg each. The swing table between our seat and that of our fellow passengers opposite was strewn with their lunch, forcing Dad to clamp the Thermos flask between his knees, hand me the aluminium lid and then unscrew the stopper. He half-filled our enamel cup with some of the flask's contents – sweetened tea made with condensed milk – and offered it to me, then poured his own portion into the aluminium lid. I followed his lead, blowing on the surface of the tea to cool it down before attempting to sip it.

After lunch, I fell into a satisfied doze, and it seemed no time at all before Dad was gently shaking my shoulder and whispering in my ear.

'Lily, wake up, *ma*. We are here. Come, we don't have far to walk.'

Gemas was predominantly a railway town, a meeting place of trains running from west to east and back again. It was also home to my mother's younger sister, Arul. Her husband also worked for the railways.

We got down from the train and made our way out of the small station past row upon row of milky-tea-coloured wooden houses on stilts, each joined to the one next to it. I found myself half-running as my short legs tried to match Dad's large strides, my head dizzy with the anticipation of meeting relatives I had no recollection of and in whose company I was to spend the next twenty-four hours.

Dad found the right house. Wooden steps led up to its veranda where, as we drew closer, I spied a slim, fair-skinned lady clad in a green-flowered cotton *sari*, which billowed out in the slight breeze. Her broad smile of recognition as we approached confirmed that this was my Aunty Arul. Three younger faces peered wide-eyed through the veranda railings: my cousins.

My sandals clattered up the wooden steps, closely followed by Dad's clumping strides. My beautiful aunty stretched out her hands in greeting; ready to pull me up the last step as she welcomed us, as was customary among Tamil Indians in Malaya, in a mixture of Tamil and English.

'*Vaanga, vaanga*, come, come inside. Eh, Lily *ma*, you have grown since I last saw you.' She patted my hot head affectionately and chuckled. I spied two gold teeth, set one on either side of her grinning mouth, glinting as they caught the evening sunshine.

We trooped into a large, square, cream-coloured sitting room, and settled into rattan chairs circled around a low, glass-topped rattan table. Aunty Arul's chatter trailed behind her as she disappeared for a few minutes whilst I took in my surroundings.

Hanging from the wooden picture-rail behind us, a black and white photograph of my aunt's wedding hung next to another faded old photograph of what could only be my grandparents. I twisted around in my seat and gazed at it. There was my now-deceased *sari*-clad *ammachi*, looking so young and fair, sitting stiffly on a stool. My stern, dark-skinned grandfather stood bolt upright behind her. There was no sign of a hand on her shoulder to soften the picture's formality.

Aunty Arul's tinkling chatter preceded her as she reappeared, balancing on a tray, glasses of fizzy orange drinks. When prompted, I picked one up and watched the bubbles travel upwards to the surface, where they exploded in little pops that landed on my eyes, making them smart, and tickled my nostrils, causing me to sneeze. Taking small sips to prolong the strange experience, I giggled as the tangy bubbles burst on my tongue.

Every time Aunty Arul opened her mouth, a chuckle escaped. I soon relaxed in her vivacious presence – although it took me a little longer to warm to her husband, a serious man of few words, who nodded at me gravely in greeting. I turned my gaze again to the photographs whilst Dad enjoyed bantering with my aunt, who threw her head back in mock exasperation.

'*Aiyyeo*, don't tease me, *atthaan*, you are a very naughty man!'

I searched for my cousins. The two older boys had disappeared, but four-year-old Alphonsia sat dutifully on a nearby rattan chair, no doubt as curious about me as I was about her. The boys had taken their colouring from Aunty Arul, but Alphonsia was as dark as her father, her ebony face and neck bathed in white talcum powder. She was slightly plumper than me and immaculately dressed in a pink flowered dress. She cast me shy sideways glances as I watched her play with her hair, two looped pigtails secured with pink satin ribbons.

Aunty stood up and beckoned to Dad and me.

'Come, I will show you round the house.'

An open doorway to the right revealed a large bedroom running the length of the sitting room, where a double bed and three singles, draped in blue and white striped bed-sheets, stood. A comforter lay across each bed, all of them encased in matching covers.

Behind the lounge, a few steps led down to the dining area. Beyond that and running across the width of the house stood the kitchen, a bathroom and an adjacent toilet – run on a bucket system, of course. In an open courtyard, to the right of the dining area, a light breeze caught the washing line running diagonally from one corner of the courtyard to the other as it casually swung to and fro. Wooden pegs like little soldiers were dotted across its length. Outside the bathroom stood a standpipe, underneath which an aluminium bucket was heaped with wrung-out washing, waiting to be pegged out. The boys raised excited squeals as they skidded bright marbles across the cement floor under the overhead washing line.

It was getting late. My aunt switched on the light as we descended into the dining area, then led me into the bathroom. An indoor bathroom! I marvelled to see clear water rushing out from a tiny spout, quickly filling up the aluminium bucket placed underneath it.

My aunt washed me, and then dusted me liberally with sweet-smelling talcum powder, making me sneeze. She passed a fresh dress over my head and I wriggled my hands into the armholes. She chatted non-stop all the while, telling me how happy she was that we had come to visit, and asking after my siblings.

'How is your *annan* Peter? He must be so grown-up now. And your *akkas*? I am sure all you girls are such a help to your mother.'

All the while wonderful smells drifted across from the kitchen a few feet away and my empty stomach growled with impatience, eager to be filled with the sumptuous treats that the aromas promised. A cool night breeze was welcome after our hot, dusty journey. Freshly washed and smelling sweet, we all sat around the wooden dining table, now groaning under its heavy burden of food. My hospitable aunt had done us proud.

A bare light bulb on a length of flex swung from the wooden rafters of the ceiling, casting a saffron mantle of light over our feast. A large blue enamel dish held a huge mound of meat, coated in a rich, thick sauce and strewn liberally with fresh pungent coriander leaves. There were two vegetable dishes, plus a big bowl of fish curry and a mountain of rice – far more food than we could comfortably eat. Aunty Arul filled our plates generously.

'Come, come eat up, there is plenty more, don't feel shy!'

I tucked into my food, savouring every tasty mouthful. The fiery spices in the curry made me gasp with pleasure. Lengths of Chinese *kangkong* greens, swirled in thick coconut milk, helped to cool my mouth, while crunchy long beans topped with strips of deep-fried bean curds cut through the thick sauce. Freshly cut slices of honeyed mangoes and sugary- sweet pink watermelon finished off the meal, the fruits' juices dripping down the sides of my mouth. I licked my sticky lips again and again, sated and happy.

After our meal, the two boys invited me to play with them on the veranda, leaving the adults to chat about grown-up matters. Nine-year-old Felix and Chandra, two years his junior, were very friendly and happy to greet me, their 'little sister'.

Felix smiled and held out his hand to me.

'Come Lily. We have a top.'

'A top of what?' I responded, innocently. The boys chuckled.

'Come on. We'll show you what to do with it.'

My eyes widened as they brought out a metal spinning top. I studied the colourful clowns painted on its surface and then, when Felix pressed down the toy's lever, watched in amazement as the spinning top blurred the clowns into a merrily skipping row, up and down, up and down.

Attracted by the noise, a pair of big black eyes peeked around the corner. Slowly, the rest of Alfonsia appeared. Shy at first, but not wanting to be left out of the fun, she eventually scuttled over to join in our play.

That simple game was the start of a close friendship between my cousins and me. Indeed, I keep a warm place in my heart for everything that took place on that day: my first awareness of life, filled with fun, laughter and plenty of delicious food.

2

'A ripe mango falls...'

Home Birth

I grew up in the very middle of a family of nine children, with four siblings above me in the ranks of age, and four below. We were the Anthonysamy clan, taking our surname from the first name of our father, as was the custom in Tamil Nadu, India, where our ancestors were born. Our home was in Sentul, a small village founded in 1880 based six kilometres north-west of Malaya's capital city, Kuala Lumpur – or KL, as the locals habitually termed it. When I was growing up, Sentul's own local nickname was 'Little India', in recognition of the ethnic origins of the majority of its inhabitants – including us.

My mother gave birth to me in 1946, the same year that the British-owned territories in which we lived were first unified as the Malayan Union. Like most of my siblings, I was born at home. But the risks of home births were very real; a fact that was brought home to me one evening during one of our customary family discussions.

The evening started in its usual fashion, with a prayer to the Almighty God who presided unchallenged over our Catholic family home and our table: 'Bless us, O Lord, and these Thy gifts, which we are about to receive from Thy bounty, through Christ our Lord. Amen.'

Dad's voice was deep and solemn, his head bowed in humble veneration. Freshly washed, he wore a white, sleeveless cotton singlet, which had a few small holes at the neckline from vigorous and frequent laundering. His slight belly drooped over a bunched-up blue-and-white-chequered *sarong*, tied at his waist. In the middle of his forehead the lime green tattooed circle from childhood creased in concentration.

'Amen.' We crossed ourselves.

Three-year-old Charlie repeated his 'Amen' a little late; his face just peeked above the table top, revealing eyes that had already started to glaze over with the promise of sleep. At the excitable age of five-and-a-half, I was still wide-awake, swinging my legs vigorously back and forth below the sturdy old wooden table. Our adored Mum and Dad sat in straight-backed, armless chairs, while we youngsters perched on high wooden stools. Our faces were bathed in the flickering light cast from above by a kerosene oil lamp, which hung from a hook fixed in a weight-bearing beam.

Night had fallen with its habitual swiftness by six o'clock, as if a window blind was being pulled steadily downwards against the sky. Now, at seven, our doors and windows were firmly shut and latched for security. The nightly serenade provided by the frogs in the back yard was reassuring in its familiarity; their united chorus echoed the cohesiveness of our family gathering.

Our eldest sister, Theresa, modestly dressed in her simply embroidered cotton blouse and long skirt gathered at the waist, passed the dishes around the table. Olive-skinned and oval-faced, she had the eternal patience of a natural mother. I had never known her to lose her temper with us younger children; she saved her taunts for her nearest sibling, Peter. But I knew her to weep for others, quietly. Sensitive to smells, she drew our teasing guffaws every time her nose quivered, retching when she passed animal dung by the roadside. Meticulous in her actions, she helped to keep our house immaculately clean.

As the hard-working man of the house, Dad was used to being waited on. Here our third sibling, dutiful Anna, rose to the occasion. Slightly darker than Theresa, with a gentle face and long, wavy hair, centre-parted and caught in two plaits, she was a balanced young soul, existing quietly in the shadow of her older sister until she learned to exert herself in her late teens.

Although officially the second man of the house, our brother Peter was still considered young enough to help himself, and he did so with confident decorum. Rosie, the undisputed family beauty, with her rosebud lips and light colouring descended from my maternal *ammachi*, claimed the chair next to her favoured brother Peter.

In the background was a gentle squeaking sound as baby Chandra, our most recent family member, dozed peacefully, swinging to and fro in his makeshift cradle as he moved in his sleep. The cradle consisted of a *sarong*, hung on an S-hook, which was then attached to a large spring on the doorway of the nearby bedroom.

Our meal that night was a fish-head curry, boiled rice, fried baby fish and long beans glistening in a coat of thick coconut cream. The fish, ikan *tenggiri*, was a type of mackerel full of fresh flavour; Mum had bargained for it at the market just that morning. A third of the fish was reserved for Dad and Peter, whilst we shared the remainder between the rest of us.

I tucked into my portion eagerly; the fingers of my right hand deftly massaging the flakes of pale fish flesh apart, then scooping them up with soft grains of rice and the green beans, all soaked with plenty of the fiery curry sauce. Not a drop was wasted as we happily poured the thick gravy, swimming with ladies' fingers (okra) and baby aubergines, onto our small heaps of rice. The baby fish were a particular treat: slashed and rubbed with pounded onion, chilli and turmeric powder and seasoned with salt, they had been fried whole, bones and all, to a state of sumptuous crispness. Crunching and slurping noises echoed around the table, with a few loud burps of appreciation. Our plates were swiped clean and fingers licked. The hot air, heavy with humidity, infused every nook and cranny and because it would spoil any leftovers by morning, every morsel of food was scraped and shared.

The fish head was reserved for Mum, who loved to suck every last bit of flesh, setting aside her favourite two parts to savour at the very end of her meal. I watched, half-intrigued, half-repulsed, as she popped the fish's eyes into her mouth, sucked on the glutinous jelly surrounds and spat out the hard, black, beady eyeballs on to her empty plate.

'Eeeh! *Ammah*, I don't know how you can eat those.'

Mum's curry-smeared mouth widened into an affectionate smile.

'That is where all the taste is, silly girl. Nearly as good as eating turtle meat.'

I wrinkled my nose in disgust. Our dining table had yet to be graced with Mum's childhood favourite meat. A teenage boy, Raju, who lived two doors away from us, nurtured a pet baby turtle and I had stroked its hard shell during its stroll on the grass when it had been nudged out from its wooden box. My body jerked in revulsion as I pictured blood dripping from the pet's flesh, its shell ripped away, its eyes bulging. Hastily I leapt down from the table to wash my hands, flicking away such disturbing visions along with the excess water. Theresa, Anna, Rosie and I scuttled back and forth to clear the table and wash the dishes, anxious to return to the table for our traditional family story-time.

This was always my favourite part of the evening on a Saturday, when everyone could relax and spend a couple of precious hours together. Our busy, tired bodies could relax and digest our delicious meal in peace, whilst we kept our minds occupied with family anecdotes and lectures from our father.

'Well,' began Dad, in his deep, strong and steady voice.

I instantly rocked forwards on my wooden stool, elbows leaning on the table and hands cupping my face, ready to be entertained. My right hand had absorbed the meal's spices and emitted a soporific perfume that I continued to sniff despite my full tummy. Dad raised his eyes to the ceiling in search of his memories, rubbing the edge of his shaven chin with his fingers.

'The early 1940s were difficult times in Malaya, thanks to the war. Things really only started to get better in 1946, the year you were born, Lily, once the *Japaan* fellows were chased out the year before.'

He nodded at me and I beamed eagerly. I wasn't entirely sure who these *Japaan* fellows were, but I was glad that they hadn't been around when I was born. Our politically astute father was keen to make us all aware of history and its influence on our lives from a young age.

Dad straightened and gripped the arms of his chair, gaining the righteous pose of a teacher facing his eager pupils. He continued with his tale.

'And the British had finally done the decent thing and started to grant us Indians citizenship after the war, even though the Malays weren't happy with that. Some of them still look upon us as immigrants. I ask you, after all these years!'

Dad's face lengthened in disappointment. I couldn't quite follow the politics, but felt my sympathy rise in line with my beloved *appa*'s indignation. Dad was very forthright in his opinions, with a slight inclination to boast that was warm-heartedly received by us and never questioned. We were all in awe of him: what he said was law, and none of us would ever question his word. He always maintained the positive attitude that everyone had the capacity to be brave, and that there was no barrier that couldn't be surmounted. He often became animated as he addressed us, deep brown eyes flashing as a fisted hand came down hard on the wooden table to emphasise a particular point.

Peter rocked forwards eagerly, so that the back legs of his stool lifted off the cement floor, as his mind took off on a philosophical tangent that was characteristic of my eldest brother.

'Just think, Lily: you were born thousands of miles from Britain, but it had already influenced your life so much! None of us would have been born here if the British hadn't encouraged the Indians to come and work in their colonies.'

'But in 1945,' Dad continued, gently drawing the storyline back, 'it was very difficult for everybody. During the war there was rationing, and after the war there was still a real shortage of food. Poverty everywhere. Do you remember, Marie,' he turned to Mum, 'how your father had changed his money into Japanese paper money? It was useless when the *Japaan* fellows left, only good for a bonfire.'

Peter sat upright again on his stool; his intelligent eyes were alight with compassion.

'Poor *thaatha*, what a way to lose his money.'

Dad nodded, approving of and encouraging his eldest son, but I fidgeted, becoming bored, not interested in the political situations that seemed to excite my older siblings; I wanted to learn more about my family. It seemed that Anna felt the same, as she piped up tentatively with a more personal question.

'Is that why we moved from *thaatha's* house, *ammah*?'

It was no secret that my elder siblings had been sorry to leave their first home: a large wooden house in Sentul Pasar owned by my mother's family, which had housed not only my maternal grandparents, but also my parents, six of my Mum's siblings – our uncles (*Maamas*) and aunts *Aathais*) – and the ever-growing gaggle of third generation grandchildren. The rambling house was set in a four-acre estate, which teemed with a variety of tropical fruit trees: mangoes, papayas, rambutans, bananas, guavas, durians, jackfruit and groves of leafy coconut palms, all thriving in the lush, humid climate. My retired grandfather cultivated a very productive kitchen garden, where he contentedly whiled away his time tending to his vegetables to cater for his expanding family – and, during the war, to provide enforced supplies to the Japanese camps.

I knew the house well and loved my visits there, playing in the extensive gardens with my many cousins. I turned to Mum, curious to hear her response – what *had* convinced my parents to exchange the freedom and space of our grandparents' estate for a single, cramped room in a shared, rented house?

'It wasn't about money,' Mum said, hesitantly. She paused to exchange a glance with my now-silent Dad, and then continued.

'While your *ammachi* was alive, everything was fine, but after she died, things changed.' A sigh escaped. 'My dear *ammah* was so beautiful, very fair. Not like your *karrapu thaatha*.' Mum shook her head again and tutted. 'She was too young to die. Nothing was the same after she died.'

Ordinarily, I would have giggled at Mum's irreverent description of my 'black Grandfather', but her reddening eyes, filled with unshed tears, held me still as I watched the familiar, faraway look flit across her serene face as she remembered her beloved mother.

I missed not having known my Grandma, who had been such a strong influence in my mother's life, and often wondered how she would have treated me. Would she have gathered me to her side and made a fuss of me, or passed by with a nod and a smile, absentmindedly acknowledging the troublesome presence of yet another grandchild? But she had died two years before my birth and I remained none the wiser. She had developed diabetes after the birth of her thirteenth child. An injury on her big toe had refused to heal and turned gangrenous. The fingers of fungation spiralling up her leg at an alarming rate reduced her and her family to utter despair. She succumbed at the age of fifty, and her death had affected Mum deeply.

'We all knew she was in pain, but she tried to hide it from us.'

Tears were welling up in my eyes in sympathy, as Mum continued.

'*Ammah* had always kept the peace between all of us, but when she was gone everybody decided they wanted to be the head of the house and they all began to quarrel. I think they missed her too. Then, one night after dinner, the men started quarrelling, and… well, you all know your *appa's* temper.'

When she turned to my Dad she smiled gently, half in affection, half in pain, but loyally defending his actions.

'Your *appa* got very angry with all of them. He was the one who went to fight in the war, and it was his war rations that helped feed the rest of the family.'

Peter's eyes sparkled wickedly, sensing an opportunity to tease his elder sister.

'Remember how *akka* was conned every time, to give away our food? Our *maamas* knew they couldn't get the better of me, so they tried their cajoling tactics on softie *akka*.'

Theresa squirmed under Peter's gaze. 'You are too hard, you. We had plenty, why couldn't we share what we had?'

'I caught Uncle Xavier hiding near the window,' continued Peter, mercilessly. 'He had passed a big spoon to *akka* and stupid *akka* had filled it with margarine. She was handing the spoon back to *maama* when I came into the room. I shouted at him, "You thief, you are stealing our rations!"' Peter chuckled throatily. 'Uncle Xavier has never forgiven me for exposing him.'

'There you go, you see, you will never make any friends if you don't share what you have.'

'You big softie, you don't know when people are taking advantage of you, that is your problem.'

'Hey, enough, you two, stop quarrelling. You are not setting a good example to the youngsters,' interrupted our mother.

'But *ammah*, just think how funny it was. Uncle must have been waiting ages for *akka* to be alone before he dared show his face at the window!' Peter continued.

Laughter bubbled around our table, and even Theresa's scowl

melted into a reluctant giggle as we all imagined our teenage uncle creeping round the outside of the house, waiting in the shadows for the coast to clear before embarking on conning his young niece. The tension in the room eased with our laughter. Dad fanned away an insistent mosquito from our table and took up the tale once more.

'I had got so fed up with these lazy fellows telling me what to do. That night we got into a big argument, after which I told your mother we were leaving and never coming back, even if we had to live in a *qudysai*. Your mother was crying. I knew she felt bad, but I couldn't stay there any more.'

A *qudysai*! If he was willing to live in a hut after having lived in such a big house, Dad must have been thoroughly disillusioned with my uncles.

Dad's eyes softened, realisation in his eyes of how much Mum had sacrificed for her family. Overcome with remorse, he took her hand in his and enlightened us further.

'First thing next morning, I set off walking, and after ten minutes I was in front of a particular house. At that time, the front of the house was not fenced in and had full view of the road. There was a bayee standing outside. He called out to me: "Uncle, I have seen you go past my house many times, you have always looked so happy – but today you look upset. Come and share a cup of coffee with me." So I did.'

I knew very few Bengali men; most of our Indian friends and family were Tamil, like us. But I knew one very well. Could it be, I wondered…

'The *bayee*, as you have probably all realised, was Mr Take Singh,' continued Dad, confirming my guess. 'He told me that his wife and children had left to live with his mother-in-law and he was living on his own. I could see it was only a small house, but he still had room for more, and he was very friendly. To cut a long story short, I asked him whether we could move into his house and pay him rent. Mr Singh was lonely, you see; he had a spare room and said we could use the rest of the house during the day when he was at work. When he showed me his spare room I knew it was small, but beggars cannot be choosers. I accepted Mr Singh's offer and we moved in almost straightaway.'

Ever shy, Mum gently extricated her hand from Dad's grip and continued the story.

'I knew your *appa* was right; we couldn't stay in *thaatha*'s house any more. Things had been said that couldn't be taken back. So we packed our things. *Appa* hired a bullock cart and we left.' She smiled at me. 'I was seven months pregnant with you. So I was… a bit scared, you know. After Mary.'

I nodded solemnly. It was common knowledge that, at the age of twenty-eight, Mum had experienced a difficult time giving birth to her fifth child and fourth daughter, Mary. My Aunty Arul was fond of reminding us on her visits.

'Your *ammah* nearly died when Mary was born, you all have to look after her now, you know.'

Running a ragingly high fever that refused to abate, Mum had received her last rites from our parish priest. The extended family members were already coming together in mourning when, against all the odds, she turned a corner and gradually pulled through. The family's relief was short-lived, however, as just a few days later the new arrival passed away in place of her mother.

I looked at Mum now, at the soft tendrils of long hair starting to escape from her neatly-pinned bun, frizzing slightly in the humidity, and dared to ask the question that sprung to my lips about the sister I had never met, but had always known about and been curious to know more.

'*Ammah*, how did Mary die?'

Tears gathered in soft-hearted Theresa's eyes. 'I'm off,' she said, wiping her eyes. 'I've heard this story before.'

Peter chuckled. 'Ah, you softie, everything upsets you.'

Dad's deep voice cut in sharply.

'Stop it, Jonah.' (Peter was always addressed as 'Jonah'. I never fathomed out why. We might as well not have been christened, for all the use my family made of our baptismal names.) 'Leave your older sister alone. She can leave the room if she wants to,' as he cast a concerned look at Mum, but she nodded reassuringly at him. Drawing a deep breath, Mum answered my question.

'We were still living in your *ammachi* and *thaatha*'s house. Mary was a few days old. I had just bathed her and placed her on the bed, drying her with the towel, when suddenly blood shot up from her *thopulu*. I couldn't stop the bleeding.'

As Mum paused, I held my breath, caught up in the emotional drama. Bleeding from the umbilical cord – why? The hiss of our pungent kerosene oil lamp broke the sudden silence. The white mantle turned yellow as it ran short of air, throwing flickering light on the now solemn faces of my family around the table. Peter jumped up to pump more air into the base of the lamp and the mantle began to glow brighter again.

Mum's nostrils flared as she continued.

'I was shouting. My mother and your *athais* came running, but we couldn't do anything. Mary went blue. A long sound came from her,

"Aaaah", and then she stopped breathing.'

Tears pooled in Mum's soft brown eyes as she relived this painful moment, so many years later. My heart ached for her, for the loss of her child. My sister's death had marked my mother; I could sense it from the faraway look in her eyes. There was a catch in her throat as she continued.

'Mary was so beautiful, very fair just like my dear *ammah*. I never heard her cry once. She looked so peaceful after she died, almost like she was sleeping.' Visibly gathering strength as she stared at a point above my head, Mum nodded with conviction: 'I knew God had taken her. She was God's child; she wasn't meant for this world.'

My eyes followed her gaze in the direction of our family altar. The portrait of the Virgin Mary with baby Jesus in her arms was lit in a ghostly fashion by the small altar light that kept vigil at all hours of the day and night. The small, red glass container, its wick floating in kerosene oil, was tended faithfully by Mum. She had sought solace for the loss of her child in religion, as was her way; but small wonder she was so scared when, three years later, she had to face the prospect of giving birth again, to me.

The beady eyes of a translucent lizard popped out from behind the Virgin Mary's portrait to assess the scene, before scrambling back to its hiding place beneath Our Lady. We barely noticed it; lizards were always appearing from behind the pictures that hung in our home. More distracting was the gentle sigh to my left: Charlie had fallen asleep, his head resting on the table. Peter quickly took charge, carrying Charlie into the bedroom. The rest of us were well settled into our seats, lost in our private thoughts. My arms were also beginning to feel heavy under the weight of my drooping head but I was anxious to hear the end of the story before giving in to sleep, so, swiftly stifling a yawn, I turned back to Mum.

'So, *ammah*, tell me, when I was born, were you scared after what happened with Mary? Did you think I was going to die too?'

'It's time for bed, Lily, you look tired, but – oh, I will tell you quickly, then off to bed, okay? Yes, I was scared. I missed my *ammah*. Luckily, Yaelumalai *paatie* helped me.'

Where did I come from? Why did our next-door *paatie* (all elderly ladies old enough to be a grandmother were addressed as *paatie*) have to help my Mum? Questions chased around my head, but I was too tired and too anxious to ask.

With an unexpected chuckle, Dad piped up.

'Marie, do you remember your sister's son, Benji, was here that day, and what happened to him?'

Mum's eyes twinkled.

'Oh yes, your Benji *annan* was visiting us. *Paatie* asked him to bring some hot water. Poor Benji was crossing the yard and, you know how big our mango tree is, full of fruit? Well, a ripe mango fell down from the tree and hit his head with a plonk.'

I laughed aloud. 'So that's why Benji *annan* teases me when he comes to visit us, about how I gave him a head injury and he has never been right since!'

'A brain injury,' laughed Dad. 'Your Benji *annan* is quite a storyteller, no one knows how much of his stories are true. But his heart is in the right place.'

'Is it really true that you got my name from the dictionary?'

I was pushing my luck now, as it was getting really late. But Mum and Dad were unusually magnanimous that night. The boundaries were being pushed and they were allowing it to happen, perhaps enjoying the reminiscing mood themselves, reliving the past through our narratives.

'Yes, Lily,' replied Dad. 'After five girls, we had run out of girls' names, and I thought you were going to be a boy. Anyway, I opened the Oxford English dictionary and there was the word "Lily", so I decided that that was it; no need for a second name. The dictionary had spoken.'

I was fascinated and opened my mouth to ask another question, but this time the yawn escaped, stretching my face to its very limits. Mum got up from the table decisively.

'Right everybody; it is getting late, enough stories for tonight. Time you little ones went to bed.'

As I settled into bed that night I thought of Mary, who was still a part of my family, having lived and breathed. She had been my older sister, older and therefore wiser: a definite presence, even though I couldn't touch or feel her.

'Good night Mary *akka*,' I whispered in the dark. 'I know you are an angel in Heaven, watch over me, keep me safe.'

As the arms of sleep crept around to gently cradle me, I fuzzily pondered on how I had been named, so arbitrarily. What if Dad had opened the dictionary at the letter X? Who knew what strange word could have been chosen as my name! My eyelids finally sank heavily over my tired eyes, and my last thought turned to my brother.

Peter was right, I realised. When I was barely a few hours old, with the help of the dictionary, a book containing the basic building blocks of their colonial language, the British had indeed already impacted on my life, in more ways than one.

3

'Sentul Palace...'

Our Family Home

Although we initially moved in as tenants, a few years later Dad bought the house in the tiny village of Retnapillai, in Sentul, from Mr Take Singh, whose decision to return to the Punjab sealed the future of our childhood upbringing.

Our kind landlord was only too willing to sell to us – and his departure meant that we now acquired an extra bedroom, a valuable asset to our still-growing family. Chandra's status as baby of the family soon passed on to his younger brother, Benny, and from him to Irene, who completed our generation. My mother was forty-two when she gave birth for the tenth and final time, her childbearing period spanning a grand total of twenty-four years. By the time Irene arrived, Mum was already a grandmother three times over, courtesy of my eldest sister, Theresa – this was not an uncommon occurrence amongst our community, where birth control was practically non-existent.

The small town of Sentul was a collection of villages – or *kampongs* – totalling a few hundred homes, some part-brick-built ones occupied by the more affluent families but mostly they were fashioned from wood, and scattered along the settlement's central spine of Sentul Road. This two-lane, tarmac road, generously scattered with gaping potholes, meandered down to Ipoh Road, where a left-hand turn would eventually take the traveller into the heart of Kuala Lumpur.

Back in the town, Sentul Road snaked past Sentul Theatre, where crowds gathered to watch mostly Tamil and Hindi movies, with occasional Chinese and English ones thrown in. Further along, it passed La Salle Boys School, a Catholic school established in 1950, where the brothers of the La Salle order educated my younger brothers. Jaded rows of railway quarters, mostly occupied by large Indian families, were tucked in between the main buildings.

The well-maintained, freshly painted St Joseph's Church loomed majestically from the setting of its large grounds. Originally it had been just a chapel, built in 1906, but then the Reverend Father Victor Herman relocated from St Anthony's Church in the centre of Kuala Lumpur in 1928, and the more substantial church came into being. The neighbourhood was enlivened by the peal of its triple brass bells during services. The church's neighbour, the Tamil Convent Sentul, had begun life as a semi-permanent wooden building on stilts in 1912 before becoming a permanent fixture later that same year, while a brick-built English convent school, about a hundred yards away, was a later addition.

Set back from the main road, and some distance from the convent school, the ever-bustling Sentul Market was especially crowded in the mornings with locals eager to sniff out a bargain. When I followed Mum round the market after early morning church services, she would purchase her meat there, but would then ignore the relatively expensive vegetables on display, tantalisingly laid out on shelves within the main building of the market, and walk instead to the roadside. There she would buy fresh produce from the housewives who displayed their wares on frayed and faded palm mats and dented tin plates. Conical piles of green and red chillies contrasted with enamel platefuls of home-grown tomatoes. Long, shiny, deep purple aubergines lay next to piles of short, globular, white varieties tinged a tantalising lime green at the base, while rods of white moolis and brownish drumsticks bulging with succulent seeds at regular one-inch intervals, slices of which would soak up the reddish orange sauce of dhal curries, were spread out to tempt the discerning housewife. Scrawny hands beckoned.

'Come, come Archie, just ten cents a pile, *lah.*'

Bangles clicked down wrists to brown leathery hands. A single jade bracelet caught the sun on the yellowish skin of a Chinese lady, selling a variety of greens. The nut-brown hands of Malay ladies pointed to piles of *Patai* green pods with plump purple seeds, delicious cooked with a paste of dried shrimps and pounded red chillies. Scrawny plucked *kampong* chickens, fine feathers still in place above the scaly joints of their feet, lay on their sides, their feet bound together with twine. I was drawn to the eddying smell of steamed pink rice cakes, a Chinese speciality. Sweetened, fermented dough steamed in bamboo trays balanced over water-filled woks, which were positioned over charcoal flames. Bargains could be negotiated with the vendors, as they did not have to pay rent for their pitches, and this made Mum's Dollars go a lot further.

A row of Chinese-run shops ran alongside the market, beginning with the shoe shop, where Dad took each of us in turn to be fitted for our first-ever pair of white canvas shoes when we were ready to commence our schooling. If we were well-behaved, and if Dad had a few coins to spare, the lucky bearer of new shoes might also leave the shop with one of the treasures that lay in the chest freezer at the front of it – the freezer's icy fog shrouded rows of rainbow-coloured ice lollies in beguiling mystery. My favourites were the soft yellow globes of durian-flavoured ice cream, topped with a shiny coat of sweet red beans: a sticky, fast-melting treat. The durian, a seasonal fruit, grew plentifully in the wild but a single tree grew in the dell in our grandfather's estate. Its thorny, hard exterior could cause untold damage and even death to any unfortunate person who happened to be in the way of a falling fruit. The luscious, yellow, honey-sweet but extremely smelly flesh was a price most devotees would be willing to pay for a taste of this goddess among fruits, and I was an ardent devotee.

Next door was another favourite shop, to which Charlie and I often headed on the rare occasions when Peter indulged me with pocket money. Here, I shared my ten cents equally with my younger brother to purchase a few treasured yellow biscuits, made from ground peas, rice flour and powdered sugar, pushed into leafy patterned moulds. The brown paper package of one-and-a-half-inch circular biscuits was tucked into our school bags for later consumption during school recess. The powder would burst open into the caves of our closed mouths, drawing coughs as some of the powder travelled up the back of our throats and into our noses. But saliva quickly transformed the powder into a soft sweet mush and our tongues would push little nuggets into our gullets, leaving the rest to be savoured and swallowed slowly.

Opposite the market, crowded GTC buses U-turned into a side lane to deposit and pick up their passengers. Here, several heavily laden Malay housewives, cooling themselves with broad palm fans, set up stalls to tempt the bus drivers, conductors and passengers into exchanging five- and ten-cent pieces for pyramids of freshly battered, deep-fried bananas, dredged with sugar, or slivers of crisp, battered, fried sweet potato. Further along, mugs of thick tea and freshly ground coffee sweetened with condensed milk were served under the shade of a wooden, tin-roofed coffee shop. My fascination never ceased as I witnessed the dark liquid magically turning a muddy colour when the layer of condensed milk at the bottom of the glass mug was stirred with a spoon.

The road ran past all this activity, continuing for a further couple of miles. Along its borders stood general provision stores, hairdressers, a photographer's, and the local, self-styled doctor, who was a personal friend of my Dad. Tucked away at one end was the Indian jeweller, where we girls had gold studs inserted into our ear lobes with the help of a red-hot needle.

Emergency phone calls could be made from the Chinese coffee shop, which was next to the noisy Malay School, and opposite stood an imposing, blue-turreted mosque. Further rows of shops led away: a young Chinese tailor's, a few carpenters, glaziers and a biscuit factory, from where we carried away bags of broken biscuits for a dollar. Beyond this, the tarmac finally ran out and a dirt road emerged.

The *kampongs* formed clusters around these dirt roads, which spread out from Sentul Road like tributaries from the mouth of a river. Here was where the people lived, in a variety of individual wooden houses fenced in by makeshift barbed wire. A combination of sweet-scented flowered hedges, which grew naturally, and wooden fences enclosed individual household compounds, while the ground was carpeted by the coarse, creeping broad leaves of cow grass that stayed short, needing no blade to reduce its height.

In the fenced off compounds, the humidity and fertility of the black earth rewarded toiling hands. Wigwams of twigs were home to snake-like long beans, whose fibrous pods enclosed soft, pink, baby seeds. Next to them stood square tents, dripping with green-veined, vessel-shaped gourds. Shiny, royal purple aubergines stood out next to the smaller, pale-green ones in the bushes, and ever-fragrant spindly curry leaf plants sat alongside the short, clumpy chilli plants.

Fruit trees towered over most compounds: clumps of stocky banana trees; delicate coconut trees, shaped into arches by the wind; spindly, umbrella-like trees with leaves arranged in spirals, crowned with ripe, amber-coloured papayas; and heavily laden mango trees.

Some Sentul villagers made their living as self-employed businessmen, running shops that catered to the needs of the local population; however, most of the local population worked for the Malayan Railways, whose largest workshop had been established in Sentul by the British in 1905. Sited on thirteen acres of land, it was here that trains were built, fixed and refurbished. The central depot was home to generations of 'railway families' who depended on it for their employment; up to 2,500 jobs were provided in its heyday. Indians brought in by the British ran the works, with a handful of Chinese and Malays.

Each working day in Sentul began and ended with the shrill tones of the depot's siren. It woke up the entire town at 6.15 a.m., and sounded again at 6.45 a.m. to remind the workers that they should have left their homes by then. A stream of bicycles then raced from the houses to the workshops, where work started with British promptness at 7 a.m.

Midday sirens announced both lunchtime for the hungry workers, and a reminder to leave home once more and return to the depot for the afternoon shift. The last siren at 4 p.m. marked the welcome 'time to go home'.

Train coaches were put together in the Sentul workshops and Dad worked with the engines. With his fellow workers, he used caustic soda to clean the engines, which were completely taken to bits, then repaired, with any broken pieces being replaced, before the whole locomotive was put together again.

We were one of the few railway families to live in a private residence, rather than in the purpose-built railway quarters. Our house was situated opposite a provisions shop, on the bend of a long dirt road that led from the Chinese coffee shop with the working telephone. To the left of the provisions shop lay a patch of open grassy land, beyond which loomed the boundaries to our home. At the end of the dirt road, a couple of miles away lived Mum's parents.

Although our house was small, a substantial plot of land surrounded it, with creeping cow grass stretching from the front and to the right of the building. Dad and Peter had enclosed the exposed frontage, with an enormous, inward-opening, corrugated zinc gate. A loop of heavy iron chain fixed the gate to a solid wooden fence post, and it was secured with a padlock to keep intruders out. The gate was our security.

An impenetrable bougainvillea hedge surrounded our house on three sides. The thorny hedge was softened with clusters of lilac flowers: open-ended lanterns, tapered at the base and flattening out gracefully, revealed bright yellow single stamens that stood proud, like the clapper of a bell. They gave off a heady perfume in the hot, moisture-laden air.

A deep stream ran alongside a path that bordered one section of our hedge. On our left, a run of barbed wire fencing was broken only by a side gate fashioned out of chicken wire. An areca nut tree – that provided one of the main ingredients of *paan* – stood against the gatepost. This gate was permanently padlocked. The backs of a terrace of three houses owned by neighbour Yellumalai, and Velu's single house on a slight rise, could be viewed through the netted fence.

Our house was constructed out of cheap offcuts from the local sawmills, which were frequently carted off by entrepreneurs in bullock carts and sold to the local community. Hairy, unfinished planks, nailed into position, formed the outer walls. I would stand on tiptoe to reach as high as I could and pull at the hairs of the wood, which came away easily with a gentle tug, allowing me to relish the thin strips of bright orange wood thus revealed underneath the sun-faded brown planks.

The floor of the main house was made from cool concrete that shone in the sunlight pouring through the open doorway, worn smooth by years of wear and criss-crossed by hairline cracks. An uncemented kitchen was separated from the main house by a foot-width passageway. The walls had been whitewashed, but relentless sun and humidity had resulted in a warped, tanned, brittle and bleached exterior, with patches incongruously set off by streaks of the bright orange exposed by my handiwork.

Rooms in the main house were divided using partitions made from the same rough, unplaned wood, containing natural peepholes that my siblings and I used to our advantage, peering at visitors grouped in the lounge from the secrecy of our bedroom. It would have been inappropriate for the young ladies of the house to be in the presence of Peter's older male friends, but these knot-holes allowed us access to life beyond the solid barrier. Giggles were suppressed and lookouts placed during our illicit transgression from our social codes of conduct; our stolen pleasures were heightened by our complicity.

Internal partitions stood three-quarters of the height of the house, leaving a gap between them and the roof in which air could circulate, providing a semblance of coolness – particularly welcome during our quieter hours in the building's two bedrooms, after the fierce sun's rays finally abated.

Palm thatch, or *attap*, topped the building, made by tightly plaiting the slick fronds of coconut palm leaves together, then leaving them to dry out to a muddy colour. The thick, smooth leaves successfully kept the rain off, while ensuring the interior of the house stayed as cool as possible in the sultry climate. *Attap* possessed similar properties to the traditional thatched roofs topping historic English cottages, although the beautiful rambling roses often adorning such picture-perfect buildings were notably absent from our tropical home.

A dining area held our sturdy old wooden table that could seat eight, around which our family meals and evening discussions took place. Adjacent to the dining area was a lounge that was big enough to accommodate all of us quite comfortably. This was filled with an eclectic hodgepodge of furniture. Placed at random, no item of furniture matched another, telling the subtle tale of poverty, where donated and bargain items were collected and planted in whatever space was available.

One particular mahogany swivel chair was a favourite of mine. I loved stroking the carved wooden spindles that stood vertically along its sturdy back, a reminder of the tall, strong tree from which the chair had been formed. Gently rounded arms invited me to scramble into its solid embrace, and I cried, 'Wheee!' as I swung from side to side in the seat, the noise of the central spring providing a creaking soundtrack to my play. I made sure not to damage it, however, as it was also Dad's favourite chair, given to him by his friends, Mr and Mrs Holmes, who had returned to their home in England after the war.

A walnut writing table, acquired in similar circumstances, stood lonely but proudly in the corner, with a concertina dome at the top hiding slim letter compartments in which Dad kept his important papers. The dome top was always locked and the key kept in a safe place known only to Dad. We loved the mystery of this 'secret compartment' and never tired of chorusing: 'Appa, show us how the desk works, we want to see the secret drawer!' Mouths wide open, we marvelled 'oooh' as he obliged us, watching the slatted wooden top disappear smoothly into the upper fold of the concertina, revealing the superb craftsmanship of this luxury item.

During family gatherings we youngsters sprawled on the cool cement floor, leaning our backs against the legs of the half-dozen wooden chairs occupied by the adults, or against the mahogany glass-fronted bookcase that held Dad's favourite books – and a home to silver fish, ousted only by sunburn. In the centre stood a glass-topped coffee table, with a rattan shelf underneath filled with Dad's neatly stacked daily newspapers and magazines from India. The youngsters dipped their sticky fingers into the bowl that sat on top of the table, their fingers often smacked out by the elders with an audible warning. A climbing plant grew in a clear bowl, sprouting variegated green and gold leaves, its twisted roots visibly entwining the few smooth pebbles that provided it with support. A common belief held that if the plant flourished, so did the fortunes of the household. As a result, many houses contained these 'money plants' in their lounges, with tendrils trained to climb and adorn the walls.

Our family altar took pride of place on the wall that faced the front door, so no visitor had to guess our denomination, while a lone black and white photograph of our parents' wedding hung on the other. While the adults talked over my head, I sat cross-legged squinting at the image of a handsome young man of twenty, dressed in a white suit, and a dark, pretty seventeen-year-old in a heavily brocaded *sari*. My chest swelled and I felt secure. My parents made a handsome couple.

As the eldest son, Peter had the privilege of his own bedroom. It held just enough space for his single bed and a wooden table. Above the table, a planed wooden shelf nailed into the wall was where Peter's schoolbooks and magazines lived, together with his comb and a jar of brilliantine hair pomade. Above his hair-grooming products hung a mirror with age spots, in a narrow, light brown, wooden frame. When I leaned against his doorway to watch him getting ready for school in the mornings, he would catch my reflection in the mirror and wink conspiratorially. I loved how his heavily brilliantined hair shone, showing the scores from the teeth of his comb.

In our second bedroom, Dad and Peter had cleverly converted the end for sleep by building a wooden platform raised above the cement floor, upon which mats were unrolled at night. Here, Theresa, Anna, Rosie, Charlie and I stretched out each night, our heads resting on half-filled pillows within threadbare cotton cases. Modesty dictated that we cover ourselves with well-worn cotton sheets when we went to bed, although during the night these were often kicked away, inviting the cooler night air to caress and cool our sweaty skin.

Halfway across the room, a sturdy beam supported a cradle, made as usual from a *sarong*. This was Chandra's bed, until he became old enough to join us on the mats. By the time Benny and finally Irene arrived our house had undergone changes and with it our sleeping arrangements.

Looming over us while we slept, like a benign teak giant, our family *almari* stood on the cement floor. Warped and faded, with streaks of old varnish still visible in the sunlight, this large cabinet held all of our clothes. On one of its doors, the one facing the doorway, hung an age-spotted mirror with bevelled edges, which we all fought over when we dressed for Sunday mass. Usually we would catch a quick glance of ourselves whenever we entered the bedroom as well, patting our hair into place or swiping a grimy line off our faces with the backs of our hands, and sometimes we used it to measure our height against our siblings.

The doorways from both bedrooms opened into a rectangular space, in the centre of which our back door was situated.

To provide them with a semblance of privacy, Mum and Dad slept on rush mats in the hall, until Peter decided to build a third bedroom for them. Equipped with nothing but his characteristic determination and whatever offcuts he could lay his hands on, Peter somehow performed a miracle, and our grateful parents then gave him free rein to indulge his expansion plans.

Over the years, our house gradually became a giant, living jigsaw puzzle, with different parts all neatly fitting into one another, and new pieces appearing in different directions, like the wings of a royal mansion house. Laughingly, we referred to our home as 'Sentul Palace'. It was rickety and makeshift; at night the whole structure would reverberate with a crash as the windows were closed: swollen and sticky with the constant rain, they needed a firm pull. The structure creaked in the sultry sunshine and trembled in the monsoon rains – but it was home, and we loved it for what it was.

General hygiene in the village was difficult to maintain. There was no collection of household rubbish by any established government bodies. Instead, Peter dug a huge hole in the ground to the left of the main gate, into which we dumped all our rubbish. A rusty sheet of corrugated zinc covered the hole, whose contents we burned periodically in cleansing bonfires, inducing coughing fits as we tried not to choke on the acrid smoke.

But, despite our own efforts to keep our home clean, we couldn't stop the more unscrupulous of the villagers. Passers-by habitually used the stream that ran alongside our bougainvillea fence as a dumping ground, never caring whether or not there was enough running water to carry the rubbish away. When the stream was low in drier weather, things would become tangled amongst the bank's ferns and catch on twigs that would rip open the parcels of newspaper. Humidity soon started the decomposing process and the stench was unbearable. I particularly abhorred the dead animals: little puppies and kittens lying stiff and cold, unwanted and abandoned. Flies were drawn in hordes to the corrupted flesh. If we heard the culprits at work, we ran alongside the bougainvillea hedge, shouting abuse at them.

'Oi, you, take your rubbish home!'

But they were always too quick for us. I heard them bolt, laughing as they made their getaway.

'Dirty rascals, you are all filthy people!' I fumed. The bougainvillea fence was a perfect cover. Their high-pitched laughter was the giveaway; these were children, used by their parents to carry out their dirty work for them.

It fell to my beloved brother Peter to scramble down the embankment, unable to avoid breathing in the stench of putrid, decaying meat filled with writhing worms, then gather up the rubbish and hastily bury it.

We were grateful for heavy downpours, when the pools in the stream-beds stretched out their glistening fingers and joined together, rising quickly to the task of clearing away the debris downstream. Peter would stand on the bank in the pelting rain, using a sturdy stick to prod the articles lying on the banks back into the stream. Standing on the path's edge, I clamped my nostrils shut to keep out the stench, taking shallow breaths through my mouth and watching my eldest brother hard at work. I felt a mixture of emotions coursing through my body: anger against the culprits, and pride swelling my chest as

I witnessed my brother's limitless energy, and the sacrifices he made for his beloved family.

Our home may have been small and poor, but it was large and rich with family love. We fitted into it like sparrows, spreading out our wings every morning to venture forth from the nest, and returning every evening to reconvene.

Growing up in Sentul, our lives were lived in a very physical sense, full of noise and sensation. We worked and played without restraint, screaming and giggling, enjoying raucous, joyous scenes, while music blared daily from every household. As children, we were unaware that we were restricted in any way. We lived our lives in the open for everyone to see; our bustling family life was lived to the full.

4

'The milkman...'

Growing Up in Poverty

'Come on Lily, time to feed Letchumi and Maarieiyee.'

Peter beckoned with his free hand, as he balanced with the other a forkful of rich grass that he had gathered the previous evening. Carefully he walked towards the lean-to shed at the side of our house and I trotted after him eagerly.

Milky white in colour and sweet as honey in nature, Letchumi was our fair and dainty princess. She was named after the Hindu goddess of wealth, who was supposedly the embodiment of beauty and grace. Maarieiyee was bigger and bi-coloured, with large patches of black splashed onto a white background. Less patient than her companion, she was quick to flick her tail when displeased. Miniature metal bells tied around their necks tinkled as the two moved forward to greet us.

Vapour rose off the quivering, glistening nostrils of our two cows. Four placid black eyes followed us in anticipation, and thick, sticky saliva dribbled from their moist mouths as they waited. Although they were tethered, with thick ropes around their necks looped into sturdy iron rings on the wall of the shed, I hung back in trepidation; their bodies towered over my short self.

From a respectable distance, I watched Peter proceed with the feed, marvelling at his bravery. His abundant, brilliantined hair had a natural wave, just like Mum's, and was swept back from his broad forehead. The V-shaped mark in the middle of his forehead, the legacy of a childhood accident, deepened as it caught the morning sun creeping in through a gap between the shed's zinc roof and wooden walls. An aquiline nose, inherited from our Dad, looked sharper from the concentration that Peter needed to feed the cows while skilfully avoiding irritable Maarieiyee's quick, sharp kick. At fourteen, his head was already on a par with Dad's shoulder.

Placing the sweet green grass in the wooden trough, Peter carefully nudged it with his feet until it sat below the animals' salivating mouths. A flick of their ears acknowledged their thanks and, heads down, the cows' munching mouths made short work of their breakfast. Once their meal was over, they relaxed, excreting green dung and steaming urine, releasing a stench that hung heavily in the humid air, quickly attracting a few buzzing flies. The first show of the day over, I retreated indoors.

Too squeamish to feed the cows, our eldest sister Theresa had instead prepared breakfast and was getting ready for the start of what would be her final year at school. Anna and Rosie were likewise preparing for the school day, while toddler Charlie was still cocooned in sleep.

My breakfast was ready, but Mum was also ready to take her turn in the shed, and I was eager to see the second show of the day. Mum's indulgent smile came into play.

'Ok, Lily, you can watch me. Once I finish, we will go and have our breakfast.'

I skipped out into the early morning once more and reached for a low, three-legged wooden stool. Positioning myself a safe distance away, elbows on my knees and hands cupping my face, I sat and made circles in the dew-drenched ground with my bare big toe.

Mum made her way towards the cows. Dressed in her familiar garb of a brightly patterned batik *sarong* and white blouse, she carried a towel, one end of which was tucked into the waist of her *sarong* on the right, while the other end was flung over her left shoulder, covering her ample bosom. She lowered herself onto a similar stool to mine and reached out to take hold of Letchumi's udder. Gently, she wiped the teats with the towel slung on her shoulders, before proceeding to milk each of them in turn with firm, practised hands. Our grey, shady surroundings quickly brightened as the sun's earliest rays grew older and stronger, dancing on the natural waves of my mother's ebony hair and lifting the dew in cloudy spirals of steam. Mum hummed to herself as she worked, throwing a look at me from time to time and giving me her 'I'm still here' smile. I watched in fascination as the creamy white stuff streamed and frothed into an aluminium pail. My ears caught the rhythmic patter of the rich liquid as it struck the empty bottom of the bucket, and then settled into a soft sloshing sound as the pail slowly filled up.

Once the task was over, I followed Mum back into the house once more, leaping along so that I could exactly follow in her footsteps, observing how the thud of her step in the yard changed to a slap-slapping sound on the natural clay floor of the kitchen. The surface was a little uneven, as there was no cement coating. I was careful not to stub my toe as I followed her in, having learnt my lesson the hard way.

In the kitchen, I watched Mum rest upon her haunches and deftly pour the milk from the bucket into the rows of glass bottles she had already laid out on the floor. She finished the task and rose, stretching slightly to release the last of the morning's stiffness from her limbs, then beckoned.

'Come *ma*, have some breakfast.'

I trotted over to a gleaming brass container with a wide body and narrow neck that stood just outside the kitchen. In the absence of a running water supply, this was how we stored our water. The neck had a wooden stopper, on which rested a brass tumbler. I tipped some water over my right hand to wash it, and then looked for a suitable spot on the floor. Brushing off some pencil-shaped ash that had escaped from the kitchen stove with my left, I sat down cross-legged, waiting with a growling tummy in anticipation of what was to come.

Mum flipped a chapatti, dampened with melted margarine, onto my blue enamel plate. I tucked in while she made my tea. Mum poured hot water from a Thermos flask into an opened condensed milk tin, washing out the remains of the sweet milk, so as not to waste a drop. The fresh milk she had just brought in was used sparingly at home; the bulk of it was intended for another purpose.

Peter strode into the kitchen, freshly showered, clad in his ironed and stiffly starched white shirt and long white trousers, now ready to leave for the school he attended: St John's School, in the centre of Kuala Lumpur. He carried two bags – one holding his schoolbooks, the other empty – and several sheets of newspaper.

As Mum left the room to check on my sisters' progress, Peter squatted down next to the bottles on the floor. Taking a sheet of newspaper, he carefully tore it into squares and crumpled up each piece tightly, then inserted them into the necks of the bottles. I watched him with curiosity; this was a morning show I had not yet witnessed.

'*Annan*, what are you doing?'

'I'm taking the milk to school,' he responded, in a matter-of-fact tone. Gently, he started to lift the bottles and place them, one by one, into his empty bag.

'See?' He gazed into my questioning eyes. 'I take all this milk and sell it to my teachers. But I must be careful – the stoppers are only made from newspaper, so I have to keep the bottles upright in the bus, and when I walk uphill to school, or they will spill.' I was suitably impressed.

Sighing in relief as he placed the final bottle into the bag without spilling any of the precious liquid, Peter fastened the bag.

'They call me *Paalukaran*. They laugh at me.'

He shrugged, reacting to my look of bewilderment and sympathy.

It wasn't fair that they called him names. He was not a milkman, just a schoolboy helping his family.

'I don't mind though. We need the money.'

Peter uncurled his lanky frame to an upright position, and gently raised the valuable load to his shoulder before departing for school, nodding a farewell and giving me a quick smile from the doorway. My sisters left to walk to their school a little later.

Devout Catholics, my parents believed that all of the children born to them were a gift from God. However, the harsh reality was that Dad's wages provided barely enough to feed, clothe and educate all of us. True, I did not experience chronic hunger, as there was always some sticky rice porridge and a vegetable of some description to fill our bellies. It was the grown-ups who would sacrifice their food for the young; the old, infirm and young were always first in the pecking order for food. As children, we only had to make sacrifices if we had unexpected visitors; then we would make do with less food, never thinking to question Mum's golden rule: 'Visitors first'. On Sundays, the only day of the week when Mum cooked meat if visitors happened to arrive, the pieces of meat landed on the visitors' plates whilst just the gravy was ladled on to our little mound of rice. A rising protest from Charlie would quickly be quelled by a 'You know the rules, do not disgrace me' look from Mum, forcing Charlie to lower his head in quiet acquiescence.

Most of the cooking took place in the cooler mornings after breakfast, whilst any children who were too young to go to school played together in the compound. As I ran about with little Charlie, our bare feet slamming into the warm earth, a distinctive aroma first wafted, then blossomed and intensified. Increasingly heady scents, released from clay cooking pots, came through the open doors and windows, floating in intoxicating waves all around us as we played: fresh curry leaves and fried cloves, cinnamon, star anise, mustard seeds. Instinctively, we drooled; you could practically taste the mouth-watering curries as housewives across the neighbourhood busied themselves creating family feasts for the day.

Mum cooked all our meals in a corner of the kitchen where a raised area of clay was fashioned into a fireplace. It had a central cavity wide enough for kindling and a circular opening on the top, where cooking pots were balanced. A mixture of charcoal, roughly hewn wood and newspaper lay close by in a wooden trough, next to well-seasoned clay pots. The clay floor turned from brown into slate grey next to the fireplace, as the ashes spilled from the wood that we used as fuel were incorporated. After completing the day's cooking, Mum's final ritual was to sprinkle water over the floor and smooth the wet surface over with the palm of her chapped hand, before allowing it to dry quickly in the reflected rays from the hot sun.

A heavy iron wok, every local household's essential cooking utensil, hung on a rusty nail on the kitchen's wooden wall, its blackened, soot-covered rounded side facing outwards to protect the seasoned interior. Pots and pans were stacked up on the floor. Clay pots of spices were housed next to pyramids of condensed milk tins on wooden shelves. The ubiquitous blue enamel plates were piled up on rough wooden boxes next to cups with chipped edges. Ladles, fashioned from wooden handles stuck through the polished half of a coconut shell, were kept within easy reach of the stove.

Everyone, schoolchildren and workers alike, returned home for lunch in the strongest heat of the day, heading back after an hour's break whilst the rest of us took an afternoon siesta. At four o'clock sharp, we sat down to a mug of sweet tea and perhaps a dry cracker, if family funds permitted, then more games outdoors followed.

At dusk, weary from our exploits, Charlie and I tramped back in, to lounge on the sitting room floor, as Mum entered to carry out her usual evening ritual of *saamburani*. She sauntered in fresh from the shower, hair washed and spread out to dry on her back. Her face was tinged a pale yellow colour from a thinly applied layer of freshly ground turmeric paste. I screwed up my nose in a familiar grimace.

'Good feed for your skin,' was Mum's response. 'My mother never sprouted a pimple in her life.'

Mum crouched on her haunches by the front door, kindling a few pieces of charcoal until they were suitably hot, then placed them in a clay container and sprinkled over some frankincense. A thick, pungent white smoke spiralled up; its initial strength made me heady and induced a rasping cough. Scrambling away over the floor to a safe distance, I hugged my knees to my chest and watched Mum carry the pot over to the wooden shelf of our family altar. She stood beneath the picture of Virgin Mary and the baby Jesus. Cupping her hand into a fan, she wafted the smoking, resinous frankincense upwards, bowing her head as she paused to say a prayer. The warm, sweet-spicy odour with an overtone of camphor permeated the room.

Her brief meditation over, she moved to fan the smoke towards her other favourite print: the Sacred Heart. This image of Jesus Christ had been a wedding present, and was a treasured possession, hanging over the doorway to the kitchen. The index finger of Christ's left hand pointed to his exposed bleeding heart, while his right hand seemed to be held out in supplication, offering you his protection if you would only believe in him. His eyes, it seemed, could see deep into your soul, and followed you around the room.

Mum's explanation – 'I have hung him over the doorway so he can always protect us' – indicated the nature of her faith, which was unquestioned and immovable.

I went outside to gulp in some fresh air, aware that the cloying smell would take a while to disperse and, with the failing light, the doors and windows would soon be shut and the harsh qualities of the frankincense intensified.

Satisfied that Christ had now sanctified it, Mum carried the clay container and made a circuit of the whole house wafting the curling smoke into every corner. This ritual not only fulfilled the spiritual need of blessing our home, but also met a practical need by seeing off the insects that invaded our home as it cooled in the evening air.

I returned to the living room in time to see Mum using the last of the embers by the altar. Bending her head forwards, she held the container in her right hand, and with her left she fanned her hair out, bending her arm at the elbow and letting her hair fall like a curtain over her bent arm. She took in deep breaths while allowing the remaining frankincense smoke to curl up through her feathered hair.

Just as we started to breathe fresh air again before we went to bed, mosquito coils were lit and left in our bedrooms. These deep emerald coils burned slowly, emitting a thin, white sliver of smoke that stung my eyes and made them water. Malaria was a very real fear at this time. At the age of thirteen, my sister Anna contracted the dreaded illness from a mosquito bite while helping my mother's oldest sister, who lived in the rural district of Kuala Selangor. It was a favourite story of Anna's, whose eyes widened dramatically as she raised them to the ceiling and, cupping her hands, she pronounced at the climax of her tale:

'It was a miracle that I didn't die!'

Small wonder that our parents were taking great precautions with the rest of us. Mosquitoes swelled in numbers in the evenings. They shrieked annoyingly in my ears as they flew past. Our whitewashed walls showed up the black specks of those mozzies who were engorged with my blood, who had been too quick for the palm of my hands. Some that didn't get away were grizzly carcasses squashed against the wall.

I fell asleep watching the tips of the coils glow red as they slowly smouldered, emitting a tinny chemical smell as the white smoke snaked its way up into the air, keeping the bloodsucking insects at bay.

*

A close-knit family, our pleasures were simple and we devised our own games. Music featured high on our list of entertainment. Peter's exercise book, his proud possession, held the lyrics to various English songs, painstakingly copied in his neat handwriting. We would congregate in his room, crammed into every available space on his single bed, our bare legs swinging with glee.

'Let's start with Lily's song!

A song of love is a sad song,
Hi-lili, hi-lili, hi-lo...'

Then they would tickle me mercilessly.

'You like that song, don't you, Lily?'

I screeched helplessly, arms and legs flailing in all directions as I squirmed to escape their groping fingers.

'Now for Rosie's song –

Rose, Rose I love you, with an aching heart.'

Rosie blushed with pride, her lips pursed and her eyes cast down to the floor.

We had many more. Our chorus of voices, mostly sopranos, mingled with Peter's deeper baritone as we sang:

'Seven lonely days make one lonely week,
Seven lonely nights make one lonely me.'

I caught my breath in a sob. The sadness implied in the lines was as blue as the seven hankies:

'Seven hankies blue I filled with my tears,
Seven letters, too, I filled with my fears.
Guess it never pays to make your lover blue.
Seven lonely days I cried and cried for you.'

The music stayed with us, setting our daily chores to a rhythm as we hummed while we bashed soapy clothes on the cement floor, or chopped up the vegetables for the evening meal. Only Theresa went squeakily off-key, her voice cracking during our family singsongs as she tried to keep up with the melody. Sometimes a particularly outrageous key would make us all stop mid-verse, groaning.

'*Akka*, you are terrible!'

Theresa's tuneless offerings never failed to amuse, and brought a smile even to Dad's eyes. 'Are all my children going to take up singing? If so, I want to know when they will start making their money from it!'

Our bathroom was Peter's favoured arena. From here, he serenaded passers-by on the other side of our bougainvillea fence, to frequent claps of appreciation and witty comments.

'*Nallaa paadurai thambi, cinemaku paadalamai* – you're singing well son, you should be a singer in films.'

Singing in an outdoor bathroom in a little wooden house in a tiny Malayan village was far from the life of a film star. But, many years later, I was introduced to the works of Robert Frost and suddenly found myself transported back to our Sentul Palace as I read some words from his poem, 'Blueberries':

'Who cares what they say? It's a nice way to live,
Just taking what Nature is willing to give...'

5

'Shared secrets...'

An Early End to Childhood

Picking up her basket, Mum called out to me.

'Coming, *ma?*'

I trotted off beside her to our productive vegetable garden, which was carefully cultivated to meet the demands of our ever-growing family. Helping my mother in the garden was our time together, when I had her all to myself and I felt closest to her. My older siblings were all at school and Charlie was too young to be of any help, although he usually toddled after us nonetheless, pulling ineffectually on hardy tufts of grass.

We bypassed wigwams of long beans, making instead for the *avurai* kai: flat, comma-shaped pods, so paper-thin that they revealed the succulent seeds within. Their crawling vines climbed over a tent-like construction of crude wooden poles and sturdy twigs. Mum guided me, showing me how to pick only the pods that were plump and mature, allowing the younger, flatter pods time to fill out over the course of a few more days. Once we had picked enough for the day's dinner, we moved on to our patch of gourds.

'I think one gourd will do for today. Here, see this ripe one: place your hands underneath and I will cut it at the stem.'

I stood underneath, supporting the juicy golden globe in my palms as my mother cut through the adjoining stem with deft strokes of her sharp garden knife. Sweeping a slight sweat off her brow with her forearm, she beckoned.

'*Vaa ma*, I think we have enough for today. Tomorrow we will make keerai curry. You can come and pick it yourself, okay?'

'Okay, *ammah.*'

I knew the vegetables she meant: a variety of creeping greens, *passi keerai*, and *ponnangani keerai*, with its maroon veins and plump maroon seeds, both of which plants appeared randomly in all corners of our garden, and were – according to Mum – rich in iron and minerals.

Armed with a wealth of knowledge handed down through generations, housewives like my mother were adept at providing a varied diet to maintain the general health of their families. I cherished the nuggets of information Mum shared with me. Each vegetable in our garden was carefully chosen for its nutritional value, and sometimes for its medicinal qualities too; many doubled as cures for different ailments.

'Better pick a few red and green chillies for the fried vegetables and the *nethilli sambal*,' she called out as she picked up the near-full basket of vegetables and walked ahead, Charlie trotting after her.

I drooled at the thought of the anchovy dish in its fiery sambal sauce and, opening my skirt like an apron, happily set to picking the elongated, finger-like green and ripened red chillies that clothed the four-foot-high bushes, dropping them into the fabric. Mum's warning floated back:

'Be careful, don't rub your eyes after you pick the chillies or they will burn!'

'Okay *ammah*, I won't.' I brushed past the fragrant curry leaf plant as I finished with the chillies, releasing a delicious warm aroma. '*ammah*, do you want me to pick some curry leaves as well?'

'Yes, yes, just a few sprigs will do.'

I followed her instructions, then hopped after her, skirt held wide with my fragrant bounty. I returned to the kitchen feeling happy, light-hearted, and ready to help Mum prepare the vegetables we had gathered.

Our kitchen window framed a clump of banana trees, from which bunches of sun-ripened fruit were plucked and set in the centre of our dining table as our traditional after-dinner dessert. Dad swore on the bowel-moving benefits of bananas, never failing to have his daily ration.

The obvious yellow fruit wasn't the only resource, however, as my innovative mother devised dishes using every part of the banana tree. Each bunch of bananas ended in a cylindrical, slightly pointy-shaped purple fruit. When its purple layers were peeled back, flattened flowers were revealed, tightly packed against the next layer. It was easy enough to prize the flowers off and chop them into bite-sized pieces. Frying them with chopped onions, chillies and cooked dhal, Mum enhanced the taste of the flowers still further with a handful of toasted grated coconut, before finishing it all off with a refreshing squeeze of fresh lime juice.

As for the versatile banana leaves, they were waterproof, large and flexible enough to wrap food for steaming, imparting a subtle sweet flavour. The aromatic waterproof leaves could also be substituted for plates, the spine across the middle acting as a natural divide between the vegetables, pickles and fried meat placed on the top half, and rice and curry served on the lower, When guests had had their fill, they folded the leaf away from them, a sign for the server to stop.

Mum's ample bottom was on display as she squatted in front of the stove. She had just finished separating and cleaning the insides of dried anchovies, a cheap and plentiful bounty from the sea that surrounded our peninsula. She balanced the *chattie* on the fireplace, pouring groundnut oil into the clay pot to heat up before crisply frying the anchovies, which filled the room with their pungent fishy smell. Using a slotted spoon, Mum lifted the golden anchovies into a bowl and held it out towards me; I took the hot bowl away from her, taking care to hold it by its cooler rim with both hands.

Next, thrusting her left arm upwards to shelter her face, Mum threw in chopped onions, tossing them deftly until they softened and took colour. Freshly pounded red chillies followed, their harsh aroma quickly reaching the back of our throats, making me cough and splutter.

'Pass me back the fried *nethilli*,' ordered Mum. The freshly fried anchovies were duly returned to the rich sauce, and the sambal lifted with a healthy pinch of sugar to give a wonderful glaze. I waited for the final touch, the introduction of the essential sour taste; holding her right hand out over the pot, Mum strained tamarind juice between her fingers while retaining the soaked pods in her palm, then placed the squeezed pulp on a saucer. I poked at the remnants, disturbing the imprint of Mum's fisted fingers still visible in the pulp.

Pouring a teaspoon of the hot cooked sauce into her cupped palm, Mum slurped it noisily, before sprinkling in a touch more sugar. The humble salty anchovies, crisped up and now swimming in their fresh, vibrant sauce, were transformed into a heavenly spicy dish: hot, sweet and sour in a proportionate and well-practised combination.

I helped Mum to prepare the rest of the day's meals in companionable camaraderie. Most of my help consisted of fetching and carrying, but I was proud to be put in charge of measuring out our precious staple for every meal – rice, which we kept in a large wooden chest. I picked up our measuring device, an empty condensed milk tin, and dug it into the heap of rice like a spade, levelling it off and tipping it into the clay pot – one full tin for every two to three hungry mouths.

As I dug particularly deep into the rice heap, the tin came into contact with something hard. I pushed my hand into the dry beads of rice and retrieved its hidden treasure: a flat Players cigarette tin, which rattled as I shook it.

'Look, *ammah*! Look, look what I found!' I gabbled, waving the tin in the air.

Before I could prise it open, Mum gently removed it from my eager hand.

'Never mind that, you carry on with what you are doing.'

My face must have fallen in disappointment, as she took one look at me and relented.

'Okay then, Lily, but you can't tell anyone about it, promise me.'

I nodded eagerly and watched, wide-eyed, as my mother opened the tin and showed me its contents: a folded-up roll of notes.

'Emergency money. I keep it in the rice box for safekeeping. Don't tell anyone, okay? I know I can trust you.'

My heart thumped: Mum and I had a secret that none of the others knew. I smiled conspiratorially at her. 'Okay, *ammah*, I won't tell anyone.'

She smiled and continued with the job at hand, while I wrapped the thought of our shared secret deep into my heart.

Later that morning I was playing with Charlie in the front garden near our family swing – a wooden board hovering in mid-air, held up by a rough rope at either side, which Peter had erected for his siblings. Our neighbour's fourteen-year-old son had popped round, as he often did, bringing payment for *sari* blouses that Mum had sewed for his mother. Crossing the compound with long, lazy strides, the *annan* (all boys older than you were respectfully addressed as 'older brother') swung on to the wooden seat, holding out his hand.

'Come on, Lily, I will swing you up high into the air.'

I hesitated, as I didn't know this *annan* very well, but he was a near neighbour and a frequent visitor to our home; besides, the prospect of being flung into the air was enticing.

Abandoning Charlie, who was engrossed in the fine art of drawing in the dirt with a twig, I stepped forward as the *annan* steadied his bottom on the seat of the swing, tilting it slightly and planting his feet firmly on the well-worn patch of bare earth beneath. He reached out and rested his hands rather heavily on my shoulders, turning me around firmly to position me in front of him but with my back to him. Placing strong hands under my arms, with one deft movement he lifted me on to his lap.

I nearly slipped off his starched brown shorts and reached out to steady myself by holding tightly to the ropes a little below where his strong hands gripped. My little legs dangled between his sturdy ones, which squeezed me in tightly on both sides. Holding me tightly around the waist with his right arm, the *annan* kicked out, starting the swing. I squealed happily it was exhilarating feeling the air whoosh against my face, swinging my little pigtails into the air.

Mum called out for me from the kitchen; but the *annan* answered for me.

'I am pushing Lily on the swing, Aunty.'

'Okay. Don't make her too dizzy.'

Moments later, while I was still enjoying myself, he lifted me up and off the swing.

'Come, let's go inside, Lily. Leave Charlie to play, he is quite happy.'

My head was still spinning giddily as the *annan* gripped my hand tightly, leading me into the house, and then to the bedroom propelling me to the gap between the wooden pallet that flexed beneath the weight of our bodies at night, and the wall of the bedroom. I looked in disappointment at the *annan*; was he putting me to bed? He smiled, bending towards my ear and whispered conspiratorially.

'Come, I am going to teach you a game. You've got to be very quiet, don't make any sound, okay?'

I nodded, eager to please.

'Here, lie down on the floor.'

The cement floor was hard on my back and I felt uncomfortable, wondering what sort of game we were going to play. *annan* knelt down beside me, his face darkening in the shadow of the room. He wasn't smiling any more.

What is he doing, why is he not talking and why is he looking at me so strangely? I was uncomfortable. He had told me not to make any noise, and I had to obey; besides, the strangeness of the situation was making me nervous. I stared up at him as his tongue protruded slightly from his mouth and saliva trickled from the corner.

He brought his hands down and lifted my dress with one hand, pulling my white cotton panties down, hard, with the other. Frightened by the strange and sudden movements, I began to squirm. I reached down to grab the elastic of my panties, and tried to pull them up but he shushed me.

'It's all right. Pretend to sleep. Close your eyes.'

Frightened and hemmed in, I did as he said and closed my eyes. I felt him shift, and then his heavy body was on top of me. I whimpered and squirmed, barely able to breathe against the weight of him. My panties were gone. His breath was loud and ragged in my ear.

A furious voice screamed.

'Get out! Get out of my house, you filthy boy!'

Mum stood in the doorway, visibly shaking. A ladle, dripping with curry sauce, was held high; her eyes blazed.

I had never seen her in a rage and I did what came naturally, which was to burst into tears; all my pent-up emotions came to the fore. Pulling up his shorts that had strangely come undone as he lay on top of me, *annan* shot off, arching around my mother and bending his body to avoid the ladle that she swung at him.

Mum strode over to me, her face working she picked up my panties with shaking hands, nodding at me to step into them.

'Don't you *ever* let anyone do that to you again.'

I shrank into my skin in shock. What had happened? I had certainly not relished being walked into the room, but this was an older person who was directing me, and we had been brought up to obey and respect our elders. As far as I knew, I had been getting ready to play a game with a known neighbour. Mum's obvious fury ignited a hot flush of shame, effusing my whole body. I felt defiled I had been made to do something shameful, something wrong. God was going to be cross with me.

Numbed into silence, we left the bedroom and I slunk away into a corner of the sitting room, hiding my tear-streaked face. The tuneful humming that had been drifting over from the kitchen all morning had ceased and a dreadful silence hung everywhere. Miserable, baffled little sobs periodically escaped my tight throat as I kept out of Mum's way and ignored Charlie's pleas to 'Come and play, *akka*, pleeeee-ease.'

The lunchtime siren boomed from the railways workshop, but I didn't hear it; I had sobbed myself into a hot, restless sleep. Nor did I hear my Dad cycling into our compound for lunch. Only when I roused myself and heard a whispered conversation flowing between my parents in the next room did I realise that he was at home. I stayed in my shameful little corner, my eyes tightly shut, unable to face my dear Dad. At the sound of the second siren Dad had to leave again; I felt his presence, heard his stockinged feet momentarily pause at the doorway before they continued towards the front door. The creak of the front door shutting gave me the courage to finally pull myself up and seek my Mum's presence.

I padded into the kitchen's doorway, my face sticky with half-dried tears, and stared at Mum, willing a smile, a softening. Relenting finally, she beckoned.

'You must never let anyone touch your body, Lily. He was a bad boy and he will never come back here again. God sees everything and he will be very cross at what happened. You understand? There are some wicked boys out there, don't go near any boys. Always stay near

50

your brothers and sisters. Now promise me that you won't talk about this to anyone, you understand? This is a very shameful thing to have happened to you and we mustn't talk about this.'

I nodded silently, shaking with shame but not knowing why.

Piling some rice onto a blue enamel plate, Mum made a well in the centre and ladled in some curry. She motioned at me with her eyes, 'come and eat'.

I shuffled in and took a sitting position on the floor, cross-legged, staring at the plate with no appetite. My right arm felt dead, drained of all life. With a supreme effort, I shoved some rice and curry into my dry mouth, choking in the process.

Her eyes softened, and my floodgates opened; I was sobbing hard now.

'I am so sorry, *ammah*.'

Whatever had happened had been a bad thing. I had upset my Mum. After lunch, my afternoon nap was interrupted with more sobbing. I prayed for my mother's silence, ashamed to face more accusatory faces when my older siblings returned from school.

Thankfully, Mum held her tongue. There was no change in behaviour from the rest of my family, and that *annan* never darkened our doorstep again. Not long afterwards, the boy's family moved away, which helped to lessen my burdened conscience. With the exception of my family members, I avoided men; my childhood had been sullied for ever and the incident set about a chain of events.

Among my various pet names in the household was one I loathed – *Muthura kundy,* literally translated as 'a child who wets herself'. I cringed every time my teasing siblings chanted it at me. To be continually reminded of an ailment that I had no control over felt cruel.

The morning after my humiliation at the hands of the *annan*, my younger brother pinched his nose as I walked past him, saying 'somebody smells round here'. Even after scrupulous scrubbing with soap, I remained highly conscious of the fact that I had lain in my own urine during the night. Every morning without fail, the sharp, smoky stink of stale urine, as strong as the smell that wafted over from our cowshed, clung to me as my crumpled night clothes clung to my body. My morale was at a continuous low. Nature had singled me out to bestow this unwelcome punishment upon me. Why me? What had I done? The mats I lay on deteriorated rapidly with the constant nightly wettings and had to be washed and aired on the clothesline every day.

Mum was sympathetic, but I received a gentle scolding from time to time, too.

'The mats rot, you know, and we cannot afford to be buying new mats, *ma*.'

I hung my head, my heart pounding in shame. Mum sighed.

'We must do something.'

After much rummaging around, a 'bed' was finally found and presented to me. Flat and hard, it was coated in olive green paint that was peeling and flaking; a few nails protruded from the wood and rusty hinges clung to its sides. My new bed was a door.

Peter wrenched out most of the nails, and hammered in those that refused to come out, until the surface reached a semblance of levelness. He then scrubbed the door with soap and hot water and laid it in place: the level front was for me to sleep on, while the underside, where the joists sat, rested on the floor.

I hated it at first. Its hinges seemed to mock me: *remember, I am a door and you are sleeping on me.* My body's movements during the night tilted it, making it tap the concrete floor in a constant search for equilibrium. A greyish pillow, the colour of clouds ready to spill their contents, held a small amount of stuffing that flattened out when my head pressed into it. This, and a torn-off length of old *sari* for my blanket, were my only night-time companions. The ragged ends of my blanket snagged on the splinters of the door as I fought with it every night.

And yet, I grew to love my bed. I clung to it, to the smell of me. My body lengthened itself on the hard boards as I stretched out at night and claimed my new, solitary domain, which was the open area on to which both bedroom doors opened. My sleeping quarters had to be moved from the family room to spare the rest of my siblings from being contaminated by my nightly habit.

If I lifted the top edge of my blanket and shook it, I could make it billow, creating a welcome breeze as it settled softly on my stretched out body. I relished the dry lightness whilst it lasted. It would be heavy and dripping wet by the morning. The sleep sounds from the bedrooms nearby lulled me into my own fitful sleep. The proximity of the back door, just a hand-stretch away, worked to my advantage: any tell-tale yellow puddles in the morning could be quickly washed out of the doorway, and my bed was stacked neatly upright against the wall during the day.

But now I had a new ailment.

'Why are you scratching yourself? Stop it, it is going to become sore.'

Anna dabbed some yellow astringent lotion on the weal's as she mouthed her laments. I had taken to scratching my body until I bled. The source of the itching remained a mystery to the family for some time until, on the same day that Anna dressed my wounds, she decided to air my so-called bed in the front garden. The harsh glare of the midday sun had an unexpected effect. All at once, bugs started fleeing from the wooden slats in the door. I screeched. 'Oh my God, what is that?' Anna turned away; her usual humorous comments had deserted her for once.

'They are *mootai kochi* – bed bugs. See how bloated and shiny they are? They have been drinking your blood at night. No wonder you have been scratching yourself. No, no, don't cry – I will pour hot water on the bed to kill them. Tonight you can sleep without having to scratch yourself. Let me look at you: here, pull your dress up.'

Sure enough, the rest of my body, normally not on view, was etched with scratch marks, some freshly encrusted and countless others dried.

'*Che, che*, I wish I had known earlier. I would have killed those horrible creatures before now.'

Moving quickly, Anna proceeded to heat up some water in our large empty kerosene tin, in which our whites were regularly boiled with flakes of carbolic soap on an open pit in our garden. She then poured cupfuls of the steaming water from a height on to the door and attacked it with a steel brush. The heat of the sun sizzled the water, which turned green as the brush lifted the flaking paint. From this day onwards, Anna set a regular cycle of fumigation in motion for my bed, but my tenacious night-time companions refused to be eradicated without putting up a fight for their survival.

6

'The mango tree family...'

Nature's Bounties

There was little time or space for prolonged periods of quiet in our household. Laughter rippled through the grounds as we engaged in outdoor games, principally using the house as a thoroughfare. The chipped blue enamel containers of prepared vegetables would tremble on the dining table top as we thundered through the house, seeking suitable places to hide from our seeking siblings. Our childish shouts and giggles mingled with the strains of music that blared out daily from the radios of neighbouring houses.

Adding to this daily cacophony were the regular toot-toots of railway engines as they shunted back and forth along the tracks. We could catch glimpses of the engines' green paint and the spiralling of the smoke through gaps in the foliage at our back fence. Sometimes the engines would gather speed and leap forward like a snorting bullock on the attack, sometimes they would retreat, at a much gentler pace.

Despite the constant noise, we had no difficulty in falling asleep; we were used to our lively environment. Mum enjoyed an afternoon nap; her head would fall forward abruptly towards her chest whilst squealing children's running feet thumped all around her. Hustle and bustle was as essential to us as breathing; everyone spoke loudly, and shouting at children was the norm – not through anger or frustration, but simply because of the practical need to be heard. Bellowing children's names whilst beckoning them from the doorway as they played in the compound was common practice.

An ancient, towering and highly productive mango tree that grew directly in front of the house dominated our large, noisy compound, its buttress base firmly rooted in a six-foot diameter of caked clay soil. Its elongated orange-pink leaves changed to a glossy red before finally turning dark green as it reached maturity. Its bark cracked in rough-edged rectangles, ready to fall off, under which numerous insects found shelter. Giant red ants, millipedes, quick to curl their multitude of tiny legs into a ball, and centipedes with their venomous claws and segmented blood-red bodies that moved surprisingly fast, sent shivers up my spine as I examined the bark closely with undiminished fascination.

Exposed roots, gnarled and cracked with age, were flattened in places with the wear of our feet as we played beneath the tree; its umbrella-like structure of branches and leaves provided us with much-needed shade from the midday sun. Brown resin exuded from the bark and branches, often sticking stubbornly to the soles of our feet, needing a scrape with our nails and a forceful pull to remove it.

The tree was our homing beacon, a landmark for the village that we could spy from as far away as the Chinese coffee shop. We were affectionately nicknamed by the locals as the *manga maram kudumbum* – 'the mango tree family'.

The fruits from our famous tree were especially large and almost achingly sweet; their honeyed aromas filled nostrils and caused mouths to water expectantly as soon as the smooth, ripe skins were split. While we played beneath the boughs, we knew to take extra care; as cousin Benji's experience proved, sun-ripened fruit could fall at any moment without warning. Some fruits would split as they landed, revealing the deep yellow, luscious flesh whose colour and flavour would tempt a whole host of hungry insects to home in and feast on it within minutes. The size and fertility of the tree ensured that there were always plenty of whole mangoes ready to be gathered for the family and for sharing with guests.

Only Peter was adept enough to climb this enormous tree. He would start his journey in the morning to avoid the worst of the heat, clad only in a pair of shorts, as the energy required to climb even at this slightly cooler time of day was enough to make him break into a sweat. He cleverly used his bare feet to grip on to the lumps and bumps in the bark, pulling himself upwards by embracing the trunk with his strong, muscular arms. As he gradually headed upwards, he cut down the occasional old or dead branch with a hefty *parang*. It was no mean feat, placing him at some risk, but a necessary task to keep the tree in its healthy condition.

It did not help Peter's somewhat fiery nature that as he carried out this essential but potentially dangerous maintenance work he was under the watchful scrutiny of our next-door neighbour.

Little evidence now remained of *paatie*'s former beauty, save the genes that she had generously passed on to her daughter. Our Hindu neighbour's once plump face now had limp leathered cheeks that hung in folds over an angular chin. Permanently clad in her traditional widow's garb of an off-white *sari*, *paatie* had deep-set, shrunken eyes, no eyebrows and elongated ear lobes that had been stretched over the years so they now hung all the way down to her shoulders, her heavy earrings studded with sparkly red stones sitting in them as though on a swing as they caught the sunlight. A matching red-stoned nose stud perched on the right side of her nose. Her great age allowed her to go topless: with no *sari* blouse to contain them, her wizened breasts hung like enormous prunes, flapping against her chest; her bony shoulders drooping forward, she used the end of her *sari* to cover her modesty.

Before our family moved into the house, *paatie* used to gain access to our mango tree via the padlocked gate in the barbed wire fencing. She had constructed a makeshift altar that she'd attached to the trunk, where she would light squares of camphor, make offerings and chant her prayers, all intended to appease the tree spirits and thus guarantee the safety of the neighbourhood. Still present a few feet off the ground, the niche, stained an orange red, marked the spot.

Paatie had helped my mother to bring me into the world. I imagined her at the altar, her bony back curved, showing the nubs on her spine as she bent over her offerings: burning camphor on a metal tray, from which a wisp of smoke curled like pencil sharpenings, and also an earthenware pot full of water, fresh mango leaves pulled off our tree and a husked coconut, the pointy end facing upwards. The leaves and coconut represented divine consciousness. The pot symbolised Mother Earth, or the goddess Lakshmi, whom *paatie* believed resided in our tree.

Thankfully, she did not pursue her prayers once our family bought the house, but *paatie* never failed to remind us of the mango tree's special significance as a holy tree. As befitted our status as children, we duly acknowledged and respected her wisdom as an elder, even though her beliefs in this instance held no real significance for us Catholics. As a mark of respect, we made sure that the bounties of the tree were always shared with *paatie*.

Whenever Peter started pruning the tree, *paatie*'s face would miraculously appear at the other side of the barbed wire fence. Despite her small stature, she could yell loud and shrill at Peter from her side of the fence, her gappy, *paan*-stained teeth in full evidence.

'*Dei*, Jonah, be careful how much of the tree you cut down. She will not like it if you hurt her, you know, she will curse you if you don't show her respect.'

'I wish this old woman would stop interfering. It is difficult enough concentrating on climbing this tree without her shouting out orders to me as well,' Peter muttered, loud enough for us to hear, but not within *paatie*'s hearing.

Mum gently clicked her tongue on the roof of her mouth and lifted soft eyes to Peter.

'She is an old lady, *thambi*.' (Mum often affectionately referred to her eldest son as her younger brother, another unexplained tradition.) 'Don't get annoyed with her. She has helped us a lot.'

'All right, all right, I know, but she is testing my patience. I will try to be nice.'

Raising his voice a couple of notches, Peter turned his head towards the old lady as she stood on splayed feet, one arm on her hip and the other shielding her eyes from the sun so that she could scrutinise proceedings.

'*Paatie*, I am only cutting down the rotten branches,' he said, trying to ignore the tuts and headshakes that greeted this comment.

Muttering under his breath, Peter hacked at the branches with renewed vigour, taking out his irritation on the tree and angrily brushing away the fragments of wood chips that clung to his sweaty skin. Even so, he was well aware that he himself was indebted to *paatie*.

From an early age, to augment our income, Peter scavenged scraps of metal from the railway's dumping site a few hundred yards from our house at the end of the shunting run. Chinese scrap metal merchants hunched close by with gunnysacks and portable scales, ready to bargain with the scrawny soot-covered child labourers who brought their dubious wares for sale. When Peter was fifteen, one such trip ended badly.

We were drawn to our doorway by strident shouts; a group of fellow scavengers had brought a hobbling Peter home, leaning heavily on another lad's shoulder. Mum stepped forward, and then faltered when she saw blood steadily dripping from a great gash in her son's foot. At four years old, and petrified by the sight and metallic scent of the blood, I screamed, but was unceremoniously pushed aside to make room for Peter to be guided into Dad's chair.

The room was suddenly full of bodies it seemed as though a hundred people had followed my brother to watch the spectacle. Some faces showed concern, but most had mouths gaping open, eyes shining in excitement at the living drama being acted out before them. I stared at my adored brother in an ecstasy of nerves. Clad only in a pair of dirtied khaki shorts, his body streaked with sweat and grime from the dumping ground and hair clinging damply to his head, he gritted his teeth to hold in the pain.

Then, seemingly from nowhere, *paatie* suddenly appeared, no doubt alerted by the tumult. Ignoring the drama, she quickly took control of the situation; her shrill voice cut through the murmur of the crowds.

'The show is over! Go away, everybody. Now!'

Perhaps surprised at the powerful voice coming from so unassuming a figure, they all obeyed immediately, muttering under their breath and casting backward glances as they dragged themselves reluctantly from the scene.

Paatie began shouting out orders. Under her direction, people ran to gather shiny deep green leaves from her hedgerow and pound them into a paste, working quickly while Peter's pupils dilated soundlessly with pain. With gnarled, yet deft fingers, *paatie* applied the slimy paste to the deep cut and bandaged it with a torn-off length from Mum's old *sari*. Then, waving aside our thanks with a flick of her widow-white *sari*, she left as swiftly as she had appeared.

Thanks to *paatie*'s swift actions and the healing properties of her homemade *valli elai*, Peter's wound healed without any complications. Peter bore the scar, visible for many years, as proof of the debt he owed to our local medicine woman.

As well as our distinctive mango tree, six coconut trees grew within our grounds. In true Malay style, we could therefore use generous amounts of coconut in our cooking. Thick coconut milk added richness to our sauces, binding wonderful aromatic spices together and giving curries an addictive flavour.

When the coconuts were ready to be harvested, specially trained men, 'toddy tappers', approached Mum, touting their skills.

'*Ammah, thaenga vetunum ma?*'

Mum nodded, giving them brisk instructions.

'All right, go ahead. But mind the children, they get curious. Shoo them away if they get too close.'

Duly shooed, we stood at a safe distance and watched the short, dark men dressed in grimy loincloths climb the tall trees, lean muscles rippling. A cloth pouch and a length of bamboo secured by a string were tied round their waists. Having approached the trunk, a thick loop made out of coconut fibres was placed round their ankles and then their legs splayed to the width of the loop. This they used for support, their ankles held within the loop as they leap-frogged, their dry, calloused feet firmly gripping the trunk as they climbed to the point where the palms fanned out. They made the whole process look so easy. Now the chopping process commenced as they cut and prized the coconuts away and let them fall to dot the grass below, carefully balancing themselves against every movement. We watched, fascinated, from a safe distance as the number of fallen coconuts grew steadily. Mum would be happy with the plentiful harvest to be stored and dipped into daily. The men slid down the length of the tree minus the bamboo piece.

'How come you didn't have to pay the men, *ammah*?'

Mum paused from her task of counting the coconuts and laying them in piles, so that they could be husked and twined together for easy transport to the open storage area beside the kitchen.

'What they collect from the tree tomorrow morning is more than enough payment for them. They use the sap they get from the flowers to make toddy. All these poor, stupid men go and get drunk on the toddy, wasting the money that they should be spending on their families.'

A deep sigh escaped as Mum looked at me and smiled.

'Luckily your father does not have this terrible habit.'

I understood. I had seen men heading past our front gate, zigzagging their way home in broad daylight, their dirty, moth-eaten singlets wet from spilled drink. How they managed to stay on the narrow path without falling into the open drain remained a mystery. One man in particular I had seen stumbling past many times, his eyes red, a sickly sweet smell emanating from his half-opened, dribbling mouth. I would shrink away from the gate, hearing him mutter as he weaved along, his speech slurred.

'Musht give the wife a good kicking, always crying, can't a hard-working man enjoy a well-deserved drink? Always money. Asking for money, like it grows on treesh. Treesh!'

The toddy had a culinary use that Mum indulged as a weekend treat whenever she had a few cents to spare or something to barter with. Before sunset, I was sent on an errand to an adventurous near-neighbour's house, clutching an empty bottle in my sweaty palm. A tumbler-full of the pungent liquor was poured in and a corkscrewed newspaper pushed into its neck for a stopper. Mum used the toddy to ferment ground rice, producing a very light batter that was perfect for our breakfast-time *dosais*. The liquor gave each springy *dosai* a distinctive sweet perfume and a slightly tangy taste. It was a sobering thought, if that's not an inappropriate description, that our life-sustaining food was someone else's devil's brew.

Thankfully, as Mum said, my own Dad did not succumb to that particular temptation. Family responsibility sat firmly on his shoulders and he was constantly engaged in the role of provider. Meat was an expensive commodity; if we were to enjoy it, when it couldn't be bought, it had to be caught. Once a month, Dad would set off to the jungle for a hunt. An uneasy cloak of tension covered the household for the duration of Dad's trip. I came to dread those evenings when I heard him announce:

'Marie, I'm going hunting tomorrow morning, so have to be up early. Make my breakfast for me and pack some food; there will be two fellows coming with me this time.'

Dad's hunting friends were fellow soldiers from the Indian National Army. One of the 'uncles' lived in railway quarters, near neighbours to my godparents, but on this occasion the other was someone I had never met. Mum sighed and shook her head, but reluctantly complied as bidden.

I hid around a corner and peeked out carefully, watching with a mixture of fascination and fear as my father oiled and greased his big hunting rifle. Black grease caught under his nails. The tattooed spot in the middle of his forehead from childhood days deepened into a darker green as he concentrated on his task, half-listening to the news on the radio, unaware of my prying eyes. He was meticulous, taking the rifle apart piece by piece and laying each down precisely in a familiar pattern before proceeding to clean the bore, then reassembling everything with the same precision, ready for the next day. I crept away silently; Dad did not like his children around him when he was handling his rifle.

I never saw him leave. Mum was engaged in her cooking in silence that morning; the steady tick-tock of the clock on the wall replaced the usual sound of her humming. I stood ready to carry the used cooking water to the vegetable patch as usual, but she poured it down the drain in her distraction. Once her cooking routine was over, Mum did what she always did when she needed comfort and reassurance; kneeling in front of the altar, she prayed. Shining tears held just behind her eyes, waiting to spill down her smooth, nut-brown cheeks.

'Please God; send my husband back home safely. What will I do with all these children if anything happens to him? I place his life in your hands only.'

The wait was unbearable. It was her prayers that brought home the danger in which my Dad was placing himself, in order to provide food for us. The twisting tentacles of poverty crawled into every corner of our lives. As I watched Mum pray, I vowed with renewed conviction that I would study hard, to enable me to earn sufficient money to ungrasp those tentacles and push them firmly away.

Dad returned, safe and unharmed. Wild boar was plentiful in the jungles, but on this occasion he brought great big slabs of particularly dark meat that he and his friends had shared among themselves. Mum took it into the kitchen to skin it while I watched. Large clots of blood still clung to the cut joint and a giant sinister bone stuck out. My mouth drew down in disgust.

'It's tiger meat. It will need a lot of spices and ginger to tenderise the meat, but it will be tasty.'

Mum smiled as both my eyes and mouth widened into the awed shape of silent 'o's.

'We are very lucky to get so much meat, *ma*. Look at the marrowbone; it must have been a big tiger. Your father is a brave man.'

I pictured the scene: the great cat creeping, my father taking careful aim, then just as the tiger launched itself at him, BANG!

A fly buzzing around my head brought me back to the present; it was drawn to the strong smell of the meat. Pinching my nose, I made a quick getaway, lacking the stomach to witness any further preparations.

As I munched the rich, dark meat later that night, pride in my Dad's prowess overwhelmed and filled my chest. None of my other relatives could match his bravery. Dad was a fighter who could never be caged, and he could outmanoeuvre a tiger, one of nature's most fearsome beasts. His only scars were leech bites that welled up on his legs, courtesy of the moist jungle swamps. Faced with the prospect of kill or be killed, and knowing that hungry mouths at home were waiting to be fed, my Dad would always face whatever danger he had to, in order to keep his family safe.

7

'Paan and parangs...'

Our Neighbours

It was a Friday evening, and Chippu – the good-looking but far from good-hearted daughter of *paatie*, and our neighbour Yelumalai's wife – was about to provide us with our evening's entertainment. No turning of the knob on our radio did we require; simply open a window and a soap-opera drama would commence without fail at twenty minutes past four each day, when Dad and our skinny neighbour returned home from the Sentul railway workshop. Within minutes, a strident female voice rose up to greet him, not with a welcome, but an accusation of some sort – and, just like that, battle had commenced.

Chippu and Yelumalai's arguments invariably took place in the kitchen that backed on to the dividing barbed wire fencing. We only needed to open our window a smidgen in order to catch every word. Full of curiosity and the guilty glee of eavesdropping, we hovered at the window until Dad strode in to shut it firmly, giving us a warning look that clearly read: 'None of our business.' Even with the window shut we could hear the drama reach its next stage: a dull thump, followed by a muffled '*Aiyyo*! Stop that!' Then the clattering of aluminium saucepans landing on the cement floor, accompanied by the same strident, shrill voice, now raised a couple of notches.

'Ohhh, you are a good-for-nothing husband, no backbone to stand up to anybody. Your children are grown-up and you *still* wet your bed!'

The voices continued to crescendo, until Yelumalai finally retreated to the open air, battered and subdued. Bare-chested, he shuffled across the ground, bending his smooth, skinny body double to dip a metal bucket into an open well. Keeping his eyes lowered, he moved his upper body sideways, tipping his now-full bucket into a grey funnel fitted onto the outside of a corrugated zinc sheet, which formed the enclosure of his open-air bathroom. The splosh as the water hit the bottom of the empty concrete tub on the inside of the bathroom could be heard from where we youngsters were gathered in play for the last hour and a half of daylight. The barbed wire between our two properties gave little privacy to our neighbour as his head bobbed up and down above the zinc partition whilst his raised hand poured tinfuls of water over his head with an air of dejection. Smothering our childish mirth, we sauntered towards our front door to give him some space and much-needed peace.

Yelumalai's two children, five-year-old son Moorthy and daughter Parameswari (Para-mace, for short) were shooed out by their impatient mother and thrust in the direction of the bathroom. They smiled and waved at us in a carefree manner; the daily drama of their household seeming to have little effect on their effervescent natures. Finally, *paatie* appeared to take in the balmy evening air, casting a resigned glance at her son-in-law's bent head. Perhaps they all sought some refuge from the irascible Chippu.

Our wounded hero quietly finished his ablutions and slunk from sight. Minutes later, *paatie* was joined by Mr Yeharmbaram and a Punjabi man, Mr Chadha, both tenants of Yelumalai. The men with their young families rented the two terraced houses adjacent to their landlord and were always ready with a friendly smile and wave for us.

Dad, freshly showered and dressed in a clean *sarong*, sauntered, barefoot, towards the fence to exchange pleasantries with the old lady and the two gentlemen. Their chatter drifted away on the night air, a free-flowing amalgamation of Tamil, Hindi, Malay and the occasional English word, as was typical in our multicultural community.

Leaning on the doorway, Mum attracted Peter's attention, as he was engrossed in the task of splitting logs in the yard. Tiny shards of wood showered him with every chop, sticking to his khaki cotton shorts and tangling in the fine dark hair on his chest, arms and legs.

'Jonah, can you pluck that ripe jackfruit? It is ready to be chopped down. Cut some up to give away.'

Peter, at sixteen already six-foot tall, obediently leant his axe against the well-worn tree stump upon which he had been chopping offcuts into smaller strips for kindling, and set about following our mother's instructions. He sat on his haunches, his long, lanky body glistening in the humid air. The V-shaped mark in the middle of his forehead was the only part of his face that wasn't bathed in sweat.

The skin of the jackfruit was the colour of hard-boiled egg yolk, dotted all over with black pinpricks; it was bumpy, but quite soft to the touch now that it was well-ripened. Used to physical work, Peter flexed his muscular arms as he deftly cut into the soft flesh, his tongue probing the inside of his cheek in concentration. I gazed adoringly at my handsome brother while I squatted on the grass next to him. Peter used a cleaver to chop the fruit into large chunks, then prized it open to expose golden, succulent, soft globes housing a single seed, all held together by long, tenacious strings, which could be stripped away to release the pods. He prized open one globe, pressing it gently to let the seed plop out, and handed me the luscious quarter-inch pod, whose honey-sweet aroma made me salivate.

'Here, eat,' said Peter, smiling indulgently, his dark brown eyes twinkling at me.

'Thanks, *annan*!' I bit into the soft flesh, releasing its sugary syrup, which quickly coated my tongue; a few chews and it was gone. As I smacked my lips in satisfaction Peter laughed.

'All right, have another one, but no more after that or you will get a tummy-ache. Have more later after dinner.' Endowing me with his special smile, he added: 'Want to give me a hand?'

I nodded. My heart singing with the knowledge that my big brother loved me, I proceeded to help in companionable silence. After peeling off sufficient for our home consumption, Peter portioned the rest and wrapped them in squares of cut-off gunnysacks that ever-practical Anna had brought out in readiness. All were neatly stacked ready for distribution to our friends. As dusk fell, we carried our bounty indoors.

Peter lit our kerosene oil lamp; the smell of food preparation stirred the air. The rest of the evening passed without further interruptions.

The following morning, Mum washed our loomed rug, which had a woven picture of the Taj Mahal in its centre in all its domed glory. Dad had purchased it with a 'mates' rates' discount from a mail-order catalogue run by his friend Gurdial Singh, a political activist and owner of a textile shop in Kuala Lumpur that was largely stocked with products from a factory in India owned by Mr Singh's relatives. Dad's pride and joy was the centrepiece of our sitting room, spread out underneath our low, glass-topped coffee table.

Peter's help was sought to hang the rug out to dry. Wisely choosing not to use our regular clothesline, as the weight of the sodden rug would have been too much for the slender jute string to bear, Peter shook it out and spread it on the sturdier fence between our neighbour Yelumalai's house and ours. His task completed, he returned indoors, unaware that his actions had been under scrutiny.

Chippu was not exactly enamoured of Peter, whose easy confidence and straight talking often riled her. If they were ever outside at the same time, she would rudely hawk and spit onto the ground, then sniff and turn her face away in disdain. Brought up to respect his elders, Peter did not rise to her insults, but his fiery nature was being tested to its limits and he noted every spit and sniff.

As soon as Peter left the compound and went inside, Chippu appeared in her garden and abuse was hurled across the barbed wire fence.

'Which rascal is trying to break our fence? Dirty rascal. He can keep his rubbish in his own grounds!'

The long, droopy hair that sprouted from the mole to the left of Chippu's upper lip shook furiously as she pushed the wet rug off the fence. It landed with a thump in a crumpled heap in the open drain below.

Spirited Rosie, my wispy imp of a third sister, six years older than me, was tall enough to peek through the large spy hole in the wall of our house that overlooked the compound fence. Scuttling to her side, I found my own smaller hole lower down, which I could just about reach on tiptoe. Rosie's hand gripped mine as she called out:

'*Annan*, she has pushed the carpet into the drain!'

Furious Peter, in no mood for a husband-bashing woman, retaliated by rushing outside and replacing the rug on the fence. Chippu refused to give in, struggling to knock the rug off again, but Peter held firm and she had to give in to his superior strength after a couple of attempts. Angrily, she stormed off to the other side of the compound, muttering insults.

The show over, Rosie and I moved away. Our soothing mother talked Peter into calming down and wisely sent him out on an errand for the rest of the day, but Chippu's tirade continued in spits and spurts as we went about our daily activities trying to ignore the abusive language, with Mum on hand to shush us.

The scorching sun soon dried the offending rug and, sighing with relief, Theresa laid it out again in its rightful place. As she did so, she giggled and offered an explanation half-seriously, half in jest:

'You know, *ammah*, I bet Chippu fancies Jonah. I have seen her staring at him sideways when she thought no one else was around. Yelumalai Uncle is such a reed against Jonah, no wonders she looks at other men. She must be frustrated, that is why she is always in a bad mood.'

Theresa's speculation drew a frown from Mum.

'Shhh, don't go spreading stories; there is enough bad blood between the two families without you adding to it. Don't say anything in front of little listening ears either.' Mum threw a sideways glance at me while I returned her gaze, all innocence.

That evening, we heard raised voices emerging from our neighbour's kitchen.

'That swaggering young rascal needs to be taught a lesson. If you are a *real* man, you will stand up for your insulted wife. Here, take the broom. Go on!'

Peter's lips curled with laughter and we all giggled at the thought of the slight, uncertain Yelumalai turning up on our doorstep to 'thrash' our six-foot, muscular brother. But no avenging angel appeared and the incident was soon forgotten by Peter – but not by the humiliated Chippu, as we would soon discover.

Not all our neighbours were problematic. Kuttan was our saviour. He lived in a single wooden house on the other side of our smelly stream. Always bare-chested, he was a bronzed, wizened bachelor with dry, creased skin that crackled like elephant hide and bare feet that were slippered with split and calloused skin. An off-white cotton *veshtie*, a length of spun cotton, was permanently tied around his midriff, begging to be washed. His white hair stood to attention like an exclamation mark. Rounded shoulders emphasised his slight hump; tracing his spinal cord with a finger would feel like a ride on a rollercoaster. A row of gapped, *paan*-stained teeth couldn't mar Kuttan's infectious smile. Next to his house stood a terrace of three cottages that he rented out, all set in undulating acres of productive fruit trees. His green fingers tilled the rich soil, producing an abundance of vegetables that he generously shared with his grateful neighbours.

Towards the end of the day just before dusk, standing on the edge of his plantation, Kuttan's familiar voice would ring out. With practised skill, Peter negotiated a makeshift bridge formed from a couple of logs thrown across the stream, returning with the bounty that Kuttan had gathered for us during his day's toil. Sometimes a whole comb of bananas, other times, vegetables, or coconuts husked and bunched together, came our way. Whatever he gave was gratefully received. In return, my father and Peter helped the illiterate Kuttan with his paperwork.

Perhaps Kuttan was younger than he looked. Either way, he certainly surprised us when he returned home after a holiday in India with a beautiful, fair-skinned young wife. Nothing fazed our parents, however; they quickly expressed their congratulations to the newly married couple and helped Kuttan's wife to settle into her new home. Mum, the untrained but well-practised midwife, soon had cause to come to her aid, helping to deliver three children produced in quick succession over three years.

The Kuttans were respected neighbours. The fact that they were Hindus and we were Catholic never mattered; in fact, it enhanced our friendship. We celebrated each other's religious festivals, sharing our specially prepared celebratory food.

I was reduced to disrespectful giggles when I caught sight of Kuttan with his jaw constantly moving backwards and forwards, chewing his beloved *paan*. This was a highly addictive concoction of beetle-nut shavings and peppery tasting *vethelai* – betel leaf. The flat surface of the leaf was brushed with toxic *chunam*, a white lime paste, then wrapped around the beetle-nut shavings, folded into a pyramid shape and its loose flap tucked in. Now it was ready to be popped into Kuttan's waiting mouth and chewed on, creating a stimulating, carcinogenic high.

'Here, what's happened? Has anyone noticed, there don't seem to be any dramas happening next door. The evenings have been unusually quiet. Maybe Chippu has come to her senses,' Peter remarked one night, as he passed the vegetable dish to *ammah*. 'About time too.'

However it was only the lull before the storm. Chippu had been seething over Peter's apparent victory with the rug, and was not about to let the matter rest. Eggs had been hatching in the viper's nest, and we were about to be bitten.

Yelumalai formed a pact with his near neighbour, Velu, a tormented soul whose troubles arose not from an overbearing wife, but from his elderly, live-in parents. A bachelor through no choice of his own, he was bullied into submission by his domineering, foul-mouthed old man, who was followed meekly and silently around by his diminutive mother. Velu's father was one of our local toddy drinkers, who saw nothing to be ashamed of in subjecting his wife and often his son to kicks and slaps on a daily basis.

But it was impossible to feel too sorry for Velu. He seemed to harbour a bitter envy towards the rest of the world, going through life with a scowl on his face and a mutter under his breath for every happy word he heard. Dad had little to say about Velu; if we complained about him, Dad would sniff and shrug scornfully, saying: 'That rascal of a father of his has never done a day's work in his life. Like father like son.' Actually this was not strictly true, as Velu was in full-time employment, an escape during the day from his abusive parent. Dad regarded hard work as something to take pride in; he could never suffer lazy layabouts.

Both Chippu and Velu shared a particular dislike of Peter and envied his independent spirit. What seemed to be little more than a harmless personal opinion turned nasty when Chippu decided to fan the flames of their mutual hatred and conspire with Velu against our brother. He needed to be taken down a peg or two, they decided, and plotted a way to do so. Aware that neither of them could match Peter when it came to physical strength, Chippu and Velu had united in the knowledge that they required help. Between them, they hired a local thug and convinced him to challenge my brother to a fight. Plying the thug with alcohol late one night, they sent him along the road that led past our house. Already in bed, we could all clearly hear the man's raised voice as he walked from one house to another, hurling abusive language that was directed solely at us.

At five years of age, I had developed a fear of the dark. I sat bolt upright, my heart pounding in my chest, utterly petrified by the sound of this isolated, disembodied stranger's voice screaming abuse at my family in the middle of an otherwise silent night. I was too terrified even to scream.

Dad appeared, shielding a lit candle.

'Come, follow me, children. Follow me into the hall.'

Charlie and I followed to where Mum, Theresa and Anna were standing next to the family dinner table. Mum held baby Chandra tightly in her arms, gripping her rosary in her spare hand and reciting prayers while continually crossing herself. Peter was nearby, bare-chested and standing tall and silent, gripping a sharp, hefty *parang* in his hands. I couldn't take my eyes off the huge flat blade, which glistened dully in the flickering candlelight. Dad held the candle lower.

'Keep it dark, so that fellow will think that we are asleep and believe it will be safe to come into our compound. Then we will wait by the gate and give him a nasty surprise,' he whispered.

Dad looked around at our fearful faces, his strong, clear eyes meeting each of ours in turn.

'Now, children, stay quiet and don't worry, your *annan* and I will make sure that this bad man will not harm us. Join your mother in prayer. God will look after us; we are good people. I want you all to be brave.'

I was confused. Why would *appa* want to give that man a nasty surprise, wouldn't it be better if that man just went away, and *appa* and *annan* will be out of danger? This course of action seemed to make no sense to me, but I placed my trust blindly in Dad's superior knowledge, even though my gut was churning cartwheels.

Re-knotting his *sarong* at the waist, Dad kicked up the hem with his right heel and tucked the gather into his waistband, effectively halving his *sarong*'s length to free the movements of his slender, muscular legs.

My Dad is strong. Despite my misgivings, pride welled up within me.

Dad reached over to Peter to retrieve then grasp the *parang* tightly. Slowly but purposefully, they ventured out into the pitch darkness, leaving our gate wide open in invitation to lure the hired man into our grounds. My eyes gazed unfocused at the gap they had just left behind, willing it to be filled again. Come back *appa*, come back *annan*, I repeated silently to myself. I was convinced that only their presence would make me feel safe again.

As my father had instructed, we kept only a single candle burning, so the house appeared to be in complete darkness from the outside. Too tired and too young to realise the implications of what was happening, three-year-old Charlie soon succumbed to sleep. I followed him underneath the table, but was far too frightened to join him in sleep, all too aware of the danger we faced. I kept my eyes fixed on the solid latch bar that usually sat across the door at night, and which now stood against the wall waiting for the safe return of Dad and Peter. Our vulnerability was greatly increased. Anyone could walk in through the unprotected door.

I had visions of the crazed thug killing my father and brother and striding through the doorway, a bloodied *parang* grasped in his hand, ready to slaughter us all. Despite the tropical humidity, I was shivering and shaking, as a blanket of cold fear as dark as the night enveloped me.

Suddenly, the night fell completely silent. The thug had stopped shouting. Perhaps he had gone, I hoped fervently. Unless... Was he, even now, attacking my father and brother? Were they already dead? The suspense was unbearable. Every minute in the unnatural quiet seemed an eternity. The only sound around me was the hushed whispers of my mother and eldest sister Theresa as they continued to pray to God for help and the night chorus of the frogs. I blabbered my own prayer: 'Help us, God, help us, please.'

Finally, there was a movement at the door – and Dad appeared, quickly followed by Peter. They were unscathed. The tightness in my chest eased and I gasped in a deep, ragged breath. The thug, Dad revealed, had taken fright when he saw the open gate and fled the scene. The danger was past.

Our parents hurried us back to bed, but I found it impossible to sleep for the rest of the night. Fear of the dark was now even further ingrained into my mind.

One week later, we realised that the situation was not over. Furious at the failure of their plotting, and under the influence of bravado-inducing toddy, Velu staggered over to lean against our fence and bellowed out, challenging Peter to a duel.

'*Dai*, Jonah, come out. Come out and fight like a man! I will take you, one-to-one.'

Good God, was he ever going to stop tormenting us? Despite

Mum's pleas to ignore Velu, Peter's anger was quickly ignited and he flung himself past her and out of the door. Angry veins in his neck stood out as he marched towards Velu, his siblings following behind in his wake. Peter's open hand slammed against our zinc gate.

The stage was set as they squared up to one another. Velu had taken up his stance on the triangular patch of grassy land outside our gate, scowling and bunching his fists. With two strides Peter was upon him, fierce and righteous anger fuelling his momentum. They set to immediately, raining blows onto each other's bare torsos. The rest of us children gathered together, shaking at the thud of fists on flesh, watching limbs flail and fall as each tried to out-punch the other. Passers-by and close neighbours quickly gathered into a mesmerised crowd, raucously taking bets as to who would emerge the victor.

I huddled tightly against my sisters' warm bodies, wincing, feeling every punch that landed on Peter. But Peter was clearly the stronger of the two. Soon he was raining lethal punches upon his opponent, who was hopping around on pole-thin legs, unsuccessfully seeking escape from the fight he had drunkenly started. Unable to keep up the momentum, Velu unclenched his fists and placed his hands on either side of his face, trying to avoid the punches. Grazes accumulated on the dark knots of his knuckles.

The battle finally came to an inevitable and humiliating end. As Velu ducked and staggered around, his *sarong* loosened, then took a sudden dive towards the ground. Not having had the foresight to sling on a pair of underpants before the fight, Velu made a very public display of himself, causing uproar among the amused onlookers. Peter lowered his fists and watched as Velu clumsily hiked his *sarong* to cover his modesty before fleeing the scene amidst howls of laughter. He never bothered Peter again.

Though it all ended in hilarity, the whole charade emphasised only too poignantly the violence that was prevalent in the society I was growing up in. I was glad of the strength and security that my Dad and elder brother gave to our vulnerable family – but my breathing shallowed and palms sweated all the same.

My dreams increased in number, becoming repetitive in their theme. I was standing on top of a mountain, gazing over vast distances – then I was falling, falling down and down helplessly, endlessly, not knowing where the bottom was. My body became weightless, my arms stretched out in front of me, desperately trying to break my fall, but the air continued to rush past as I gasped for breath, hurtling helplessly into a vast void.

A thief broke into our grounds not long after the incident with the thug. Although his intentions were successfully thwarted by Peter and Dad's quick response the intrusion only served to increase my nightmares. I feared nightfall and needed an adult to accompany me to the bathroom; I scuttled to and fro like a frightened rat. Peter's efforts to allay my fears were a losing battle.

'There is nothing out there that can hurt you, Lily. Come on, get on my back, I will take you round the compound.'

Unable to refuse my elder brother, I let him ease me on to his shoulder and held on tightly to his neck. With furiously thumping heart, I was carried around our grounds. At first my eyes remained firmly shut, but then slowly, getting used to the rhythm of Peter's walk, I opened them, letting them adjust to our surroundings. Peter flicked the switch on his torch and I followed the beam of the winking yellow eye, which shone ghostly in the inky blackness of the night. He took me to all the dark corners while my back itched with fear. With a stick in his hand, he prodded the undergrowth.

'See, there is no one hiding anywhere. It is quite safe.'

The scurry and loud croaking of frogs heightened my fear of the darkness as we skirted the bougainvillea's undergrowth. I was glad of my remoteness from the ground I didn't fancy one of those creatures jumping on to my feet in the dark. Although calmer than before, I wasn't completely happy until we returned to the house.

That night I lay awake for some time. I heard the creaking of my little brother moving in his sleep on his bed. A fierce protectiveness gripped me: no one had better dare to harm my beloved brothers and sisters. I got up and tiptoed across to where Charlie's gentle breathing rose and fell from his young chest. I watched him for a while, feeling my palpitating heart slowing its beat in line with his peaceful slumber, then crept back onto my plank bed. I sobbed myself to sleep.

Halfway through the night, I woke once more. A familiar smell filled my nostrils. I felt cold. Rising, I trod my way carefully, eyes slowly growing accustomed to the dark, to where Mum and Dad were sleeping on the mat in the corner of the sitting room. I tapped on Dad's shoulder.

'*Appa*. I wet myself again.'

8

'A nice young man...'

First-born Leaves Home

I fashioned cups and plates out of mud and balanced them carefully, one by one, on a stack of firewood to bake hard in the hot mid-afternoon sun. Charlie was squatting nearby, dipping his chubby toddler fingers into the pool of mud I had created. Mum was busy in the vegetable patch, while Theresa and Rosie had disappeared into the house a few minutes earlier, armed with the day's washing. Peter was probably pottering about in his room, and Anna would have been boiling water for our four o'clock tea. Through the front doorway I could just about see Dad's feet, casually crossed at the ankles, and no doubt stretched out in his favourite armchair with his Saturday paper.

Hearing a noise at the gate I looked up from my play and caught sight of Innasi, my paternal uncle; he weaved into the yard on his motorbike, a stranger riding pillion behind him. Uncle Innasi lived in the agricultural village of Serdang, where the British conducted horticultural experiments in the purpose-built Serdang Agricultural Centre. The vast, fertile area of land surrounding the College's buildings provided ideal growing conditions. Seeds and seedlings imported from all over the British Empire found a welcome home. Grafts were cultured and those of the local workers who were fortunate enough to find employment at the centre often smuggled prize plants out to give to selected friends and relatives. The bounty of the centre's succulent crops was sold to the workers at competitive prices. Uncle Innasi, who was employed there, had presented us with an often admired and prolific cocoa plant that flourished by the side of our front gate. We prized open the pods to reveal the flesh-covered seeds, then dried the seeds in the sun, but never actually succeeded in producing any edible cocoa – instead our small mouths chewed on the bitter seeds and spat them out in disgust.

Serdang was a couple of bus rides away from Sentul. It wasn't a planned visit; but in our open-house culture, friends and family often dropped by without any notice, assured of a warm welcome at any time of day. Tall and slim, with a complexion the colour of heavily milked tea that was a shade lighter than that of either Theresa or Peter, the stranger jumped off the bike first. He ran a hand quickly through his dark, wind-ruffled hair, styled in a side parting, revealing a wide forehead whose broadness spoke of some intelligence (according to our family lore). The sun's glare highlighted three shiny scars on his forehead, but these did nothing to detract from his attractive features. The outline of his long legs was emphasised in pressed, slate grey trousers, and he wore a full-sleeved, cuff-linked white cotton shirt that was unbuttoned at the neck, allowing a few wiry tufts of hair to peek through. It seemed he was dressed to impress. My uncle alighted from the motorbike and called out his familiar greeting of mock bewilderment.

'Eh, Lily, Charlie, how you have grown!'

Shy in the presence of the stranger, I had no answer for him and dropped my eyes to the ground, hiding my mud-stained hands behind my back. Charlie ran to hide his head in Mum's *sarong*, spattering it with mud from his hands. My curiosity piqued, I turned to my mother.

'*Ammah*, who is this other uncle? Is he related to us?'

She half-cupped her mouth and whispered in response: 'No, *ma*. Never seen him before. Must be Uncle's friend.'

Folding his paper, Dad stood up to welcome our guests and ushered them into the house; we all followed, curious. A shy smile played round the stranger's lips as he was introduced first to my parents and then to Peter, who sauntered from his bedroom into the sitting room. After a few minutes, Mum left the men to converse and found the rest of us clustered round my bed space, trying our best to eavesdrop on the conversation. She turned to my eldest sister.

'Theresa, *ma*, go and put your best *sari* on, the Kashmir one, and hurry back to make some tea for all of us. Bring it into the hall.'

My eldest sister gazed at Mum, expecting an explanation, but none was forthcoming. Her brow furrowed in quiet rebellion and her small mouth half-opened like a hungry fish, a protest forming on her lips, but Mum shook her head. Seeing the worried look in Theresa's eyes, Mum spoke softly:

'Look, just go for now, I will explain later. Go *ma*, don't worry, it is all good news. He looks like a nice young man, doesn't he, heh? If you don't do this, it might seem rude to your Uncle. You don't have to stay for long. Just hand the tea and then you can go back and join your brothers and sisters.'

Defeated, Theresa turned away, shoulders drooping in resignation; she trudged into the bedroom. Charlie shadowed her as usual, trotting along with his left hand outstretched towards his *akka*, the thumb on his right hand firmly jammed into his mouth. A few minutes later, Theresa reappeared, looking enchanting in a soft, light blue *sari*. I beamed at my sister as she turned towards the kitchen and beckoned to me.

'Come and help me, Lily.'

We left a curious Anna and Rosie behind, craning their necks around the corner to get a view while listening out for Chandra, who was asleep in the bedroom in his *sarong* cradle.

Her lower lip quivering slightly, Theresa led the way to the kitchen, Charlie clutching at her legs. My smile faded as I felt her distress and I decided that complete silence was called for as I solemnly followed her instructions.

Slowly, Theresa measured out our precious black tea leaves into a large aluminium container; once she had re-boiled the water on the stove, she added it to the pot. Thick, sweetened condensed milk and sugar were then stirred in until the right golden colour was reached; the very colour of the stranger in our sitting room. Blowing on a teaspoonful, she tasted a drop in the palm of her hand before straining it into the five stainless steel tumblers that I had placed for her on a wooden tray.

I followed at a discreet distance and joined Anna and Rosie to spy, as Theresa tried to walk into the sitting room gracefully while a persistent Charlie kept a firm hold of the loose end of her *sari* that fell over her shoulder. Mum put her hand out to the clinging Charlie, but he sidestepped, refusing to be parted from his beloved sister. Distracted, Teresa stumbled slightly, but quickly regained her poise as she made her way across the room to give our visitors the first offering, before turning to our parents and Peter. Keeping her head downcast, not making eye contact with anyone, she then softly retreated to the safety of the bedroom, her little shadow padding after her.

Mum cast a warning look at us, shaking her head in a silent command – 'off you go'. We scuttled back into the sanctuary of my bed space, eager to quiz our sister.

'*Akka*, do you know what is going on? Who is that man? Why did Mum tell us to leave them?'

Theresa put her hand up, sketching a gesture of helplessness in the air.

'Don't ask me, I don't know,' she whispered impatiently. 'Go, go and play.'

She walked back to the kitchen, seemingly lost in thought. Reluctantly, we left her and went out to continue with our games, our curiosity at the strange scenario quickly forgotten.

But the following weekend this performance was repeated, and then again for a third weekend. Theresa became more and more pensive, but would not tell us anything. At the same time, there were a lot of whispered conversations between my parents. Anna and Rosie concluded that something was definitely afoot while I sat nearby, trying to understand the mysterious adult tone that had suddenly crept into their conversations.

One evening after dinner, my father made an announcement that was to change the dynamics of our household. Us younger siblings looked wide-eyed at each other as we discovered that our sister Theresa was to marry the young stranger who had been visiting us: Mr Arokiasamy.

Amid the excited chatter that ensued, Rosie piped up with the most important question.

'*Appa*, will that uncle come to live with us now?'

'No, no. *Akka* is going to live with him.'

Silence fell abruptly. A look of horror was mirrored on every face. Arokiasamy lived in Serdang, near our Uncle. Serdang was like the other side of the world, we agreed amongst ourselves, in whispered conversations. How could we bear to lose our older sister, who seemed like a second mother to us?

Together, we formed a protest group and pleaded with Theresa, begging her not to get married; we wanted to stay together.

'You cannot leave us, *akka*. Tell *ammah* and *appa* you don't want to go.'

She looked agitated. Her eyes shone with tears and suddenly they came tumbling down; she attempted to wipe them away with the back of her hands but as the tears began to course more steadily, she used the arm of her blouse to mop her face, increasing our sense of bewilderment and vulnerability.

'I cannot tell them that. I am the eldest and I have to get married. I am eighteen now. None of us can stay at home forever.'

Her arms outstretched to encompass us all, Theresa explained that my parents were anxious for their first-born to make a suitable marriage. This was a duty she had to perform.

'He seems to be a nice man, a nice man,' she repeated over and over again, her voice lifting in optimism.

Theresa had always been very attached to her siblings even the squabbles that she and Peter regularly exchanged paled into insignificance against our family ties. Their squabbles stopped abruptly as soon as the engagement was announced. An unfamiliar silence descended on the whole household at this time, almost as if we were in mourning. Sometimes I felt as though our family pictures should have their faces turned to the wall: a traditional mark of respect that denoted a death in the family. Instead, wedding preparations were being set in motion.

As a non-school attender, I was Mum's shopping companion, accompanying her on strolls into the heart of Sentul, and returning with bags of groceries. Soon after Theresa's engagement, we took a trip to our local Indian goldsmith. Mum proudly announced her first-born's impending marriage, to a chorus of excited congratulations, and took a seat as she investigated the merchandise for some suitable wedding jewellery. I peered into the back room, where skinny apprentices in sleeveless singlets were bent almost double over the intricate work they were engaged in. Hissing acetylene-flamed lamps were gripped tightly in their hands, sparks flying everywhere. I was surprised that their hair wasn't singed from the flames. Mum made a few preliminary choices, and then made an appointment with the shop owner for a home visit.

In the middle of the following afternoon, the goldsmith arrived with a case full of gold bridal accessories. Examples of exquisite craftsmanship were carefully laid out on, our glass-topped table as all the females in the family gathered around to gaze and gasp. Theresa picked up four thin gold bangles and looped them over her slender wrist into an armband; the precious metal caught the light, twinkling tantalisingly in the sun. Anna, Rosie and I watched in fascination as calculations were made and bargaining swung back and forth.

After my sister had made her modest choices, the discussion centred on the most important item, the *thali* – a thick gold chain through which was looped a central flat piece that resembled a carved doorway. This was held in place on either side with threaded gold baubles. The *thali* symbolised the marriage. Traditionally it was the choice of the bridegroom and his family; however, in the absence of Arokiasamy's immediate family who were residing in India, our future brother-in-law was grateful to hand over this responsibility to my parents.

The following day, Dad returned from his Saturday half-day's work, grabbed a quick shower and lunch, then he and Mum made their way to Dickson Road in Kuala Lumpur, which teemed with *sari* shops. (Today, this same street has been renamed Jalan Masjid India: the name has changed, but the *sari* shops remain.) They returned with a selection of brightly coloured, embroidered *saris*, draping a part of each over Theresa's shoulder and asking 'What do you think of this, *ma?*'

Furniture was delivered and stacked in the bedroom, taking up most of the floor space: a wardrobe, an occasional table and rattan chairs. All formed part of my sister's dowry. It was traditional to negotiate a financial dowry that an Indian bride would have to provide for the prospective groom, but Catholics on the whole had dispensed with this practice by now. Instead, the bride's family provided more practical items of gold jewellery, silk and gold-embroidered *saris*, and household goods.

As the buzz of preparation crept into our daily lives, our mourning period abated; the air seemed thicker somehow, pulsing with excitement. I was curious to know everything that was going on and my young age made it particularly easy for me to creep in on family conferences. Quietly, I sat in a corner and listened as discussions revealed that, since my future brother-in-law's relatives were not around, the wedding would be held in Sentul, in our house.

My parents were clearly overjoyed with their good fortune. Dad concluded:

'Our prayers have been answered. What a nice young man, we are so lucky he wants to marry into our family.'

'He doesn't seem to mind that we have such a large family, and he a clerk in the Serdang Council office!' Mum too was overwhelmed and grateful.

'He will qualify for married quarters.'

'Theresa is lucky. *We* are lucky, to get such a fine young man for our first son-in-law.'

'And if the first one is right, we will be fortunate with our future sons-in-law,' uttered Dad with conviction.

Arokiasamy was from the landowners' caste of Odayars, similar to us; despite our Christian faith, old cultural beliefs dictated this as a necessary consideration. Making no demands on us, he was happy for my parents to take all the necessary decisions.

The date for the wedding had to be determined by my parents' resurrection of an old Hindu custom whereby Indian elders consulted almanacs to determine a propitious day. The months in the almanac followed the cycles of the moon and its astrological influences. Certain months were avoided as being unsuitable for a prosperous future. Christmas was also to be avoided, to keep the celebrations separate. The wedding was eventually set for February of the following year, a day that was anticipated with mixed feelings.

That Christmas, the last with Theresa living at home, was a subdued affair. As the forthcoming nuptials were to follow soon after the festive celebrations, our ever-practical Mum announced: 'We might as well sew new Christmas clothes for everybody, then store them safely to use for the wedding.'

When February came round, all the preparations were already in full swing. One week before the auspicious day, the dry goods for the wedding feast arrived. Separated from the main house by a two-foot passageway, our little kitchen had never seen such plentiful supplies. Everyone was in high spirits, looking forward to the first wedding in the family.

That night, Rosie was stretched out on a wooden bed that Peter had built against the back wall of our house; I was on my customary door bed on the floor beside her. Having had a busy day sprucing up the house and the compound in preparation for the wedding, we both fell asleep almost immediately. But in the middle of the night I woke up groggily, feeling unusually hot and sweaty. I could hear Rosie's movements from above, seemingly equally restless. There was an unusual sound outside, like paper crackling.

Seconds later, all hell broke loose.

'Rosie, Lily, get up quick! Run, run out of the house, NOW!'

Hasty hands pulled us up. Everyone else was awake. Bewildered, rubbing the sleep from our eyes, we followed the rest of the family outside, to the sound of shrill shouts. I recognised Dad's voice, unusually shaken, then the familiar voice of our neighbour's tenant, Mr Yehharmbaram. Nearing the open doorway, I saw a glow in place of the expected pitch darkness; and there was heat, immense heat. The sight that greeted us was nothing but chilling as Rosie and I stumbled into Anna's shaking back.

A rush of fear struck me forcefully. Through the blur of sudden tears, I saw our kitchen, engulfed in flames. Cruel, snarling orange tongues, fanned by a gentle night breeze, were eating away the little wooden building at a breakneck pace. Baby Chandra was screeching in Mum's arms; three-year-old Charlie clung to a stricken Theresa.

I peered around for my Dad; he was already lowering a bucket into our well, shouting orders to us.

'Jonah, go and open the side gate; Mr Yehharmbaram is coming to help us. Quick, all of you, bring whatever container you can.'

Mr Yehharmbaram, a well-built ox of a man, and our Punjabi neighbour, Mr Chadha, dashed across to help, followed by their wives, who stood ghost-like in the flickering reflection of the flames, murmuring their sympathies to Mum. Yelumalai and Velu were noticeably absent, but dear old *paatie* stumbled into the compound, seeking us out. Dependable Mr Kuttan, alerted by the noise, had crossed the rickety bridge across the stream in the dark, accompanied by a couple of his tenants, whom he had roped in to help too. They merged into the human chain that had quickly formed; only Kuttan could be distinguished in the reflected light by his shock of silver hair, which stood up and shook as he worked.

Dad drew water from the well, while the rest of the men passed buckets to and fro along the chain, as well as any other containers that were at hand, flinging their contents at the vicious flames. A mound of sand, part of one of Peter's projects, was close by; unable to keep still, our little hands joined in the rescue project, filling every available utensil with sand and aiming it at the flames. Some found the target, while others went awry in our fevered, anxious state.

A sudden rush of wind swirled the heat and it lunged out at us, forcing us to stagger backwards as one. Bottles of cooking oil bought for the wedding feast exploded in the intense heat and a fountain of sparks shot into the night, like fireworks shooting in all directions; I felt an answering explosion of shock and hurt in the very heart of my being. Acrid smoke billowed its way towards us, finding every pore, inducing fits of rasping coughs. Only gradually, thanks to the combined efforts of everyone present, was the fire brought under control.

Exhausted, and unable to do anything more until the sun rose, we all retreated to bed and a fitful sleep, the main house thankfully spared and remaining intact. A couple of hours later, when morning broke, the sight of the charred remains of our provisions reduced us all to tears. Flames had licked out the kitchen's windows and door, leaving charred, indelible scars. The wooden supports were so blackened by smoke that the building was clearly unsalvageable. Solemnly, we ringed the ruins in a silence that was as thick and black as tar. Eventually finding a shaky voice, Dad instructed us to stay at a safe distance, as he and Peter set about looking for evidence of anything that could have started the fire.

Yehharmburam's wife had woken up at three in the morning to prepare a feed for her baby. Noticing a bright light from her kitchen window, she had called out to her husband to investigate. It was his shouts that had woken my father, who dashed out to discover our kitchen's *attap* roof already engulfed by flames.

Frowning as he scanned the ruins, Peter beckoned to Dad.

'*Appa*, look, there is a pile of burnt-out rags. And see here, there is a pool of petrol.' He pointed to a glistening area near the bucket system toilet. 'The rags must have been soaked in petrol, set alight, then thrown on the roof. Look.'

Dad moved over to investigate further, and discovered that the latch on the little gate next to the toilet had been forced.

'Okay. Don't touch it Peter, we had better let the police look at it.'

Grim-faced, Dad left for the police station to make his report, whilst the rest of us stood round the ruins helplessly, not knowing what else to do. None of us had the heart to indulge in meaningless games. As we waited we heard scuffling feet in the lane on the other side of the bougainvillea hedge. Glances were exchanged as we recognised a well known voice in conversation with another man in a deliberately loud voice.

'Dai', they are still alive, 'dah'. We didn't do a proper job, did we?'

The voice belonged to Anthony, the second son of an orphan Muthusamy, whom our maternal grandfather had taken into his home and treated as his own, nurturing him alongside his seven children and arranging his marriage to a protégée of the nuns who ran an orphanage.

We froze. These words were clearly meant for our ears. Mum placed a finger to her lips. We were rooted to our spots, eyes fixed on Mum, not daring to breathe. My heart thudded in familiar fear. Dad wasn't here were they going to force their way into our house? Thankfully, on this occasion they were happy to leave us with the threat of their words; we heard their footsteps receding. Mum let out her breath.

'Come children, let's go inside the house and pray to the Sacred Heart.'

The framed photograph of the Sacred Heart of Jesus, hanging over the doorway between the main house and the kitchen, was still in place. However, the heat from the flames had caused the glass to crack and smoke had curled its way in, causing some minor discolouration.

Mum raised her cupped hands to the picture.

'Look children, Jesus was looking after us. He stood between the kitchen and us and saved us all. We must all kneel down and thank him.'

When Dad returned from the police station, he found us on our knees reciting our rosary. Mum got up to greet him and he sighed.

'The police cannot do anything, they say. But at least a report has been lodged.'

Dad was in agreement with Mum's course of action.

'Yes, Marie, it is truly a miracle that saved us all. I will go to St Anthony's Church later and light some candles in thanksgiving.'

Thus was our disaster reclaimed, and now deemed to be a miracle. How quickly we children learnt to accept that placing our trust and faith in God saved us from evil.

Soon, the full story emerged. It was well known that Anthony had always resented what he perceived to be the second-class status accorded to his family, in comparison to my grandfather's blood-related grandchildren. He held this opinion despite the fact that Grandpa had provided his adopted son with a plot of land adjacent to his own property, and helped to erect a house for the new family. In his quest to cement relations with my grandfather's 'blood family', it appeared that Anthony had secretly chosen Theresa to fulfil all his aspirations. When news of my sister's impending marriage reached his ears, he realised that his well-laid plans were about to be ruined – and had hatched his grizzly plan of revenge. Just whom Anthony had been talking to in the lane was never revealed. We therefore had no proof of any other party's involvement but suspicions were raised, and suffice to say this event did nothing to improve relationships with our two heartless neighbours.

Peter and Dad made plans for a new kitchen to be incorporated within our main house, to minimise the risk of further attacks. Their plans, however, had to be postponed for the present, as the wedding took priority.

Family weddings were always celebrated in style. Relatives naturally played a large part in the proceedings – which meant that, as in most cultures, this was also a time when family politics inevitably came into play.

Mum's younger brother, my Uncle Leo, was particularly well known within the family for his arrogance; Uncle Leo was dark-skinned like my mother, with a triangular jaw that jutted in your face and a straight nose that quivered in a permanent state of impatience, and from which regular snorts emitted. Flattened moles like squashed raisins were arranged on his brow, above his hollow cheeks. Despite his almost permanent frowns he could belt out either a series of orders or collapse into laughter cackling like a goose. He looked incongruous with a body too short for his legs.

Uncle Leo and my proud Dad had a long-standing silent feud, stemming from the family-splitting argument that had forced my mother to abandon her parents' home many years before. Family bonds remained strong, however, and when news of the arson attack so close to the big day became public knowledge, Uncle Leo came up trumps for us.

One afternoon a few days before the wedding, a car pulled up outside our gates and we heard an insistent blaring of the horn. As I was close by, Mum asked me to investigate.

'Go and see who that is.'

I dashed outside, snatching up the keys for the padlock as I went. The corrugated zinc door of the gate had seen better days by now and it hung on rusty iron hinges. Unable to reach the official peephole even standing on tiptoes, I resorted to creating my own. Humidity, rain and sunshine had marked copper-coloured vertical lines along the gate's grooves where rust had worked its way into the zinc, forming dusty lacy patterns. I poked the closest one with my finger, opening up a tiny hole. Fixing a squinting eye to the hole, I saw Uncle Leo sitting waiting in his car, his impatient fingers already tapping the wheel. Aware of his short fuse, I hastily tugged at the heavy iron chain, which clanked noisily. The rust made heavy work of moving the gate, which creaked in greeting as it swung open, almost matching my Uncle's high-pitched voice as he screeched at me through his open window.

'Go quick child, and ask your mother to come. And bring some help with you.'

I needed no second command and turned on my heel to carry out his bidding.

'Archie *akka*, I have brought you some provisions for the wedding,' my mother's brother called out, as soon as she came into view. 'Tell your children to unload the car.'

I saw Mum's step falter and stop as if stumped by the appearance of her brother who paid rare visits to his older sister. Stepping out of the vehicle, Uncle Leo slammed the door shut and, as we scurried round to the open boot, he stood aside and watched with his arms folded. He had done his bit.

Flustered with gratitude, Mum started to thank her brother, but he brushed away her comments with a flap of his hand.

'No need, *akka*, no need for thanks; just hope there is enough.'

Working speedily, we soon emptied the car of its treasures: rough jute sacks of rice; two varieties of dhal, deep yellow split dhal for curries and the smaller, lighter-coloured dhal for spicy, deep-fried patties; jars of cooking oil to fry lightly battered crisp fresh vegetables; tins of QBB ghee, to add extra buttery richness to the dhal, and the sweet rectangular slabs of kesari, made with crunchy semolina flour; newspaper parcels containing curry powder, spices, sugar, loose tea and ground coffee and two dozen tins of condensed milk. All non-perishable necessities, to feed large numbers of wedding guests, who always arrived early and left very late.

As soon as we had removed the final items, Uncle Leo leapt back into the car, waving aside our smiles and thanks, and sped off; the whole episode was over in less than fifteen minutes. Mum walked back to the house deep in thought, no doubt wondering what my

Dad was going to make of this generous gift. I never found out his reaction.

I knew my own, though: wonder and immense gratitude for this proof of the enduring strength and generosity of the family bond, which has stayed with me to this day.

The auspicious day finally dawned on Saturday, 25 February 1952, when, five months before her nineteenth birthday, our eldest sister Theresa Anthonysamy was married to Arokiasamy Arulanthoo. She would take on his first name as her surname, and as the surname of their future children, as was the Indian custom.

We were all up earlier than usual, partly through natural excitement, partly through necessity; we still had plenty of final preparations to complete. The morning sun dappled a pattern of light and shade over a huge canvas marquee that stretched across the grounds of our home. Two tall banana trees, heavy with green fruit, stood upright like proud sentries at the entrance. The compound was full of bodies, helpers strewn about the grass, who were hard at work making our decorations. These were fashioned from young, pale yellow coconut leaves, a contribution from our grandfather's estate, which we wove into long plaits with intricate cut out patterns. These were then going to be secured on lines of twisted rope, leading from the front gate to the marquee. As the number of plaits grew steadily, I ran around helping to stack the finished products in a pile. Mum issued a warning from the kitchen.

'Lily, keep Charlie away from handling the leaves! The edges are sharp and he will cut his fingers.'

I shooed Charlie away from the snaking yellow braids and went back indoors, where Chandra, still unsteady on his spindly fourteen-month-old legs, leant on the doorframe under the watchful eyes of Anna and Rosie. With racing hearts, we all stood with pride and watched Peter and his friends hang up the pretty plaits to trail from the banana trees to the tops of the zinc gate, that had received a fresh coat of white wash, swaying gently in the breeze and enhancing the grandeur of the occasion.

Anxious to create a real festival atmosphere, Peter had approached Dad to discuss the music, which was a must for every local celebration, and especially for such a joyful occasion as a wedding. There were no laws or restrictions on noise pollution everyone within earshot would enjoy the music as it reached out to proclaim a proud message of happiness, fun and celebrations to the neighbourhood, as well as providing an invitation to join in.

Not owning a gramophone himself, Dad had borrowed one for the occasion from my Eurasian godparents, Mr and Mrs Alexander, who were neighbours to my grandparents. They had built up a close relationship with our family by offering and receiving mutual help during the war years. To cement their friendship my parents had approached tall and sprightly Mr Alexander and soft-spoken, wavy-haired Joyce, both of whom were happy to accept the role of godparents to my parents' sixth child. In true neighbourly spirit the now middle-aged couple were pleased to help to make the wedding a success for their old friends.

Peter and his pals practised playing the Alexanders' collection of records over and over. All the songs were of course in the language of the Eurasian family – English – which suited Peter's taste: My Truly, Truly Fair, by Guy Mitchell; Beautiful Brown Eyes, by Rosemary Clooney and, of course, Unforgettable, floated richly in the soft baritone voice of Nat King Cole.

I was allowed to take my turn in cranking the handle of the HMV (His Master's Voice) gramophone. I could not be trusted however to place the needle on the revolving groove, as this required a steady hand; a nervous twitch or clumsy move would scratch the borrowed vinyl.

When Peter's back was turned, I surreptitiously poked a curious finger into a little compartment that fitted neatly into the side of the machine. Unfortunately, as this housed the spent needles, my reward was a stab on my outstretched finger, drawing a big red blob of blood. Ouch! I swallowed the exclamation as it rose in my throat, eager to avoid a scolding from Peter, and hurriedly wiped the bloodstained needle on my dress, replacing it quietly in the hope that no one would notice. Sticking my finger into my mouth, I slid off my stool and sneaked into the kitchen, where I applied some soot from the underside of the wok to the throbbing spot on my finger, having witnessed my mother on countless occasions applying the same remedy to cuts.

It was nearing midday when the hired cooks arrived, riding a laden bullock cart. Clattering along the lane, the bullock pulled up at the gateway to our house, frothing at the mouth. A sturdy wooden shaft resting on the dented shoulder moved up and down slightly as the bullock's great sides heaved with deep breaths. Half a dozen muscular men jumped off the cart and tethered the animal to a pole outside the gate. Seizing a spade from the cart, a swarthy man with a length of cotton looped round his head, to keep perspiration from his eyes, proceeded to dig shallow pits for cooking fires midway between the charred remains of our kitchen and the well. The others unpacked massive cauldrons; baskets brimming with prepared vegetables and mysterious newspaper packages piled high on much wider and flatter rattan baskets.

'Lily! Where are you? Time to get ready!' Anna's anxious voice emerged from the depths of the house.

'Coming, *akka*!' I left the bustling compound and scurried indoors.

We took turns to bathe and dress in our worn only once newly tailored outfits, helped and hustled in turns by a handful of relatives who had arrived early to lend a helping hand. Mouth-watering smells wafted over from the back of the house as we wrestled with sleeves and buttons, giggling at each other.

As soon as I was ready, I skipped into the main bedroom for my first glimpse of the bride, where two female relatives had spent what seemed like hours getting Theresa ready. Eyes widening, I gasped.

'Oh, *akka*!'

My eldest sister looked a picture. Her slender figure was draped in a glittering *sari*, the main body of which was a rich gold, made with gold filigree its three-inch border and the pleated shoulder piece was a deep magenta, packed tight with embroidered flowers. A gold brooch anchored more pleated *sari* material over her shoulder. A matching magenta blouse sported a V-neck and modest elbow-length sleeves. A solid gold, two-inch belt inlaid with a scattering of tiny twinkling diamonds, borrowed for the occasion, circled her slim waist. Long pleats fell gracefully from her waist, swinging as she bent forwards slightly to slip her feet into golden, medium-heeled, open-toed slippers.

The aunties shooed me out of the way as they bustled about Theresa.

'Nearly there,' one of them said, and she picked up a white, billowing mass from the bed. Carefully, she framed my sister's young face with the veil and secured it in place with the sparkling gold wedding tiara, studded with pearls. A long trail of lace was meticulously arranged to flow gently behind the bride. The veil was a present from Sister Raphael, Dad's older sister, who was a nun; orphans in her convent had embroidered the white lace. Everyone openly exclaimed over the exquisite handiwork, as my sister finally emerged from the bedroom in all her finery.

The first family wedding generated its own magic. The wedding ceremony was held at four o'clock in St Joseph's Church, where the rickety wooden pews overflowed with guests. Malayan weddings were elaborate affairs and numbers were often in triple figures. Those included that day were not just immediate relatives and friends, but also many more distant relatives, neighbours, workmates of my father, friends of my brother; the list went on and on. I believe Theresa and Arokiasamy had between two and three hundred guests.

The Catholic wedding mass took around an hour to complete.

Holy vows to last a lifetime were exchanged before the priest. The groom looked resplendent in his anglicised, tailored, inky-blue suit, with a folded white handkerchief tucked into his breast pocket, a white long-sleeved shirt with gold cufflinks and a golden tie knotted at his collar. His feet stood firm at the altar in highly polished black shoes.

A couple of willing aunties stepped forward to gather Theresa's veil to the side, leaving room for Arokiasamy to fix the catch of the *thali*, the symbol of marriage, at the back of her long neck. Tears fell, then laughter and applause broke out. Like a flash of lightning, I had gained a new brother-in-law.

The newlyweds led us all out of the church, where we discovered that Dad's local connections had procured us a police presence, ensuring a jaw-droppingly smooth journey for the wedding party along the main Sentul Road. Our procession was preceded by a troop of traditional Indian musicians, creating a joyful fanfare on flutes and *tabalas*. Their rounded bellies were draped in white cotton *veshties* – a long piece of lightweight cotton fabric, usually white, wrapped around the hips and thighs, with one end brought between the legs and tucked into the waistband, thus resembling baggy, knee-length trousers. I loved the sound of the Indian drums, which were played with both palms and fingers, beaten rhythmically to produce a powerful, almost hypnotic sound. Dominating the medley was a *nadaswaram*, a South Indian wind instrument traditionally played at weddings, blaring out intoxicating music. I swayed to the beat of the music as we made our way home, lightheadedly acknowledging smiles and waves from the whole village.

As we reached our home, we found a motley crew of onlookers gathered by the front gate, eager to catch a glimpse of the new bride and groom resplendent in their magnificent attire. Our two feuding neighbours had naturally been left out of the wedding invitations; nevertheless, they had both found excuses to be in their compounds just as the wedding party came into view, casting interested but surreptitious glances across the fence. Our celebrations were not marred by their obvious sourness, however. I was flushed with pride; my heartbeat responded to each musical note, and every comment from the crowd.

'Ah, look at the bride she looks so pretty, eh? And did you see the groom, so fair and so handsome, *lah*. The Anthonysamy family have really managed to catch a good man for their daughter.'

Basking in reflected glory, I danced to the pulsating beat of the *tabala*, giddy with joy, as the piercing melody of the flute blared out the Indian wedding march. So immersed was I in the excitement that I had temporarily forgotten that my sister's departure was fast approaching.

Groom and bride were guided to an ornately decorated raised dais, where they bent down towards the dust at their elders' feet, staying low until the elders rested reassuring hands on their shoulders, then indicated for them to rise.

'Enough, you have shown your respect. Bless you both. May you prosper jointly in your new path in life.'

Our guests then trooped into the marquee, removing their shoes and slippers at the entrance before stepping onto rows of woven mats laid out on the floor. As they entered, they passed my twelve-year-old sister, Rosie, who graced the doorway, dressed in a silky pink *paavaadai*, a long skirt with a gold-embroidered border that sat on her ankles, topped with a matching puff-sleeved silk blouse. A simple gold necklace, just above the neckline of her blouse, shone bright against her milky, coffee-coloured skin. I watched in admiration as she smiled, offering richly scented sandalwood paste towards each guest in a silver salver, which the guests acknowledged with gentle nods of their heads. They dipped their fingers into the salver and applied a dab to their foreheads, following an old Hindu tradition that marked the sacred 'third eye'. Next to Rosie stood my equally well decked out cousin Elsa, who sprinkled fragrant rose water lightly on the guests from highly decorated silverware, as a sign of welcome.

Everyone seated themselves in groups on the mats. The guests mostly divided up according to gender: the men congregated together, sitting cross-legged, while the women sat more modestly, some with one leg placed across and the other tucked around to the rear. Those with babies sat with both feet tucked to one side, gathering their youngsters to their bosoms. Sweat from the humidity soon mingled with talcum powder to form a white paste between rings of neck-fat on the better endowed of our female guests. A heady scent rose from the ladies' hair, which was decked with strings of white jasmine flowers, mingling with the equally sweet aroma of perfumed water. I inhaled deeply, savouring the sweetness that vied now with the rich odour of cooked spices that was beginning to pervade the air within the marquee.

Now that the Catholic mass was over, it was time for the traditional Indian ceremonies. In many ways, Christian converts in our community were still rooted to their ancestral Hinduism. With head bowed correctly, as modesty dictated, Theresa placed a heavily scented jasmine garland, bound loosely with golden strands, around her new husband's neck; as he returned the gesture, he exercised his right to scrutinise his new bride full in the face. A proud and satisfied smile played on his face, to the satisfaction of the close family. Theresa had now earned the right to address her husband: *atthaan*. As Indian wives did not use their husband's first names when they addressed them, *atthaan* was the polite form for use not only by the bride, but also a right bestowed on her siblings. We had each acquired an *atthaan*.

Acting out his role of catechist, or caretaker of the church, my grandfather began proceedings by blessing the newly married couple in front of the seated guests. Well versed in all ceremonies, he drew the sign of the cross first on his new grandson-in-law's forehead, then on his eldest granddaughter, meanwhile entertaining the Indian guests, who were in the majority, with age-old religious songs in Tamil. His distinctive baritone voice induced electric chills down our spines. I held my breath in awe as my grandfather's voice rose in a strong crescendo until it reached a peak, prompting loud spontaneous clapping at the finale.

The time approached for the older generations to bestow their individual blessings, and they crowded forward to outline the sign of the cross on the newlyweds' foreheads then press money into their palms. Some close relatives and the more affluent of the guests placed gold chains around the couple's necks and pushed rings onto their fingers. Overawed by the sparkling gold, I turned to my mother.

'Ooh, *ammah*, look, they have so much jewellery! They are going to be rich, aren't they?'

Smiling in amusement, Mum whispered back: 'they have to be careful with that, ma. That is for their future. If they need money unexpectedly, they can use their jewellery, you see.'

Many families invested their money not in stocks and shares, but in gold. Unlike the ups and downs of local currency, which many amongst our community had experienced over the years, gold never lost its value. In times of hardship, when money was scarce, jewellery was often hocked to pawnbrokers, and then reclaimed at a later date when funds became available. In later years Mum confided in me that her own mother had hidden nuggets of gold in a covered clay pot; my young Mum was roped in to make an inventory of them on a regular basis, the numbers entered into a ledger and placed within the pot before returning it to its hidey-hole. My *ammachi* was thus educating my mother at an early age in good housekeeping and the importance of gold in any household, and in her turn Mum was equally keen to hand down these practical skills to her own offspring.

Ceremonies over, the tent was cleared for the much-awaited part of the day: the wedding feast. Kerosene oil lamps, tied to the internal marquee supports, cast a whitish glare over the guests as they re-seated themselves cross-legged on the mats at the tent's periphery, leaving the centre clear for ease of serving. As dining space was limited, the remaining guests gathered in groups between the partly-lit garden and main house to wait their turn.

Practised hands placed banana leaves in front of the diners with lightning speed. Food slopped over the edges of the stainless steel buckets, containing ghee rice perfumed with crushed cardamom, mutton curry, dhal curry and a variety of vegetables, some cooked with thick coconut milk and spices, others with sweet and sour flavours. Guests dipped their right hands into the piles of food before them, scooping up portions of deep-fried battered ladies' fingers, crunching into crispy poppadums and scooping thumb and forefinger pinches of spicy lime pickles into their hungry mouths. Efficient fingers swept over the leaves, picking up every morsel. The leaves, still glistening with a film of curry remnants, were also used for dessert: a sweet concoction of rice vermicelli, sago, plump raisins, golden, ghee-fried cashew nuts and thick coconut milk, all fragrant with cardamom and coloured richly with saffron. Globules of melted ghee floated to the top; that I too quickly scooped up with cupped sticky fingers, slurping appreciatively.

Duly sated, our guests trooped to the back of the tent, where a *sarong*-clad boy poured a tumbler full of fresh water for the guests to first wash their hands, then drink from cupped hands. Men dried their hands on the gold-trimmed cloth that they had draped over their shoulders to mark the celebrations; women shook their hands dry and wiped their children's curry-stained mouths with a swipe of their wet hand.

Lively chatter continued throughout. Relatives who had not seen each other for long periods fell upon one another with loud cries, forming tight little circles, eager for the gossiping and speculation to begin.

And begin it did. Ignorant of the sub-plots developing around me, I mingled among the guests, eavesdropping on their conversations; not until several years later did I learn the full implications of the pantomime being played out in front of me.

With assessing eyes, the visitors openly discussed and admired the other daughters in the crowd who were of marriageable age: young maidens, decked out in their finery, sat in a suitably subdued manner. They held their hands respectfully in greeting to their elderly relatives, while surreptitiously casting sideways glances at the handsome sons who had dutifully accompanied their parents, wishing themselves anywhere but under this scrutiny by prospective in-laws. Parents made mental notes on the suitability of the attending youngsters, savouring the titbits of gossip that surfaced, pondering over different families' welfare. Marriage scouts, elderly married women with years of experience, were a common sight at weddings, scouring the crowds for suitable families, matching castes, professional churchgoers and those that lapsed. Ideally they favoured strict non-smokers and teetotallers.

As the celebrations drew on late into the night, I felt my eyes begin to sting with fatigue. My younger siblings had already been put to bed; so far I had managed to avoid my Mum's questing eyes, but I knew my time would soon be up, and I lingered outside, drinking in the scene while stifling successive yawns.

Groups of men shared *paan*, their jaws moving together in rhythm as they chewed and talked work and politics. A handful of guests who had travelled from long distances started to lay themselves out in the tent, seeking comfortable spots for sleep; little bedding was required in the hot and humid climate, making accommodating a large group of people easily manageable. Women loosened some of the pleats from their *sari*, providing enough loose material to provide cover both for themselves and for their children resting their heads on their folded arms, hands tucked under the backs of their necks for support. Children used the bosoms and tummies of their mothers for a soft resting place for their heads. Men shook loose the folded, gold-trimmed cloths that had been draped over their shoulders, bunching them up to fit snugly under their heads for an instant pillow. Loud snores soon echoed around the tent. Unable to keep my eyes open any longer, I finally crept into my corner and curled up, falling into a deep sleep.

The following morning, the guests woke in their crushed *sari*s and crumpled *veshties* and emerged from the tent to crowd around the well. In small groups, they coated the pads of their index fingers with ash from the wood fires to brush their teeth, before swilling their mouths out with a dash of water cupped in their hands from the filled bucket.

Back they went to the food tent, to feast upon a lavish breakfast of steamed rice cakes and soft spongy *dosais* soaked with dhal curry, served on fresh banana leaves, after which most finally said their thanks and took their leave. The thickened air of excitement was gradually losing its layers.

Later that afternoon, the bride and groom were decked out once again in their wedding outfits for the final stage of the celebrations. There was sufficient room in Uncle Leo's car for me to squeeze my little self in next to Mum and Theresa as the car made its way to our local photographer's shop on the main Sentul Road. Mum lightly dusted their faces with talcum powder; Arokiasamy's brilliantined and oiled hair received its final combing. We spread Theresa's embroidered train out on the floor and tweaked the tiara, all under the direction of the experienced middle-aged Chinese photographer. Amid glaring hot lights, my sister sat on a strategically placed chair while my new brother-in-law perched on its arm, imitating the pose of countless other brides and grooms. The two smiled in time to the count of three as the cover was taken off the aperture, taking an upside-down image of them. The groom showed his teeth but Theresa remained subdued. One week later, when the black and white prints were collected, the perfectly posed and captured images generated appreciative oohs and aahs from us all.

I felt elated in the presence of my brother-in-law, who had raised our family's status and allayed my parents' concerns. No longer would they have to worry about where they might find a man to marry into such a large family, with so many girls needing to find husbands. Our fortunes had turned: now we were the lucky family who had gained such a good-looking and prestigious eldest son-in-law. Best of all, our newly acquired family member had a ready, friendly smile for all and was truly appreciative of the variety of foods that my mother kept preparing in his honour.

Our beaming faces were just settling into semi-permanence, when the inevitable dreaded day of parting arrived. Three days after the wedding, my sister and her new husband left for Serdang to set up home in the married quarters that my brother-in-law had recently been allocated, reflecting his new marital status. Slowly and sadly, we helped to load the hired van with the married couples' new treasures: a brand new double bed with a latticework bed-head, an *almari* with a mirrored door to hold my sister's trousseau, and a dining table and chairs; all the furniture that my parents had bargained for my sister.

When the moment of departure finally arrived, eyes reddened all round as hot tears coursed down our cheeks. Carefully balanced on Anna's hip, baby Chandra looked around in bewilderment at his family gathered in various degrees of distress. Young Charlie, sensing separation, was particularly distraught; clinging to my sister's legs in desperation, he refused to let go. Theresa was like a second mother to him and, like the rest of us, Charlie was devastated as he became aware of his impending loss.

'*Akka*, don't go, don't go. Stay, *akka*!'

Dad was forced to physically wrench Charlie from his precious daughter, prising his son's locked fingers apart gently; the sight raised an audible sob from the gathered crowd. Our neighbours craned their necks over the barbed wire fence to catch a glimpse of the family drama. Theresa's shoulders shook; overcome by emotion she succumbed to the sorry tableau before her. My new brother-in-law stood by patiently;

but, caught up in the emotional scene, he endeared himself to us when we saw tears in his eyes, too. Despite this and many other signs in his favour, I struggled to accept that my married sister had to begin a new life, a life away from us.

Charlie moped around the house for days. Heartbreakingly, we would discover him standing by the doorway, waiting for the gate to open to the presence of his beloved older sister. Always prone to sleepwalking, Charlie's night-time wanderings now escalated for a time. Thankfully, the reinforced front door kept our brother indoors, but he was often found in the morning curled up on his haunches like a frog, fast asleep either under the dining table, or behind the rattan settee.

We all experienced his pain. Tears were never far away from anyone's eyes; we recognised the void that Theresa's departure had created in each one of us and forced ourselves to go about our daily activities. Marriage was part of family life, after all; our life, though different, was forced to go on.

9

'The English girl...'

Preschool Days

'I will let Sister Raphael know you are here, sir.'

Dad lowered himself into a high-backed leather-bound chair, while the nun who had greeted us at the entrance hall disappeared down a long corridor. Comfortable chairs were dotted around the spacious, high-ceilinged room. Ever curious, I trotted over to the arched windows that overlooked a cemented courtyard. Roses grew in abundance in concrete tubs placed in measured distances from one another. Pairs of young girls, boarders dressed modestly in loose, high-necked, below-the-knee cotton dresses, skirted the concrete tubs and glided across the courtyard towards the covered corridors, their heads held close together conspiratorially. I surmised that they were whispering, as no sound of voices drifted though the open windows. Were they novitiates who had taken a vow of piety, I wondered – there was certainly an air of humility around them. I was half expecting to see the rosary dangling from their hands.

The building nestled halfway up a gently sloping hill, a *bukit*; a cool breeze from the surrounding dense forest drifted through the open windows. A carved, full-length statue of the crucifixion on a marble plinth took centre stage in the waiting room. Dad looked up at it and crossed himself in respect and I quickly followed suit in response to an inviting glance from him.

Soft footfalls drew my attention; my gaze was drawn to my aunt's serene face as she approached us. A gentle smile that reached her eyes revealed rows of pearly white teeth in her obvious joy at catching sight of her much loved eldest brother and his fourth daughter. Clad in her nun's garb, she wore a white peaked cap that draped in folds to her shoulders, emphasising her beauty; it framed an oval, light-skinned face, warm brown eyes, a straight nose just like Dad's and a soft but strong mouth. A greenish dot tattooed in the middle of her forehead matched my father's. They looked so alike no one could mistake the blood connection between them.

She inclined her head at us in greeting; her soft voice was controlled, even.

'*Annan* and Lily, how nice to see you both! How is the rest of the family? And how is *unnee*?'

Dad confirmed that Mum was well, and the two adults continued to exchange family news, each clearly comfortable in the other's company. Dad was obviously proud of his younger sister and spoke to her with undisguised warmth.

Tea arrived, to be served in dainty china teacups and saucers, accompanied by a plateful of plain Anne-Marie biscuits. I tucked into them gratefully, taking care not to consume too many for fear of appearing greedy. My aunt glanced at me with twinkling eyes and graced me with her gentle smile.

'You have brought up your children very well, *annan*. How old are you now, Lily?'

'Six, Sister, and I will be seven this September.'

'So you won't be starting school for another year, then?' She turned to my Dad.

'Look, *annan*, I know the principal of the Tamil Convent in Sentul very well. I can arrange for Lily to join the standard one class there. Sister Florence is my very good friend; she will look after Lily. There will be no need for school fees.'

Dad's eyes lit up as he turned to smile at me. The prospect of free schooling for his daughter, which he could not afford to provide, could not be turned down.

'What do you say, Lily, would you like to go to school for a few months? You can join the English convent school next year, after you turn seven.'

Attending the Tamil School and mastering squiggly Tamil alphabets would prove to be a new challenge. I nodded vigorously, excited at the prospect of entering the mysterious world of school. Not that it would be my first experience of learning; always game for a challenge, Peter had been keen to help his siblings. His active mind never at rest, he devised a unique method for teaching; I was his favourite willing guinea pig.

'Lily, look carefully. Take your time and tell me: what letter is this?'

'Is it A?'

'And this?'

'Is it W?'

Peter had procured a large piece of cardboard, in the middle of which he had cut out a window. He would pass this crude device over the pages of an English book, isolating each letter of the alphabet and getting me to identify each one in turn. Once this well-established pattern was set between us, I quickly progressed to recognise words, and not long afterwards I was reading basic children's books in English.

Thus, a magical new world opened its doors to me at the early age of six, one that would change the course of my life. I felt my life becoming richer as I acquired the tools that would help me to escape into another world, a world peopled with mysterious blonde-haired girls and boys, who lived in houses surrounded by animals very different from the ones I was familiar with. I was quickly drawn in, fascinated and eager to explore new pastures.

It wasn't long before my family bestowed on me a new nickname: *Vellakarachi*, 'the white girl'. The name seemed particularly apt: not only did I have my nose in an English storybook at every opportunity, but, for reasons unknown, I also spoke slightly differently from everyone around me, speaking proper English and leaving out most of the Malaysian slang.

'This little *Vellakarachi* will go far,' my Dad would announce with an indulgent smile, ruffling my hair.

Did he ever suspect how true his words would become?

As soon as I could read, I was desperate to become a schoolgirl; I was kicking my heels at home, impatient for the months to pass. Dad had arranged this meeting with his sister in response to my eagerness, and I was grateful to him. It would be fun to attend the Tamil Convent and get a taste for school.

Half an hour passed in pleasant conversation. Then Sister Raphael was required to attend to her prayers, and we took our leave on the understanding that the following week I would be taken to the Tamil Convent in Sentul for registration. As we left, I turned my head back to absorb the atmosphere of the sprawling, cream-coloured, double storey building that was Bukit Nanas convent school. Through the window, I spotted a couple of nuns walking along the corridor above the courtyard, their heads bowed slightly and hands tucked into their sleeves, a picture of piety. So this was where my mother and my aunties had attended school, all those years ago. I was duly impressed. I skipped along with a light heart, humming happily. It was my turn now; I was about to become a *student*.

My much-anticipated school days finally arrived. Rosie led me on the tarmac road past the main wooden Tamil School building, branching off to the left until we came upon the first years in the grounds under the shade of a fragrant frangipani tree. Groups of girls were at various stages of play. Heads bobbed as some girls jumped the squares, moving up the rungs of a ladder of hopscotch, finger-drawn in the dirt. Others tossed and caught stones, placing the five stones in a pile as they deftly caught each in mid-air. A few groups were engaged in a new and to me unfamiliar playground game. Bunched-up frangipani flowers fixed with rubber bands were heel- and back-kicked to a count, and the person who reached the highest count without allowing the bunch to fall to the ground claimed victory. I looked forward to learning this new game.

Curious eyes followed me as the newcomer. We reached the brick-built classrooms on the ground floor that adjoined the left arm of the main English Medium School. The rear of our imposing St Joseph's Church added its own shadow, while a wire fence with a latched side gate kept the schoolchildren away from its grounds.

After introducing me to my class teacher Rosie politely took her leave. The peal of the assembly bell cut short our conversation and I was motioned to the tail end of the jostling row of Class 1A, lined up parallel to Classes 1B. A chorus of greetings gradually hushed as morning prayers in Tamil commenced. Having attended the early Sunday mass in Tamil with Mum, I was able to follow the prayers with a minimum of mumbling.

In my first-ever classroom, a massive blackboard faced pews of wooden desks that could accommodate six students each. The desk was separated for individual use by wooden dividers. Half a dozen little writhing bottoms parked themselves on a single long wooden seat. The desks stood on either side of the central aisle. A groove near the top edge of the desks had been bevelled out to house chalks, with which to scribble on our slates.

I was a year younger than the rest of the pupils; in fact, I wasn't an official pupil at all. I stood apart from the rest, my outsider status emphasised by the fact that the obligatory wearing of the school uniform was waived for me. My fellow pupils were impressed.

'Hey, Lily, is your aunty really a nun?'

I flushed with pride; my heart raced as I unsuccessfully tried to suppress the self-satisfied smile that played around my lips. Few could boast of the ordination of two nuns in one family; I eagerly informed them that Sister Martha, younger sister to both Dad and Sister Raphael, was a teaching nun based in the northern town of Taiping. But my pride was soon squashed with the realisation that my new respected status came with a price: responsibility.

My teacher, and Sister Raphael's friend, was Sister Florence, a jolly, rounded Tamil nun with polished cheeks devoid of powder. From day one, she took a special interest in me. Both kind and fair, however she expected high standards in both my studies and in my personal behaviour.

'Now, Lily, you should be an example to the others. You come from a good family, you know, and I have to report to your aunty about your schoolwork, so work hard and don't let her down. You hear?'

She revealed a row of pearly white teeth that shone brightly against her dark skin. Her eyes sparkled behind her round, gold-rimmed glasses. The message was loud and clear. I was a pupil in the class purely because of my relationship with my aunt; as this realisation set in, the net tightened.

Hmm, my life is going to change. Schooldays have started; the next eleven years are going to be just studies, exams, and passes or failures.

Had I really bargained for that?

But the standard was set now for the rest of my school life. My childhood days gained structure; apart from weekends, my days of following my mother around the house came to an abrupt end. I knuckled down to hard work, making sure that I completed my daily homework. My formal education in Tamil had begun. This, even at standard one level, was to stand me in good stead later in life. The brain is extraordinary in its retentiveness, as I realised at the age of sixteen when I had to recall what I had first learnt at the age of six.

I spent my afternoons poring over Tamil books, lent to me by my new benefactor, Sister Florence. My older sisters were my sounding board and, eager to perform well at school, I bullied them into helping me with my work, following them around as I clutched my homework, begging them to check my spelling.

'Please, *akka*, ask me what the opposite of these words is, I'll see how many I know.'

My long-suffering sisters Anna and Rosie gave in with good-humoured groans, knowing that there would be no peace for them until I had completed my homework. We all held to our parents' strict ethic of work before play.

As well as nurturing our book knowledge, Sister Florence stretched her responsibilities to include lessons in deportment and personal hygiene.

'You have to be clean, girls. Haven't you heard the phrase "cleanliness is next to godliness"? You must take daily baths, and don't just pour a couple of tinfuls of water and think you are clean. Soap and scrub, soap and scrub.'

Gripping a pretend towel in her hands by its two ends, she moved her round body from side to side, backwards and forwards. 'This is how you dry your body, especially your back where you cannot reach.' Every ensuing bath-time, Sister Florence's demonstrations induced me to rub my body with renewed vigour, seeking godliness, until my back felt red-raw.

One fateful day, Sister Florence made a special announcement that made me prick up my ears.

'Girls, those of you who want to go to the cinema, remember to bring fifty cents by the end of the week.'

I danced home in anticipation of a treat, only to be pulled up short by Mum.

'You know I don't have spare money for luxuries like that. Sorry, *ma*.'

I should have known better than to ask for the impossible. I arrived at school next morning with a heavy heart, forced to acknowledge that this was the pattern my life was to take: we could not afford school outings. The heavy cloak of poverty wrapped itself tightly around me, and I could not shake it off.

Later that morning, as I raised my head pondering the answer to a question, I noticed a classmate a row away from me untie a knot in a corner of her handkerchief and extricate a coin, before re-knotting the handkerchief and pushing it into the back of the open-sided desk. She glanced around the class to check that no one was watching. She caught my roving eye and forced a swift lowering of my head.

That little scene refused to go away. The wrapped up coins floated before my eyes, goading me and taunting me, so tantalisingly within reach. During recess, I hatched a plan. If only I could somehow manage to lay my hands on that money, I could join the girls who could afford to go on the cinema treat. The wrongs of what I was planning I refused to dwell on. Temptation was all-powerful. Just before the end of recess, I dashed into the classroom before the others trooped in. Quickly delving into the recess of the desk, with shaking hands, a dry mouth and a rumbling tummy, I extricated the handkerchief and undid the knot to reveal a stack of coins. Counting out fifty cents, I knotted the remaining coins into the handkerchief again and pushed it back into its original position.

The fifty cents burnt a hole in my hot palm and I stacked them into the far corner of my desk. My hot hands were shaking as the others walked in and took their seats. My eyes were firmly glued to the back of the girl I had just robbed. Silently, I prayed that she wouldn't check the contents of her handkerchief, but retrieve it when it was time to go home.

Every breath I took screamed *thief, thief.* The enormity of my actions came home to roost. I was desperate to replace the wretched money, I followed the girl's every movement with a thudding heart, but it was too late. My luck had run out. My skin prickled and my hands sweated as I noticed her delve into the back of her desk. My head lowered to my slate. Her shriek of outrage seemed to be aimed directly at me, and I looked up to an accusatory finger pointing straight at me.

'Sister, I have lost some money. I know who stole it. That girl, she saw me put the money away. I know it was her.'

Tears of justified anger were coursing down the accuser's cheeks. I trembled as Sister Florence towered over me.

'Now Lily, did you take the money?'

'No, no I didn't,' I stammered. 'I brought my own money for the school outing. That is all I have.'

My face must have been my undoing. Sister Florence's sad face spoke volumes. I cringed, trying to cover my guilt.

'Well, all I have to do is ask your sister Rosie if your mother gave you the money, then we can clear this up.'

I sobbed out loud. 'No!'

My body shook with shame and sobs as I stumbled through my confession in front of the whole hushed class. All eyes were on me, hands held to open mouths as a thief was apprehended.

'Sorry, Sister, sorry, my mother couldn't afford to give me any money. I wanted so much to go to the cinema.'

Under stern scrutiny I retrieved the money and held it out in my shaky sweaty palm.

The look of disappointment on Sister Florence's face hurt far more than what followed – a well-deserved lecture on the evils of stealing other people's property. I couldn't have shrunk any further. I made my apologies and hung my head for the rest of the lesson, trying to squeeze my body into an invisibility that was impossible to obtain.

After class I hid round the corner. Every passing moment was agony until Rosie came to collect me; my best course of action was to make a full confession. She heard me out in silence, and let out a deep sigh.

'Well, you have learnt your lesson now. No more stealing. We may not have money, Lily, but at least we must maintain our dignity.'

Thankfully, there were no further recriminations. After a couple of days, even the girl I had stolen from relented her hard stance against me. Rosie did not report me at home. Sister Raphael did not chide me during my future visits. This was an early lesson I never forgot.

Rosie had already completed her Tamil studies at the convent and was enrolled for her English education at Loyola School, also in Sentul. I walked to school with her each day, pacing my steps with hers, never failing to enjoy our chatter as we walked, catching up in sisterly fashion. Every morning she would see me safe within the school grounds before continuing her journey to her own school, just a couple of hundred yards away.

A few weeks into my new school days, I was scribbling on my slate, twirling the white chalk between my fingers to keep the writing end sharp, when I became aware of Sister Florence's white-robed figure standing next to my desk. She stood so close I could smell her freshness. The silver-coloured ring on the fourth finger of her left hand sparkled: a symbol that she was God's bride. I looked up with a mixture of reverence and inquisitiveness.

'Come,' she said simply, with a look I found difficult to fathom. She beckoned me to follow her to the door.

My classmates craned their necks in curiosity; a few even crept up to the door to eavesdrop, but one stern look from Sister Florence was enough to send them scurrying back to their desks.

'Lily, you have got to be very brave. I have to tell you something,' her voice low and gentle. 'It is your *akka*, you see, your Rosie *akka*. She has been taken to hospital. But don't worry, Lily, I am sure God will look after her.'

'But... but...' I stammered. Suddenly my safe little world did not feel safe any more. 'What is wrong with her?'

'I don't know, *ma*. All I was told is that it is something to do with her stomach.'

Tears stung my eyes and I felt tightness in my throat, before bursting out crying. My *akka* in hospital! Was she going to die? You had to be seriously ill before you were taken to hospital; so far no one in the family had ever been hospitalised.

I felt the soft pad of Sister Florence's hand on my cheek. She pushed a crisp white cotton handkerchief into my hand.

'Now, now, Lily, if you pray to God, everything will be okay. You must put your faith in God. He won't let you down.'

I have no recollection of my journey home. Everything passed by in a blur. Having reached home, I found Anna on her knees in front of the altar, hands raised in prayer, toddler Chandra curled up in her lap.

Charlie sat cross-legged on the floor with a look of bewilderment. As I hovered hesitantly in the doorway, Anna looked up, her face shone with streaked tears, and beckoned to me, her right arm stretched out, hand half-cupped upwards, offering support. I ran across to my sister and joined her in prayer.

'Please God, please look after my sister and send her safely home.'

With a catch in her throat, Anna informed me that Mum had left for the hospital. Our prayers were interrupted when Dad rushed in, throwing a concerned glance at us.

'That's right, girls. Pray for your sister.'

After a quick shower to wash off the grime from work, he too set off, reiterating 'don't forget to pray hard for your sister now' over his shoulder as he left.

Time dragged while we waited at home, the atmosphere grey and melancholy. I missed the reassuring presence of Theresa, who was far away in Serdang, ignorant of what was happening at home. Peter arrived back from work, to be confronted by his anxious siblings. He soothed us, and we drew strength from his reassuring presence whilst Anna busied herself preparing our dinner.

After what seemed an eternity, Dad returned home, looking grey. His stubble seemed to have put on a spurt. His normally upright shoulders slumped forwards as he sank into his chair and broke the news. Rosie had undergone emergency surgery for a burst appendix. Mum had stayed on at the hospital to look after her.

'Will... will she be okay, *appa?*'

'Yes, *ma*, she will. The operation was successful. She just needs time to recover now.'

I had no idea what an appendix was, but was simply grateful that God had answered our prayers. We learnt later how close Rosie had been to death: failing to reach the hospital in time could have ended in tragedy, a situation too horrible to contemplate.

It was a long, slow week before we saw Rosie's soft smile again. Throughout her hospital stay, I missed her sunny presence; we had never been parted before. I couldn't visit her. Devoid of her company my walks to and from school were lonely. At night I dreamt of Rosie lying in a strange bed with great white bandages tied round her tummy, writhing in pain, unable to walk, reaching out to us and unable to connect. My hand stretched and grasped air.

When she finally returned, we treated her to a heroine's welcome. Charlie and I refused to leave her side, happy to perform any tasks she requested, so grateful to have her home safe and sound. The drama over, normality returned to our household.

10

'Communists and smallpox...'

Visit to Serdang

Every few months, Mum would travel to Serdang with Charlie or myself in tow, to visit her newly married eldest daughter. Sympathetic to Theresa's homesickness, my brother-in-law welcomed her family members into their new home, especially once Theresa gave birth to their first child, baby Charles.

The trip to Serdang from our suburb involved two bus rides along both tarmac and unmade roads, and lasted approximately three hours; a journey that seemed to take forever to an excited six-year-old.

One such trip took place during a period of significant communist activity in certain individual regions but also in the country as a whole. After the Japanese occupation ended in 1945, the British made moves towards granting Malaya Independence, though it remained a member of the Commonwealth. Many of their ensuing policies favoured the Malays, whom the British recognised as the rightful citizens of Malaya, to the dismay of the immigrants who had been actively recruited by the British. Unaware of or deliberately ignoring the unfairness to individuals, the British had followed their Commonwealth policy of divide and rule to the letter.

My Dad's keen interest in politics often led to repeated shakes of his head in the contemplative quiet after dinner, as he made comments on the current situation.

'The Chinese owned most of the tin-mining companies. They had a good head for commerce; see, even our provision shop owner, Kitchi, is a hard-working family man. The communists helped the British to overthrow those *Jaapan* fellows, and for that the *Jaapan* fellows targeted them. The Chinese suffered during the war and how were they repaid? So many of them have been crowded into kampongs and there are barbed wires round them keeping them in like animals in a cage.' I had no idea what he was talking about.

Some of the Chinese leaders went back to the jungle to begin their own guerrilla war against the British, wreaking their revenge by murdering Europeans on Malayan estates. The British, recognising that some of the grievances of the rural Chinese were valid, brought in measures aimed at placating the more moderate people and set aside villages for Chinese occupation in the above mentioned conditions, mounting a major offensive to segregate and defeat the communists.

A state of emergency was declared in 1948. The British High Commissioner, Sir Henry Gurney, who introduced military security and conscription measures to fight the insurgency, was ambushed and killed in 1951. There followed a massive crackdown on the movements of the Chinese. Forays into the jungle began in a big way, resulting at times in some barbaric practices. We heard many a rumour of the disembodied heads of Chinese communists put on display by angry British and Malayan troops to deter others from joining the communist cause. Gruesome photographs reportedly appeared in local newspapers not that we ever saw any evidence of that.

These were troubled times. General communist activities continued until 1954, but sporadic events continued to occur over a further period of twelve years. It was July 1960 before the British emergency regulations were repealed, by which time around 11,000 lives had been lost. From 1958 onwards, the vacated villages were opened, the rounded up Chinese helped with resettlement and a semblance of normality returned to the country.

One of our journeys to visit my sister and brother-in-law took place in 1953, over a year after Sir Henry Gurney was killed and at the height of the British crackdown. Mum and I were sitting halfway down the bus among our fellow travellers, comprising mostly of women of Indian and Chinese origin. I gazed dreamily through the window as we jolted along, enjoying the sights of rubber plantations, tin mines and rows of wooden houses as we drove past small villages.

We were heading down a long, straight road lined with palm trees, when the bus jerked to an abrupt halt, tyres squealing in the dirt. I heard a sharp, simultaneous intake of breath from all the passengers, including my mother, who grabbed my hand and squeezed it, whispering:

'Sit very still, and don't make a sound.' I looked up at her in anxious enquiry.

Two stern-looking Malay policemen boarded the bus, intimidating in their khaki uniforms and with large black rifles in their hands. I froze. All conversation ceased. During this time of political unrest, the rules were strict. Travelling with food items was prohibited for fear of communists hijacking and looting the buses. Police undertook regular checks on bus routes to ensure passengers complied with the rules. The men slowly and silently made their way down the aisle, using the tips of their rifles to prod the baskets and bags that sat on the passengers' laps and by their feet. They glared threateningly at each traveller in turn, daring traitors to reveal themselves. People broke out in sweat, adding to the discomfort of the humidity and dust. The backs of my legs became wet and my skin slipped and slid on the seat.

Some of the women were rudely prodded, indicating for them to rise. Nearly all of those selected for this treatment were of Chinese origin; clearly the surmise was that communist sympathisers could be smuggling foodstuffs for distribution to the rebels. I cringed when the ladies were being shouted at.

'Oi, *awak, turun, turun, pergi, pergi! Get down, get down, go, go!*'

The women were herded off the bus like cattle. I didn't dare turn my head and openly watch where they were going, but out of the corner of my eye I could see them being herded roughly into a tiny corrugated tin hut by the side of the road. The building was roofless – just a paper umbrella lay across the top of the tin 'walls'. It was quite a while before the women came out again, hurriedly re-tying the strings that held their trousers up and shaking as they tried to compose themselves.

The police, I later discovered, often set up such makeshift booths along the roadside, where recruited women could search the ladies more thoroughly in relative privacy. I felt fear radiating from my mother. She started to retch and pressed a handkerchief to her mouth. I glanced at her, alarmed; was my mother okay? Why was she feeling ill? Mum pulled out her 'good morning' branded towel from her cloth bag and cleaned her mouth. Her head leant back against the seat, her dark skin pale as a yellowish tinge crept in. She closed her eyes for a moment but, sensing my concern, reclaimed my hand in hers and pressed it reassuringly. My heart raced with anxiety for my mother, coupled with a fear of the policemen.

'Are you all right, *archie*?' A concerned lady leant over from the seat across the aisle, addressing Mum with the familiar, friendly Malay term for 'woman'.

Mum whispered something in her ear.

The lady tutted and her eyes grew round; she leaned over and patted Mum's hand. I sat perplexed, looking from one face to the other. What was happening? Why was Mum so scared of the policemen?

Although we carried no prohibited items on us, Mum knew that the police were incredibly strict and eager to make an example of rebellious communists. Anyone suspected of helping the communists would be immediately arrested and imprisoned. I didn't dare look up at the policeman as he sifted through my mother's bag, which held my clothes, a *sari* for my sister and some baby clothes that Mum had sewn for my sister's two-month-old son, her first grandchild Charles. Finally, he grunted and left. I blew out air through my nose while my mother muttered long-winded prayers that rolled on and on, fingering her rosary beads frantically.

Eventually, the Chinese women were ordered back onto the bus; it seemed no one was to be arrested on this occasion. Once they had taken their seats, a policeman instructed the bus driver to move on and everybody around me finally relaxed as our journey resumed.

But I could not relax. The menacing attitude of the rifle-bearing policemen stayed with me, my stomach clenched and I badly needed to relieve myself. But Mum informed me that we had another fifteen minutes to go before we reached Serdang. Pressing my legs together tightly, I tried to sit still, squirming every now and again to keep my bladder tightly closed and hoping and praying that I wasn't going to wet myself. My carefree sightseeing ceased and my sole concentration for the rest of the journey went into holding in my wee.

Thankfully, our journey continued without incident and we arrived in Serdang. We were visiting my sister's family in their new living quarters, which reflected my brother-in-law's recent promotion at work to chief clerk. The main house was a large square building on stilts, set well back from the main road. A veranda graced the full width of the house and the rest was divided into a large sitting-cum-dining-room to the right; the other half split into two adjoining bedrooms to the left, with a bathroom located at the rear end. A short flight of stairs from the back led to a covered, cement walkway that terminated at the doorway of the ground level kitchen.

Extensive grounds surrounded the house. To the right of the property stood a productive mangosteen tree. Its branches almost reached the ground, weighed down with ripe, reddish-purple fruit, containing sweet, juicy, tangy, pearly white segments. A rambutan tree sat a few feet away. The ground to the left of the house was tilled by my green-fingered *athaan*, and a variety of lush vegetables had been cultivated there.

I was full of our recent adventure and eager to tell my sister all about it; however, halfway through my account, Mum took Theresa aside and whispered in her ear. Theresa's eyes grew wide; her mouth formed a round, soundless 'oh'. Puzzled, I decided that Mum must still be upset; she couldn't do justice to Theresa's freshly prepared lunch.

A couple of hours later, Mum bade me farewell and left to catch the bus home from the bus stop conveniently located close to Theresa's house. I was to spend the couple of weeks of my school holidays with my sister and her little family.

My first day passed happily and I soon managed to push the incident on the bus to the back of my mind. I accompanied Theresa on her visits to her friendly neighbours' houses for coffee and tasty titbits, where I was introduced and welcomed. Then they cooed over baby Charles.

The next morning, I woke up unwell, feeling incredibly groggy. I had to drag myself to the dining table for breakfast. My sister had made *dosai* and coconut chutney, one of my favourite dishes; but I could hardly eat. I was tired and my mouth felt dry and coated despite my vigorous tooth-brushing exercise. I tried the food, but couldn't taste a bite; I could have been chewing paper.

Athaan looked at me closely.

'She doesn't look well. Look, her eyes are red – feel her, see if she is hot.'

Theresa placed a cool palm against my thumping forehead and nodded.

'Yes, she is hot. Very hot.'

'Hmm,' he grunted. 'Better take her to the dresser.'

Once her husband had left for work, and after tidying up the remains of breakfast, my sister bathed and fed baby Charles, then hooked him onto her hip and held out her free hand to me. Off we set to get me checked over.

It was nine in the morning and we were the first patients at the medical centre. The 'dresser' worked at the local medical centre, where all government officers' families received free medical treatment. Such individuals had often experienced some level of medical training, but were not fully qualified doctors. A tall man with a slight hump and a gentle manner examined me carefully. Using a small, flat, wooden instrument, he looked in my mouth, instructing me to stick my tongue out and say 'aah'.

I did everything he asked slowly and mechanically; I was starting to feel very woozy.

He cast an anxious look at my sister.

'I am afraid I have some bad news for you,' he murmured in a low voice. 'Your little sister has got smallpox. It is very dangerous and contagious. You must take her home straight away and nurse her on her own. Don't let anyone near her – especially your baby.'

Theresa stiffened in shock whilst the 'dresser' continued with his instructions.

'Give her plenty of young coconut water to keep her cool. If she recovers, it will take about three weeks. You had better let all the others who have come to your house recently know about this, so that they can keep a look-out for a high fever, which will be followed by blisters on the body.'

If I recovered? I looked up at my sister in bewilderment. Theresa looked visibly shaken, concern for me clear from her facial expression, but combined with fear for her precious little baby.

'How am I going to tell *athan* when he comes home?' I caught her shaken whisper.

Her gaze returned to me her composure disturbed and her face reflecting the fear in my own eyes. She drew a deep breath; her lips quivered as she tried to compose herself.

'Never mind,' she reassured me, soothingly. 'We will just have to manage and pray to God.'

The journey home was a blur. Once we were there, Theresa hurriedly prepared the back bedroom for me, and then crouched down to look me in the eyes with great seriousness.

'Lily, ma, you have to stay in this room; you cannot come out at all. If you do, you know what will happen to Charles, he is only a baby – please, stay there.' Responding to the terror on my face she added: 'Sorry, *ma*, so sorry. But I cannot do anything else!'

Theresa drew the windows shut, reaching on tiptoe for the top latch, and closed the door gently, leaving me in a sunless room. Strips of light from around the window lay on the wooden floor. Slowly, I curled my weak body onto the fresh white sheet that my sister had spread out on the floor. There was nothing to do now but wait.

It wasn't long before a raging high temperature set in. I was soon drenched in sweat and felt far too weak to move around. Everything became blurry and my grasp of time swiftly disappeared. I existed now somewhere between sleeping and waking. The walls of the bedroom disappeared and shadows magnified.

Days passed. I was delirious most of the time, with only ghouls and ghosts for company. The sole activity I managed was to drink the fresh coconut water that Theresa placed by the door from time to time.

Theresa was forced to nurse me all by herself. While I was ill, the emergency laws made it difficult for my mother to come to my sister's aid, as only the most necessary of journeys were undertaken. Theresa had a tough time caring for her critically ill sister and her precious little baby son at the same time. Smallpox was a well known killer disease, no other visitors could visit the house and offer their help; nor could she leave the premises. Thankfully the productive vegetable garden enabled Theresa to prepare meals, and my brother-in-law on his journey back from work purchased the necessary provisions.

I was cocooned in a black cloud, drifting in and out of consciousness, hearing voices in the distance. During my more lucid moments, I shook violently and uncontrollably with fear and loneliness. When I called out in desperation, my sister's sympathetic voice drifted through the closed door, reminding me sadly that she could not enter the bedroom.

'Just push the sheet to the door, Lily, then move away,' she instructed. 'I will pass a clean sheet for you, and I will leave you some coconut water, too. Here.'

The door squeaked open, just wide enough for Theresa to pick up my soiled sheet and push a clean one towards me.

Nights and days merged. My sleeping pattern was out of my control in my delirious state; sleep during the day resulted in sleepless nights. My fevered imagination latched onto the events of my recent bus journey, conjuring up bloodthirsty communists who were creeping around outside, desperate for food, trying to find their way into the house. Every little noise magnified and translated in my fevered brain into the stealthy movements of a communist. What if they entered and killed all of us while we were asleep? I sobbed into the hard floorboards with fear and pure exhaustion.

Spots popped up over my body, only a few of them, but they were incredibly large. Two huge ones appeared on one leg and three on the other; another couple ballooned on my face, one on my hairline and another on my forehead. The one on my back pressed into me like a small, hard bead, forcing me to lie on my front. I retched when the spots filled out with a watery liquid. My body did not seem to belong to me. Aliens were taking hold, controlling me.

Was it prayer that saved me? Was it luck, or was I simply destined to live? I will never know. Whatever the reason, my skin eventually cooled and my vision and appetite slowly returned. I became acutely aware of the light outlined by the windows and the firmly shut door. My ears picked out the footsteps of my brother-in-law leaving the house in the morning, and his return steps in the evening. The day was given life by Theresa's soft padding as she went about her housework, along with gurgling baby noises and attention-seeking tantrums.

I woke to birdsong, loud and clear. Daylight washed away the gloom of the night; my ghouls and ghosts had been laid to rest. I felt for my spots; they too were gone, my scabs were dry. I called out to my sister with my progress report. Freedom tasted sweet as I was allowed out of the room where I had been incarcerated for three long, lonely weeks. My eyes adjusted to the sunlight. The bathroom mirror revealed my drawn face, eyes that had sunk low into grey sockets. My caked lips held red cracks, yet I smiled despite the pain. Against all the odds, I had survived. Nothing could beat me now. Mumps, measles and chicken pox were a piece of cake. The precautions that Theresa had undertaken had worked.

On the day of my release, Theresa's neighbour's mother, Perianayagum, volunteered to oversee my post-smallpox bath. A respected elder and knowledgeable in folk medicine, although smallpox was beyond her ability to cure, she could help with the aftermath. The midday sun warmed my bathwater in a large tin tub; it stood on the cement strip next to the open drain that surrounded the house. Turmeric stirred into the water turned it the colour of sunshine, whilst a sprinkling of deep green neem leaves floated on the top like gems. Tropical neem trees were often referred to as 'nature's drug' and were especially popular in ayurvedic preparations, such as those that my Dad used from time to time to stem the psoriasis that plagued him. Persistent patches on his right arm and the hairline on his neck were troublesome spots. He associated his ailment with the greasy and grimy working conditions of his job, noticing an improvement whenever he was away from work for a few days.

Under the watchful eyes of Perianayagum *paatie*, her daughter Anthoniama and my grateful sister all gathered chatting under the shade of the fruit trees as I stood on the narrow strip of cemented area, weakly but happily bathing in the sun-warmed water, contemplating my narrow escape. How many people could claim to have survived the killer disease of smallpox? During the twentieth century, it is estimated that smallpox was responsible for somewhere between 300 and 500 million deaths. Thanks to luck, fate, or simply my sister, I am not counted among them. The scars on my legs are visible signs of my suffering as a scared six-year-old, and have remained so all my life.

As soon as I was well enough to travel, I returned home to a rapturous welcome. My miracle recovery was news for the entire neighbourhood to gossip about. But life carries on as usual despite miracles, and I quickly settled back into my new education regime. Mum continued to be tired and sick most days. Anna left school to help at home.

11

'Kakka and Kitchi...'

Shopping Trips

My smallpox episode had heightened my feeling of invincibility. I had stared death in the face and he had backed down. I was cocooned by my family's love and protection. I would soon start 'proper' school, and I was growing up. What could stand in my way?

Perhaps pride goes before a fall, or perhaps confidence at such a tender age was never built to last. Either way, I was reminded once more of my vulnerability all too soon.

In general, Mum favoured the Chinese provision shop on the main Sentul Road, but if she required sundry items in a hurry I was dispatched to an Indian Muslim's smaller convenience store, just a few yards from our main gate. Kakka's wife and children lived in India and he ran his shop with the help of a fellow countryman, but one member of his family had recently returned to Kakka's side, and now his shop helper took the form of his softly-spoken teenage son. I liked being served by the shy newcomer and was happy to agree to Mum's request one afternoon to nip to the shop for some margarine.

I scanned the shop for the teenage son, but his welcome presence was absent; the middle-aged Kakka was on his own for once. The margarine tin I needed to purchase was stacked on the top shelf, and Kakka turned to me, raising a thick bushy eyebrow. He clicked his tongue, rubbing the thick silver bristle on his chin with one hand, while the other was propped at his waist.

'Come, Lily, I cannot reach the tin. I have to lift you to reach it.'

I took a step forward, then paused, uncertain. I gazed at his round, bald head, beaded with perspiration. His familiar face had taken on a look that induced an uneasy sensation. My mouth dried out as he moistened his thick pink lips, his piercing black eyes fixed on me. A memory from the dim and distant past struggled up from deep within, screaming a warning; a tremor shuddered through me. I had seen that look before.

Distaste overwhelmed me and I dropped my eyes to Kakka's off-white singlet, unwilling to meet his gaze. The singlet's trimming, dotted with a line of holes, was stained yellow with sweat under the arms. A rounded belly hung over the shopkeeper's bunched-up belted, none too clean *sarong*. He wiped perspiration from his hands on his *sarong* and stepped towards me.

I stiffened. Railing inside against being lifted by this shifty-looking creature, I glanced around nervously, hoping to see the smiling face of his son, or indeed anyone, a fellow shopper perhaps. *Please, please, somebody – anybody. Where is everyone?* But no reprieve appeared. I was trapped. I prayed silently for this loathsome task to be over quickly.

Before I could draw breath to argue, Kakka leaned forward and grabbed me under my arms, hoisting me up to the top shelf. One hand gripped the top of my left arm and the palm of his right hand balanced my buttock. With lightning speed, he shifted his grip, slipping his index finger to the side and pressing it between my legs. His chewed nail scratched and hurt me.

Petrified and trapped, I tried to reach for the tin as speedily as I could, but Kakka had other ideas. Encouraged by the continued absence of shoppers, he sought to prolong my predicament, lifting me close to the tin and, as I reached out, yanking me away just far enough for my hands to grab air. A nasty gurgling sound emanated from his disgusting throat, as he pushed his finger in further. Furious and terrified, I yelled, kicking my feet at his hand.

'No, no, let me go!'

He looked around hastily, checking to see if anyone had heard, then met my eyes again. Realising I was set upon spoiling his fun, he moved me forward so that I could grab the tin with both hands, which I did with desperate haste. As he reluctantly lowered me to the ground with a final stab of his finger, I fixed him with a stare, exhibiting as much loathing as I could muster. I cringed inwardly when I saw the man's eyes twinkle in response, as though we shared a fun secret. His tongue lolled as he licked his lips once more, slowly and deliberately, confident in his power.

I turned and sprinted home on shaking legs, burst into the kitchen and slammed the margarine tin onto the table, then ran out again before Mum could stop and question me.

I hid, needing to be alone. My mind raced as I wondered what I could do, knowing all the while that I was trapped. I felt unable to disclose what had just taken place to my mother, having experienced her accusatory silence once before. Besides, Kakka was well liked by my family, who had benefited hugely from his generosity. During Muslim festivities he would present us with piles of chapattis and large pots of biryani rice, ingratiating himself particularly well with my father and brother. He had enlisted their help when burglars had struck in the middle of the night. The neighbourhood ties ran deep.

There was nothing for it, I decided. I had to suffer in silence and couldn't tell anyone. Still shaking, I washed myself thoroughly with copious amounts of soapy water before pulling on a fresh pair of panties, thrusting the used ones down to the very bottom of the washing pile. The urge to throw them away was overwhelming, but the sum total of my white cotton panties was a paltry four, and Mum would be certain to notice if one was missing. Questions to which I could provide no satisfactory answers would soon emerge.

In the meantime, I had questions of my own. Was there something wrong with me? Why were these things happening to me? Was it my fault? Had I unwittingly drawn attention to myself?

My confidence shattered, I withdrew into my shell. My secret thoughts ran endlessly on the incident, until I learned to force the memory away, closing a part of myself down. Yet I still had restless nights, waking sobbing from nightmares where Kakka's leering face was pressed into mine. My distrust of men grew, and my bed-wetting habit increased in frequency.

From that day onwards, I avoided stepping into the evil man's shop at all costs. Mum's shopping requests were handled by bribing Charlie to shop on my behalf; however, this came at a price. Ever the shrewd businessman, my younger brother demanded five cents for every time I approached him. Faced with few options, I soon accrued a considerable debt that I was unable to settle for a time, not until Peter commenced work and treated me to occasional pocket money.

I couldn't avoid shopping forever, and nor did I want to: I was unwilling to appear lazy. Instead, I volunteered to shop at Mum's favourite Chinese shop, which was a little further away but offered better prices than Kakka's convenient shop.

I set off on my first shopping trip after the incident to purchase sugar and condensed milk. My pony-tailed hair was pulled firmly away from my face to keep me cool; beads of sweat trickled down my neck. I wiped them away impatiently with the back of my hand, feeling self-conscious. My faded print dress was a hand-me-down. The waist rode high and the hem fell just above my knees, doing nothing for my self-respect as I walked towards the main road.

Face set straight ahead, my slippered feet flew past the dreaded

Kakka's shop and hit the dirt road that led to the tarmacked Sentul Road. The dirt surfaces were fairly solid, made accessible for motor vehicles with the help of pebbles that were transported to our streets by bullock carts and hammered in periodically by the collective effort of a few well-to-do and conscientious residents. The combination of heavy downpours and the tyres of the motorcars pushed the pebble and mud mixture into two ribbons, with a raised grassy mound running along the centre. I scuttled along in the hot sunshine, swinging an empty string bag at my side; my hasty feet raised dust that settled on my moisture-covered toes.

More relaxed now, my feet took me past a wooden house on stilts, where I would sometimes call in to purchase foot-long dark green drumsticks that resembled a multi- knotted finger and hung in clumps from a sparsely leafed tree. The swollen knotted parts encased succulent seeds. Mum chopped the long vegetables for curries and the *paatie* made a few dollars. Halfway along the track, just past Mr and Mrs Kandasamy's bungalow house with its pillared columns and shining black car parked in the porch, I hit the creaking planks of the rickety wooden bridge that was strong enough for just one car at a time to creep across.

Here, the air reverberated with excited squeals that floated across from the Malay primary school to my left. Malay girls, their dark hair tied up in pigtails and ribbons, played hopscotch, or jumped over swinging skipping ropes. The students were dressed in traditional *sarongs* of pale blue and overlaid by white, long-sleeved *kebaya*. The friendly ones waved as I walked past and I waved back, but a few stared and poked their tongues out at me.

Trying not to let their rudeness affect me, I turned my face away and continued on my journey, clutching tightly within my damp fingers the few coins that my mother had parted with. I passed gossiping housewives hanging out their washing. I had just cleared the terraced houses, when out of the corner of my eye I caught the presence of three teenage boys, their backs lounging against a tree. I knew what to expect as soon as I spied them.

'Oi *paappa, enga pouraie? Naangalum varummaa?' Oi girl, where are you going? Can we come with you?'*

They laughed and leered. I tried to ignore them but their chanting grew.

'Stupid Sentul rowdies,' I muttered under my breath, speaking out loud to reassure myself. I felt their eyes on me and turned my head away, deliberately crossing to the other side of the road. They didn't follow me and I continued on my way.

My sisters had often returned home after being verbally accosted during school and church outings. They vented their frustrations among themselves.

'Dirty rascals, they don't know who they are messing with. If we report them to *appa* they will be taught a lesson that they will not forget.'

Thankfully we had never been threatened with physical harm. We recognised some of the boys as regular troublemakers with too much time on their hands; however, aware of the fiery tempers that both our Dad and eldest brother possessed, and fearing for their safety if they attempted to confront the gang, we maintained our silence.

I reached the end of the dirt lane; on its left-hand corner stood the Chinese coffee shop from where we made any necessary phone calls. Some of the shop's wares – soft rice buns filled with sweetened black bean paste, and my favourite, savoury pork-filled buns – were being arranged on circular woven bamboo trays by the wizened old lady with a remarkably straight back, clad in her widow's black garb, a single substantial jade bracelet circling her wizened wrist. Despite her age she earned her keep in her son's shop. She was muttering in Cantonese to her daughter-in-law in the background. The familiar sweet and savoury smells made my mouth water. Too bad, I had no spare funds to purchase any.

Repressing a sigh, I looked left and right, then crossed the road, glad for the shade thrown by the corridor that skirted the row of shops. The barber's shop my Dad frequented was in demand, as usual; a Chinese man in shorts and white singlet and two Indian men, one clad in an off-white *veshtie*, the other in a *sarong*, both in short-sleeved singlets too, were parked on wooden stools, engrossed in conversation as they waited their turn for the lone barber's skills. Rising from his stool, the Chinese man hawked and spat on the roadside, then pressed a thumb onto his right nostril and blew snot out through the other, before returning to his interrupted conversation. I skipped out of the way, nausea rising from the pit of my stomach. This was a common habit, especially among the Chinese; I could never get used to this disgusting practice.

Chinese opera blared from the radio as I entered Mum's preferred provisions shop and smiled at the owner, a diminutive Chinese man affectionately nicknamed 'Kitchi' by his customers (meaning 'little' in Malay).

A queue of shoppers was already ahead of me and I waited my turn to be served as Kitchi bustled around, clearly rushed off his feet. When he reached me, he paused to steal a quick moment to revive himself: he dipped his chin into his chest, then arched it back; placing the padded edge of one open palm under his bony chin, he supported the side of his head with the other, then proceeded to wiggle his head from side to side, until a loud click was forced.

'Ahhh, that's better,' he sighed.

I had witnessed my father perform this ritual on a regular basis, although I was never tempted to try it; the click set my teeth on edge. Revived, Kitchi now gave me his full attention as I delivered my order in Malay.

'*Satu kati gula, dua kati tepung tolong, Kitchi. Oh, dua tin susu lagi.*'

I was fond of Kitchi: he was a friendly man with a twinkle in his eye, with no dark undercurrent of meaning. His equally tiny wife, dressed in a starched flowered jacket and matching loose cotton trousers, stood on a wooden chair behind the counter, her head swaying gently to the music as she stacked bright green tins of Milo onto the shelves. I gazed at them longingly, imagining the milky drink with its rich malty chocolate, frothing up to the brim enticingly. But I was under strict instructions, and constrained by an even stricter budget.

Kitchi's two children were perched on stools in the corner, dressed in matching flowered shirts and soft white cotton shorts, prattling in Cantonese as they sucked on sweets that had coated their pink tongues a bright red. When they turned to smile their baby teeth was also tinged a slightly paler red. They nodded at me, their rimless, coal-black eyes shining in recognition and welcome. I was only a couple of years older than them, but being older commanded their respect. *Lucky them*, I thought, *they can have a full meal every day. And I bet they enjoy a cup of Milo before they go to bed, and can dip their hands into the sweet jars whenever they want.*

Peeling my envious eyes away, I watched Kitchi weigh out the sugar, balancing his rust-flecked scales with one *kati* metal weight, then he poured the sugar into a newspaper cone before deftly folding the top over and tucking the end in securely. Sweat poured off his forehead as he worked in the heat and he dried his palms on his khaki shorts while tiny rivulets ran down his sleeveless white singlet, darkening it. Repeating the same process for the flour, he placed the packages into my string bag, together with the tins of condensed milk that were on my list of purchases.

His deft hands worked with lightning speed on the black abacus. I handed over the money and passed my tongue over dry lips as he delved into the biscuit container, placing a couple of cream crackers in my hand and enquiring politely after my mother as he did so. What a kind-hearted man he was. Warmth spread from deep within me, as my battered faith in men took a small step towards renewing itself.

I walked back with my purchases, munching appreciatively on my crackers. Rather on the dry side, they clung to the roof of my mouth, needing a lot of spit and tongue- twisting to dislodge them before I could swallow them; but they were a treat and well worth walking the few hundred yards to the shop. I couldn't afford pork buns or Milo, but at that moment I felt that these cream crackers, given with warm generosity that asked for nothing untoward in return, were more than a worthy substitute.

I reached home and handed Mum my purchases with a lighter heart.

12

'One less mouth to feed...'

Separation

A few feet away from the foot of our centrally placed well, I heard water splashing dully on the concrete floor and a lighter splash as it hit the sides of the corrugated zinc sheets that enclosed our open-air bathroom. A smile thinned my lips; Dad was showering. It was imperative for me to hurry: he would be expecting my company at the eight o'clock mass.

Dressed in my Sunday best, I hastened into the kitchen. The delicious aroma of freshly made porridge, our Sunday morning treat, drew me to the pot. Lifting the dancing, clattering lid, I feasted my eyes. Globules of fat from rich coconut milk glistened enticingly on the surface of the mix, breaking into eddies as the porridge bubbled like a hot spring. Leftover rice from the previous night had been reheated in freshly squeezed thick coconut milk and sweetened with palm sugar. Nutty, lightly cooked green peas swirled throughout like gems. A sprinkling of crushed cardamom seeds added an even more enticing aroma.

I clanged the lid back into position and swallowed my saliva. The sound of Mum's slippers slapping at her heels could be heard as she reached the front door and I heard her call as she paused to kick off her outdoor slippers.

'Rosie, Lily, somebody! Come and take this bag from me.'

She looked weary. Beads of sweat glistened on her forehead from the effort of carrying the string bag. Anna followed close behind, out of breath and weighed down by more string bags bulging with potatoes, onions, garlic and ginger. They had both attended the six-thirty mass and, as was customary, visited the local market on their way back.

We took turns to attend to attend early mass with Mum. On

such occasions I would have accompanied Mum to church and then followed her to the market. An enormous brick building with a high ceiling, the market contained cement stalls spread in rows from the central walkway. Wooden poles were fixed overhead, from which hung large metal S-hooks bearing produce. Dry goods, fruit and vegetables occupied the front stalls, but one could smell the fish stalls situated a third of the way into the building well before they came into view. The cement floor was always wet and slippery with melting water from the cracked ice that kept the fish fresh.

Meat stall-holders were grouped towards the back, blood and guts highly visible with fresh carcasses hanging from their steel hooks. Mr Ansari, a Muslim Indian gentleman with a distinctive goatee beard as white as the sparse hair that was drawn across his shiny ovoid head, always greeted Mum warmly. Father to six children, he understood all too well the difficulties faced by housewives with large families. After weighing the one *kati* of meat that was Mum's weekly purchase, he would throw in an extra lump or two of meat along with the marrowbones that imparted a particular depth of flavour to our curries. He was repaying Mum for her loyalty. She would thank him as she handed over notes wrapped around coins, kept tied in a knot in the free end of her *sari*.

That Sunday Rosie and I had agreed to attend the later, rather livelier English Mass when the rich voices of the choir singers, supported by Peter's powerful contribution, would echo from the domed raised dais towards the back of the church. This service attracted a younger church-going audience in the main.

Rosie was in the bedroom, changing into her Sunday best. I ran across to Mum, hooking the fingers of both hands onto the bag's handle and gently easing it from her heavily indented right hand. She smiled gratefully, massaging her hand to encourage the blood flow, before laying it protectively onto her rounded belly and going into the bedroom to change into her home *sarong* and blouse. Mum's tummy was heavy with baby.

With a sweeping motion, I plonked the bag onto the dining table, noticing that blood had already soaked into the *Strait Times* newspaper from the shopping. Lifting the meat packet, I took care to place my fingers on the unstained print, but one finger punctured through the softened newspaper. In disgust, I chucked the parcel unceremoniously onto an enamel plate on the table. The blood stained the sky-blue plate immediately, turning a deep maroon, the colour of a *sari* blouse that Mum had been working on the day before.

The metallic smell hit my nostrils. *Yuk.* I turned away from the dead meat, expelling my breath forcefully to rid my nostrils of the smell, with little success; I rushed to the kitchen doorway to draw a fresh breath. I reached for the cup that bobbed on top of an old bucket full of water in the doorway, to wash off the offending stain. As part of his daily morning routine, Dad topped up this bucket and the concrete tub within the bathroom with water from our well, leaning the bucket against the kitchen wall on the cement surface that ran three feet wide round the well. This open cemented space was our general washing area, where prepared food was washed, and pots and pans freshly scrubbed to shine and dry in the morning sun. Plates were lathered and rinsed and laundry was thrashed on the slate grey surface.

When we returned home from mass Rosie reminded me, 'Lily, don't forget, Uncle James is coming this afternoon.'

My heart sank. Had that day dawned already? I helped myself to a bowl and meekly sat down to eat, but the creamy porridge tasted bitter in my mouth. I dreaded what was to come.

In keeping with tradition, Mum's second younger brother, our Uncle James, had set off to India in 1953 on an extended family holiday, and returned as a happily married man. Our new Aunty Emily's belly was also rounded with baby like Mum's. It wasn't long before Uncle James, concerned that his young wife was lonely during the day, approached his elder sister with a mutually advantageous scheme. If he could relieve her of one of the many mouths she had to feed, he could also supply a companion for his wife. He had already made his choice. A little girl that my aunty could fuss over was ideal.

With the plaintive voices of the church choir still ringing in my ears, I left our family home in the company of my Uncle. Peel road was miles away from Sentul on the outskirts of Kuala Lumpur. I was leaving my familiar home for somewhere strange to live with an Aunty I was not acquainted with. My Uncle kept up a lively chatter throughout the journey, but I could barely respond. I was quiet and subdued.

We approached a tree-lined avenue with rows of brick-built, semi-detached houses, and approached one whose frontage was edged with white tiger lilies. Holding my hand, my Uncle led me up a tarmac path to a solid wooden door. My seven-year-old legs wobbled. I wanted to take two steps back for every one forward. My mouth was hanging open in wonder. Polished cars stood on driveways. Well-fed children in starched clothes stared openly as they pedalled shiny tricycles up and down the street. This was alien territory; even the air smelt foreign.

The heavy door creaked open into a spacious sitting room. My stomach felt as empty as the vast space I was walking into. My aunt rose to greet me.

'Come, I will take you upstairs to your room first. We can leave your bag, I will show you where the bathroom is.'

Aunty gently led me through the house and into a bedroom, *my* bedroom. They had meticulously planned for my arrival. I had my own little bed with several toys arranged invitingly on the pillow. My bedroom at home, a flat old door in an empty space walled on three sides with a walkway through, was in stark contrast to this enormous room with a single bed, a large almari and a glass cabinet that was pressed to the wall. At the flick of a switch an electric ceiling fan whirred overhead, stirring the humid air into cooling caresses. Clear corners remained devoid of piled-up dirty washing, and there was enough room for a dozen feet to play. Aunty Emily disappeared momentarily into her bedroom then re-emerged, coming up behind me and placing a hand on my shoulder.

'Come Lily. You must be hungry. Come, eat.'

I followed her into the kitchen, uncomfortably aware of the noise that the pad of my feet made in the silent house. I perched uneasily on the edge of a stool and looked at my plate, a mound of rice, chunks of curried meat and thick gravy and stir-fried vegetables and mini crisp poppadums around the edge. It smelt delicious, but I poked at it and played with the meal, hardly able to swallow the unusually plentiful dinner.

Night gathered outside in shades of grey that darkened as my loneliness deepened. The relative safety of daylight was ebbing. The laughter of children became fainter and died out altogether. Uncle clicked a radio on and retreated behind a newspaper. Popular Tamil songs blasted out and Aunty Emily's feet began beating time, her mouth working to the tune while her crochet needle flew in and out. A few ignored toys were scattered on the coffee table, no eager hands to fight over them here. I fingered my book absently, feeling my throat gradually tightening until it hurt. Tears pricked the back of my eyes.

The clock struck eight and Aunty Emily looked up.

'Come *ma*, time for bed.'

I crept into my comfortable bed obediently, but couldn't sleep. After a while, I heard the door to my aunt and uncle's room creak open. The light switch clicked and the line of light under my door disappeared, throwing me suddenly into black darkness. The fear of darkness spread its gnarled fingers in a firm grip that tightened round my heart, making it palpitate until it seemed to squeeze the breath out of me. The house was still; the click-click of the chitchats magnified. I missed the sounds of my large family and began to sob in short breathless gasps, training my eyes on the shadows cast on the window. I cried myself to sleep.

The following morning I woke to a wet bed. My crumpled dress clung damply to my shaking legs. I stood contemplating my next course of action, staring at the reflection of my tear-stained face in the glass cabinet. When I scrutinised my face, I could see aspects of my family. There were my sister Rosie's shrewd eyes, Anna's filled-out cheeks, my mother's nose and the shape of my father's feet, the second toe longer than the big toe, the same inward turn of the little toe. *Who is this girl? She belongs in Sentul, not here.*

The door opened to my smiling aunt. She took in the scene at a glance. Unperturbed, she ushered me into the bathroom. Thankfully my Uncle had left for work. I could not have looked him in the eye, smelling as awful as I did. By the time I had showered and dressed in fresh clothes, Aunty Emily had laid out my breakfast – but, once again, my appetite had abandoned me.

'What is the matter, girl? Why aren't you eating your breakfast? Is there something else you want?'

Her tone was soft, kind and concerned, opening the floodgates of fresh self-pity. In between sobs I choked out, 'I... I... I want to go home.'

'But you've got everything you need here: nice bed, new clothes, and sweets to eat. Is there anything else we can get you?'

I shook my head, as the tears flowed unchecked.

'Are you worried about the bed? Don't worry about that, the mattress will soon dry in the hot sun. It is my fault, I should have covered the bed with some plastic, I forgot.'

Her distress rose in line with mine. 'Stop crying now, what is your Uncle going to say? He'll think I've been unkind to you.'

I sniffed hard and tried to stop, but an image of my family rose before me. My longing was too strong. 'S... s... sorry, *atthai*,' I sobbed. 'I want to go home!'

She sighed then patted my head.

'Okay, *ma*, I know how you feel, because I miss my family too. But I cannot take you home now. We have to wait until your Uncle comes back from work, and then I will tell him. Now wipe those tears and eat something, or you will starve. I will finish my cooking then we can play with your toys, yes?'

I shuddered, and gave a weak smile of gratitude for my aunt's understanding. She had neither scolded, nor tutted at me. She was a lovely lady – but she wasn't my mother. My place was at home with my family.

Lunch cooked and kitchen cleared, Aunty Emily sat beside me as

I twirled the end of my plait and practised my alphabet. My hopes up slightly, I had done marginally better with my lunch. Aunty took an afternoon nap, while I tossed and turned on the settee, uncomfortable in the silence. The day seemed to stretch out interminably; every minute was an hour. Soon I was answering my aunt in monosyllables until she stopped trying to engage me in conversation. My eyes were glued to the doorway and my heart jumped as I finally heard the key turn in the lock.

'Hello Lily,' my Uncle greeted me, warmly. 'Have you had a good day?'

My lip trembled in response and I burst into fresh tears.

'Oh dear, what is the matter, why the tears? Emy, what happened?'

'She wants to go back home, she has hardly eaten anything and I have tried everything, *athaan*. Look at her face. She is not happy. I think we have to take her back.'

Uncle James clicked his tongue on the roof of his mouth; his face drooped in sympathy.

'I am sorry, you don't like it here, *ma*.' He caught Aunty Emily's eye and nodded to her before turning his attention back to me.

'Never mind, we tried. I suppose you are missing your brothers and sisters. Okay. Wait till I have had my shower and my tea. Get your bag together, Lily, *atthai* and I will take you back to Sentul.'

I hopped, skipped and jumped to what had briefly been my very own bedroom, eagerly pulling my neatly arranged clothes from the *almari*. I could have lived in comfort here, looked after and cared for by loving relatives. But I had briefly tasted separation from my family and been devastated by the experience. Nothing could replace them in my heart.

Our next visit to Sister Raphael bore no similarity to our previous one. Changes were afoot. Sister Raphael had been advised of her imminent transfer to Seremban, a small town forty miles south of Kuala Lumpur and a couple of long bus rides away from Sentul.

'*Annan*, I have spoken about Lily to Reverend Mother concerning next year's schooling. It should be fine for her to join the English convent school – but she must continue to work hard.' I beamed; I was already committed to work. But her next words removed my smile instantly.

'And *annan*, I have already asked for a place at the boarding school for Rosie, to join me in Seremban. I hope you don't mind; one less mouth for you to feed. And, think about this, Rosie may want to join our order and your family will then be blessed.'

'I've got no problems with that. I will speak to Marie and Rosie.'

My heart sank. The pain of separation was still palpable for me: Theresa's departure, Rosie's hospitalisation and my own brief experience at Uncle James's. With leaden steps as heavy as my heart I followed Dad home.

Rosie did not react favourably to the news of her imminent departure.

'I don't want to become a nun! I will go and be a boarder if that is what you want but there is *no way* I will become a nun.'

'All right, all right, no one is forcing you to follow in your Auntie's footsteps.' Dad held out his hands in a placatory gesture. 'But becoming a boarder at the convent is a privilege that few girls get. Consider yourself lucky, Rosie, *ma*.'

Rosie took to padding around the house, unusually subdued. Her spontaneous laughter, her jokes, her pranks, all ceased. I missed my sister the tomboy, who swung from trees and jumped down from fearsome heights: Rosie the joker, who played pranks on our cousin Raja when he visited our house.

'You are not my *annan*,' she would retort to Raja, during one of their frequent scuffles. 'I don't have to address you respectfully just because you were born one day before me.'

'You, *Kuchi Biru*,' he would reply, referring teasingly to her spindly legs. 'Respect your elders, or else.'

Then they would chase one another around the compound and fall exhausted in a heap, much to the family's amusement.

But now Rosie was quiet and withdrawn. Decisions had been made for the greater good and family compliance was expected. We trod carefully around her. She was to leave for Seremban after Christmas. Rosie, much like Theresa before her, was to leave a considerable gap in our young lives at home. In my quieter moments of solitude, in the build up to Rosie leaving, I wondered: was this what growing up would bring for all of us?

13

'From Our Lady to Allah...'

Religion

Rosie strode into the living room and flung her school bag onto the settee. A deep disgruntled sigh escaped her. I placed my book face down.

'What's wrong, *akka*?'

'Just something Rani said at school today. She was bragging about Shivaji Ganesan's latest film.'

I nodded in sympathy. None of us were immune to the magnetic lure of our local cinema but we were in the middle of Lent, a time of abstinence and sacrifices.

'Maybe the film will run until after Lent, then you will be able to go and see it, eh, Rosie *akka*?'

'Maybe. We'll see,' she retorted, not convinced.

Religion shaped our lives. It identified us all and created communities within communities. Judgements on character were attributed to religious fervour. Practising believers made for law-abiding citizens. It stood to reason that if you bowed to rules and regulations therefore you must be a good person.

The Anthonysamys practised Catholicism to the full; our lives were dictated by the Commandments. We were God's chosen people and as such constantly reminded of our privileged position. Only believers could gain entry into the Kingdom of Heaven and on the last day when the world came to an end, we would be judged. Our time on earth had to be accounted for and we would cower in shame when a list of our sins was read out.

'Oh the shame of it. The theft of those coins during my Tamil School days will become public knowledge,' I thought.

I reached a firm resolve. Commit as few sins as possible. To guarantee the safety of our souls, lest God should send for us whilst we slept, we daily implored God's forgiveness. On bended knees by our beds we sought our guardian angel's protection.

'Keep watch over me tonight dear angel and guard my family. Dear God, if I don't wake up in the morning please forgive my sins.'

I envisaged a benevolent guardian angel wrapping me in its protective wings and a smiling God raising his hand in blessing. I was a firm believer.

During Lent we abstained from our favourite activities. We fasted and abstained from meat and other favourite foods. No weddings were planned during this period. The Muslims fasted for forty days before Hari Raya Puasa or Eid; similarly, Lent was a preparation for the feast of Easter, when the miracle of all miracles was manifested through Jesus rising from the dead.

I took such rites very seriously and firmly believed that my sacrifices during this holy forty-day period brought me closer to God. There was a link, a chain. I felt a compulsion to make as many sacrifices as I could conjure up and a count was made at the end of the day. I aimed to break my record.

Enthusiastic as I was for Lent, nothing could outshine the preparations for Christmas. In the days leading up to Rosie's departure, Christmas was drawing near, and it was time for my annual new dress; a much-anticipated change from the dresses fashioned by mixing and matching remnants and hand-me-downs or when hems were let down to coax a few more months of wear. Sensing my anticipation, Mum addressed me calmly.

'Lily, go with Rosie *akka* to our tailor and choose what dress you both want for Christmas. Your *akka* will help you choose a pattern and Ah Chin will know what material we can afford.'

No second bidding was necessary. I followed Rosie on winged feet; just past the mosque on the main road, a row of wooden shops with rusty tin roofs stood alongside each other. We made for the second shop where Ah Chin, a Chinese lady in her late twenties, sat by her Singer sewing machine. Her bright eyes were fixed on the material she fed to her needle, a measuring tape draped round her neck. I could hear the chatter of her children's voices from the open central doorway. She greeted us with a soft smile, her rimless eyes sparkling.

With racing heart I looked through her pattern book, where sylph-like Caucasian ladies struck poses in beautiful dresses. My finger pointed to a pattern sporting a square neckline, bows to the back and a double-layered skirt.

'Rosie *akka*, do you think I can have a dress made just like this one?'

'If Ah Chin can tell us we can afford it, then maybe.'

Our tailor guided us to the bales of material that lined the wall of the shop, expertly directing us to the ones within our agreed budget. I chose a light blue taffeta, my favourite colour, as worn by Our Virgin Mary. Rosie plumped for a cream-coloured material. Our measurements were duly taken and scribbled in Chinese characters into Ah Chin's order book. I skipped home light-heartedly, following close behind my beloved sister.

At home, another Christmas preparation was under way. Bare-chested, Peter stood on the grassy area of the front compound, bending strips of shaved bamboo and securing the ends with jute string. Twenty-one separate pieces of translucent paper had already been cut to size and were weighted down by pebbles on the grass. I sat on my haunches, watching his careful movements in fascination. The bamboo skeleton now complete, Peter gently picked up a piece of the white translucent paper and dabbed it with glue concocted out of tapioca starch and hot water. Concentration was etched deeply on his dripping forehead; one rogue finger could easily slip through the delicate paper and ruin it.

'Here, come and help me finish off.'

I balanced the structure as instructed while Peter glued each piece into place, leaving a gap at the top end where a candle could be placed on a metal cap. He held the finished product up to gasps of admiration: here was our very own, beautiful, shining star of Bethlehem. Carefully, Peter carried it indoors and stored the star in his room to keep it safe.

The grand launch took place a few days later. A pulley system was devised to raise the star to the topmost branch of our rambutan tree. The homely event grew to theatrical proportions in the presence of an admiring crowd, both within our grounds and from the passing pedestrians who traipsed along the lane beyond our fence. The air resounded with the clapping of hands as the star found its new tropical home. The glow in our hearts matched that of the single white star as it swung gently in a soft breeze, heralding the arrival of the greatest festival in our Catholic calendar. On Christmas night and for the following fourteen nights, a candle gave life to Peter's star, casting a ghostly glow in the darkness.

Our celebrations this year were marred somewhat by Rosie's imminent departure. Theresa, gently rounded with baby number two, joined us for the festivities, along with her husband and the bouncy eight-month-old Charles, whose existence had ensured that my newest brother, Ben, had been born into unclehood. Their presence helped to ease our heartache, proof that departure wasn't forever. Whilst Theresa and Anna remained at home to nurse the little ones, the rest of the family, decked out in our finery, joined groups of our Catholic neighbours as we all walked in crocodile-fashion to attend Midnight Mass.

Bobbing pools of torchlight picked out the ruts, potholes and large pebbles. Despite numerous attempts at covering the lane with gravel, the ruts reappeared, regular as clockwork. Our shoes squelched on the muddy patches and crunched on the sandy spots until we reached the ghostly-lit Sentul Road, enabling us to admire one another's newly tailored Christmas attire. Our excited chatter matched our festive spirit. Puffed-cheeked and chest pushed out, my double-plaited hair, finished off with matching blue ribbons, tapped my back in time to my strides. I was showing off my beautiful taffeta dress, made to perfection by Ah Chin: the sashes were tied into a bow at the back and the layered skirt fell gracefully from the waist to just below my knees. My hands slid up and down on the stiff taffeta, raising a mouse-like squeaky note. I loved this dress and wore it to death.

We joined the surging, tightly packed crowds mounted the steps of the church and passed through the great side doors, aiming for the front third of the high-ceilinged building. We dipped our fingertips in the holy water held in the half-moon-shaped fonts and crossed ourselves before making for the polished wooden pews. The sweet smell of incense mingled with the warmth of burning wax from tall candles that ringed the approach to the altar, which was sparkling with richly embroidered drapes.

The congregation, mostly Indian but dotted with a smattering of paler-skinned Chinese and Eurasians, arranged themselves in family groups, with the exception of those proud offspring who swelled the choir or served as altar boys. The most pious and the elderly occupied the front few pews. Families padded out the middle rows while the young and impatient filed into the back rows. Latecomers filled any standing space. We exchanged nods of acknowledgement, followed by a swift appraisal of the Christmas finery, before bending towards threadbare, tapestry-covered kneelers.

High mass was celebrated with the choir at full throttle, sending thrills down my spine. We openly and joyfully proclaimed our beliefs and beat our breasts with a fisted right hand as we repented our sins.

'Mea culpa, mea culpa, mea maxima culpa.
(Through my fault, through my fault, through
my own grievous fault.)

Those old enough to receive Holy Co'mmunion walked up the aisle to the altar with their heads held high but bowed them respectfully when returning to their seats, as the worshippers acknowledged the

127

saviour's presence within their humble bodies.

Hard-earned notes and coins were dropped into hovering collection bags. Our voices rang out loud and clear in both prayers and song.

I fell asleep against Mum while mouthing prayers; the tinkling of the bell during the offertory failed to waken me. Just as mass was coming to an end, I woke with a start, my neck stiff where Mum had rested my head on the arm of the pew. I joined in with the final blessing as the sign of the cross was drawn in the air towards the congregation.

'And the blessing of God Almighty, the Father, the Son, and the Holy Ghost, be amongst you and remain with you always.'

'Amen,' we chorused in dutiful response – and, duly blessed, the congregation began to disperse.

Once we reached home bleary eyed we could not retire to bed until we repeated our obligatory family prayer of thanks, imploring God's mercy on behalf of all our loved ones, and waited in anticipation for that special drink. Dad passed round our annual family treat: a schooner of sweet sherry, from which everyone took a sip, the fumes never failing to induce a round of coughs. The mouth-watering cooking smells that originated from the kitchen meandered through the house. Sniffing the smells, we made our way to our beds for a few hours sleep.

Our communities were nurtured around church attendances; our family basked in a greater solidarity that elevated us above our poverty. Within the high-ceilinged building we were united with the rest of the congregation in a classless environment of fellow believers, where the poor rubbed companionable shoulders with the wealthy. Dressed in our fine Sunday clothes, our bowed heads covered in white embroidered lace, we were truly a congregation. No Catholic family stayed away from Sunday mass without reason, and any absence was a point of discussion.

'Where is young Mary? I don't see her. Is she okay? Will she be attending evening mass?'

Once the service was over, there was gossip at the church doors and in the grounds, while the few waiting cars revved impatiently. 'How are you? Family okay? We are going to the market; are you coming? We can talk on the way.'

Obligatory evening prayers, at home, required distractions to lighten the half-hour daily ritual. Strictly clock-watched by us, we were expected to remain kneeling on the hard cement floor throughout the recital of the Holy Rosary; however, all too often the littlest ones fell asleep on the laps of the adults, or just sprawled on the cement floor, while others fidgeted and sat on their haunches. We committed to memory all the requisite prayers in English, dissolving into uncontrollable and unsuccessfully smothered fits of the giggles when Tamil-School-educated Anna repeated her prayers parrot-fashion, mispronouncing her words.

'Hail Mary, full of grace, the Lord *ees* with *ee* blessed *thart anon* women, and blessed is de fruit of thy *hom*, Jesus.'

A loud clearing of the throat and a disapproving nod from Mum often had the desired effect, at least until the next mistake occurred. Dad determined that the thread of prayer was not to be broken and tactfully ignored Anna's mistakes. With knitted brow he solemnly nodded towards the individual whose turn it was to dedicate the first decade of the rosary. Four other individuals were chosen likewise for the remaining four decades. Each dedication was made to a worthy cause: a sick relative who could benefit from our collective imploring's to God; a member of the household preparing for an important exam or on a job-hunt.

Fridays were marked as confession days when we were cleansed of our sins.

'Bless me Father, for I have sinned.'

I would assiduously compile in my head a list of my sins against God. Non-attendance of mass due to laziness, or failure to say my daily prayers; sins against my neighbour, including jealousy towards my friends; sins against myself, have I been conceited, impure in thought, word, or deed? All my activities and innermost thoughts of the week were fully examined and confessed, followed by the final assertion: 'For these and all my other sins which I cannot remember, I am very sorry, I firmly resolve not to sin again, and humbly ask pardon of God, and of you, Father, counsel, penance, and absolution.'

Returning to the pew and mouthing my penance with bent head, I was suitably subdued, aware that my sinful soul was at that very moment being washed clean in the blood of Jesus Christ. Routinely I made renewed vows not to commit these sins again.

Saturday evenings were dedicated to novena attendances, when prayers were offered to Our Lady and favours sought. The Sabbath remained sacred, as a day of rest. Attendance at Sunday mass was compulsory and no heavy housework was allowed.

Being brought up as a Catholic – and, later, educated in a convent school, where strict Catholic teachings were reinforced with morning assembly prayers and religious studies – forced an orthodox way of life on me from the moment I was born and blessed. Babies were baptised, so that our natural mortal sins could be washed away to allow God to take up residence. Our godparents promised to help guide and raise us to become good practising Catholics.

Communities in Sentul and in the wider region of Kuala Lumpur respected one another's beliefs. I grew up within a community where religious rivalry did not seem to exist – conversely, mutual respect for one another's beliefs was celebrated.

'Just because our neighbours are not Catholics doesn't mean we should consider ourselves superior to them. They are all God-fearing people and we should respect their beliefs. The Kutans are Hindus, but they are good Hindus, see how he practises neighbourliness, and shares his produce with his neighbours. After all, our ancestors in India were also Hindu before they converted to Catholicism.'

The doorways of our multi-national and multi-religious community proudly displayed religious artefacts and pictures for the eyes of all passers-by. Wooden crosses, with or without the crucified Christ, hung on nails hammered into front doors; Hindus hung framed photos of their numerous deities; pictures of half-moon crescents and stars represented the Malay faith; and the Chinese houses burst with colour as the intoxicating smoke curled from burning crimson joss-sticks on matching crimson miniature altars erected against walls or hung from plinths in their courtyards.

The largely Indian community of Sentul was dominated by Hindus, with a Christian community coming a close second; the majority of the Christians were Catholics but there was a smaller minority group of Methodist worshippers too. At the tender age of seven, during my first year at Sentul Convent, my classmate Nadira was my sole Muslim friend; at a later stage, after an amalgamation of schools, three Muslim classmates joined, enabling me to expand my knowledge of other religious beliefs. I understood that the Koran was the equivalent of our Bible. I observed the correct way to greet our Muslim elders: Dad would drop his head in respect and offer his hands, saying *Salaam Alaikum*, peace be unto you. Their Allah was equivalent to our God. Our cultural and religious differences but also the underlying similarities between our beliefs was acknowledged and respected.

The grand lead-up to important local festivals stirred up excitement within every household. Housewives grouped to gossip and undertake collective cooking sessions. Rice cakes and *achi muruku* and *atharasam* were my particular favourites: crisply fried swirls of savoury soft dough perfumed with caraway seeds were squeezed out of patterned sole plates into boiling oil. Measured quantities of rice, green pea and chickpea flour soured in vats overnight were then enriched with generous helpings of sugar and ghee, the resulting sweet sour dough was hand-patted into ovals and deep-fried to a rich caramel colour. The mounds of cooled produce were shared and packed into empty biscuit tins. Youngsters were roped in to help their mothers cart everything back to their respective homes.

Tradition dictated that we share our festive food with our neighbours, especially people of other denominations. Before maturing into a teenager and being forced to take a more demure back seat appropriate to my budding womanhood, I acted out my delivery role by balancing heavily laden trays covered with hand-embroidered tray-cloths to our near neighbours, and gratefully pocketed the rewards, small change that was eagerly thrust into our moist little paws.

Christmas Day dawned with our eager faces crowded in freshly decorated doorways and newly curtained windows, scanning for visitors. A constant flow of relatives, friends and neighbours from other faiths would arrive from breakfast through till supper to pay their respects and rejoice in their friends' celebrations, partaking of the delicious food that my mother and sisters had prepared. After attending Midnight Mass it would take them until the early hours of the morning to get everything ready.

The noise level during Chinese New Year reached new heights every year; it was their belief that the noisier the celebration, the luckier the year. Red paper from firecrackers would litter the streets. Red joss-sticks burned continuously throughout this period in the Chinese temples as visitors offered prayers for a prosperous New Year. The young were encouraged to visit the oldest and most senior members of their extended families, parents, grandparents and great-grandparents, who rewarded them with *Ang Pows* – money placed in gold-patterned, shiny red envelopes, generously bestowed on all visitors.

My school holiday visit to my Aunty Ava, Mum's younger sister, coincided with the celebration of Chinese New Year. I accompanied my aunt and my cousins to her rich Chinese neighbours. We were ushered into the presence of their revered grandfather, an unusually tall, elderly Chinese gentleman with soft, long, white hair and long buffed fingernails. He was dressed in richly embroidered red satin robes, with upturned red satin embroidered shoes. My cousins and I were beckoned forward and an Ang Pow placed in our outstretched hands. I muttered my thanks and backed away to the safety of my aunt, overwhelmed by the rich furnishings and the satin hangings on the walls. As we left the imposing brick-built house, I was quiet in contemplation of the opulence I had just witnessed in what was clearly a wealthy household. When I reached the normality of my aunt's house, I peered into the red envelope and was delighted with such a very generous gift: coins totalling a whole dollar rolled on to the palm of my hand.

'Aunty, look what that Chinese uncle gave me.'

'You are a lucky girl, aren't you? Don't spend it: you can save it in your moneybox when you get back home. And here, take this, too,' she added, pressing more coins from her purse into my hand.

On the fifteenth day after New Year, the Chinese celebrated *Chap Goh Mei*, when they – and sometimes we – would traditionally partake of glutinous sweet rice dumplings brewed in soups. The air was thick with magic as Chinese families walked the streets at dusk, carrying red transparent lanterns often in the shape of animals – roosters, dragons and fishes – all sparkling with scatterings of glitter. The lighted candles made the lanterns glow like giant fireflies as they swung in rhythm to the accompaniment of excited chatter.

The most memorable of Muslim celebrations was *Hari Raya Puasa*, the festival of Eid at the end of Ramadan. Great importance was attached to their 'breaking the fast ceremony' every evening at the designated time. The few Malay girls that sauntered with their families on the main road looked splendid in *kebayas*, embroidered tops, and ankle-length skirts, while the boys strutted in *sarongs* and long-sleeved tops, their waists drawn in with lengths of golden silk cloth, and *songkoks* (conical-shaped traditional hats) perched on their heads.

Our house was too far from the local mosque to hear its calls to prayers, but I had been in the vicinity many times when Arabic quotes from the Koran were blasted out through loudspeakers. Muslim men, their heads covered in white skullcaps, dressed in colourful *sarongs* and wearing loose tops, hastened towards the elaborate mosque with its colourful minarets.

Malay cakes, locally referred to as *kueh*, were mostly made from rice flour, but my favourite was a wafer-thin pancake fragrant with *daun pandan,* screw pine leaves: a sword-shaped leaf that imparted its essence when crushed or cooked. The pancake was generously filled with a mixture of desiccated coconut and brown sugar, then rolled and coated in more juicy grated coconut: a sweet-toothed treat. Pyramids of plump, honey-sweet dates abounded during this time of the year.

Through joint celebrations and delicious foods, a multicultural and multi-religious community created a peaceful coexistence. Our festivals, rituals and celebrations helped our community to map out each year.

Local celebrations commenced with Chinese New Year and its red envelopes, followed by the Hindus' *Thaipusam* and a visit to the nearby wonder of Batu Caves. Lent, with its sacrifices and fasts, culminated in Easter. *Hari Raya Puasa* ended the Muslims' fasting. All Saints' Day heralded the glorification of our Catholic saints, whilst All Souls' Day entailed a visit to the graves of our loved ones, where candles were lit, flowers strewn and prayers offered for the departed. *Deepavali* (This is how the locals spelt it)celebrated the Hindu festival of lights, and then of course the end of the year culminated in the greatest celebration of our lives: Christmas. Finally, Mum's familiar phrase, 'An old man is dying today, leaving his twelve children behind,' rang in our ears as another year drew to a close, leading on to a new beginning, with hopes, aspirations and New Year resolutions.

14

'Tigers on the prowl...'

Primary School

Anna parked her bottom on a low wooden stool in readiness to prepare the meat and vegetables for lunch, her skirt lifted and stretched between her legs. She swung the sharp cleaver repeatedly, bringing it down with a thud on the well-worn wooden board with each stroke. She used the water from the bucket to rinse the chopped meat. The natural incline of the cemented area that circled our well ensured that everything drained into the shaped channel that flowed into half-cylindrical concrete drains, emptying their contents into the open drain that ran alongside the back fence. The stained concrete drains necessitated a weekly scrub with wire brushes to release the algae that greedily claimed residence.

The zinc door banged shut, as Dad emerged from the open-air bathroom in his freshly laundered *sarong* that clung damply to his thighs, his bare chest flecked with water. He dried his sparse wet hair with a threadbare blue towel. Dad's St Anthony-like bare patch had developed at an early age, retaining just enough strands of hair that could be combed across to cover his shiny pate. The lack of an abundance of hair did nothing to detract from his good looks, however: he cut a dashing figure in any crowd. Dad and I crossed paths. I held my hand out for his towel and made my way to the freshly vacated bathroom while Dad walked into the kitchen. A neem twig hanging from the corner of his mouth slurred his speech. An empty condensed milk tin, its lid prized off, held Dad's selection of neem twigs, flattened at one end to splay out like a brush, which he used in place of a toothbrush.

His muffled voice called out to me from over his shoulder.

'Lily, I am going to take you to the English convent to talk to Reverend Mother about your enrolment, so wear something nice.'

Whoopee! My heart skipped a beat; I had been eagerly waiting for this day when I was to follow in my mother's footsteps. I would have expected my mother's generation to have had a Tamil education but she had been privileged to be educated in English. I never worked out why my older sisters had been settled into the more traditional medium of Tamil, attending our local Tamil convent school. With no plans for me to continue at the Tamil School on reaching the official school-going age of seven, my Dad had, to my immense relief, decided on an English education for me.

I hurriedly showered and changed into my Christmas dress; the knee-length, light blue taffeta dress was beautiful. Nine months on it still fitted me, though its layered skirt now fell just above my knee and the waist was riding an inch higher. The two lengths of material that hung at waist level ready to be tied into a bow were frayed a little with wear and the dress had lost its shine, but it was still my best. I drew on my only pair of shoes, white canvas with a strap across, now well-worn from attending the Tamil School. Cuticura powder slapped all over my face, I walked with comb and ribbon in hand to Anna, who was busy washing her hands. She shook the water off, slapped her wet hands on the sides of her skirt and then proceeded to fashion my bow and plait my hair.

The night before the auspicious day (which was to be my first at the English convent school), I followed Anna into the family bedroom. From Anna's index finger a freshly ironed uniform swung on a wire hanger. She rose on her toes to hook it over a corner of the rickety old *almari*. The puffed short sleeves and the rounded collar of a white blouse peeped from under a navy blue, square-necked pinafore, with three equal-sized pleats to the front and rear, starched and ironed to perfection. I gazed at it longingly; all it required to bring it to life was my face, arms and legs.

The outfit hung proud. My underclothes were displayed next to it on a separate hanger – a pristine white cotton petticoat and matching panties trimmed with a quarter-inch of embroidered white lace. Mum's handiwork was written all over them. Her own convent school education had set her up with life skills. The whirring of *ammachi*'s practical present, a hand-driven Singer sewing machine that Mum often referred to as her 'saviour', was heard most evenings. She produced *sari* blouses and children's clothing, exquisite smocking panels on dresses, embroidered with raised pink roses and green-veined leaves, all made to order for the local community. The hours spent painstakingly sewing, often under candlelight, provided the much-needed petty cash to supplement my father's wages. Remnants of material were cleverly turned into mix-and-match dresses for her girls. Mum had used a template to sew the uniform that I was busting to put on.

My white, ankle-strap canvas shoes received a fresh coating of Blanco, a ritual I'd seen my older siblings perform on a weekly basis. I swirled a clean wet rag in the hollow, scooped up some of the paste, and applied it in sweeping motions before smoothing the ridges with a finger dipped in water. Eyes scanned my surroundings for a sunny spot: the shoes were balanced on a piece of firewood, pointy ends facing upwards with the rubber heels planted on the cement floor. I hurried back to where I had left the quickly drying Blanco. Anxious to escape a telling-off, I carefully wrapped the waxed paper round the block once more and returned it to its home – the shelf in our bedroom.

Anna was to accompany me on my first day at proper school. Anna, at the tender age of sixteen, had been forced to shoulder responsibilities greater than other cousins of similar age. Mum was pregnant again her childbearing years had taken their toll on her and she needed help with household tasks. Anna's under achievements in school made her the ideal candidate as a home help. She was up at five, sizzling chapattis on the hot griddle for Dad's breakfast, preparing his flask of tea and then cooking the family's portions. She never raised her voice in anger and we youngsters took advantage of her passive nature, often getting the better of her whilst she just resigned herself and carried on with her lot.

Her faced beamed childishly as she showed off her new pair of red clogs and some colourful hairgrips with which she had been presented for services rendered to relatives. She developed a habit of hoarding her new things in a battered old suitcase under her bed. Some years later when preparations were being made for her wedding we teased her rotten when her well-kept secret was unearthed. Resourceful Anna had been engaged in gathering her trousseau throughout her teenage years. It seemed natural for Anna to fall into a second mother's role that she played to perfection.

'Lily, go to bed early, you need to be up by six-thirty tomorrow. You need to have your bath and get ready for school.' She patted my head affectionately.

We were early risers, waking with the sun. School commenced at seven-thirty. The hot and humid weather dictated an early start and the bonus of a one-thirty finish gave us ample time for afternoon play.

I had endured a restless night, wound up tight with excitement; the butterflies in my stomach had fluttered dizzily. A gurgle of wind had circled round and round my system, forcing me to turn over onto my tummy to halt it. Tension leaded my head, with no obvious answers to questions I asked of myself. 'Who are going to be my classmates? Will any of them become my best friend? I hope they will like me!'

I woke up to Anna's call.

'Lily, *endheri* (get up) ma, time to wake up.'

Dawn was breaking outside as I rolled off my wooden plank of a bed. I had wet my bed as per usual. I dripped as I walked with my towel tucked under my arm. The big concrete container in the outdoor bathroom brimmed with cold water from the well, rippling in the gleam of the early morning sun. This was courtesy of Dad's duty, before he cycled off to work. The cockroaches nestled in the cracks of the wooden supports scuttled away as I poured the cold water over me, gripping the wooden handle nailed across the diameter of an empty margarine tin. Splashes of water hit my bare skin; I shivered violently in reaction to both the change in temperature and the anticipation of my new adventure.

I climbed into my pristine white-laced trimmed knickers and let the elastic snap snugly against my talcumed stomach. Two shiny vaccination scars gleamed on my right upper arm. Would the girls in school notice my disfigurement? Anna helped me into my starched uniform and fitted the belt round my waist, the fastener fixed just right to allow a comfortable, finger-width space between the belt and my body. Into the belt she looped a starched, neatly folded and ironed white handkerchief, with the embroidered motif sitting uppermost. A fruity smell wafted across as Anna poured a measured amount of gingerly oil, made from a mixture of sesame seeds, coconut oil and other aromatic oils, into the palm of her hand. She rubbed the oil between her palms and then oiled my hair from head to tip. My hair was parted with a huge black big-toothed comb, combing out the tangles that had formed while I tossed around restlessly during the night. I cried out when she found a particularly difficult knot to untangle and used her two fingers to part the stubborn strands.

'Stand still! It is difficult enough without you wriggling about – you want to look smart, don't you?'

I blinked my tears away. Anna drew the comb through my hair several times before she obtained a perfect parting then proceeded to create two neat plaits, tying the wispy ends with white ribbons in tidy bows. I let out an 'ouch' as black hairgrips were pushed into the sides of my hair to keep unruly strands away from my face. Shaking a generous amount of white Cuticura powder from the orange and yellow tin into her hands, Anna slapped them on both my cheeks; I drew my lips in as she smoothed the white powder over my face.

'Lift your face up,' she ordered, and proceeded to dust the remains of the white powder over my neck. My whitened face was a contrast to my nutty-brown arms and legs but I felt finished off. Happy with her creation, Anna nodded her approval.

My mother broke a raw egg into a glass. She held out the glass, and wiped her egg-wet hand on her *sarong*.

'Now, drink this quickly, you are going to need all your strength today, it being your first day and all.'

'*Chee*. It looks horrible,' I shuddered, shaking my shoulders.

I took one look at the bottom of the glass. The yolk looked harmless, but the clear sticky fluid surrounding the yolk made me queasy.

'Do I really have to swallow it raw, can't I have it cooked?' My plea fell on deaf ears.

'Raw eggs taken on an empty stomach are good for you, you know how much eggs cost, you are lucky to get one, so you had better take it. *Appa* left strict instructions!'

My sister moved forward determinedly and threatened to pinch my nose and force the egg down my throat. I was backed into a corner. An egg that could have been used to enrich the family meal had been sacrificed for my good health; I took the glass and gulped its contents. I managed to stop the urge of physical sickness by sheer willpower as the egg made its slimy way down my throat. This ritual became a familiar 'treat' before I sat for important exams. Over time, I became expert at swallowing raw eggs.

My school bag was collected from where it lay patiently on the glass-topped table. Anna took my hand in hers and Mum followed us to the front gates. We waved goodbye and set off. I looked back for a final glimpse of Mum as she stood in her faded flowered brown *sarong* and white cotton blouse with its rick-rack edge, washed to an almost grey colour. Her trademark white 'good morning' towel was arranged diagonally over her ample bosom and slung over one shoulder. Warmth spread over me as I caught the whimsical smile that played on her face as she proudly watched her latest little school-goer set off.

I had used this familiar path the previous year during Tamil School days, however the half-hour walk remained a challenge to my little legs. Initially we walked alongside the railway tracks, which ran behind our house before deviating to the left down a slight slope. We followed the well-trodden path through the rubber plantation. It wasn't massive, like the dedicated 'rubber estates', but covered a good few acres. The path of the short cut wound across the plantation through the short green undergrowth, beneath towering rubber trees. The early morning dappled sunshine picked out the wisps of vapour as the heat dried the overnight dew on the leafy vegetation. Everything around me took on a magical glow, reflecting my excitement and pounding heart.

There were two private dwellings within view in clearings among the rubber plantation assuring a safe journey through the short cut. The aunty and uncle waved as we passed by and we acknowledged them with a cheerful, 'Good morning aunty, uncle!'

'First day at school then, Lily. Growing up, eh?'

My glow returned. We continued to negotiate our way carefully over a rickety wooden bridge that crossed a gurgling stream. See-through minnows darted about at the edges. Rows of narrow wooden houses in various stages of disrepair sprawled on either side of the stream. Bronzed four- and five-year-olds waved to us, some clad in their underwear; others in shorts, knee-deep in the stream. They used empty condensed milk cans to catch the ever-slippery minnows whilst the rest played in the grass outside their houses, running around the legs of their early rising mothers who were hanging out their washing, their babies cradled on their backs.

We followed the unmade dirt road, skirting a few rich folk's bungalow houses contained by slatted wicket fences with guard dogs barking a warning. We finally joined the main Sentul Road. I tightened my hold on Anna's hand, as there was no pavement; the dirt road converged on to the busy tarmac road.

We passed the bus terminus, where scores of school children poured out of the GTC bus, and joined the laughing, chatting crowd of convent schoolgirls. Those with money to spend stopped to enjoy early morning treats at the roadside stalls, which were doing a roaring trade in *ice-kachang*. Bowlfuls of hand-shaved ice, creamy red beans, creamed sweetcorn and squares of black seaweed jelly, all sprinkled over with both deep red sugar syrup and brown palm sugar syrup. A swirl of evaporated milk seeped into the shaved ice – a colourful, inviting concoction. All the flavours mixed with a spoon produced a slushy mixture, an amalgamation of flavourings that looked mouth-wateringly good. The Malay housewives were already set up with their banana and sweet potato fritters as they tempted the schoolchildren to part with their tuck shop money.

My chest swelled to be part of this teeming mass, looking distinctive in our convent school uniforms; now I was part of this identifiable group. The early morning sun was hot enough to scorch the fine soil that skirted the road. Clouds of fine dust swept over us with the passing traffic. I could feel the heat of the tarmac through the soles of my white canvas shoes. Beads of sweat appeared on my forehead with the pace of our walk. I clutched my plaited rattan school bag and fingered the spine of the exercise book with my name proudly written across the front. A well-sharpened pencil, a wooden ruler measuring up to six inches and a square of white eraser sat in a plywood box. Its sliding lid, with a groove for a thumbnail on one end, was embellished with coconut trees and feathered bamboo fronds under its high gloss varnish.

Another package, prepared by Anna and still warm to the touch, enclosed my elevenses: breakfast chapatti wrapped with a generous spread of ghee. I anticipated enjoying that later; I could already taste the soft dough and the rich ghee, a treat to replace our usual spread of Stork margarine.

After Sentul Market and a few more railway quarters we reached the tall gates that led to the school grounds. Within them stood the wooden-terraced Tamil School on stilts, the brick-built double storey English School, and our local Catholic Church, St Joseph's.

The journey had seemed much longer than usual. I shadowed Anna into the school hall where she presented me proudly to the nun in charge. With a nod and a wave I was motioned to join the group of nervous-looking fellow newcomers.

The presence of Reverend Mother Martha, the school's principal, on the raised platform emphasised the solemnity of the occasion. As her deep blue Irish eyes settled gently on the latest additions to her school, her smile broadened and her rosy cheeks heightened with colour. Sister Bernadette was our Portuguese import. Her surly face was a study in contrast to the home-grown calm of gentle Sister Beatrice. I caught Bernie's all- knowing eyes, grew uncomfortable and turned away. The nuns belonged to the order of The Holy Infant Jesus and were covered in white habits from head to toe, leaving only their faces and hands in view. They looked distinctive and an aura of mystery surrounded them, commanding respect: God's chosen people.

A few new recruits looked ready to burst into tears: eyes filled with water, lower lips quivered and there was much wringing of hands as the mothers moved away. I suffered no such qualms. I looked forward to the experience of school – but was totally unprepared for what happened next.

'Children, I want you to form a single line one behind the other, that's right, keep to a straight line. Come, come, no pushing take your time,' the voice rose a notch. 'In a straight line please!'

Sister Bernadette took little steps in her rubber-soled shoes, her expert, shrewd, light brown eyes scanning every inch of uniform. Totally unexpectedly, she hooked her bony finger under the hem of our skirts to inspect our underclothes, giving rise to some squirms and a few perplexed looks, as the new pupils searched their mothers' eyes for reassurance. For their part, the parents stood respectfully by, possibly congratulating themselves and silently expressing relief at their foresight in having provided clean underclothes for their children. A lecture on the importance of cleanliness followed, a strict requirement from all pupils. Any deviation from this rule was not to be tolerated and we should expect to be sent home immediately. Thankfully this bizarre procedure was not repeated but over the course of my student years a few girls were sent back home for arriving in a dirty, untidy uniform or shoes.

Once we were organised into our classes, we filed crocodile-style into our own class. Anna took her leave and I settled into my allocated place. We were grouped according to our reading abilities. My table companion, Geraldine, a Malayayalee girl whose parents originated from the Malabar Coast in south-west India, flashed her dimples. Short, black, curly close-cropped hair framed a face with a pointy chin and eyes that spelled mischief. Her nails were bitten to the quick. She later exhibited a flair for caricature. A friendship was forged between us from that day: all other classmates, paled into insignificance. The dainty, doe-eyed daughter of Mrs Chin, our form teacher, was our table companion. I was unaware at that moment as to how my school days were going to be influenced by Geraldine. She was our undisputed leader, talented, jolly, innovative, her ability for humour inexhaustible.

When the bell rang for recess, we trooped to the tuck shop. I parked myself on a wooden bench, clutching my ghee-soaked brown paper parcel, and unwrapped it on the narrow wooden table that ran across the width of the rectangular dining area adjacent to the tuck shop at one end. The ghee had congealed to an unappetising scum. My morning anticipation of the treat rapidly turned to one of shame. I took in the scene. My classmates strained on tiptoe to decide which of the tempting items displayed on the stepped shelves to purchase. They delved into their purses, parting with their twenty or thirty cents for their final choice. My mouth watered as I gazed at the plates of *meehoon*, the hot bowls of egg noodles swimming in spicy soup with crispy fried fish balls and bean curd slices bobbing on the surface, topped with a sprinkling of crunchy beansprouts and a spoonful of glistening anchovy sambal.

A pretty Eurasian classmate came over to join me. Her almond-shaped eyes were distinctly Chinese but unlike the straight hair of the Chinese she had softly curled, light nutty-brown hair.

'My father is Eurasian and my mother Chinese,' she said.

Her dimpled smile humbled me. This gorgeous creature had deigned to speak to me!

'I have a brother who looks more like my father,' she went on. I nodded, suddenly struck dumb. Lily De Rozario clasped dainty peanut butter sandwiches. Sensing my curiosity, she explained the contents.

Ashamedly I confessed, 'I have never seen peanut butter before, thanks for explaining.'

With one hand desperately covering the oily chapatti, I nibbled at it and my pleasure and anticipation of the morning diminished in a few minutes. My 'poor girl' status had been established on day one.

In direct contrast to Lily, Collette, another Eurasian girl, was the greatest bane of my life during those first few months. She seemed to smell my feeling of inferiority. I tried to hide it for as long as I could but the inevitable had to happen – like blood from a gash that seeps into the orbit of a shark, Collette smelt my vulnerability and saw me as easy pickings. Hands on hip, Collette faced me one day in the playground.

'You are so black you are just like a devil. I will call you *Hantu* from now on.'

My gregarious heroine, Geraldine, who was within earshot, was quick to rise to my defence.

'If Lily is a devil, then you must be a white ghost! You leave Lily alone or else.' Geraldine struck up a threatening pose to match Collette's, who walked off muttering under her breath as she cast a furious backward glance in our direction.

It seemed I had gained a friend for life, ready to fight my battles even before she got to know me. Ironically, a few months down the line Collette and I developed a friendship. Our paths home lay in the same direction. I was invited for tea and we played hopscotch. Included in our game was her younger sister, Maureen, who was much darker-skinned; her colouring matched that of her father, a man who clearly had some Indian blood in him. He was plump and swarthy and given to issuing orders in a booming voice. Collette's dainty auburn-haired mum stood her ground with him, gently but firmly. She was the perfect lady. I learnt to use a knife and fork at their dining table when pressed to stay for tea, cut into iced cakes on decorated china plates and drank tea from a dainty china teacup and saucer.

Table A continued to progress. Reading and writing came easily to me. Geraldine provided light relief. Exercise sheets had marking squiggles in their corners. Coloured sheets blossomed into paper flowers. Plasticine came alive in Geraldine's hands: her figures were given shape and life, whilst my stick figures compared very unfavourably. But I was the reader. I devoured books feverishly: indeed every book on the fold-up display cabinet was soon devoured, one a day.

My thirst for books unquenched, I found an ally in both the B and C streams. Nadira's father was an Indian Muslim and her mother native Malay. Nadira was a willing C stream mate. She borrowed books from her class to feed my ferocious appetite and she was repaid with friendship and companionship during our walks home. We bid farewell outside our zinc gate. Nadira craved company. Her only younger sister had mental problems and was unable to attend school; she required constant supervision by her uncomplaining and patient mother. I became Nadira's borrowed sibling. We visited each other's homes on a weekly basis. I learnt to accommodate the wild, unpredictable behaviour of her younger sister, and we included her in some of our games under Nadira's Mum's supervision. No explanations were given, and gradually I realised that she had been born as she was. Nadira's tall, silent but kindly father walked me home at dusk with a chatty, skipping Nadira for company.

On the final day of our second term, the clashing of cymbals drew our attention to the open doorway of our classroom. Two double-storeyed corridors of classrooms commenced from the main entrance, and covered steps led away from the central area down an embankment, culminating in the tuck shop area. Our classroom was on the ground floor at one end of the corridor, the furthest away from the main entrance. Beyond our classroom a strip of grassland led to the foot of a high, open-netted fence that enclosed our school grounds. Tall wild *lalang* grass swayed in the breeze behind the fence. The commotion, which was getting alarmingly louder by the minute, seemed to originate from the direction of the tall grass. A confab with a worried little runner prompted Mrs Chin to issue sharp orders for our four classroom doors to be pulled shut and bolted. The room was thrown into twilight that even the four electric light bulbs failed to penetrate.

'Carry on with your work until I tell you to stop,' she said.

Her voice was unusually wobbly. The noise outside grew in intensity and everyone's concentration wavered. Frightened looks were exchanged as our pulse-rates increased. After a long break the noise slowly receded, then stopped altogether. A knock on the door heralded an all clear; welcome daylight flooded in to relieve our blinking eyes. Another whispered conversation took place and finally Mrs Chin was able to enlighten us.

'Apparently some men were chasing off a tiger, but don't worry, they have managed to move it away from the area. They are bound to have caught it by now, so you are all safe.'

A tiger! I marvelled. *What a dramatic ending to my term!*

My numeracy skills gradually improved. Daily homework completed as soon as I reached home earned me the right to indulge in my passion for reading. End of year exams assured a place in Standard Two for both my best friend and me but sadly Nadira remained in C stream. I was selfishly and secretly glad that a future source of a fresh supply of books was guaranteed.

The end of our first year was marked with a treat. We trooped into the school hall with the B and C stream girls. The hall buzzed with excitement. We squatted on the floor and waited for the projector to be set up. After a few abortive attempts the screen came alive. Oohs and aahs came from all around as we were pulled into the magic screen.

Little Heidi stole my young heart: the spectacular views of the mountain covered in snow, that magical powdery stuff that I craved to touch, then the green of the mountainside during the summer months when apple trees groaned with shiny red apples that Heidi's teeth crunched into. My fingers itched to reach out to a red apple and my mouth wanted to experience that same crunch of the crisp white flesh, to lick the juices that would run down from my mouth. I could dream. My legs twitched with the desire for a run up the mountainside in the company of blonde, blue-eyed Heidi and Peter the goatherd. I longed to catch snow with my bare hands and take in lungfuls of crisp cold air. I closed my eyes. It was an impossible dream that could never come into fruition.

Our lay teachers were mainly Chinese and Indian, but there was one European lady, our second year teacher, introduced to us as Miss Old Dog. This raised a titter among the pupils. I cannot say for certain whether we pronounced her name correctly. She could have been Miss O'Dowd, or any other similar-sounding name, but neither she nor anyone else put us right, so to our continued amusement she was always referred to as Miss Old Dog. Punitive Miss Old Dog, with her pock-marked skin and her red face, mopped her brow constantly. She found it difficult to handle Geraldine's impetuous mischief so she gave up, pretending not to notice.

We chanted our times tables: 'two ones are two, two twos are four...' and so on. Twelve inches equal one foot. Three feet equal one yard. All of this was learnt parrot- fashion. Exercise books were chosen with the times tables printed on their back covers.

Lily Grace was another Indian classmate. With Lily De Rozario, my lunchtime companion, this meant there were three Lilys in one class, causing some confusion. A lack of a second name to distinguish me during the calling of the register, I answered 'Yes, present' to the shout of A Lily, A in reference to my Dad's Christian name Anthonysamy.

The Sikh girls travelled in by bus from brick-built houses on the outskirts of Kuala Lumpur. Diminutive, pretty, fair-skinned Jaswinder flicked her two long, jet-black braids seductively. Stocky Narinder and sophisticated Jagdish both vied for Jaswinder's affections as she held both their strings firmly in her dainty hands. Meanwhile ebony-skinned, rich little Indian beauty Indira was shadowed by sloppy but intelligent Selvamalar, who could boast a doctor and a lawyer for older sisters. Buck-toothed Rajaletchumi studiously scored above ninety percent in all subjects.

My Chinese classmates, though, were businessmen's children. As for Geraldine, her sister was on her way to study at medical college, her father was an important figure in politics and they lived in a large detached bungalow in an expensive area adjoining the more working class Sentul. I didn't really fit in with that crowd. My position in school had already been established whilst in standard one. Within my first few weeks Mrs Chin summoned me to her desk, explaining that I had been awarded a scholarship.

'What does that mean?'

'It means you don't have to pay any school fees.'

'Oh.'

'The office people told me.'

I walked back to my desk with mixed feelings; I felt a rush of anger and shame but was thankful that my parents did not have to fork out for my school fees any longer. I had no idea how the award of the scholarship had come about.

I blurted my news to my mother as soon as I reached home.

'It is because of Sister Raphael that you got that scholarship. She told your *appa* when he went to visit her. You know how difficult money is for us. It is because you already know how to read and write that she was able to get the scholarship for you, but you do have to work hard to keep that scholarship going.'

What was I supposed to make of this news? I had mixed feelings. Great that the family was exempted from paying fees but not so great that the scholarship was intrinsically connected to our poverty. I was in receipt of special privileges that segregated me from the rest of my classmates. I felt I had been reduced to a charity student.

From then on, each month I would sit clasping and unclasping my hands, nervously cracking my knuckles, my eyes cast down on an open book but unable to take in any words or images, as my classmate's names were called out and they walked up to the teacher's desk clutching the envelopes containing their fees. My name was obviously omitted, magnifying my embarrassment. I huddled further into my seat with hunched shoulders and wished I was invisible, humiliated; I wanted to be inconspicuous. Poverty seemed to cling to me and I was powerless to shake it off. Thankfully my guardian angel Geraldine protected me from ridicule and my own academic achievements elevated my position within the classroom.

15

'You won't marry like us...'

Teenage Years

Throughout our childhood, Dad stipulated that we should be fluent in English. He would bestow his all-knowing look on us as he declared 'It will help you when you start school.'

English tripped off our tongues with family and friends but we stumbled when switching to my parents' native language, which was Tamil. Our aunties, the four brides of my mother's four brothers, all of whom hailed from adjoining villages in India, were happiest reverting to their childhood language, a language of comfort, familiarity, security. My gorgeously *sari*-clad, heavily bejewelled aunties, looking like ghosts because of the perfumed white powder liberally dusted over their faces, were cosseted in the lounge drinking condensed milk tea, sweetened further with spoonfuls of sugar. Their bangles clinked as they gesticulated animatedly, fingers flexed and un-flexed, knuckles cracked, as they exchanged news about their immediate families and from their relatives in India.

'Come and greet your *atthais*.'

I swung on my heels slowly and obeyed Mum's bidding, taking temporary leave of my daydream by placing my book reluctantly on the table. I took care to use the flap of the dust cover to mark the page where I had just been transported to a village where the Secret Seven were in hot pursuit of their suspect. I greeted my relatives' presence with hands raised to waist level, palms pressed together: *Thosthuram* – welcome. I was careful to answer their questions in Tamil for fear of being chastised.

'It is important to speak in your mother tongue; otherwise you will forget your culture. Our roots have to be nurtured, our knowledge passed on to the next generation. They need to know where their ancestors came from. All this English business should be restricted to your schooling.' All nodded in agreement.

The language barrier did come in handy right at that moment.

'Mmm, it's okay for you,' I muttered to myself in English, my head bent to avoid being detected. 'Our parents want us to talk in English and, just because you don't know how to, you expect us to speak to you in Tamil.'

With no greater knowledge of the importance of cultural practices at that stage in my life, I was convinced that my parents were right. If we were to attend an English School, then we had to practise our English. What did these old-fashioned aunties know, anyway?

Of course, I would never have dreamt of confronting them with my rebellious retort. They were my elders and I knew better than to be rude. Our lives were disciplined by manners. I bided my time and made a quick getaway when I could, leaving the visitors to the grown-ups so that I didn't have to speak to them in a language that, roots or not, I was not terribly good at. I knew what the turn of their conversation would be, having heard it many a time before. Desperate to be beyond observation, I disappeared into my bedroom book in hand, and soon lost myself once more.

The gist of these family conversations generally centred on marriages – whose son was marrying whom, whose family boasted eligible sons and daughters, who was soon to take a trip to India and would they be able to deliver parcels to their families there? Such uninteresting material was not meant for young ears. I was also aware that gentle Mum did not contribute much to their conversation, just sat among them smiling politely, nodding her head when appropriate and generally managing to keep the cohesiveness of the group going without divulging too much family information herself. It was obvious that my aunties looked up to my mother, never failing to remark on the loving relationship that my parents enjoyed or the discipline that my parents imposed on their children and the general happiness that was evident despite our restrained circumstances. My chest swelled with pride when I caught their praise. We might not be as rich as my aunties' families, but they still envied ours and I would not have changed places with them even for the luxury of eating meat every day.

The English influence flourished everywhere in Malaysia. Mountbatten Road was named after Lord Louis Mountbatten, Campbell Road after Douglas Campbell, who was the state of Johor's first British adviser, and Robinson's, the big department store, sold much sought-after and valued British manufactured products.

'Goods made in England are always the best. They are built to last. Quality stuff, you know?'

The bosses of large firms were mainly British. My Dad had worked for the English before World War II broke out and he valued his relationship with his English boss. I listened enthralled to details of this foreign man, who had clearly been particularly fond of my beloved Dad.

'He was a good man. He would invite me to his house and his wife made me feel welcome. He had two children who were very polite, and always called me "Uncle". His wife wrapped up food for me – cheese sandwiches and corned beef sandwiches.

"Take these to your wife and children Mr Anthony," she would say.'

I had often partaken of Dad's presents, and enjoyed the creamy and smoky tangy flavours. My thoughts returned to the memory of my first train journey and I smiled. I could see in my mind's eye 'the Englishman as he tucked into a mysterious, flat, white and yellow concoction with obvious relish' – at last the mystery was solved.

'I ran errands for my boss, such as buying his cigarettes, and he always gave me tips.' Dad gave a half smile of remembrance and then sighed and became serious. 'True gentlemen, the English. They were very good bosses.'

Dad's relationship with the British was a great source of pride and prestige. None of our relatives enjoyed the same connections as he did. He sighed again as he gazed at a point on the wall behind me, then remembered aloud.

'Life was good under the British. What a shame the Japaan fellows came. They hated the English. They took them all prisoner. Some of the Europeans managed to escape but those who didn't were sent to detention camps. I don't know what happened to my boss. Poor man, I couldn't do anything to help him.'

It was obvious that Dad had been deeply affected by what happened to his boss. His eyes glistened as he reminisced, and I felt mine moisten in sympathy. War was so cruel.

Dad's fondness for the British influenced his way of life. Despite his insistence that we conversed in English at home, he continued to throw Tamil sentences into the mix when he engaged with Mum and older relatives. We therefore grew up multilingual. Our communication with the wider community was conducted in Malay.

Our Malay was really a pidgin form of Malay, or what was known as 'market Malay'. Local stalls were in the main owned by the Chinese and in order to make our money go further, we bargained in Malay, the common language of communication between the various different nationalities. From a young age, we could all communicate effectively in three languages, often combined together in one single sentence.

'Go and *mandi*, your *kaallu* is filthy!' my sister would remonstrate when she spied my dirty feet, courtesy of playing barefoot within the grounds. She was sending me off to wash them utilising the Malay word for bathing and referring to my feet in Tamil. As this manner of communication was second nature to us we never realised the peculiarity that an outsider would have observed.

The majority of the Chinese population living in Kuala Lumpur was from the Canton province of China. Although I could recognise some of the spoken words in no way was I able to converse in it. Mum, however, had mastered a smattering of Cantonese from associating with her previous Chinese neighbours, and playfully taught us a few words. *Thaa sigh yeeah*, I will beat you. *Lai-lai*, Come, come. She had also mastered some Japanese during the occupation, and we learnt to count to ten, chanting in unison as we played: *ichi, ni, san, shi, go, roku, shichi, hachi, kyuu, juu.* Our multiculturalism was derived from a variety of sources, but the English language was my major love, nurtured from an early age by our mother.

Mum had also been blessed with a rich voice and loved to exercise it after her day's work was done. Her convent education meant that religious songs featured greatly in her life. I knew she was particularly happy when she was humming to herself and I edged over to listen.

My favourite memory of her was of her sitting on the rattan chair in the sitting room. I would park myself by her feet on the cement floor and gaze at her as I fingered the safety pin she had pinned to the sleeve edge of her blouse in readiness for emergencies. The pin might be used to draw elastic through the waistband of cotton panties, or string through her petticoat, the undergarment for a *sari*.

'Leave it alone.' She smacked my hand playfully and eyes raised, her clear soprano voice rose in song.

Mary from thy sacred image,
With those eyes so sadly sweet,
Mother of perpetual succour
See us kneeling at thy feet.
In thy arms thy child thou bearest,
Source of all thy joy and woe;
What thy bliss, how deep thy sorrows,
Mother, thou alone canst know.

When mood dictated, we would continue to sing half a dozen hymns at a time. A peace descended. Mum would sigh, eyes vacant and stare, lost in thought. We would sit for a few minutes in companionable silence, each wrapped in our own thoughts, before recommencing our daily routine and breaking the magical spell.

Dad's favourite form of relaxation was more practical – reading. His two favoured books, Winston Churchill's autobiography and Nehru's letters written whilst in prison, still in their dust covers, took pride of place in the mahogany, glass-fronted book case, along with a copy of the Oxford English Dictionary. He would sit in the comfort of his swivel chair and choose his book. It usually fell open at his favourite chapters, his strong fingers curling over the tops of the pages, eyes rounded and flashing, eyebrows raised, brow knitted, pupils dilating and constricting with passion as he read excerpts from the book in a voice deep with feeling. He would raise his voice a few notches here and there, as he peered over his bifocals every now and again to monitor everyone's undivided attention. Having missed out on education at an early age, he educated himself after his marriage. Education was therefore a burning desire for Dad and he would go to any lengths to find the money to educate his children. Unsurprisingly, a lot of importance was placed in our household on education, education and education.

Despite the existence of various ethnic schools, English became more and more popular and we were far from the only family who spoke it as a first language. However, just like the colloquial dialect spoken in various English cities and counties, our English was subject to local slang. Words were introduced that clearly identified the speaker as native Malayans, softly peppered with floating interrogatives – *lah*? There is no translation for the word, simply because it doesn't mean anything; it's like a verbal punctuation mark.

Come here, *lah*.

Okay *lah*, okay *lah*, I'm coming!

Thus was my multicultural heritage clearly etched into my own speech from a very early age. But it was English that I felt most comfortable with – and I loved practising my skills at school.

Each year I was impatient for December to come, for my trip to Anthonian Stores, which specialised in school textbooks. Clutching my book list for the next academic year that commenced in January I paced up and down, impatient for Dad to return from work.

Chow Kit Road, where the store was situated, was a bus ride away, en route to Kuala Lumpur. Immediately after we arrived I detached myself from Dad, lovingly fingering the covers of the pristine books and savouring the musty smells of the unopened pages. I watched my pile of books grow before my eyes. The assistant, sensing my excitement, smiled indulgently.

'Your daughter obviously loves her books doesn't she? Don't worry, *paapa*,' using a term of endearment often used to address little girls, 'I will wrap them up very carefully for you.'

He handed me the brown paper packages, which I placed carefully in my cloth bag, and Dad parted with his precious money. On reaching home the brown paper packaging was removed carefully and reverently. I gloated over the freshness of my new books. The excitement of a fresh story raised my pulse as I slipped down on the cement floor, back resting against the wall. My English books were my first choice: the pristine pages soon engulfed me in their magical stories and carted me off to another world.

One of my initial tasks was to claim ownership. I inscribed my name on the first page of every book with a freshly sharpened pencil: A Lily. The books were then covered, to preserve their newness, in sturdy brown paper that Dad brought home from work, cutting around any grease-soaked patches. My name was written again halfway down the cover.

As I moved up the classes year after year I was introduced to the classics. They transported me to a world of lush meadows, beautiful countryside, and great big country mansions filled with gentry folk who spoke in quaint English. Ladies in crinoline dresses attended coming-out balls, personal servants at their beck and call; horse-drawn carriages, wigged gentlemen, calves in breeches, the magic and opulence of upper-class gentry – I was captivated by all of it. I envied these people the cool weather that allowed them to wear long, flowing, elegant dresses whilst I bathed in sweat in my cotton knee-length ones, needing to take a couple of showers a day to keep cool and failing miserably.

My books were my pride and joy, and took pride of place on the homemade side-table, a square of wooden shelf propped up on bricks. The shortest book stood at one end and graduated to the tallest at the other. Vigorous hand-washing was performed before I handled my books; no marks or dog-ears were evident that could ruin their virginity. Neatly torn-off strips of exercise book paper served as bookmarks. The pages crackled between my fingers. I smiled involuntarily as I lovingly ran my finger down the spines of the stacks of shiny new books, plop plop plop: mine, all mine. I fed off my books. They were my oxygen. I treasured them so much that I became fiercely proprietorial and warned off my younger brothers. 'Don't you dare touch my books and dirty them.'

Despite my obsession, I kept track of my ultimate goal and passed exams as required. Hours were spent memorising my times tables;

verses from poems were repeated verbatim, such as Daffodils by William Wordsworth, Abu Ben Adam by Leigh Hunt and Young Lochinvar by Sir Walter Scott.

I was an enigma to my sisters, who failed to understand their little sister.

'You cannot be our *thangachi* (younger sister), *appa* must have picked you up from some dustbin. Maybe your real parents didn't want you, *appa* felt sorry for you and brought you home.'

My heartbeat slowed, I felt alienated by a separateness that was exhilarating as well as painful as I pushed my back against the wall and braced myself with one leg flexed, foot against the wall, and one sole down. I wanted to disappear when they teased me. I couldn't share my inner thoughts with them, my deep desires, dreams and aspirations. I was aware that I nursed book-learnt attitudes and expectations of life but I resented the aspersions that were cast about my beginnings. I wanted to belong to my family; I loved them too much to let them think that I was just an intruder, that my parents could be strangers.

However the remarks they made about my future I tolerated, as I knew that there was some truth in them.

They would laugh, 'We are only teasing! My, you are so sensitive. This girl won't get married like us,' continued my sister Theresa, flicking her head in my direction, 'this one isn't going to fall in love – her head is always in the clouds.'

Too right I wouldn't. It was acknowledged that my sisters would accept arranged marriages to strangers. They conformed to the rules of Indian society; they knew the exact dimensions of their cage and were content to reside within its confines. Theresa had already proved that. I envisioned marriage to a boy I did not know or love; I shivered involuntarily and failed miserably to make the mental leap. Unlike them, I was eager to grow wings and make my escape. My love of books had broadened my horizons, and I was no longer content with my surroundings. I craved to see and experience more of the world I lived in.

As I have mentioned, my family's nickname for me was the *Vella Karachi* – white girl. They reckoned that I behaved like one. For example, I tended not to pick up the local slang. My teachers often selected me to read texts aloud to the rest of the class and I was picked for parts in the annual school plays. I even dished out presents from a bulging sack, dressed as Father Christmas, to the excited juniors. I represented my school with fellow students in inter-school quizzes.

The years passed and we reached standard six. Soft-spoken, gentle classmate Sheila confessed to daily secret meetings with her boyfriend at the bus stop. The first stirrings of sexual awareness were aroused. When is a handsome boy going to look in my direction? Mixed sex parties were already being hosted at Geraldine's more progressive household, thanks to her older brother and sister, but Geraldine was impervious to them.

'I see my brother with his girlfriend. I am not interested in boys: more trouble than they are worth.'

'Wish I was in your household, I would like the opportunity to mix with boys.'

16

'Arrogant young Minerr...'

My Parents

'Marie, (Dad's nickname for Mum) I'm off to St Anthony's Church.'
Dad spoke from the doorway, clutching a packet of white candles in
his hand.

His prayers must have been answered, because we soon heard the
awakening rattling cough and ensuing putt-putting of his Lambretta
scooter, which announced Dad's successful departure on the nine-mile
journey to his favoured church named after his favourite saint.

The ring of hair that enveloped his otherwise baldhead was
regarded as a testament to St Anthony's wisdom, and as the patron
for lost things his help was sought frequently. 'Pray to St Anthony,
you'll find it,' would be declared with great conviction. The rows of lit
candles beside his statue were a testament to promises made and also
fulfilled, having been placed there by grateful devotees. The flames
cast flickering shadows on the life-size, chocolate brown-robed monk
as he circled the child Jesus protectively in his arms, a benevolent smile
etched on his face.

A substantial stone building, St Anthony's Church stood in its own
vast grounds, which stretched away from a gentle gradient to its left.
The peals of the bells rang out joy, hope and celebration, sentiments that
truly resonated with the congregation. Chanting processions assembled
on the grounds to the left and snaked their way to the church, skirting
the edge of the grounds. These were always headed by the priests,
followed by the altar boys, each of whom balanced something in his
grasp – the giant crucifix came first, followed by consecrated candles
in their sconces and smoking goblets of frankincense. Then followed
the congregation: women with covered heads, young girls with fancily
embroidered veils pinned to their glossy hair, children tripping along
shadowing their families and men in Sunday best. All strode along with

heads held high. The glittering procession, accompanied by the sound of everyone's voices raised in haunting hymns, drew the crowds, who lined the embankment on the main Pudu road. We walked past them puffed up with our own importance. We, the chosen, were part of a blessed Kingdom; our place in Heaven was assured while the non-believers eyed us with awe.

Although St Joseph's Church, much nearer home, was our established parish church, attendance at St Anthony's held a special significance for both our parents. The ornate building was impressive with its massive window panels of kaleidoscopic stained glass, which were resplendent showcases for scenes from the Bible. Events in the life of St Anthony stood high on either side of the main marble altar that was itself inlaid with plant and floral motifs. The elaborately carved tabernacle, where the consecrated hosts resided, took centre stage. It never failed to induce humility and a sense of privilege in me as I knelt to pray in front of the magnificent statues, flanked by row upon row of candles whose flames sent gentle wisps of grey smoke curling up towards the lofty ceiling of this awe-inspiring building. I closed my eyes and inhaled deeply the soft scent of the melted candle wax that hung heavily in the humid air. The constant addition of freshly lit candles forced down the spent and still warm wax.

It was within the yawning shadows of this imposing building that Dad had spent his childhood days as my Mum's neighbour. A covered flight of grey stone steps led uphill from the side of the church. The red slate roof, was upheld by timber painted a contrasting black. Black wooden balustrades ran the length of the walkway and ended at the top of the slope drawing to a halt in front of the heavy carved wooden doors of the grand residence of two priests.

Dad described the interior of this building in hushed tones. Two storeys high, the house was of British architectural design, featuring high ceilings, well-proportioned rooms, and a grand hallway that led to the main sitting room scattered with a profusion of cushioned chairs and carved pieces of dark wood furniture. A line of ceiling fans cooled the air. The hallway was in constant use when the priests held audience with the general public. An imposing study led off the main hall. My maternal grandfather – affectionately nicknamed Chocolate *thaatha* – in his role as the catechist, responsible for the daily activities of the church, was privileged to enter this inner sanctum to discuss church affairs with the Holy Fathers. (My grandfather's habit of secreting little rectangles of dark chocolate in his coat pockets had earned him this nickname from his grandchildren. His hand would dip into his pocket in their presence and then a pleasing smell of chocolate would emerge, as the silver paper was carefully prised open to reveal the mouth-watering treat. Chocolate *thaatha*'s eyes would twinkle as he pressed pieces of chocolate into eager little hands. The hand warmth commenced the melting process but every brown streak was always licked clean.) My paternal grandfather was also employed in the same place, as head chef in the detached kitchen that stood to the back of the priests' house.

A not-so-grand but well-maintained row of wooden, two-bedroom houses stood a little to the left at the foot of the hill. Employees of the church were fortunate to be living in these houses with their families, in close proximity to their place of worship and work. It was in two of these houses that both sets of my grandparents had lived. When my Aunty Arul's husband eventually took over my grandfather's role of catechist, I enjoyed many school holidays with them during my teenage years, renewing ties with my cousins, Felix, Chandra and Alfonsia. The family had spent a few unrewarding years in India trying to make a living but were forced to return home.

I drew comfort from sleeping in the same bedroom that my Mum had occupied as a child; the peeling walls, imbued with voices and images from the past, seemed to reach out to me and envelop me protectively. Aunty Arul assured me no changes had been made to the building; it was just as she remembered it as a child.

'We had two big beds in this back bedroom,' she would sigh in reminiscence. 'We girls slept on one and the boys on the other bed. Your *thaatha* and *ammachi* slept in the smaller front room and if we raised our voices in play or became boisterous with bed-time games, your Chocolate *thaatha* would bang on the partition wall.'

The precious times I spent with my mother were never wasted. She had interesting stories to share and with my insatiable curiosity for family history I gleaned from her the tale of my adventurous maternal grandmother, who had married and followed my grandfather to the 'The Land of Gold'.

Chocolate *thaatha*, Savarimuthu Odayar, was born in Malaya in 1890 to Indian immigrants. At the age of seventeen, following commonly held practice, my grandfather set off to India; his family had their roots in a village called Nagarikathaan near Trichy, in arid scorching Southern India, where he intended to find himself a bride.

Chocolate *thaatha* first encountered my beautiful *ammachi* while taking a walk through Nagarikathaan. A bit of a tomboy, the thirteen-year-old girl, christened Nayanapoo, loved to climb trees and was on this particular day sitting partially hidden among the branches of a tamarind tree in her front garden, chewing on sweet, fibrous stumps of sugar cane and revelling in her privacy. She spied a stranger, dressed in his fine clothes from Malaya, walking purposefully along the dirt track, kicking the dry soil as he took in the sights of the rural village – and no doubt eyeing all the pretty girls he passed by as prospective brides. She shifted her position to get a better look. Hearing a rustle in the leaves above him, my grandfather glanced up to see my grandmother's large dark eyes peering down at him. Flashing his teeth in a broad grin, he shouted up to her:

'Oi, *pullai* – little girl – what are you doing climbing trees like a boy? *Irru dee*, you wait, I am going to marry you and put a stop to your tomboy habits.'

My grandmother, feeling safe in her high perch among the branches, replied cheekily: 'Ha! When I get married I won't marry a *karrupan* – black man – like you! Mind your own business and keep walking, you *veili nattaan* (foreigner)!'

Little did my Grandma know that this 'black man' was instantly charmed by both her beauty and her spirit, and would be true to his word. Following her family's approval of a very welcome proposal from overseas, and thanks in no small part to the promise of the material comforts that such a liaison would bring to the rest of the family, my Grandma Nayanapoo swiftly found herself subject to a traditional arranged marriage at the tender age of thirteen. This young girl, plucked from her innocent tomboy childhood, entered the strange new world of marriage, with its physical expectations and the unquestioning obedience expected from a good wife. She had to leave the only home and life that she had ever known and move to the strange new country of Malaya, thousands of miles away from her familiar little country village in India.

The couple settled initially with the extended family in Kuala Selangor, situated by the coast about forty miles away from Kuala Lumpur, moving in later years to Kuala Lumpur itself. Young Nayanapoo Savarimuthu had thirteen children – amongst them my mother, Lourdes Mary Elizabeth (known as Marie). If miscarriages were taken into account, Mum would have been the sixth child, a position that I proudly shared with her, but she was the third-born live child in 1915.

My father, Anthonysamy Savarimuthu (coincidentally he shared the same surname as my mother, a common name among the Odayar community), was born in a small rural Indian community called Kumulunguli, also based relatively near the southern Indian town of

Trichy. Kumulunguli was nicknamed *Vaanam partha bumi*, a land beneath a vast expanse of sky where there was hardly any rainfall for long periods of time. One of the few crops that the cracked, caked yellowish earth would reluctantly yield, like a petulant teenager, were saplings of a giant, umbrella-like pine tree called saukai, a special type of tree used for wood-burning. All landowners, including my paternal grandparents, cultivated *saukai*, hoping Mother Earth would answer their prayers for a fine crop to sustain their family. The mature trees were felled and sold to local contractors, who carted the tinder-dry trunks and branches to the cities, selling them for a good profit as firewood. The cleared land was allowed to lie fallow for a while in order to recuperate before being coaxed into production once more by the landowners.

To supplement their income from the *saukai* crop, my father's family also reared goats, whose restless, adventurous spirit made them well suited to finding suitable grazing fodder in the sparse land and who were highly prized for both their meat and milk.

My grandfather could see no advantage in educating his son. They lived in a village where there was land to be cultivated and goats to feed and milk: what would be the benefit of wasting time and money on education? From an early age, my Dad therefore grappled with the feisty goats, learning to keep them in order with a switch of his sturdy stick, seeking out the ever-elusive grassy patches to fatten them up so that they would yield good quantities of their precious milk. Small wonder that my father soon earned the predictable but uncomfortable nickname of *aadu ohtti* – the goatherd – amongst the school-attending village boys.

To supplement his daily lunch of gruel, made from a crude mixture of cereal, water and salt, my innovative father devised his own recipes using whatever ingredients he could find around him. Tamarind trees grew abundantly in the barren conditions and a short climb rewarded him with the sight of a handful of long, ripe tamarind pods, hanging invitingly from its branches. He twisted the tops off the thin brown pods, which were about the length and shape of his index finger, then used the pods as a vessel when milking the goats, becoming adept at catching their milk in these makeshift containers. The pulp in the tamarind pods – often used in Asian cooking to impart a sour taste – curdled the milk at the same time, resulting in a delicious concoction that my father much enjoyed. To quench his thirst, he often lay on his back under a goat, squirting the fresh warm milk straight from the teat into his open mouth. This was no mean feat, involving a great deal of skill as he twisted and turned to avoid a painful kick from the indignant goat. His took his afternoon naps in the fork of a tree and then returned home with his charges at dusk.

It was thanks to the British that my father was able to retire, at the age of eleven, from his first career as a goat-herder. When the British first came to Malaya in 1786, they signed lucrative treaties with rich Malay sultans in order to establish a new branch of their Empire – for which they needed the help of skilled, cheap labour. Thanks to their existing colonial ties with India, the British were able to offer South Indians this work in Malaya – the so-called Land of Gold – providing a great lure for many poor villagers, who rushed to take up the offer. A majority of the Indians were initially employed in the building of government buildings and homesteads, which replicated British architecture, grand colonial constructions that remain in Malaysia to this day. Later, more Tamil immigrant labour was needed when the rubber tree was introduced into Malaya from Brazil. The new rubber plantations that sprung up around the country in the late eighteen hundreds were very labour-intensive.

Emigration continued in drips and drabs from India. The new settlers in Malaya sent their hard-earned money back to relatives in their home villages, which went a long way to easing their poverty – a trend that was not lost on my paternal grandfather, eager as he was to support his now-expanded family of my father and two younger daughters. Thus, the lure of money, together with an inherent spirit of adventure, tempted my paternal grandfather to follow some of his friends and up sticks to set sail for Malaya with his wife Maria Magdalene and three children in 1921. They arrived safely, settling for the first few years in a rubber plantation.

Granddad followed in the footsteps of other immigrants by taking up the harsh life of a rubber tapper. Their day commenced in pitch darkness at three-thirty every morning when their families were still asleep in bed. A sharpened knife was used to remove a thin layer of bark along a downward spiral on each tree trunk. The spiral allowed the latex to run down to the collection cup, which was a half-coconut shell. Starting the collection during the night ensured a longer time for the latex to run, as this had to be completed before the drying rays of the sun hit the tree trunks. Young Anthony was not yet up to these challenges, as the workers risked snake-bites, leeches and tropical insect bites in addition to the risk of contracting malaria. Colonial labour was cheap and living conditions were harsh.

Travelling priests who visited the plantations to administer Sunday service spotted the family's plight and took an interest in this young Catholic lad, offering him a job as assistant to the catechist at the oldest established church in the area. St John's was originally built in 1883 in Kuala Lumpur for expatriates and Eurasians but later became a popular destination with immigrants. Priests from the church travelled to the surrounding estates to spread the word of God and offer Sunday mass to the European managers' families.

The priests' proposal was a two-pronged one: if young Anthony accepted the job offered to him, then his father could escape his harsh working conditions and become a part-time cook for the priests. His father gratefully accepted this new position and so Dad commenced travelling to nearby St John's church daily. Education was once again denied him.

The youngsters from both families had attended the same schools: a girls' convent school, Bukit Nanas, was situated at the crest of a hill, and St John's School that nestled in the foothills educated the boys. Dad grew up in the shadow of his neighbour's sons, my educated uncles, the foundation of their later squabbles thus being laid down at an early age. Whilst working at St John's Church Dad managed to sneak off from time to time to hide behind the doors of the nearby St John's boys' school classrooms to eavesdrop, but suffered great humiliation if he was caught playing truant. Despite a lack of education my father relied on other talents to get by, using his good looks and charm to his advantage and earning the nickname *Minerr* – Jack the Lad. The little education he did gain came later, from a kind-hearted little girl, Dad's neighbour – later to be my mother. Though five years his junior, she shared her homework time and introduced Dad to the alphabet.

Dad's mother, my grandmother, referred to as *appayie* – father's mother – found employment at the Englishmen's golf course, working seven days a week to supplement her husband's wages, retrieving golf balls that went astray. Her one night off a week, Saturday, was spent cooking for and sharing the day with the family before she deserted them once again after an early start, to attend six-thirty mass. She trusted her older daughter to manage the household and care for her younger sister who was eight years her junior.

Appayie was a resourceful woman and a fast learner. She learnt to communicate in English and the English gentlemen, no doubt appreciative of her hard work, tipped her generously. The generation of that era were happy to be employed by their English masters in order to earn a living but within their own households they were a proud people. Hard work was applauded, community spirit abounded and flourished, and sacrifices were often made for family obligations. The only times *appayie* was unable to fulfil her role at work were due to miscarriages, which sadly had been a fairly frequent occurrence. But none, of course, were as tragic as the final time, when she gave birth to another son: a week later, God claimed both mother and child.

Heartbroken, my grandfather returned to India in 1928. My Dad, at eighteen years old, was old enough to look after himself, and remained in Malaya. Grandfather, who had by now been working as a part-time cook for both the church and the convent, gained assurances from the nuns at the convent where his two daughters were day school attenders that they would be looked after. The Reverend Mother, sympathetic to a fellow Catholic's plight, struck up a bargain that offered this solution: the girls would become free boarders on the understanding that they would enrol as novitiates to the nunnery. The older daughter, Innasiamal (older than my mother by one year), had already experienced her calling, but her younger sister, Irudiamary, required some coercion.

Grandfather, in his forties, was an eligible widower. He married Maria Selvam, who was a couple of years younger than his older son. The year 1937 saw them return to Kuala Lumpur with their own charming young son, Francis, who soon won his step-siblings' adoration. His pregnant mother bore twin daughters a few months after the family's arrival. Once again, nature claimed one of the twins within two weeks but baby Mary survived. A few years later prolific grandfather added son David to the crowded household.

It was after my birth in 1946 that my paternal grandfather returned to India once more with his young family, leaving behind my by-now-married father and his blood sisters. Having completed their novitiate training, pious, gentle older sister ordained Raphael became a skilful cook at the convent, following in her father's footsteps. My life and education was strongly affected by her influence. The feisty, academically-minded, younger sister, ordained Martha, found employment as a schoolteacher at The Convent of the Holy Infant Jesus, having to transfer away from Kuala Lumpur to a lesser town called Taiping towards the north of the country. It was a town known for its large number of Chinese immigrants, who had flocked to work in the tin mines during the nineteenth century.

Deaths seemed to plague my Dad's family. David died tragically at the age of twelve. He had been drinking milk from a conch-shell, standing by the well. No one had noticed him dive into the swollen well to retrieve his drinking vessel. No male help was around to rescue him in time.

When broken-hearted Grandfather eventually died in 1952, my father undertook to provide financial support for Uncle Francis's education. Francis's exceptional academic achievements were a great source of pride. Dad waved the pale blue aerogrammes. 'Look, your clever Uncle is the class's number one pupil again. You should all follow his example.'

Eventually Francis chose a celibate life, dashing Dad's hopes of secular achievements for his talented younger brother. Nevertheless, Dad supported his choice of career. Uncle Francis successfully completed his studies for the priesthood in the balmy town of Bangalore but the angel of death once more spun his own devious plans. I had dreamt of my Uncle Francis lying in bed with a bandaged tummy. I recounted the dream to all-knowledgeable Mum, and awaited her interpretation breathlessly. She offered her usual palliative prayers and these quietened my pounding heart.

A telegram arrived that very morning. Dad's lunch break was filled with audible cries of grief from him that chilled the air. A week later a letter of explanation arrived from the seminary. The night before his ordination, Uncle Francis had succumbed to peritonitis, the very same complication of appendicitis that Rosie in later years thankfully survived. Mum cast a speculative look in my direction and shook her head; how come I had dreamt so uncannily about my Uncle's condition? The previous deaths had occurred before my time but this death was particularly poignant. The house went into mourning. The faces of framed photographs were turned to the wall. Black armbands appeared on men's sleeves, changed to white for church attendances. It was years before Dad could talk about his stepbrother without resorting to his handkerchief.

Mum was born into a family of thirteen siblings. Only eight survived into adulthood. My mother's eldest sister, Mary, was married and settled with her three children in Kuala Selangor where my grandmother had begun her life in Malaya. With the eldest of his four daughters already married, Chocolate *thaatha* was well aware of his responsibilities to his other daughters. Mum had now reached the magic age of seventeen. Schooling was over and she helped her mother at home whilst acquiring household skills. Parents with marriageable daughters at home were naturally anxious for them to be settled and my grandparents were keen to establish a suitor for their next daughter.

My father's attention was directed to the softly-spoken but self-possessed girl who had demonstrated such kindness to him with his reading struggles. He began to look at his shy helper with new eyes. As his romantic intentions became more serious, it didn't take long for my father's good looks and persuasive manner not only to win my mother over but also to convince her own mother of his suitability as a son-in-law. However their potential union encountered its fair share of opposition from Mum's youngest uncle.

Curious to know more, this became a topic of our after dinner reminiscence sessions.

Mum took up the story.

'We were all in the front room: my *chithappa* – younger father – Uncle Soosai was visiting us when the subject of my marriage proposal was brought up. *chithappa* became furious when he heard who had asked for my hand in marriage. He never liked your father you see. He thought he was an irresponsible young man. My Uncle had a lot of influence over his older brother, your *thaatha*; just because *chithappa* was English-educated he could always influence his older brother. Anyway, he got angry and started shouting at my father.

'This arrogant, young *Minerr*, with his fancy clothes and no proper job will not make a suitable match for my niece!'

Dad looked at Mum in mock anger, puckering his lower lip. 'Fancy calling me an arrogant *Minerr*! If I had known that's what your uncle called me I would have told him what I thought of him.' He turned to us. 'Your timid mother did not tell me what had been said until after our wedding and it was too late by then, the opportunity was lost.'

Bestowing on Dad one of her soft smiles, Mum continued: 'Knowing your hot temper I decided not to tell you about it. Anyway, my father tried his best to win Uncle round but *chithappa* threatened, "If you go ahead with the marriage after I warned you about that fellow, then I will not come to the wedding." I stood quietly in the corner crying silently. I was so scared, wondering what your *thaatha* was going to do. He was so upset at being spoken to like that by his younger brother. He went into the bedroom and didn't come out. The whole house went quiet.'

Chocolate *thaatha* was eventually persuaded by his wife to reflect on his daughter's future happiness. *Ammachi* had already fallen for her future son-in-law's charms. The final and more important consideration was that both families belonged to the same caste, the Odayars.

The caste system was an important part of our culture. Indians were socially divided into four main groups. At the very pinnacle were the Brahmins, greatly revered in their professions as teachers, scholars and priests; next came the Kshatriyas, the producers of kings and warriors. Our group, the Odayars, was the largest group, and we were the agriculturalists. Then the fourth main group, the Traders, followed us. Finally, on the lowest rung, hung the Untouchables, who were expected to undertake all the undesirable jobs that no one else was willing to perform. The social divide was hardly ever crossed, which helped to maintain people's identity and pride. Hence marriage within the caste was actively sought-after and encouraged, so Chocolate *thaatha* agreed to his daughter's nuptials.

'What happened to *thaatha* Soosai, did he come for the wedding?' we asked.

'No, he didn't, but once we got married and your father settled down and found a job everything else settled down too.'

Despite sharing the same caste, there still existed a social divide between my parents. Although both families were landowners, my Dad's fortunes were in poorer India, whilst Chocolate *thaatha* was a relatively rich man. His money was partly inherited wealth and partly generated through gambling; horse racing in particular was one of his favourite pastimes. *Ammachi*'s prudent housekeeping ensured sufficient funds to set their daughter up for the future.

My parents finally became engaged with the blessing of both sets of grandparents and were married on 8th October, 1932, at the ages of seventeen and twenty-two. *Ammachi* bestowed on her daughter a pair of diamond earrings and a large diamond ring. The earrings were studs, a single central stone encircled by five smaller ones. The ring numbered nine stones, arranged in a diamond shape and set in twenty-four-carat gold. The ring and earrings caught the light, shining out a myriad of colours when Mum wore them to weddings and functions.

After their marriage, my parents set up home, renting an extension to a lawyer's house, living independently but within close proximity to the rest of the family. Theresa, their first daughter, arrived two years later much to the jubilation of their adored son Peter. Dad took his marriage responsibilities to heart and with financial help from his new father-in-law, renewed his interest in studying. He attended evening classes with remarkable dedication and obtained sufficient knowledge to apply for various jobs. He was passionate about passing on to his children the benefits of education.

I had grown up with an awareness of my Dad's love of English food and eventually learnt the source of his unusual tastes. These had originated from his father, my grandfather, who as cook for both the priests and the nuns at the convent had become an expert in foreign dishes under their tutelage. The ever-generous nuns, aware of Grandfather's home circumstances with a working wife, allowed him to take home any leftovers. No doubt some food from the priests' tables found their way into the household too, particularly as my Dad was roped in to help the priests with various odd jobs, for which payment in kind was forthcoming.

One day Dad was sitting at the table tucking into a musty cheese veined with blue fungus. Catching my eye, he cut a corner off.

'Here, try this.'

I instantly spat it out in disgust, as it released a cloud of green spores, which promptly shot straight up my nose and made me sneeze furiously. I gulped down some of Dad's water, swishing it round my mouth before swallowing it.

'Yee! *Appa*, how can you eat this?' I asked in mystification. 'It is bitter and horrible. I like Kraft cheese, but not this horrible stuff. It tastes awful.'

Dad chuckled, and patted my cheeks playfully.

'You never know, when you grow up, you might go to England and find that you like eating cheeses like this. They are an acquired taste.'

'Chee, I won't!' I declared emphatically. 'There are plenty of other nice things to eat, thanks *appa*. Anyway, when am I ever going to go to England? We don't have money for that.'

'If you study hard, and do well in your exams, I will send you to Australia or to England for further studies.'

I looked up at him with a thumping heart, wanting to believe him. Seeing all those places that I read about over and over again would be a dream come true! But, just as quickly as my heartbeat had quickened, it slowed back down again. This would never become a reality. There were too many of us and we were too poor. Miracles didn't happen to humble mortals like us!

Dad saw the doubt clouding my eyes; he looked me full in the face, eyebrows raised in a solemn expression. I focused on the greenish dot in the middle of his forehead that took on greater intensity.

'Don't forget, if I make a promise, I will keep it.'

I relaxed. I suppose I could always enjoy dreaming about going to England, even if such a thing never materialised.

Mum's voice brought me back to earth again.

'It was from the *Vellakara* priests that your *appa* got his taste for foreign clothes and shoes.'

Dad chuckled.

'Father Perissoud passed his old shoes on to me when his new ones arrived. He even passed on his clothes, because he was the same build as me. He liked me, you see. I used to help him with various things from time to time.'

'But your father wasn't satisfied with the clothes the priest passed on to him. He ordered shoes from somewhere in London,' Mum continued with an indulgent smile, pretending to chide him. 'What a vain man Dad was!'

She threw him a fond look. She had always been so proud of the good-looking young man who wanted to marry her. How romantic. As I have already said, Dad had a most engaging smile and invariably won over any ladies. They smiled at him coquettishly and he basked in their admiration, engaging in harmless flirtation, but I did find this embarrassing at times. When I was out for a ride with him on his Lambretta, beautiful young women walking by would often draw Dad's eye. Embarrassed, I would turn my gaze away if the young women responded to his intense stare or acknowledged his appreciative nod; their step would quicken a pace, their heads would be lowered. All this would happen in a flash, the whole scene being re-enacted half a dozen times before we reached our destination.

But Mum merely smiled, safe in the knowledge of her husband's steadfast love for her. Seeing their love for each other never failed to make me feel proud of my parents.

'Wow, he must have been quite a catch. I am so glad it was my lovely mother who married him,' I would think to myself, wrapping my arms across my chest and hugging myself.

I had always known my Dad as a tall, handsome man with lightly tanned skin and deep brown eyes that shone with steely determination when faced by his enemies, but softened with love for his family. His aquiline nose, high cheekbones and broad forehead spoke of intelligence. He was strong both physically and mentally, and never displayed fear in any situation nor of anyone, meeting every situation head-on without hesitation. There was a degree of arrogance in his brisk, upright stride that was a legacy of his years in the army. His calloused hands were often covered with the grease and grime of engine oil from his work with the nuts and bolts of the train engines, which even harsh carbolic soap failed ever to remove completely, but there was strength and a surprising tenderness in them too.

A self-taught man, Dad described himself as a 'leading hand' at work. He was responsible for the maintenance of the steam locomotives in the Sentul workshop and took great pride in his job. He also displayed a huge appetite for life.

Dad traipsed to the Indian 'dresser' whose apothecary shop adjoined the row of wooden stores on the main Sentul Road. He had developed a friendship with the dresser who, despite his lack of a doctor's qualification, successfully dispensed pills and potions for a variety of ailments. Many a time the dresser had examined me for cuts and grazes or persistent temperatures and sore throats. With his rotund figure, he was an amiable man, and instilled us with confidence in his diagnosis. His white pestle and mortar came out and he dropped white tablets into the bowl, ground them into a fine powder and then deftly divided this up onto individual thin paper sheets. With practised hands he folded them into rectangles, tucking the ends in carefully to seal the contents inside. Throughout the procedure he and Dad continued their political conversations, with Dad perched on a wooden bench in the consulting room, which doubled as the treatment room.

I woke up one morning with a slight earache, which became progressively worse by late afternoon. Dad returned from work and noticed my agitation.

'Why are you pulling your ear all the time and making that face?'

'It's hurting, *appa*.'

Armed with a knife he set off determinedly and returned with an elongated frond of variegated dark green leaf. I recognised the source, clumps of them grew plentifully on the slopes of our nearby stream that Peter spent hours grappling to keep free of discarded rubbish. Dad proceeded to warm the frond over the naked flame of a candle, by gripping the ends and twisting the middle to release gelatinous lime green drops.

'Come *ma*, lay your head on my thigh, now turn your head to the side.'

Lifting the edge of my throbbing ear, he dripped the precious liquid in, and it slid inside soothingly. By nightfall my earache had disappeared. For all his apparent verbal arrogance, Dad was truly compassionate. A great soft spot for his children manifested itself when he sat by our bedsides, reduced to holding our small hands in his strong ones when we fell ill. His eyes shone with unshed tears and he would be husky-voiced as he spoke gently to us, mopping our brows. If necessary he would scrape a few cents together to purchase medicine for us.

My soft-spoken mother, gentle and calm, was made of sterner stuff in her dealings with her children. Mum had a practical, unsentimental outlook on life and was not given to grandiose gestures. When we fell ill, she would appear, cup in hand, with instructions:

'Drink this, you will get better soon,' and gently chide us if we protested. 'Don't choke on it, sip it gently and it will go down.'

She never raised her voice. If she was upset in any way, she resorted to her lifeline: prayers. She knelt at the altar, her face engulfed by a spiritual flame of unshakable faith, eyes often at the point of filling with tears. She implored her lord and master for help; it was here her well-judged decisions were made. On the rare occasion when Dad requested her company for a show, she would invoke her 'we cannot afford it' reply. She lived a life of sacrifices.

When provoked, Mum's face would snap shut like a drawer and if we were naughty in front of visitors a shake of her head and her finger to her lips was sufficient warning – *don't you dare show me up in front of strangers.*

Her ebony skin was inherited from her father. It was soft as silk, velvety smooth to touch. Her jet-black hair, flecked with grey in later years, fell in silky, glossy waves, spread on her back in the shape of a winnowing tray, wide at the top and narrowing to the apex of a triangle. Scissors had never snipped her split-ends. The natural waves rippled like spent waves on the beach. After she had washed it, she would throw her face forward and flick the residual water from her hair, which would explode in tiny droplets all around, swiftly to evaporate in the heat of the day. Her blouse would be damp where her freshly washed and towelled hair hung down. Once dry, she rubbed gingelly (sesame) oil from her scalp right through to the tips of her hair. Her fingers flew and coiled her hair into a bun secured with Kee Aa pins with ridges halfway down for grip, held in her mouth until she was ready to put each one in. She perfected the art of producing a tight, shiny ball at the nape of her neck, looping silky netting over this if she was going out. All this she achieved without the aid of a mirror.

The youngest children missed out on Mum's undivided attention. There were too many of us and too many household demands on her. Cuddles had to be snatched. I rested my head on Mum's lap as she sat on the settee, luxuriating in the few moments of closeness. I felt totally safe as she placed the palm of her soft hand on my head. To love Mum was to be soothed, comforted and secure. Her calming presence was everywhere. Her imprinted roped slippers discarded by the door assured us of her presence somewhere safe indoors. Life began and ended with Mum.

When Chocolate *thaatha* retired from his catechist job, relocating to his four-acre estate in Sentul, all his children followed, whether single or married – including their spouses and grandchildren. It was during their stay with the extended family that Anna and Rosie arrived to boost our family numbers. It was whilst they were living in the family home that my sister Mary made her brief appearance into this world. Mum and Dad now had five of their eventual nine children to nurture. Dad was following in his own father's footsteps.

17

'From pet to table...'

Survival

'I've been thinking about chickens.'

I shut my book and raised my eyes. Dad's plans were always grandiose. 'Always go for the best, and if that is not possible, go without. It is not worth doing things by half measures.' He lived by that principle.

'If we cleared some of the land in front of the house we could raise some chickens,' he went on. Every new idea was mapped out on Dad's face as it occurred to him, with a twitch here, a blink there, a creased eyebrow or a pursed mouth. He conveyed his enthusiasm to Peter, who listened with an animated expression and then dashed off to his room, returning with sheets of paper and a sharpened pencil. Plans were sketched, erased and re-sketched. Off they went to survey the plot. Between the two of them they then cleared a third of the vegetable patch whilst poor Mum stood in resigned silence, watching her plants being uprooted.

Within a week necessary materials were listed and purchases made. Dad held the sturdy poles whilst Peter, balancing on a makeshift ladder, hammered them home. Rolled up chicken wire was deftly unrolled and nailed into place: the chicken coop had been constructed. Charlie, Chandra and I balanced on our wooden seesaw – another of Peter's constructions, made especially for his siblings – and watched the progress from a safe distance. A wooden-framed door with chicken wire stretched across it was hinged into place and a wooden latch made to keep the door shut.

Once Dad and Peter withdrew indoors, curiosity got the better of us youngsters. My Japanese slipper-clad foot moved forward, my eyes focused on the new construction. Suddenly I emitted a bloodcurdling scream as an excruciating pain shot up my left leg as something sharp pierced the pad of my foot. A piece of rusty metal had sunk into my flesh. Dad and Peter rushed out of the house.

'Oh my God, quick, Jonah, pick her up, bring her into the house. Marie, Marie!' Dad exclaimed.

The slipper from my right foot fell off as I was carried into the sitting room and laid on the couch. Dad knelt down and I caught sight of a discreet nod from him to my brother. Following this cue Peter placed his hand on my face and turned it towards him. I let out another ear-piercing scream, frightening myself. Was it really me screaming?

My father wrenched the left slipper away, causing deep pulsating throbs of searing pain to travel all the way up to my thigh. My mind strayed, momentarily disordered by the pain. I was drenched in sweat – from both the pain and the humidity. My dress clung to me as I lay on the settee. Avoiding my gaze, Mum passed something to Dad from her clutched hand and through a haze I could just make out Dad scraping match-heads on to a piece of paper. Another nod was aimed at my brother; this time I started screaming in anticipation.

'Are you ready?'

Peter nodded, as he cupped one hand over my mouth, the other grasping a slipper that had been thrust into his hand.

'Lily, Lily, keep still!' he implored, as tears formed in his own eyes.

My seven-year-old foot was held tightly in my father's hand. Mum hovered behind the settee next to Peter and held out one of her hands for me to grip. I felt a gentle swipe with something soft, the pressure of a finger on the pad of my foot and then I heard the strike of a match. A sharp pain shot up right through the marrow of my leg. I could see rather than hear Peter's slippered hand as it came towards my foot. I fainted.

When I came to, I was lying on the settee; the blood that had fallen on the cement floor was being mopped up. The family gathered round me. Charlie and Chandra's saucer- like eyes were still big with tears though some had run down their cheeks. My mind was fixed on my wounded foot. The pain grew steadily, mounting in intensity until it seemed to saturate my consciousness. My breath came in gasps through gritted teeth but eventually I settled into a sob and sipped on the tea that Mum proffered.

After a few hours the pain settled into a dull ache, allowing me to enjoy the treats the family bestowed so generously. I made the most of this rather painful escapade and the barbaric treatment I had had to endure. It seemed to have done the trick though, as bar a tell-tale scar, I experienced no further ill effects.

Meanwhile, the men's chicken coop was proclaimed a success and it soon started to fill up. Apart from the local breed, Dad introduced some specialist, imported chickens. The rowdy, noisy Rhode Island Reds fought for their territory like unruly adolescents, in contrast to the well-brought-up, ladylike white Leghorns. Cockerels with brilliant combs strutted about and chased after broody hens. All the chickens were forever clucking and pecking at grain and the smell of chicken poo soon mingled with the spice rich air. Every morning we collected our rewards: toasty-warm brown and white eggs with downy feathers still clinging to them. Very few eggs were reserved for home consumption. Most served effectively within a barter system. I set off in the style of Red Riding Hood with my basket of eggs, stopping periodically to massage my fingers criss-crossed from its rattan handle. The eggs were exchanged for bottles of medicinal neem oil or earthenware jars of fresh, thick, natural yoghurt. I could never resist a quick peek inside the jars to inhale the sour smell and marvel at the sumptuous yoghurt within. Its surface usually sported a yellow, cracked crust, which looked just like parched earth whose cracks had filled up with rivulets of water.

Dad's favourite meal was yoghurt mixed with a little water to relax it then poured into the centre of a plateful of rice. A sprinkling of salt for taste, a skinned raw onion and a fresh green chilli or a spoonful of fresh lime pickle were the only accompaniments required to make this dish into a king's lunch. Sitting beside him I enjoyed my plateful too, minus the green chilli and raw onion; it was worth the morning's walk.

The chickens satisfied our yearning to have our own pets. We made our choices, and then christened them. We poked our fingers through the chicken wire, teasing the chickens, whilst monitoring our individual pet's progress. When we threw handfuls of chicken feed through the fence, we aimed it near our favourites. Predictably, tears were shed and tantrums displayed, making it very difficult for our mother, when it was our pet's turn to feature on the menu. All our wiles were used to the full as we desperately tried to influence her choice.

'Please *ammah*, can you kill one of the other hens and leave mine for now?'

We were painfully aware of the inevitable but there seemed no harm in trying.

Weekend jobs in the kitchen involved the preparation of vegetables and grinding the coconuts to obtain the much-used coconut milk from the flesh. I was roped in when Anna was absent, for example during her 'have to go and help our relatives' spells. Mum split each coconut in half deftly using a flat-bladed *parang* knife before handing me the two halves. Our coconut scraper, which rested against the wall when not in use, was placed flat down on the floor. This kitchen essential was a clever piece of equipment, consisting of a curved steel bar, like the head of a cobra ready to strike; one end had a serrated crest for scraping and the other was fixed to a narrow wooden base. Sitting sideways on the base, clamping my dress between my knees, I had to lean forward, cupping the hairy, half-shell of the coconut in both hands, then roll the sphere over the blade's zigzag edge to scrape the soft, white flesh against the serrated scraper until the coconut had yielded every juicy bit of flesh, reducing the half to an empty shell. The lethal serrations drew blood from my index finger, especially during my early efforts, but satisfaction was guaranteed as the grated coconut pile grew into a mini-hill on the enamel plate below.

Cupfuls of water were then added to the gratings, and the mixture massaged and squashed to coax it to release its milky fluid. The first milk extracted was used mostly at the end of cooking as a thickener for curries, as well as providing a delicious sauce for vegetables and Indian sweets and deserts. Adding more water to the squeezed-out gratings produced a lighter fluid, which added volume to the daily curry. I entered the kitchen as usual to carry out my chores when my mother announced the dreaded words.

'We will have chicken curry today. Lily, I need your help.'

'Oh no, I hate this job.'

My shoulders went into an involuntarily spasm; even the heat of the mid-morning sun failed to warm my spirits but I had no option. My brothers were too young; Anna had been dispatched to my Uncle Leo's house to assist my pregnant aunty. It was a Sunday, and coupled with church attendance it was also our meat-eating and foraging day.

Unable to refuse, shoulders slumped and suppressing a deep sigh, I made my way to the back of the house. Mum was ready, squatting on the cement floor, gripping the selected chicken's head and pulling its neck taut, its yellow scaly claws, edged with sharp toenails, held firmly under her splayed feet. A freshly sharpened knife was poised in her other hand.

'Now hold the bowl just here,' she said, indicating with her chin.

I could barely look at the struggling chicken. I placed the bowl as near as I could to where Mum was directing me, and then averted my eyes and pursed my lips in revulsion. I felt Mum draw the sharp blade across the chicken's neck in one deft movement. My muscles tensed as the vibration travelled up my arm but I was forced to turn my gaze back to position the bowl as the blood squirted everywhere, hissing like a lit Christmas sparkler. A fine film of warm magenta fluid sprinkled the grey cement floor, patterning my arms and my clothes. After the initial spurt the blood settled into more of a downward flow.

'Now, keep the bowl close to the neck so you can catch all of it.'

The chicken initially thrashed about furiously but as the bowl started filling, lost its momentum. Nausea was overcoming me as I offered silent prayers for the process to be over. The chicken had given up its fight. My face must have expressed my revulsion.

'Watch, watch and learn.'

With a heavy cleaver, Mum cracked the bones apart right through the breastbone, neatly prizing off the plump breast meat to be marinated in toasted ground spices and dry fried. The rest of the carcass was soon jointed, the steel cleaver making short work of dismembering it. The heart was sliced through and the soft slippery liver cleaned of the green bag of bile, ripped away without any spillage. The kidneys were halved and the inner ribbed layer of the gizzard, with its collection of crushed stones, deftly peeled away. Despite myself I was morbidly fascinated with Mum's skilled handling of the whole procedure. In the strong sunlight her hands glistened with the melting fat. The carcass lay in the enamel bowl. Nothing was wasted; the intestines were washed, cleaned and curried. The blood, a useful source of nutrients, was poured into the curry towards the end of the cooking time, ensuring that it kept its soft consistency when cooked and didn't turn rubbery.

I left the scene as fast as possible, rushing to the open-air bathroom to scrub off the tell-tale spills; I had just taken part in a murder, I thought dramatically. I dared not recount my barbaric weekend activity to my fellow pupils.

I could hardly bring myself to eat lunch that day but it was futile to display any squeamishness. 'One day, you will have to kill chickens to feed your own family, so you might as well learn early.'

'Not if I can help it,' I muttered under my breath.

My favourite chicken, Meena, was a beautiful, dainty Leghorn lady and it broke my heart when it was her turn for the cooking pot. Thankfully, Anna was around and I was spared the slaughtering ritual. I hid myself in the bedroom, my salty tears drying into lines of stickiness. My protest went as far as refusing to eat her, helping myself to plain boiled rice and vegetables with no gravy to moisten the rice. My parents, whilst sympathetic to my feelings, held to their commitment to the family as a whole, over and above my selfish sentiments.

'Everybody's pet chickens have to be eaten one day you know.' An early lesson was learnt the hard way.

We partook of our customary four o'clock afternoon tea with a cream cracker for dipping. Bits of cracker always broke away no matter how quickly I dipped and retrieved them. When I tipped the cup to sip the last of my tea I had to exercise extreme caution as the broken bits of biscuit had by then reduced to a brown mush, which tasted like mud when accidentally swallowed. Having eaten only rice and vegetables earlier on this day, a single cracker and a cuppa proved insufficient to quell my growling stomach. By evening I was experiencing serious hunger pangs and at dinner I felt compelled to dip my chapattis into the curry – though I stubbornly avoided the chicken pieces much to my brother Charlie's amusement.

Sensing my need for a diversion, our dinnertime anecdote centred on the Japanese occupation. Mum launched into one of her favourite stories, chuckling softly as she reminisced.

'Everybody was in a hurry to get to the shelter as a raid was imminent, but everyone thought that someone else had taken baby Elsa – in fact she had been left behind! Luckily, I was one of the last to leave the house and, realising what had happened, I gathered her up in my arms and ran across to the shelter. Your Uncle Leo and Dayavu *atthai* were so upset when they discovered that they had left their baby daughter behind. Thank God I had seen her.'

When the all-clear siren was given, my Uncle and aunty were reunited with their daughter thanks to Mum's quick reactions.

As she finished that tale, Mum's face became overshadowed as she recalled a poignant scene that had always haunted her.

'When we left the shelter we saw this headless Chinaman going past on his bicycle. The bomb blast must have cut off his head whilst he had been out cycling. I watched, horrified, as his bicycle hit a stone that was lying at the side of the road and the body just fell to the ground. It was still shaking.'

Equally horrifying tales of the Japanese soldiers' vengeance against their sworn enemies, the Chinese, raised goose pimples on our skin as we listened. The young Chinese girls of my older sisters' ages were particularly vulnerable. Girls became 'boys' overnight, their hair cut short. My mother continued:

'When we had any inkling of a raid, *ammah* rolled our Chinese friends' daughter in a straw mat and leaned the mat against the wall. The soldiers did their usual search of the house and we were lucky that they didn't look too closely at the mat.'

If discovered, the girls fell prey to the soldiers, and the lives of their families were for ever altered. Hands cupping my face, I sat at the dining table and listened, mesmerised.

'Do you know what? The worst thing was when I walked to work at the war factory where I was a machinist. The *Japaan* soldiers stood on the street corners, and we had to bow to them when we went past – but one day when I looked up there was the head of a Chinese man stuck on a pole. Aeiyyo, I had to walk past this head! See what we had to put up with during the war.'

She shivered at the horrifying memory and I shivered with her.

'We had no choice, the soldier who was standing there made sure we looked at the head, otherwise he would have hit us with the barrel of his gun. Your *appa* was away fighting and we were on our own. Luckily we were living with your Chocolate *thaatha* and *ammachi*.'

I was so thankful that I had been spared the horrors of war.

'I fought against the English...' said my father.

My eyes widened in surprise. I could scarcely believe it. Although I knew Dad had served in the Indian Army – his uniform was folded and stored in the top shelf of our *almari*, being brought out from time to time and packed away again with fresh mothballs – his respect for the British had always been beyond question. Dad's lips quivered at my childish astonishment.

'Hmm-mm, not literally, *ma* – I was stationed in Jitra in Burma' (a township very close to the northernmost tip of Malaya where the peninsula narrowed to a thin neck) 'my platoon didn't come up against any British soldiers there. But if the British had found out about my army career in the Indian National Army, they would have thrown me in prison when the war came to an end.'

Then Mum piped up, throwing an accusatory glance at Dad but one tinged with understanding. A gentle smile played around her lips.

'Your father only joined the INA after he listened to a speech by Subhas Chandra Bhose. That man hated the British because of what they were doing in India. He was doing a tour you see all the way from India. Your father heard about it, you know how he has a nose for these things, and there was no stopping him. He went to Singapore to hear this man's speech and when he came home he had already volunteered to join that man's army.'

Mum shook her head at Dad. She had obviously disapproved of his impulsive action but mindful of his patriotism was not prepared to try to change his mind. I wasn't surprised, aware as I was too of Dad's devotion to his motherland. The realisation that he could contribute a great deal to India's struggle from overseas must have been a temptation impossible to resist. He was renowned for taking his life in his hands and striking forward, never letting caution dictate the way he led his life.

Mum had certainly succeeded in diverting my attention away from Meena's fate. I admired the resilience of all the people who had had to endure such gruesome times. Their experiences had shaped them, toughened them. They possessed qualities that truly engaged my admiration.

18

'Generosity to cousin...'

Holidays

I set off along the railway line, past miles of open-wire fencing. The grinning faces of the railway workers pressed against the fence. Both their wolf-whistles and the admonitions of the older workers rang in my ears.

'Leave the little girl alone. Haven't you got sisters?'

Although flattered, knots formed at the back of my neck, and my steps faltered a little but, face firmly averted, I stared straight ahead, intent on reaching Uncle Leo's house. My feet slipped awkwardly on the railway sleepers and I stepped back on to the dirt path as soon as I could. A bottle of neem oil that my aunt appreciated was wrapped safely among my clothes. But I was unprotected, and in the baking sun. Perspiration formed unsightly half-moons beneath my armpits. My talcumed face was covered in rivulets of sweat that trickled down from my damp hair.

I hurried along the well-trodden path as best I could, reaching my destination half an hour later. A row of three terraced, brick-built houses with fenced off frontages faced the local police station, ensuring a week's sleep free from fear. At the front of the house on the left there was a profusion of orchids, some trained on bamboo stakes whilst others hung from strung pots. Although this riot of colour dazzled the eye, Uncle Leo's frontage next door was equally impressive. His garden was edged with a line of candy pink and crimson roses behind which grew a few vegetables; then there was a big clump of aloe vera and every Indian household's must-have, a curry plant. The roses wafted a fragrant welcome to visitors. When I called out, leaning on the padlocked gate, cousin Agnes appeared jangling the keys.

My two aunties, clearly not long woken from their afternoon

nap, acknowledged my presence with a smile and a wave of half-cupped hands.

'Come ma, come in Lily, how is everyone at home?'

Annie, the eldest daughter and the darling and beauty amongst all the siblings, acknowledged my presence with a brief nod. Rounded Elsa emerged from the passageway carrying a tray with glasses of evening tea and a platter of biscuits. She threw a dimpled smile in my direction. Little Steven, their only son, and shy Angeline, the youngest of the brood, interrupted their floor game and moved aside to let me pass. The twins had been born in the same year as me. Antoinette had been generously offered for adoption to Uncle Leo's childless older brother, Anthony, whilst Agnes stayed with her birth family. As my school holidays were spent in both households, I developed a close and lasting relationship with the twins.

An electric fan in the centre of the room stirred the humid air; I stood under it momentarily relishing the breeze as it dried the rivulets on my face. Framed photographs of Uncle Leo's wedding and group pictures of the family hung above the seating area whilst an altar took pride of place on the narrow shorter wall. I was familiar with this room. It was good to be here.

Wealthy Uncle Leo had amassed a fortune through a combination of hard work and luck: he was a successful car salesman of Cycle and Carriage fame, a flourishing business based in the heart of Kuala Lumpur. However Chocolate *thaatha*'s addiction to gambling also ran in his son's veins. The word was that Uncle Leo was the envied owner of a few racehorses; just how many was anyone's guess. He played his cards close to his chest. He was also the first amongst the relatives to own a car. His wealth raised his status within our extended family. Of average height, with sparse hair that was approaching the first stages of baldness, his beady eyes under surprisingly bushy brows missed nothing. The sharp toot of the car horn was always an announcement: 'Come and help unload.'

Despite his rather harsh 'I am the Lord of the manor' strut, he was a good provider for his family. After all, hadn't he purchased a lovely brick-built house for his family? Didn't he chaperone his family to church in style in his Peugeot, a commodity that few families could afford? Not to mention dropping his children off at school in his car too. He could afford private tuition to boost their grades and purchased lots of books to expand their knowledge.

Every afternoon Teacher *atthai*, my aunty's older spinster sister (a teacher in the Tamil School by profession, who lived with her married younger sister) conducted a quiz based on the 'three Rs' – reading, writing and arithmetic – as well as history and geography.

'Name the principal islands that make up Japan.'

'Honshu, Hokkaido, Shikoku, Kyoshu,' flowed off my tongue.

I was so grateful for these extra lessons but they only took place during short spells in my life. Agnes, my contemporary cousin companion, was not an avid reader herself but generous in allowing me access to her books, enabling me to indulge in my favourite pastime. I hid behind chairs and in remote corners of the house away from prying eyes. I earned my keep by helping in the kitchen, laying the table and folding up the laundered clothes. I passed many a pleasant week in the company of my cousins, where food was plentiful and I was included in family outings.

Uncle Leo's fiery temper was reserved for his immediate family and siblings. Although we trembled when he returned home in the evenings I remember him for his kindness and thoughtfulness.

'Right, get ready you little ones, I am taking you shopping. Lily, you come as well.'

When I acknowledged his generosity, he treated me to one of his rare smiles and winked at me. He was fond of his sister's children. Packing us into his Peugeot, Uncle Leo drove us to the more expensive shopping areas of Kuala Lumpur. As he sped through the traffic there was pin-drop silence from his subdued passengers, a testament to his 'children should be seen but not heard' rule. The Bata shoe shop was our first stop.

'Now line up everybody and get measured.'

Not knowing quite where to put myself, I hung back. A finger wagged at me.

'You too, come on.'

I came forward with mixed feelings. Uncle Leo's open-handedness highlighted my own parents' poverty. My rich cousins knew of the financial difficulties faced by my cash- strapped parents. I did not relish my position of 'poor cousin, we have to be kind to her'. Whilst not wanting to appear ungrateful I was uncomfortable; I fixed the shoebox under my arm and wished my parents had made the purchase instead.

'We will go and get some dress material now, we can go to Pudu for that.'

The shop assistants recognised 'money' as soon as my Uncle walked in with his troupe of potential customers. Bales of taffeta, voiles and satins shimmered on the serving tops. We were not measured formally but just by the assistants' trained eyes, and soon yards of material were being cut and packaged. When we arrived back I was quick to hide my embarrassment, the new canvas shoes quickly hidden amongst the clothes in my bag.

Equally generous Aunty slipped a brown paper parcel into my hands before I left.

'Give this to your mother; she will know what to do with this.'

The parcel held lengths of silk to be sewn into *sari* blouses. My aunt was fond of her sister-in-law and never failed to remind my mother of her good fortune.

'You are lucky *un-nie*, (sister-in-law) even though you are poor, you are rich in love.'

Another venue for my holidays was Uncle James's house. Lovable, loud, jovial Uncle James was the quite the opposite of his older brother Leo. Uncle James and Aunty Emily and their young family had by now moved to Galloway Road, only a ten-minute walk away from my grandparents' old haunt – St Anthony's Church. A few houses away on the same side of the road lived the youngest of my uncles, Uncle Xavier and his family. St Anthony's Church seemed to wield its magic, throwing its net out and successfully catching our family so that we were drawn to that locality. Arriving for a week at Uncle James's house I made no requests to return home this time, unlike my very first trip. Although the boys were very friendly, I enjoyed a special closeness with my cousin Josephine, the only girl in her family of five.

Return visits from any of my cousins were always a treat. They made no complaints of our basic fare. My mother's rule that visitors should always have the best was followed to a T. Food placed on the table was first offered to visitors. Pieces of meat mysteriously landed on their plates whilst we were happy with the ladled gravy – no disappointment was ever expressed. Our cousin Raja, Mum's younger sister, Aunty Ava's only son, often came for school holiday visits. With only one younger sibling Raja was drawn to the fun and laughter in our crowded household.

'Boys, go to sleep, stop making so much noise; I have to get up for work in the morning.'

A few moments of silence would follow Dad's plea but cousin Raja's irrepressible humour soon surfaced again. He was just a couple of years younger than Peter and the cousins were close. Raja's quick wit and humour reduced everybody to stitches. It was impossible to settle down to sleep until late at night as the house reverberated with peels of laughter originating from Peter's room where Raja was ensconced. Dad failed to maintain order and his regular breathing soon edged into full-throated snores that mingled with our giggles as we drifted off to sleep, our sides aching.

Raja *annan*'s younger stepsister, Grace, was a talented linguist who could jabber away in various dialects of Chinese. She was fluent in Hakka, Cantonese and even the most difficult, Mandarin. She was a bit of a tomboy and not very domesticated but her dimpled smile was infectious. During my stays with her family, I was willing to undertake the housework, which she abhorred.

'*Akka*, you are so good, thank you for doing my chores for me, I hate housework.'

Initially my Aunt Ava's family lived in Sungei Besi, a town on Kuala Lumpur's periphery. They lived within a mainly Chinese community and every morning I stood by the window, elbows resting on the windowsill to cup my chin. I was fascinated by a wizened old Chinese lady, dressed all in black, who followed the custom amongst elderly Chinese folk of carrying her wares to sell them at the local market. Despite her age, she displayed remarkable strength. A wooden pole was deftly balanced, arching across her back and hanging at the ends of the pole that dipped at either end were two woven baskets overflowing with vegetables.

A rich Chinese family lived within sight of my aunt's house. Here the contrast between two old Chinese ladies from different backgrounds stood out starkly. The grandmother, who was the head of this wealthy family, had extremely tiny feet, encased in black embroidered velvet shoes that peeked out from under her black silk full-length trousers. Aunty Ava explained to me this bizarre Chinese practice. The matriarch had had her feet bound as a baby to retard their growth. The children's feet were tightly bound with a cloth, which bent all their toes into the sole of their feet but left the big toe free. A stone was used to crush the arch and this process of binding feet lasted for years. Ladies with these tiny feet were supposed to have an erotic effect on their husbands as they tottered about and often attracted very rich men to whom they were either married or for whom they became concubines.

I realised that those tiny feet must be a source of a great deal of pain, as I watched the old lady totter about. It also made her really quite an elderly woman, because the practice of feet-binding virtually came to an end in the early 1900s. Aunty further informed me that the old lady came from a very important family in China and that feet-binding was carried out on all the girls from influential families. This family could well have been refugees from the Maoist regime. Malaya was home to vast numbers of immigrants, economic as well as political migrants.

19

'Reverend Mother in swimsuit...'

Schooldays

My companion Nadira and I were often caught in the almost daily downpours on our way back from school. Black thunderclouds raced in, followed swiftly by lightning and deafening thunder, as though the sky was being ripped apart; the ferocity of it promised havoc below. As the clouds spilled their contents the sheets of rain drenched everything in seconds. The initial large drops thudded on our skin and made us flinch. Quickly we took our shoes off and placed them safely in our plastic-covered bags, then waded through the rushing, murky water, feeling with our bare feet for the wooden planks that crossed the stream.

The violent rain turned the dirt road through the rubber plantation into a river of mud. We revelled in the sensual feel as it caressed our toes, squelching yieldingly. Faces raised, eyes closed and heads thrown back, we delighted in the huge drops of warm, heavy rain that fell on us like a natural invigorating shower. Our royal blue uniforms became ever darker in the drenching rain, and our pigtails dripped constantly, the white ribbon plaited into them streaming behind us in the wind. As I negotiated the narrow lane that skirted our rhododendron fence the open stream alongside bubbled and gurgled with brown water, sweeping the sides clean of discarded rubbish, and engorged with bobbing, broken-off branches and twigs and discarded rags. I looked like a drowned rat as I waved goodbye to Nadira by the front gate. Loud shouts and giggles from the lane announced the arrival of my equally soaked brothers. Depositing my school bag inside, I rushed to beat the queue, heading for the emptied oil drums, now overflowing rain tubs that had been strategically sited under the gutters.

Clad in a *sarong* modestly drawn across my breast I was already pouring cans full of water over my soaped hair and body when the boys joined me. Their skinny, bronzed bodies were clad only in printed cotton underwear that billowed just above their knees. For the next ten to fifteen minutes we ducked and dived to avoid the arches of sprayed water, gasping when the arch found its target. We played until our fingertips and toes turned soft white and wrinkled and only gave in when we began to shiver in the rain-cooled air. I had first go with the family towel before passing it along to the others. Our wet clothes were a pile by the kitchen door as we dressed quickly in anticipation of our treat.

Mum sat cross-legged on the floor, rolling out balls of dough made with wholemeal flour, water and salt. A burning hiss of melting Planta margarine on the flat iron wafted across. She turned the circular flat breads and puffed them up by deftly applying pressure at various spots. Then she piled the brown-speckled cooked chapatti on a nearby plate. In an earthenware pot, placed on the circular cloth pot-holder and brimming to the top, was green pea *sambal* made with soaked green peas, coconut milk, dry red chillies, sautéed onions and popped mustard seeds. We ate with fingers still puckered from their long contact with water. Our hands became shiny with melted fat as we tore bite-sized pieces of chapatti off to scoop up the slushy, spicy green peas before tucking them into our salivating open mouths.

Satiated, we made for the bedroom, dragging wooden stools along for the younger ones to stand on. I balanced my bum on the windowsill and rested my back against the frame. The network of streams outside created by the flowing rainwater eventually came together into one main, fast-flowing current, which gurgled past our window. With practised hands we folded old newspapers into boats and launched them into the flow.

'Look, my boat is first! Come on, come on, keep going! Oh Charlie, look, your boat is turning over.'

A disgruntled moan came from beside me.

'Mine has sunk, not fair,' grumbled the disappointed Chan, as he turned away from the sorry sight of the waterlogged boat nose-diving into the mud.

We enjoyed the thunderstorms during the day but night-time storms, besides keeping us awake, intensified the darkness outside and added to the fears of the night.

My early friendship with Nadira got lost in the wider world of new students, especially as we did not share the same classroom, but my very first friendship in primary school remained steadfast throughout. Geraldine was the indomitable clown of the class, a jack-in- the-box who popped up everywhere. Her grin so irrepressible, giggles so infectious and pranks so outrageous meant that our school life became one big adventure. Gangly Geraldine, with her mop of curly hair kept under control with a boyish bob cut, flourished. A permanent twinkle dazzled in her hazel eyes as she devised her next escapade, wondering how and when she was going to pull it off. She had an unerring ability for getting away with things that no one else could. Largely thanks to her antics, we were officially recognised as the 'naughtiest class in the school'.

Year six, when I was thirteen, stood out as a particularly fun year. An amalgamation of schools in Kuala Lumpur resulted in fresh students from surrounding schools joining us. Thankfully my classmates also consisted of a handful of former friends that included Geraldine, but we were amidst strangers. I was surprised to be appointed class monitor – a responsible position that I found increasingly difficult to fulfil, thanks in part to my bosom buddy. One of my duties was to make sure that work progressed when the teacher had to leave the class for any length of time; of course this was show time for Geraldine.

A twitch of her face or a twinkle in her eye threatened the birth of a ruse, a plot that was gathering flesh before it reached fruition. She was a talented mimic and also a gifted artist. One day she sprinted to the blackboard with a piece of borrowed chalk and with a few deft strokes drew a caricature titled 'Reverend Mother in swimsuit'. In general the nuns commanded our respect, so depicting our Reverend Mother in scanty clothes reduced the class to tears of guilty laughter. Unpopular schoolteachers were similarly caricatured in amusing poses. Our mirth, which we were unable to suppress, mingled with a slight wobble of nervousness. The new recruits to our class were won over by Geraldine's clowning, and enjoyed these regular interruptions to our daily routine. None of us attempted to snitch on our skilful and creative classmate.

However, responding to complaints made against us by the teachers of neighbouring classes, Mrs Thomas, our class teacher and Geraldine's real-life aunt, had set a trap. Having made a very obvious retreat one day, Mrs Thomas hid behind an open door towards the rear of the classroom. Geraldine, totally oblivious, was in full swing. One vigilant student caught a glimpse of Mrs Thomas's dress through the gap in the door and managed to alert her neighbours. The rest of the class cottoned on one by one. Their laughter petered out, which totally perplexed Geraldine.

'What is the matter with you lot? Why are you making funny faces at me, Norma? Lily, what is the matter with you?'

At this point Mrs Thomas decided to make her presence known. Her high-heeled shoes clicked up the central aisle. She assumed her usual pose: head bowed slightly, one hand contemplatively under her chin, and the other across her ample behind. Geraldine made a dash to her seat, shocked but unable to suppress her nervous giggles. Mrs Thomas had difficulty in hiding her own amusement but meted out her punishment just the same. Discipline had to be established and implemented. Thus Geraldine landed herself in trouble yet again, but surprisingly I was let off lightly despite failing in my responsibilities. Mrs Thomas was fully aware that I had been lumbered with an impossible task. No one could control Geraldine.

Each class was divided into four teams, Red, Blue, Green and Yellow. The team colours were permanently displayed on the blackboard, as were the points awarded to each person for academic achievements and crosses for bad behaviour. Geraldine's typical reaction to her steady accumulation of crosses was 'Let's see what happens once she runs out of space on the black board. Who cares anyway?' Perhaps surprisingly, none of her team members seemed to mind, a testament to Geraldine's popularity.

At the completion of that year, we sat for our first government exams, the results of which determined our placing for the following year. The thirty most promising students were streamed off into Form One A, the rest into B or C. This milestone in our academic careers meant that we had entered secondary education, and were now just over halfway through our schooldays.

Most of the sixth year students had re-grouped in Form One A. Friendships cemented during the previous year strengthened still further. We became bolder in our escapades. Banned comics, collected for swaps, were secreted in the upturned umbrellas that lined the wall at the back of the classroom.

If there was one single nun who could inspire anyone to join the nunnery it was our beloved Sister Beatrice. Our form teacher, she was young, probably in her mid-twenties. She certainly didn't seem to be much older than my sister Theresa. Bespectacled, angelic, softly-spoken, pious Sister Beatrice had an older sister, a fellow nun who was working with the poor in India, whilst their only brother was a serving priest in Africa.

'I have to fetch something from my room. I need to borrow one of your umbrellas, girls.'

The nun's living quarters were adjacent to the school above the classrooms where I had sat during my Tamil schooling months. An open-sided corridor connected the two buildings. Wind was swirling the rain against the closed windows of our classroom.

A shocked silence descended. We watched with bated breath and guilt-ridden faces as our saintly teacher's soft-soled, unhurried steps reached the back of the classroom, hands in customary fashion resting in her cuffs. Her every step increased the feeling of doom in our breasts as we hoped and prayed – but luck failed us that morning. Sister Beatrice lifted one of the umbrellas and a comic fell out with a resounding thud. In pin-drop silence, without any change of expression, she methodically inspected the rest of the umbrellas and to our utter horror our guilty secrets were soon piled high on the spare desk. The atmosphere was tense. I wished the floor would open up and swallow me. Sister Beatrice unhurriedly walked back to the front of the class carrying the armful of confiscated comics. Her voice was calm, infinitely more cringe-inducing than if it had been raised in anger. Her face remained serene.

'You know the rules, girls. I am so disappointed in you. I thought I could trust you. You will have to stay back after school for detention and write out a hundred times "I will not bring comics into school".'

One morning, about a month into our school year, a newcomer stood next to Sister Beatrice, whose arms were crossed and hands slipped into her sleeves as usual. She waited patiently until we had all taken our seats.

'Good morning, Sister,' we chorused.

'Good morning, girls. This is Andrea, your new classmate. I hope you will all make her feel welcome.'

Restraint showed in our every move, but our eyes focused curiously on the stranger. A nervous smile played around her generous mouth. She had deep blue eyes and a mop of shoulder-length reddish hair, which framed a plump face dusted generously with freckles. Even the fine hair on her arms and legs was reddish. I caught her eye and gave a welcome smile and she responded immediately as though anxious for any form of acknowledgement.

'Andrea is from Hungary. Look it up in your map books, girls.'

Andrea came to sit in the empty seat to my right, casting me a nervous smile. She was a big-boned girl, well covered, and she smelt of roses. She automatically turned to me for guidance, and I was happy to oblige. A friendship sprang up between us almost instantly. During the course of the week we discovered a connection.

'He is a good boss, Mr Burgh. You look after his daughter.'

Both our fathers worked in the same department. Their Malay chauffeur dropped off Andrea and her older sister Erica at the entrance to the convent every morning. Then the sisters parted company as each headed off towards their respective classmates.

Andrea and I quickly grew comfortable in each other's company. I was invited to her house most Saturday mornings but one Saturday when we hadn't made any plans a short sharp sound of a horn outside was followed by a knock on our gate.

I was certainly pleased to have Andrea's company, but ill prepared for her surprise visit. Her broad smile and twinkling eyes had an 'I've surprised you' look. I groaned inwardly. The stench of the drains was at its worst. My brothers stood in line and gawked at the stranger. Did Andrea recognise the bright green paint that covered the frontage of the house, courtesy of Sentul Railways? I had donned my flowered hand-me-down skirt with a broken zip. Without a safety pin, I had tried to tie the ends together but they stubbornly refused to stay knotted: a twist to the right or left, bending down to pick something up or standing on tiptoe to reach up, loosened the knot instantly.

In the end we played hopscotch in scratched squares on the ground, with me gripping the ends of my skirt with my left hand. Andrea didn't bat an eyelid and took it all in her stride, whilst I hoped for the ground to open up and swallow my embarrassment and me. I knew envy. I wanted a slice of her wealth, her red hair, her deep blue eyes, fair freckled skin, shiny patent shoes and pristine white socks as I stood bare-footed in my skirt and blouse that hadn't seen an iron. I valiantly swallowed my pride. But when she smiled at me, my envy dissipated. I wanted to be like her, not be her.

Crossing the railway track at the back of our house I walked the steeply rutted, muddy-banked path past half a dozen dilapidated wooden houses topped with rusty zinc roofs and enclosed by rickety wooden fences. The path broadened out on reaching the front yard of our family friend Grace's rambling house. Sometimes I came across Gracie *akka* or her well-endowed mother hanging out washing.

'Off to your *Vellakarachi* friend's house, are you?'

A smile and a nod was my answer.

When I reached the spot where the barbed wire fencing had been prised apart, wide enough to twist my body through, I stepped out on to the soft, well-tended golf course. I cut a path across it, skirting the flag-poled circles of the greens where the softest green grass was being fed by sprinklers. As I neared the road that led to Andrea's house I caught a frantic wave of hands. She stood on the balcony of the clubhouse and beckoned to me to join her. Once indoors my gaze was immediately drawn to Andrea's older sister, Erica. Her skin was so transparent that you could count the pale blue veins. Her cheeks were the colour of rose petals. Her eyes were an electric blue, speckled seductively with golden sparks. She was draped around the lithe, bronzed body of a handsome Sikh boy, who was striking an elegant pose against the bar. His superior smile spelled out a message for home-grown simpletons like me.

'I own this gorgeous creature, who will do anything for me.'

I felt increasingly uncomfortable, but was completely mesmerised as my gaze was drawn to witnessing a kiss for the first time as Erica performed, yes, performed, seemingly for my benefit. Her lithe body twined around the equally self-centred young man. They seemed to be eating one another as they played to their audience. The elderly Englishmen, all golfers, raised their eyebrows as they leant against the bar cradling their drinks. My embarrassment intensified, aware that a pantomime was being played out for my benefit, to embarrass me, and put me firmly in my place: I was a little nobody in a much-washed cotton dress, who presumed to mix with her betters. I was furious with myself. The spectacle had sent tingles down my spine. Why hadn't I looked away?

Andrea took my hand and ignored her sister's display.

'Erica is a right show-off, don't mind her. She is just trying to shock you. Come on, let's go outside and leave her to her young man. I am used to her theatrical ways, she always manages to get away with it. My parents never tell her off; she is spoilt. I don't let her bother me.'

Still reeling from what I had just witnessed, I was grateful to be led away to their house. It was a large detached wooden house on stilts, surrounded by immaculate gardens, situated in a tree-lined avenue. Servants were always at their beck and call. I was honoured to be friends with an occupant of this affluent neighbourhood, where I was made to feel welcome as Andrea's close friend.

Andrea's parents took us shopping on Saturday mornings to The Cold Storage, a grocery shop in Weld Road that catered for expats and those who could afford it. To my relief, Erica never came with us, obviously too busy making up to her boyfriend. I gave the golf club a wide berth after that, not wishing to make a fool of myself again.

'You can choose something, is there anything you want?' asked her parents.

'No thank you.'

'How about an ice cream? What flavour?'

Sensitive to my feelings, Andrea piped up with her own choice so that I could make mine too. I made every mouthful of ice cream last as long as I possibly could as it dribbled deliciously down the back of my throat. As we left the cool of the store to walk back to the car, I took larger mouthfuls before the sun's rays did their job. I crunched up every last crumb of cone that hid the remnants of the delicious mixture.

Invariably I was invited to stay for lunch, which would be meat in a thick gravy or mince-stuffed chillies with vegetables in a light broth – a touch bland for my taste but interesting nevertheless. I was invited to stay over once, sleeping in a spare bed in Andrea's bedroom. We talked in whispers until sleep overcame us. Mr and Mrs Burgh were kindness itself. They made me feel very special. I was their daughter's best friend and was treated with great respect, for which I was grateful.

It was an interesting year for me, as I cultivated a friendship with Europeans who, until that point, had existed only in books for me. A year later the Burgh family moved to Australia because of another job change. Tearful farewells were exchanged. Unable to afford the stamps to keep up a correspondence, my wonderful friendship with Andrea came to an abrupt end.

At school, the students divided themselves into two camps, those who were fans of either Elvis Presley or Cliff Richard. I could not contribute to the knowledgeable chatter of the rival groups. I was not familiar with the gossip magazines and did not have time to listen to English stations on the radio as I had books to entertain me. This restricted my friendships somewhat. I could count on one hand the number of friends' houses I was allowed to visit: those of Nadira, Andrea and Geraldine. My relatively wealthy classmates often got together for birthday parties but I reluctantly had to make my excuses. Unchaperoned visits to unknown families were not permitted. 'You are a young girl; once a young girl's name has been spoilt there is no future for her. We are only telling you for your own good, one day you will thank us.'

We were now pupils of Form Three, an important year, when we had to sit for our second government exam: Lower School Certificate. By now we had won ourselves a few adversaries, one of whom was our school secretary. She was roped in to help the teachers from time to time and made no effort to disguise the contempt with which she regarded us, a feeling that was totally reciprocated. Sister Bernadette, our form teacher for that year, was the antithesis of the soft and demure Sister Beatrice, who was blessed with a great sense of humour and tremendous tolerance. Short and wiry, Sister Bernadette's beady, shrewd eyes missed nothing. She was of indeterminate age with wrinkles round her mouth and a shading of downy hair over her upper lip, and an almost permanently creased forehead. Her mouth screwed up in disapproval as though she had just swallowed a sour buah kanna – a preserved sweet and sour prune. Her short fingers were claw-like in determination. She had our measure, and was determined to suppress our independent spirits.

Our monthly test papers were handed out and placed on our desks face down. Our disdainful young school secretary walked in briskly, her black patent shoes echoing on the cement floor, all starchy and with a 'look at me I am important' swagger. As this was her first job after leaving school she could not have been more than three or four years our senior.

'Girls, I want you to carry on with your exam. I have to leave you for a while and Janet is going to oversee you. Behave yourselves whilst I am gone and I will expect Janet's full report when I get back.'

Sister Bernadette – or Bernie as the pupils nicknamed her – having handed over the invigilator's role, gathered her files and got ready to leave us to the tender mercies of the puffed-up Janet. As Janet turned round to face the class, a self-satisfied smirk appeared on her elongated face. Her short haircut indicated an efficient secretary's persona. Our eyes focused on a large mole on her lip, which looked like a flattened goat poo. Janet surveyed us with a 'you may think you are smart, girls, but I am the important person now, you are all under my supervision' expression.

'Now Janet, don't put up with any nonsense. I know who the troublemakers are,' went on Sister, as Janet's self-importance and our resentment both grew.

'Please remain quiet and get on with your work. The teachers next door will report to me if there is any noise from this class.'

Throwing the sternest look she could muster, Bernie walked out. Janet strutted about in her superior manner, a smug, lopsided smile playing around her lips. The mole seemed to be growing bigger. You could read exactly what was in her mind: 'I've got them exactly where I want them now. They dare not play any of their tricks, not now, not after sister Bernadette's warning.'

However, gullible Janet was no match for enterprising Geraldine. The class worked in silence on our test paper, filling our Parker pens from time to time from the glass inkwell sunk into the right hand corners of our wooden desks containing Parker's Quink in royal blue. Faint titters were quickly suppressed. I looked round for guilty faces, but couldn't detect any signs. Head down, I continued with full concentration until another titter erupted. A second scan round the room still revealed nothing. Deciding to ignore any further interruptions I once again applied full concentration to my work. Just as I was about to put my pen down, Janet walked past my desk in her invigilator's role. As she did so she cast an eye over our test papers. I placed a cupped hand over mine. What cheek, I thought, she is not our teacher, and has no right to look at what we have written. I cast another disbelieving look at Janet. Her white cotton skirt, rigid with starch, was generously splattered with blots of royal blue ink. Oh my God, I thought to myself, Geraldine has been up to her tricks again. That's it, we are going to be in serious trouble now. What on earth are we going to do, for there will be no escaping Bernie's wrath.

Without drawing attention to myself, I surreptitiously glanced round the rest of the class and each one of my friend's faces reflected mine – the same aghast look mingled with suppressed laughter. Geraldine, having finished her exam, was playing with the inkwell. It had a hinged brass lid that she was lifting and letting fall with the tip of her nail, her face inscrutable. Thankfully, before our suppressed laughter had a chance to erupt, Bernie returned and relieved Janet of her duties.

'Thank you Janet, did they behave themselves?'

'Yes Sister.'

'Okay, you can go now. Now girls, pass your test papers to the front and then you can go for your recess.'

We filed out, fit to burst, marvelling at our narrow escape. We grouped together during recess laughing uncontrollably until our sides ached. A few of us sobered up sufficiently to admonish Geraldine.

'You shouldn't have done that you know. What if we had been caught? Anyway, we know Janet can be a pain, but destroying her white skirt...' I shook my head. 'You will have to go for confession this Friday you know. You have gone too far this time.'

Recess over, we filed back into our classroom still in the grip of hysterical laughter, which immediately froze in the chilly atmosphere. Bernie was standing at the desk with one hand resting on the shoulder of a furious, tearful Janet while the other hand gripped a cane. Once we had returned to our desks, the cane hissed as it came down hard on Bernie's desk. I winced.

'Well, who was it?' hissed Bernie, her white face contorted with rage.

We shuddered, thunderstruck, silent, guilt written across all our faces.

'Own up, or say who did it. None of you will be leaving this class until you give up the culprit.'

A solid wall of silence greeted Bernie. The next ten minutes seemed an eternity. Bernie's laboured breathing was clearly audible. Janet's accusatory eyes were fixed in Geraldine's direction. Janet had no proof that it was Geraldine and none of us were going to give her up. In the mood Bernie was in, Geraldine could face suspension and none of us wanted that for our favourite friend, even if she fully deserved it on this occasion. Unable to break our solidarity and totally frustrated, Bernie's full wrath was vented on us.

'You will all go to hell! You think you are clever hiding the culprit? God knows everything. He has eyes everywhere, you cannot hide from him.'

Incensed as she was with rage, her voice shook just as much as her finger as she pointed at us. 'He can see every one of your guilty faces. Yes. You are ALL guilty now. Sinners, the lot of you! You can all stay back after school and write a thousand lines in neat handwriting: I WILL ALWAYS TELL THE TRUTH. And you Catholic girls make sure you go to confession and confess your sins. Shame on you! I am very disappointed in all of you. You will be reported to Reverend Mother.'

We later endured Reverend Mother's reproaches with bowed heads, suitably chastised. Reverend Mother had always commanded our respect and we were truly sorry that we had hurt her. Wisely, she did not pursue the matter and we got over this episode in due course. Geraldine's antics came to a temporary halt but the irrepressible naughtiness surfaced every now and again, perhaps just a shade subdued.

As a group, we were noisy, cruel, clever, talented, and above all inseparable. In true musketeer style, it was one for all and all for one. Because of our loyalty to one another and our ability to maintain our academic standards, the teachers tolerated us and were even amused by us at times. There was a reluctant admiration from the senior students too, who could not understand how we got away with as much as we did. Those school day relationships had a lasting impact on us all and our bonds remained strong.

20

'Our lives' "ten commandments"...'

Houseguests

'*Ammah*, Margie *ammah* is here!' This was a cry repeated most evenings. Margie *ammah* was an eccentric widow, a larger than life character whose status almost equalled a man's – a remarkable achievement for those times. Widowed relatively young, in her mid-forties, this formidable lady, affectionately referred to as Margie *ammah*, lived a mile away in a back lane behind the lively, smelly Sentul Market. She cycled over to us at least four or five times a week, seeking stimulating conversation with Dad and later, when my older sister and her family moved back in with us, my eldest brother-in-law would be drawn into their conversations too. A woman cycling was itself an unusual sight at that time, but then Margie *ammah* was a pretty unusual woman. Forced into employment to provide for her five children when she was widowed, she had educated all her children through her own stalwart efforts. Her employed eldest daughter was married and lived in government quarters as a near neighbour to Uncle James. The elder son, David, was embroiled in a controversial love affair with Stephanie, a work colleague who was a Malayalee. David's Tamil genealogy and humble upbringing meant that her well-to-do and sophisticated family did not regard him as a suitable match for Stephanie.

'What can I do? She is a good girl really, I have no problem with her, but you know what our society is like. My poor son won't give her up either. *Che. Che.*'

Two more daughters, Cecelia and Margie (from whom Margie *ammah* earned her nickname), were both at secondary school whilst her second son was in his third year at junior school.

Margie *ammah* dismounted from her bicycle, unhitched the tuck she had made in her *sari* to keep it out of the bicycle chain's teeth, and settled her machine against the side of the house before entering. She claimed visitor's rights at dinner and parked herself next to Dad. She burped like a man after the meal and expelled air whilst seated, lifting her bottom sideways without the slightest embarrassment.

After dinner, Dad, my brother-in-law and Margie *ammah* made their way to the sitting room, where they plunged into their monsoon of politics and put the world to rights. Margie *ammah*'s high-spirited vocabulary of English sentences peppered with Tamil and Malay words turned the dark nights into something comic. Mum gravitated deferentially to an available chair and joined in the general chat with a nod or an occasional 'ahem'. She tactfully suppressed her amusement and often busied herself at the sewing machine. My eyes focused on the opening and closing of the blades of the scissors as Mum, using the owner's blouse as a template, precisely cut the *sari* blouse pieces making sure the borders matched. She had to peer at the fabric as she worked in the glow of the lantern, making sure that she faced the kerosene oil light so as not to cast a shadow on her patterns.

Us children were reduced to the margins, and engaged in our own games. A brief affectionate glance would be thrown in our direction from time to time or a hushed 'sssshhhhhh' if we raised our voices in excitement and cut into the adults' lively debates.

Margie *ammah* was employed as a nurse at a general practice. She was both vocal and entertaining, and a great raconteur. Despite the close proximity between them, she always spoke louder than the others as if addressing the deaf. She amused her listeners with outrageous tales from her workplace, possessing an unusual talent of being able to inject humour into any mundane story and thus reduce her spectators to fits of laughter. As an experienced nurse, she was a supplier of valuable medicine for our family ailments. When I developed an unexplained rash on both my feet that soon developed dry painful cracks she arrived with a bottle of permanganate of soda.

'Dissolve a teaspoon of the crystals in water and soak your feet in it for ten minutes every day, then dry them well. See how you get on for a week.'

She gave these instructions with authority, in a 'bound to have the desired effect' tone. The crystals left a purple residue on my feet but as predicted, after two weeks of this treatment my feet were restored to their original smoothness. One up for Margie *ammah*!

Dad relaxed in his customary chair, striking a pose, which suggested that he was expecting to be waited on. Coffee arrived. After a suitable time, a dipped finger served as a thermometer to gauge the temperature of the coffee. The enamel mugs were passed around to the men who bent their heads in acknowledgement and continued their conversation as the server, usually Anna, returned surreptitiously to her perch. Dad slurped his coffee off the rim and smiled his appreciation. The conversation became a drone in the background as I pressed on with my studies until around nine, the children's bedtime during the week.

Mum bit off the thread and folded the *sari* blouse, laying it carefully on one side.

'That's ready for Letchumi to collect tomorrow.'

Undaunted by the lateness of the hour, Margie *ammah* left an exhausted gathering as she set off home on her bicycle – but she always managed to leave some vestige of herself behind, such as screwed-up man's handkerchief or the daily newspaper in which a particular job advertisement or article had been circled with a pencil. Mum laundered her handkerchief to hand back at Margie *ammah*'s subsequent visit. Dad picked up her paper and read it front to back.

The widow's youngest son was the first of many to lodge in our already crowded house. As a working mother, she had little time to oversee his education.

'Rosie *ammah*, can you help me out? Thambi Raja is giving me so many problems. He won't study you know. I take the *rothan* (cane) to him, but that fellow, no matter how much I hit him, the *rothan* bends but not him! Nothing doing. His report bookmarks are all red, red, red, red, every month! I don't know what to do *lah*. I thought I would ask you. Peter is a good teacher. I know he taught Lily to read, and if there is anyone Thambi Raja will listen to, it will be our Jonah. What do you say Jonah,' using his pet name and appealing to Peter's generous nature, 'do you think you can help Thambi Raja?'

Faced with a plea from a widow from whose help our family had benefited, and Peter's natural inclination to rise to a challenge, prompted his agreement, to Margie *ammah*'s obvious relief. So it was that ten-year-old Thambi Raja became a family addition for the next two years. A shy boy, he had few words. Short and well rounded, with wavy hair which had a tendency to fall over his forehead, Thambi Raja was in awe of our family. Aware of his mother's high regard for us he was on his best behaviour. Under Peter's guidance, Thambi Raja's grades improved, and a few blue marks began to replace some of the red ones in his monthly progress report. He blended into the family, sharing my brother's four-poster bed and going on to La Salle School in Sentul. After two fruitful years with us, he returned home to complete his education and eventually joined the Malayan army. Forever grateful to our family, he never failed to visit. My parents and Peter had earned Thambi Raja's, and his mother's, eternal gratitude.

More often than not Dad's distant relatives helped swell our numbers when youngsters required temporary accommodation with job transfers to Kuala Lumpur. My cousins often enjoyed their school holidays with us too. Every visitor was absorbed into our family effortlessly; the closeness was all due to Mum's efforts. The general sleeping arrangements naturally remained flexible in order to accommodate any visitors who happened to stay, the children sharing my siblings' bedroom whilst our parents vacated theirs for adult guests, opting for the hall again.

Our houseguests were in the main on a par with us, apart from Cousin Mary and her four children. As the result of an advantageous matrimonial liaison, they were very different from us. She had fallen in love with a Hindu boy from a wealthy family: Ramachandran held a prestigious job with a French firm, Socfin Company, that dealt with rubber products, so the family were mainly stationed in rubber plantation estates. There was a lack of good schools in these estates, so my parents came to the rescue.

A jeep pulled up at our gates, Socfin Company emblazoned on its sides. Cousin Mary's husband, a handsome soft-spoken man, broad-shouldered and with a gentle smile that always hovered on his lips, stepped down. He helped his family of four little girls out – although the third girl, with a boy's haircut and wearing boys' clothes, surprised me. She and the youngest one clung to their father's hands on either side while Cousin Mary walked ahead with her older two. Shy Rita held back a little but bright-eyed, ebony-skinned Jenny skipped ahead ready for adventure. This was their first visit to our paint peeling house, sprouting extensions in various directions just like the old woman who lived in a shoe, with children falling out of doorways. My wide eyes fixed on the number of suitcases and brown boxes that were unloaded and stacked in our back room.

Wealthy Cousin Mary had come prepared to cook, but was forced to share Mum's small kitchen. Our family traditions were challenged. There was the appetising smell of meat cooked not just on Sundays as was our norm but enjoyed two or three times a week by my cousins' family. Used tins of condensed milk were thrown on the rubbish heap without the lid having been prised right off to enable every last drop to be swilled out. Such evidence of obvious wealth extracted a sigh of envy.

The riddle of the girl dressed as a boy was explained to us in hushed tones by Mum. Disappointed with their failure to produce a son, the third daughter, Florence, was renamed Raja (King), and was being raised as boy. It was a sensitive subject for Cousin Mary and we were warned to play along with the plan. Care must be taken not to jeopardise our good fortune, for every extra cent in the form of

Cousin Mary's rent for her single room was greatly appreciated. So we acquired four extra siblings. The shy eldest, Rita, kept me company on the way to the convent, traipsing through the rubber estate without complaints about the length of the journey. I took pity on her and shared the load of her school bag.

Six months later Mary announced her husband's transfer to Damansara Heights. They were offered a large bungalow to move into and good schools could be reached by means of car-pooling. We bade tearful farewells to our cousins but maintained our contact.

People came and went in our house. The landscape of it changed constantly and we miraculously kept packing everyone in. When our house was rebuilt in 1957, accommodating visitors became less difficult. We had then acquired seven bedrooms, and the older children looked forward to enjoying privacy for the first time but prudent Mum, ever practical, had her own ideas. Strapped for cash as ever, she rented out the largest of the rooms by persuading Peter to convert an open space into a second kitchen and a lean-to bathroom for the tenant's personal use. There was never a shortage of tenants and Mum had to turn customers away. Her caring nature came into play once again as she became midwife to pregnant tenants, and helped to feed and clothe their young children.

Mum's attitude to life was a learning curve for me. She was full of well known maxims by which she lived and they became our family's 'ten commandments':

1. *Live within your means*
2. *A stitch in time saves nine*
3. *Don't beg borrow or steal*
4. *Tell the truth and shame the devil*
5. *The devil makes work for idle hands*
6. *Cut your coat according to your cloth*
7. *Treat others the way you want others to treat you*
8. *Do not leave till tomorrow what you can do today*
9. *Dushtherai parrthaal dhura poh (Keep your distance from bad people)*
10. *If you don't have a good word to say about anyone, don't say anything at all*

Mum's commandments guided our lives.

21

'From Corporal to Psychological...'

Surrogate Dad

Life in the Anthonysamy household could be compared with that of a racecourse. Challenges were faced boldly, victories celebrated and losses borne courageously. This was largely due to our very own holy trinity – Dad, Mum and Peter. Peter's quest for knowledge mirrored Dad's: both were cast from the same mould and constantly encouraged and challenged one another. In turn, Peter shared his knowledge and aspirations with the younger generation. Our multi-talented father's busy life meant that he was fully involved in union affairs and local politics, so the responsibility for the discipline of the younger children often fell to Peter.

Peter's own diverse talents were well suited to this surrogate father role. His monthly subscriptions to psychology magazines paid dividends. The guinea pigs on whom he could practise his theoretical knowledge were well within his reach – his siblings, nieces and nephews provided ample opportunities. Corporal punishment was the norm of the times but Peter favoured the 'reward technique', where good behaviour was rewarded and punishment spared on owning up to misdeeds. Peter lined us up in the sitting room when he returned after a day's work and any culprits' knees trembled as he stroked his lower lip with his thumb, and fixed his all-seeing gaze on us.

'I will know if you are lying, so you had better tell the truth.'

The V-shaped scar on his forehead, the legacy of a childhood skirmish, seemed to us to act as a third eye. There was no escaping its scrutiny as feet shuffled and throats were cleared. Punishments were few and far between, but there is always an exception to a rule, and in this case it took the form of my little nephew, Winston.

When my eldest nephew Charles, Winston's older brother, had inadvertently set fire to the nylon window curtains in the dining area whilst experimenting with a box of matches, he panicked, beseeching his younger brother to shoulder the blame. The tell-tale charred remains of the curtains could not be spirited away, as someone in the family would certainly have questioned their absence. The frightened perpetrator was confident that Winston, with his open smile, would willingly take the blame. Hadn't he done so countless numbers of times before, apparently happy to suffer the physical punishments that made others cringe? Peter was initially unaware of the subterfuge but soon cottoned on.

'I've heard enough, Winston. Now will the real culprit own up?' he demanded, cutting the younger boy's protestations short.

Unable to lie when faced with a direct question, the shamefaced Charles eventually had to admit his guilt and was duly punished. Winston was given a serious talk about the evils of white lies and Peter's experiment of avoiding punishment for wrongdoers was abruptly abandoned.

However our eldest brother's experiments with learnt behavioural skills were regularly demonstrated to visitors to the house. Baby brother Ben, adorable at the age of four with coal-black eyes, centre-parted wavy hair and a skinny frame dressed permanently in miniature shorts, was usually roped in to be Peter's ideal subject.

'Benny, lie down on the floor and close your eyes, and don't open them until I tell you to. Don't listen to anyone else, obey only me, do you understand?'

Nodding his little head, Ben obliged, stretched out like a rod, motionless, eyes screwed shut, chest hardly moving. His fisted hands were held tightly to his sides and his toes flexed to the ceiling. No one could get Benny to open his eyes.

'Benny, *annan* is not around any more, he has gone out, he has forgotten about you! Come on, get up *dah*.'

But Ben resisted all cajoling. Only Peter's voice held the magic. Ben's eyes would flick open at his command, adoration reflected in them, his mouth wreathed in smiles: 'I hope you are pleased with me.' We hand-swiped the floor dust that clung to his bare back, seeing no harm in such play at the time, as we blindly placed all our faith in Peter, the darling of the family.

'Hey, it is the end of the month isn't it, where is your report book?'

'I'll get it *annan*.' I fetched my slim report book and handed it to Peter, confident that he would be pleased with the blue pass marks.

Peter always signed our monthly school progress report books and kept a check on our educational progress. Charlie's attempts at hiding his report book, awash with red marks of failure, were often thwarted and he faced punishment on a regular basis. Helplessly I witnessed Charlie kneel on the sand outside our front door for anything up to fifteen minutes, his knees indented by the grains of sand. Sometimes Peter resorted to a lesser punishment, ordering Charlie to sit down and stand up fifty to a hundred times while holding his ears with arms crossed. A lesser punishment it may have seemed but nevertheless it was humiliating and not without physical pain. My heart ached in sympathy but I was powerless to intervene and had to suffer in silence as I witnessed Charlie build up unspoken resentment against Peter. Throughout his punishment Charlie remained stoic and refused to cry but all the while the hushed quiet of the house spoke volumes; everyone disappeared into the corners of the house to try to become invisible.

My mother was always busy with housekeeping and making ends meet so was content to leave all matters of discipline to her trusted son. Without fail, Dad handed over his monthly salary to her and without fail she was reduced to tears. Withdrawing the pin from the bun at the nape of her neck, she used it to slit open the envelope. The slim pile of notes lay on her palm. She knew instinctively that it was insufficient for the family's needs. Wiping away her tears, I watched my long-suffering mother turn to God for guidance. On her knees, her eyes raised in complete veneration, her arms rose in supplication as she prayed. Aware that Dad was doing his best for his family I was unable to fathom who was to blame for our poverty. I was heartbroken by my inability to control events.

'God tell me, what am I going to do with this money, who am I going to pay this month? I will leave it all to you, only you can help me,' prayed Mum, letting the tears flow unchecked.

Then she anointed herself with holy water from the glass bottle, and dipped her little finger into the glass container of the everlasting light on the altar, to check that it had sufficient oil to feed the wick. She genuflected and with a heartfelt sigh wiped her face with the good morning towel from her shoulder before going about her work once more.

At that stage of my life there was nothing I could do to help her but as I notched up the years, one after another, my resolve strengthened with each one. I gripped my hands together and gave voice to this resolve: 'I have to earn money to help my family.'

I repeated this sentence over and over again, to etch it even more firmly in my mind.

Mum was not blessed with the material comforts that her siblings enjoyed, but she was blessed with a pride that prevented her from seeking financial help from them. She never failed to remind us of her uncle's objections to her marriage and the derogatory remarks made about my father's inability to provide for his large family. She always made the most of what she had, her entreaties reserved for the Almighty's ears alone.

Peter's role as the next breadwinner required his wellbeing to be of great importance, a matter that became a family undertaking. Unspoken but understood by us, we did not question it when Mum's back was bent over the stove as she prepared his special breakfast, a nourishing dish of khali – finely ground green peas and ground rice, enriched with a beaten egg, loosened with fresh cow's milk, sweetened with sugar and glistening with rich ghee. The ghee had been a gift from a kind relative returning from India. The fragrance was unmistakable; our mouths drooled involuntarily at the slightest whiff. The precious ghee bottle was tucked away safely beyond the reach of young hands. Accepting that this special breakfast was to maintain his health did little to appease Peter's guilt. He was enjoying such food at the expense of his siblings, so Peter took pains to share his treat, a tablespoon of *khali* left unfinished in the bowl. His kindness did not go unnoticed. We adored him all the more for it. He left the breakfast table licking the rich concoction from the corners of his mouth. 'I couldn't finish the *khali*, you can finish it off, okay?' to whoever happened to be lurking in the vicinity. Every last scrap was licked up and savoured.

Despite his almost feminine soft side, Peter could fly off the handle if his privacy or belongings were tampered with. His room was his kingdom, and no one was allowed in without invitation. His books and magazines, his most precious possessions, were neatly arranged on wooden shelves. The rest of us shared a comb whilst Peter luxuriated in his very own. After a full day at work Peter emerged from his shower. When he picked up his comb to run it through his wet hair, he discovered a long black hair caught between its teeth. His room reverberated with his bellow.

'Who used my comb, own up! This long hair can only belong to one of you girls!'

The comb whizzed out of his bedroom and smacked against the wall. Predictably his question was met with total silence. Well aware that nobody would dare to own up, he relented. 'I want my comb washed and put back in my room and don't any one of you even think of using it again.'

His quick temper often sparked a clash with Dad and my long-suffering mother was forced to make the peace. The tension in the house remained palpable until Peter's temper was eventually brought under control with the application of his newfound passion – psychology. He became an ardent convert; Peter never did anything by halves. His hobby produced a positive outcome though. A semblance of peace descended as rows with Dad became less frequent, but this was only achieved after a major explosion that devastated the whole family. He purchased a set of body building equipment. Piles of different sized weights were delivered to the house, including a lethal-looking steel bar on which the weights were balanced at both ends. Excitement buzzed all day as we awaited Peter's return from work.

'Has it arrived?'

A chorus of 'Yes, it is in your room.'

Peter arranged the equipment in his inner sanctum. We crowded round the doorway, jaws slackened in awe, whilst Peter grinned with satisfaction. Systematically he arranged the equipment, stacking each weight according to size, and then commenced his exercises. His muscles rippled with each stretch and retraction. Sweat dripped from every pore within a few minutes of the beginning of his routine.

'Wait a few weeks and see, my muscles will look just like the body-builders' in the magazines.'

But Peter's euphoria was short-lived. That night when Dad came home an almighty row erupted.

'You've got more money than sense! How much did it cost, eh? Get rid of it. We could be eating for months with the money you have wasted!'

Uncharacteristically, Dad threw in a few swear words too. The two of them were dangerously close to becoming physical as they locked eyes, their shoulders squared.

Peter thankfully concentrated more on his verbal argument, defending his right to spend his own hard-earned money. Dad was having none of that.

'I have worked hard for this family, and educated you so that you could get a decent job. Now it is your turn to use your money sensibly, to save for your future and to provide for your family, not to throw it away on useless junk!'

Horrified at this major clash between our two favourite men, and unable to take sides as we were sympathetic to both their viewpoints, we were reduced to seeking refuge in the kitchen. Mum attempted to make peace. She managed to persuade Peter to retreat to his room and then took Dad's hand and guided him to their bedroom where she tried to make him see reason. But neither of them would give in.

Next we heard a loud bang as the front door slammed: Peter disappeared for two nights. Our anxiety reached heights we had never before experienced. Sleepless nights followed, appetites were suppressed, prayers flowed freely and red eyes greeted red eyes. A very subdued Dad spent fruitless evenings calling at my brother's friends' houses. When Peter finally returned a couple of days later and the subject was dropped. Peter kept his equipment and continued to pump iron.

Male voices could often be heard raised in banter, as well as the thud of weights crashing to the ground, as Peter and his friends enjoyed the self-made gym. They all wanted rippling muscles and rock hard torsos. Typical young men, their shrieks of laughter, their camaraderie, the thumps and slaps on the back were reserved for themselves. The door was kept firmly shut to contain their world. Young girls' prying eyes were kept firmly out. The appearance of a head round the door and a click of Peter's fingers was all that was required for Anna to hurry to the kitchen to fetch cups of tea and Mum's spicy potato curry puffs to fuel their energy-sapping pastime.

Peter's generosity was evident from his very first employment as a clerk with Telecoms in 1955. The bulk of his salary was handed over to Mum but he was allowed to retain an allowance with the expectation that he would accumulate savings for his future. He beckoned me to him.

'Here, take this and buy something in the tuck shop, then tomorrow I want to know what you bought. Don't simply put the money away; I am giving you this because you study hard and your report card showed good marks. Spend it on yourself, okay?'

I accepted the treat in the spirit in which it was given, with a grateful smile and a thudding heart. I felt privileged and special, but these feelings were mingled with sadness. My younger brother did not share in the good fortune. As I have said, Charlie exhibited limited interest in his studies. Attending school was a chore he couldn't avoid, but that was as far as his commitment stretched. Peter would often press five cents into my palm but an extravagant ten if my grades were exceptionally good. Aware that Charlie's grades could never earn him similar rewards, I shared mine with him.

On our way to school we stopped at the Chinese stores and excitedly ran our eyes on the rows of glass jars arranged on the shelves. The Chinese shop assistant counted out my choice of sour pickled plums, granules of crystallised salt clinging to their wrinkled surface. I would salivate as I anticipated biting off the dried flesh from its black central seed that would set my teeth on edge and make my lips dry and sore. Charlie favoured little round cakes made with pea and rice flour pressed into flower-mould bases and covered in translucent rice paper. Our bargains were tucked into our schoolbags to be consumed later during our school recess. The following evening without fail Peter demanded an account. I kept Charlie out of the picture. I was being rewarded for my scholarly achievement and if I disclosed my generosity, my treat could be withdrawn or worse, it could draw Charlie into unwanted limelight. We continued to enjoy our morning shopping for as long as Peter's generosity lasted.

Peter was also willing to spare some cash for necessities around the house. Money spent on education was deemed justified spending, hence with Dad's agreement Peter invested in individual wooden desks for his younger siblings, convinced they would serve as an encouragement for our study. They took pride of place in the room, which doubled as our afternoon-nap room. Instructions were issued. After school, home-lunch-homework was to be followed by an afternoon nap before evening play. These instructions were invariably broken. It was fun time. Our productive rambutan tree's branches brushed against the windows of this room. The fruit's hairy but soft exterior easily peeled off to expose honey-sweet white flesh centred with an almond-shaped seed in the centre. The fruit hung in clusters, a fresh green colour when unripe but changing to a rich sunshine yellow when ready to eat.

'Hey, come on, let's pluck some rambutans!' Eight-year-old Charlie, our ringleader in mischief, would clamber out of the window.

Chandra, two years younger, moved cautiously but was half-coaxed and half-bullied into helping his older brother. Quietly so as not to waken Mum from her afternoon nap, they desperately attempted to contain their excitement as they clambered up on stools placed underneath the windows and swung out on to the soft earth. Uncharacteristically Charlie was not a keen tree climber but successfully coaxed Chandra to do so. Chandra wrenched bunches of ripe rambutans down and threw them to the ground where Charlie was waiting. Charlie and little Benny then passed the fruit to me and I stuffed it into our shiny new desks with a nervous 'I should not be doing this' giggle and a worried whisper: 'Chandra come down, we have enough already, otherwise we will be caught.'

Reluctantly my brothers returned, giving little Ben a leg-up. We sat cross-legged on the floor, gorging ourselves on the stolen fruit. Gentle snores from the sitting room assured us of Mum's blissful ignorance. All the evidence – peel, seeds, leaves – was gathered up in a newspaper and successfully disposed of in the large rubbish pit in the front garden, which was conveniently covered with corrugated zinc. I loathed the job but was determined that every scrap of evidence should be removed. When I lifted the cover, the reek of decaying vegetation hit my nostrils, forcing me to cover my nose with the back of my hand. To complete the subterfuge, I tucked the peels under other rubbish with the aid of a twig.

This childish prank was, in essence, thieving. The rambutan trees provided a source of much-needed cash for the family. Local Chinese stall-holders came to inspect our trees when the fruit first formed, paid a deposit to reserve the stock, and then returned to harvest the ripened fruit and settle their accounts. Despite warnings, we had helped ourselves to some of the forbidden fruit, hoping that the purchasers would be none the wiser.

Handyman Peter often had to repair holes in the roof with fresh attap. This regular task was particularly necessary during the monsoon season. We scurried to bring in Mum's lime pickles drying in the sun and tugged at washing on the line before the fierce sheets of rain came down like knives and drenched us in a couple of minutes. Wave after wave of howling winds slapped the walls, whistling through gaps and holes, closely followed by peals of thunder and blinding lightning in its wake. The torrential rain never lasted more than an hour but it could rain three or four times a day, ceasing as abruptly as it had started. Sometimes we heard the thunder in the distance first, and then very swiftly the torrential rain would follow.

As soon as any holes became apparent, Mum leapt to fetch her collection of dented aluminium buckets and placed them strategically to catch the drips. We were warned to be careful not to kick the buckets aside as we rushed through the house. After a particularly fierce downpour, the cement floor resembled a miniature pond. All hands were called on deck to use our brooms, fashioned out of the spines of coconut leaves tied together at one end with twine. The twigs, splayed out at the far end, effectively swept the majority of water out of the open doorway. Any remaining dampness was mopped up with old rags. Thankfully the tropical heat dried the wet cement floor very quickly and we could walk about again in safety.

Our roof served as a breeding ground for a rather less romantic natural phenomenon: mice. A batch of these little beauties was discovered in the eaves of the house during one particular roof-mending task. Peter found several tiny cute pink babies, silky-soft to touch, and so new to the world that their eyes were still closed. He invited his younger siblings to look at them and of course we instantly fell in love with these adorable, helpless creatures, and became desperate to adopt them as our pets. Crowding around Peter, we pleaded with him, clamouring in chorus: 'They are so cute; can we keep them?'

Ever practical and fully aware of his responsibilities, our eldest brother had to regretfully halt this burgeoning love affair. Lanky Peter looked down on us clustered at his feet and explained gently: 'No, you cannot. Mice carry diseases and they will multiply rapidly and eat our food supplies. Sorry, but we have to get rid of them.'

Our faces fell, our shoulders drooped: childish disappointment was clearly evident from our tiny, expressive frames. We all knew better than to argue with our big brother – whatever he said was unwritten law in our household. We watched mournfully as he took the little babies away, thankfully disposing of them out of our sight. I suspect the poor creatures were drowned, but Peter spared us the ordeal of witnessing this ritual.

'Who is that sounding their horn outside our gate?' The gate opened to reveal Peter on his brand new blue and white Lambretta. The younger boys' squeals resembled those of the zinc gate as it swung back on its rusty hinges.

'*Ammah*, come and see, it is *annan*. He has got a scooter!'

Peter pulled up, grinning broadly as we crowded round him excitedly.

'All right, all right, come on, you can all get on and we'll go for a ride.'

Seven-year-old Charlie, five-year-old Chandra, two-year-old Benny and Charles all clambered on while the rest of us watched fascinated. Charlie and Chandra were joint pillion riders, squashed against one another on the back seat. Benny and Charles squeezed themselves into the space between Peter's body and the wire basket attached to the handlebars, Peter's legs on either side enclosing them and ensuring their safety.

Vroom, vroom: he kick-started the engine.

'Hold on tight. Toot, toot, are you enjoying yourselves?'

I could sense their huge excitement as I followed the Lambretta as it bumped along. Peter took them a little way along the dirt road and then they put-putted their way back to the house. They clung to one another, shrieking loudly, as the wind rushed past. Thrilled with his latest acquisition, Peter threw caution to the wind and drove straight through the sitting room and into the kitchen with his load, much to Mum's amusement and the thrill of the young ones who were all screaming in delight.

Peter's new mode of transport had been bought on loan. It was his pride and joy and was washed and polished to a high shine every weekend. The bike would be pulled on to its kickstand, parked under the shelter of the zinc-roofed veranda, and Peter, arms crossed, would gaze at his handiwork with admiration.

Peter's surrogate father role continued to flourish as Dad's interest in politics and his active participation in local and parliamentary elections expanded. After a full day's work at the railway, Dad began to spend more of his evenings at the Malayan Indian Congress. This party had been formed in 1946, a month before I was born, by none other than a fellow Indian National Army comrade. Mr Thivy, unlike Dad, had been held at Changi Prison for anti-colonial activities. On his release he had founded his party originally to support India's Independence, which was gained in 1947, but soon the group shifted its focus to the fight for Malayan Independence. Dad threw himself with a passion into politics again. Candidates for the Alliance (a party formed in 1954 by a coalition of like-minded Malays, Chinese and Indians) gathered at our house before wIrene's alking the dirt roads of rural Sentul with megaphones, wooing the vote of the rural masses. When Mum provided afternoon tea for the canvassers we were privileged to meet with the candidates, and basked in their reflected glory.

The Railwaymen's Union was also gaining popularity and Dad was earning a reputation as an articulate orator, admired for his ability to hold a crowd's attention. Monetary rewards for his speeches he did not spend on himself but instead used part of them for treats for his beloved children. We were bursting with excitement, dressed in our Sunday best, standing in the foyer of the Odeon while Dad queued for tickets for the great film that was on every Catholic's lips: it was 1956, when Charlton Heston thrilled everyone with his portrayal of Moses in 'The Ten Commandments'. The magic of the big screen, the parting of the Red Sea, the sight of the Burning Bush – the whole four-hour, epic journey was etched in our memories. Cinema trips were a luxury rarely indulged in. On this occasion Dad had either saved specially or delivered more than his usual quota of speeches. Our evening's entertainment culminated with a trip to the Chinese food stalls in Chow Kit Road.

'OK, you go and choose what you want to eat from the stalls. Don't worry how much it is going to cost. Leave that to me. Place your orders then come and sit down here.'

We tucked into bowlfuls of hot curried noodles using chopsticks to deftly pick up the tasty morsels. Our salivating mouths savoured the taste of the delicate fresh prawns and the succulent mussels, golden fried tofu, crunchy beansprouts and bobbing slices of spring onions. Bringing the rim of the soup bowls to our lips, we noisily slurped the intensely flavoured soup, which also contained fresh chilli and anchovy paste. Charlie plumped for fried kuey theow – fried flat white noodles in a savoury chilli and soy-flavoured sauce scattered with crunchy toasted sesame seeds. In the dimly lit noisy outdoors our father's eyes shone benevolently.

'Now I want to talk to you all seriously. You know I will do anything for you and the only thing I want in return is that you all study hard. You cannot get anywhere if you don't study. I don't worry about you, Lily; but you boys, Charlie and Chandra, you have to work harder. Ask your sister to help you. You will, won't you ma? You must make sure they do all their homework.'

I nodded in agreement, aware that Dad was demanding the impossible. I had made various attempts in the past to teach my younger brothers but quickly became irritated at their lack of immediate understanding. Was this a reflection of my own shortcomings as a teacher? I was reluctant to convey Charlie's disinterest in his studies to Dad. Charlie knew only too well how proud Dad was of my educational prowess. The blue pass marks in my monthly report book matched his red fail marks.

'Now, don't tell your mother how much I have spent tonight or she will only worry. Okay? Now eat, eat and enjoy, I like to see you enjoying yourselves.'

Being able to point at and choose golden *jalebies* and *ladoos*, dripping in ghee, from the tantalising displays in the glass-fronted cases in Indian restaurants, or enjoying platefuls of fried noodles in a Chinese restaurant, were highlights of our lives, remembered and savoured over weeks. Quality time with our Dad was a treasured time for us.

These trips were not discussed in any detail with our Mum as instructed, mindful as we all were of her need to save every cent. She did not pry, merely saying 'I am glad you all had a good time.' Her later conversations with Dad were not revealed but the audible sighs and shakes of her head did make me squirm with guilt.

While Dad continued to immerse himself in politics and union affairs, Peter reliably played his part, assuming an easy authority as the second man of the house.

22

'Obsession leads to near disaster...'

Hobbies

'Here, I have got a present for you; I picked it up on the train. Someone must have read it and left it behind.' Teasingly, Dad brought out a book from behind his back and held it out. My eager fingers curled over its spine.

'Wow, *appa*, one of Enid Blyton's *Famous Five* books! Thanks, *appa*.'

'I had to be quick before someone else picked it up. It must be your lucky day,' he said, smiling indulgently, eyes twinkling.

'*Five Go To Smuggler's Top*,' I murmured, running my fingers lovingly over the illustrated dust cover and hardly able to contain my excitement.

'Go on, I know you want to read it straightaway.'

No second bidding was necessary. The hard cover was turned back even before I reached the sanctuary of my room, so eager was I to discover the latest exploits of the Famous Five. My delight was increased yet further with the knowledge that this was the very first storybook I could call my own. With a flourish I inscribed 'This book belongs to A Lily' inside the back of the hard cover.

I followed the story closely as George the tomboy smuggled her pet dog, Timmy, into the secret tunnel, to keep him hidden. Then her cousins, Julian, Dick and Anne, helped her to free kidnapped Uncle Quentin from the clutches of the evil villain. I drooled as they drank copious amounts of ginger beer and tucked into their ham sandwiches. I could almost taste the tongue-tingling spiciness of ginger – a familiar taste. Ham I could not imagine, but was convinced it had to be heavenly.

Although Enid Blyton was one of my favourite authors, I was such an avid reader that I didn't discriminate in my choices. All my storybooks were however based in Europe, kindling an interest in travel. This became a real yearning, and consequently an impatience to visit the world I had seen in my books.

My younger brothers' interests lay in boyish games while Rosie, six years older than me, had matured into an eligible young lady. I failed to bridge the gap between us and so trod the path of a loner. Reading became my gap-filler, my escapism, representing a withdrawal from the realities of everyday life; and as my reading opened up exciting new worlds, I devoured the stories and lived the adventures. Like me, Hansel and Gretel had experienced poverty. I snuggled in the warmth of the autumn leaves that blanketed them in the forest. I reached up, broke off a piece of roof, savoured the chocolates and biscuits that Hansel and Gretel gorged on. I shook with fear as I faced the evil witch. I took a leisurely walk in an English garden filled with laden apple trees. I stood on tiptoe, plucked a juicy shiny red apple and pretended to wipe it clean on my dress sleeve.

I had once witnessed a European lady do exactly this whilst I waited with Mum for our bus in Foche Avenue. A tall, blonde lady with crimson lips and high heels had clicked her way past us, fished a shiny red apple from her beige bag and proceeded to polish it against the sleeve of her blouse before biting into the crisp white flesh. My mouth watered and the tip of my tongue found the corner of my mouth. '*Che, che,* Lily, it is rude to stare at people especially when they are eating. Look away now,' Mum had admonished. I looked away reluctantly but continued to savour the apple in my mind. Thus I lived in my imagination from a very young age, a world created within the magic circle of my books.

Evenings were the favourite time for indulging in my reading habit. Homework was completed immediately after lunch, so I was free for the rest of the day once my household chores had been completed. I rushed through these, had a refreshing shower and then sat on the veranda in a rounded rattan chair, my favoured perch. My right foot would be pulled up to rest on my left thigh; one hand held my open book while the other played with my toes, which was totally unladylike and would have drawn a strong rebuke if an adult had seen me. I rested, waiting for my favourite moment of the day before I reconnected with the characters in my book. The five o'clock show was about to begin.

Let me explain. Rows of spider lilies, or 'five o'clock lilies' as they were called, hugged the path to the gate. The white, spidery, elongated leaves formed a nest for the stems, each crown bearing four or five flowers. At around five o'clock every evening the flower heads unfurled their dainty petals in succession until the full beauty of the whole newly-born flower raised its head in glory and basked in the gentle warmth of the evening sun. Their full fragrance lasted all evening and the petals stayed unfurled until the following morning. Then the increasing heat of the day forced the fronds to fold back into an elegant oval shape once more. The following evening the process was repeated. The magic spectacle of these plants unfolding in front of my very eyes never failed to delight me. Thanks to Peter's love of gardening we were treated to a wonderful display in our front garden all the time.

Sometimes Charlie crept up on me when I was engrossed in my book, intent on teasing me and sabotaging my peaceful enjoyment. He would wave his hand between my face and my book to attract my attention. I would slap his hand away impatiently and attempt to return to the book's private world as I followed the story, journeying with the characters and sharing their pain and their joy. I was right there with them as they walked through the damp London streets, barely able to pick out the way in the gas-lit cobbled alleys. I was completely immune to the hardness of my rattan chair. The real fading light outside failed to stop my journey, until the words on the page began to play hide and seek and my pupils were reaching their maximum dilation; then Mum's sharp call would cut in. 'Hey, Lily, you are going to spoil your eyesight straining like that. Come inside and wait for the light to be lit before you go on!' I could hear her tutting as she shook her head in disbelief. Reluctantly I slipped the torn newspaper bookmark in to mark my place.

My obsession with reading almost ended in disaster – a potential second house fire but this time not caused by an outsider with a score to settle. The lack of an electricity supply meant that we relied on kerosene oil lamps and lanterns. As dusk spread its grey fingers every evening around six, it signalled that the lantern-lighting ceremony needed to be put in motion. It was deemed a privilege to perform this ritual once one was considered old enough and responsible enough to do so. A set routine like a soldier's orders was followed: no deviation was tolerated. The lantern required a special wick, a 'mantle' made of strong silken thread woven like lace. A glass globe then encased the magical mantle. It was a marvel that such delicate-looking material possessed so much strength, expanding when lit to become bulbous and luminous. The bright white light thus produced was enough to light up our entire lounge, where the family congregated in the evening. A rounded metal base held the kerosene oil. In order to maintain a uniform brightness, a piston attached to the base had to be pumped with air periodically, and only designated persons were allowed to touch the by now very warm base.

Despite the closed doors and windows, insects buzzed around the white glare, pitting their bodies against the hot chimney and frying to death. Their dried limbs wreathed the rim of the gaslight, and their lifeless wings fluttered in the slightest of breezes. The rest of the house was lit in a ghostly yellowish light provided by smaller kerosene oil lamps hung on nails at strategic places on corridor walls. Their chimney glass too often enclosed dead flies that had had their lives singed away as they were lured by the yellow glow.

The mantle was replaced at approximately five-day intervals, depending on how much the light had been used. Bedtime was fixed at nine o'clock out of economic necessity, as even kerosene oil came at a price. After lights out, I was forced to find alternative methods if I wanted to carry on reading – strictly forbidden to youngsters, this was usually candlelight. If I was desperate, Dad's torch (used occasionally on his night prowls) was borrowed without his knowledge or consent and so it had to be used sparingly.

To lessen the chance of detection I pulled up the bed sheet right over me and then flicked the torch's switch to light up my opened book. This silent, private world was disturbed only by the rustle of the pages as I turned them over. My eyes quickly adjusted to the glare of the mustard yellow light. When the need for sleep stole up on me, the torch found a home under my pillow, wedged between it and the wall.

Whilst I was totally absorbed in my book one night the battery ran out of juice. Anxious to pick up where I had left off, I resorted to candlelight, the lit candle stationed on a wooden stool beside my bed. To obtain the maximum light, I positioned the stool so close to the bed that the flame flickered with every turn of a page. The gripping story kept me reading for far longer than I should have done. The flickering light across the page had a mesmeric effect and words started to slip away from me... my eyelids drooped shut. The candle continued to burn whilst I slept, my fingers clutching my book to my chest.

I was in a deep sleep when it was time to wake for my early morning studies. It felt as if I had just dropped off when the persistent shouts of my Dad's raised voice stirred me. I had drawn the latch on my door to stop my family discovering my night-time habit, and having failed to wake me by tapping on my bedroom door, Dad had resorted to a different method. The partitions between rooms only came up part way, not reaching the high ceilings, as adequate circulation was necessary to cool the air. Dad was not relishing balancing on tiptoe on a wooden stool to peer over the six-foot high partition, as he attempted to rouse me with his yells.

In dawn's emerging light a solid pool of wax could be seen, surrounding a tell-tale twenty-cent-size charred hole, in the centre of the stool. The reality of a near-miss fire in the middle of the night was all too obvious.

'Lily, Lily, *yenderi, yenderi* (wake up, wake up)! Look at the stool, you silly girl, look how it has burnt. My God, you could have caused a fire and killed us all!'

Dad was rightly furious. He expected an eleven-year-old to behave much more responsibly. This was only the second time I had been the recipient of my father's anger. The first I had not warranted, thanks to Anna, but this was certainly due to my own carelessness. The burnt smell from the stool was a stark reminder of my carelessness. Unable to stomach breakfast, I dressed quickly and quietly and left for school subdued, deeply regretting my immature behaviour for the rest of the day. When I returned to my room after school, the offending stool had been removed. Everyone seemed to be avoiding me, increasing my feeling of isolation.

My night-time reading came to an immediate halt. Dad instigated a ban: no more storybooks for me, only schoolbooks were allowed. The family was placed under strict orders to report any breach of this rule. I was mortified by what had happened, my throat dry, my breaths short and sharp. Dad's disappointment proved a bitter pill to swallow: it was devastating, and my eyes were constantly filled with tears waiting to spill. I wandered around like a lost soul, utterly dejected. The family seemed oblivious to my misery, as I sat with my homework spread on the dining table, unable to tackle it with my usual enthusiasm. I could hear my brothers playing in the front yard, their squeals of laughter wafting over, but I felt no compulsion to join them. My make-believe world, my means of survival in a crowded house, was denied me, and it was all my own doing. It was so difficult to accept.

I didn't give up though. My mind seethed with ideas to outwit the ban and I devised a plan. I placed a book strategically on the kitchen windowsill, picking it up on my way as I announced to whoever was in the vicinity, 'I am going to the toilet if anyone is looking for me.' The toilet was situated just a short distance from the kitchen. Luckily no one seemed to notice my subterfuge. Trips to the outside toilet became a pilgrimage.

Our primitive toilet or latrine was a three foot wide, unpainted wooden hut on stilts, with three steps, worn in the centre by constant use, leading to a latched wooden door. One squatted over an open hole in the floor hugging one's bent knees – quite a precarious position to maintain. A big black plastic bucket was positioned strategically beneath the hole, and its contents emptied in the early hours of the morning by 'night soil collectors'. The Untouchables, the caste employed for this special task, were at the bottom end of the hierarchy of workers, a group excluded from mainstream society and mostly employed in poorly paid, often dangerous and unskilled work. They carried out the jobs that no one else was prepared to do. They were socially segregated, barred from interacting with persons of higher castes. The staleness of poverty clung to them tenaciously. One might have hoped that having migrated to another country this segregation would not be strictly adhered to, but it was, testament to the fact that the caste system was alive and flourishing, imported from India and practised in Malaysia. The collectors would arrive at around four in the morning to avoid the early risers, and discreetly cart the night soil away.

I took my time in the toilet, one hand cupping my knee whilst the other clutched my book. I became totally immersed; neither the flies buzzing in and out of the hole, drawn to the decomposing faeces, nor the foul smell emanating from the bucket spoilt my concentration. The crude hut became my sanctuary for a few precious minutes. I was taking a chance, so my ears were constantly alert for the sound of advancing footsteps that would require me to make way for someone else.

Our toilet paper consisted of newspapers torn into rough squares, threaded on string and hung on a nail inside the toilet. It was a tricky manoeuvre trying to balance my book at the same time. After a visit to the toilet, I had to traipse along to our outdoor bathroom to wash myself clean. My book had to be hidden from the next customer so I pushed it into the waistband of my skirt. A tinful of water from the concrete tub had to be splashed over the rough cement floor that had absorbed the cruel heat of the sun before I could squat to wash myself. Then I retreated to the house and reluctantly secreted my book away once more.

Dad woke up half an hour early every morning to indulge in his early morning pastime before getting ready for work, shouting out his wake-up call loudly as soon as his alarm sounded. 'Time for studies, come on, wake up!' Trying desperately to shake the sleep from our eyes, hot from our beds, Charlie and I shivered in the early morning chill. Early morning was popularly believed to be the best time to study, hence these rude awakenings every weekday morning. Yawning in protest, we pulled out our books. I could hear Anna in the kitchen preparing breakfast for Dad: the fire being stoked, the flat iron griddle being heated up, and the sizzle of the first *dosai* as the frothy batter hit the hot iron. Charlie, whose interest in studying was almost non-existent, expressed his protest by leaning back in his chair, his book lying open idly on the dining table that doubled as our desk while he crooked his knees under the table ledge for support. Rubbing his hands across his eyes and yawning he proceeded to tilt his chair still further, precariously balancing it on its hind legs. Then he cracked his knuckles, which sounded like twigs being trampled on. An irritated Dad gave a despairing shake of his head.

Checking the time, Dad tuned in to All India Radio, raising the volume and adjusting the reception so that he could listen to the latest political news from his motherland. 'Hey, Charlie, get on with your studies, I didn't wake you up for you to sit and yawn. Lily *ma*, see what he is reading and help him.'

I muttered under my breath. 'What's the point, Charlie is not interested anyway.'

I tried to do as Dad asked, but soon gave up when his attention was fully engaged by the news. Fresh from his bed, bare-chested, with his *sarong* tied round his midriff and mouth slightly open in concentration, he turned the radio knob carefully, and grating sounds tickled our ears as he located the right wavelength. He was glued to the news and we watched as his whole body reacted.

'*Aiey-yo*, the stupid man has no brains, how could he do that? *Che, che*. They will never learn.'

He threw his hands in the air with frustration, his eyes flashing in indignation. Not wishing to incur his wrath we lowered our faces into our books, suppressing our giggles behind our hands. I grabbed my opportunity; opening the largest schoolbook I possessed, I reached sideways, my fingers groping in my school bag for my storybook, and stealthily placed it inside the open spine. I became so engrossed that I even earned an appreciative nod from Dad as he passed by to get ready for work. Although I squirmed inside with guilt, my book proved too much of a draw. I continued to impress everyone with my studiousness, and nobody seemed to be aware of my subterfuge!

After a few months, as my grades remained favourable, my father relented.

'*Appa*, pleee-ease can I read my books again?' The please was pleadingly elongated.

Dad nodded, head inclined slightly, pretending to contemplate; an indulgent smile played around his generous mouth.

'Yes, you can but remember this – you can only read for a few hours after you have finished your homework. Otherwise the ban will be implemented again immediately. No reading in bed either. That is strictly not allowed as we don't want a repetition, do we?'

I nodded quickly in agreement, elated. I'd got away with it! With lightning speed I fled to my room where a brand new book was burning a hole in my schoolbag. I read and re-read my books. I knew the endings yet I read them as though I didn't. I savoured the details I had missed when I skim-read during the first read, impatient to discover the ending. There was so much magic trapped in the pages, waiting to be discovered again and again. My one regret was my inability to convince my younger brothers to discover these treasures too. There was one exception: my cousin Ignatius, the youngest son of Chocolate *thaatha*'s younger brother, Soosai, the man who had opposed my parent's nuptials. One year younger than me, Ignatius, or Iggy as he was known, shared my passion for books. When our families met up, our heads close together, we excitedly exchanged views about our latest reads.

'I am on the third book in the series.'

'How about the Secret Seven? Have you read the latest, *A Puzzle For The Secret Seven*?'

I had found a fellow bookworm, someone who shared my magical world. We whiled away the time with promises to look out for one another's recommendations.

My crazy reading habits were a great source of leg pulling for my family.

'Hey Lily, remember how you used to pick up and read every piece of scrap paper as you were sweeping the floor, even a torn-up sheet of newspaper didn't escape your scrutiny. How about that time at the dining table?'

This was a well-recounted story; family, friends and relatives, all had their ears bent while I squirmed visibly. I had returned from school one day and sat down to lunch. Shafts of sun from the window fell across the blue Formica table, picking up the golden lines and squiggles incorporated into the design of the tabletop. My lunch companion, my book, emerged from my bag as usual. I was so engrossed in it that my family had crept up behind me and removed my plate without my knowledge. Eyes still firmly fixed on my book, I reached my cupped hand towards what I thought was my plate for another mouthful; but my already food-encrusted fingers hit the Formica with a soft thwack, sending a spray of curry covered rice across the table. Peals of laughter came from my siblings who were hiding behind the triple-jointed screen; their laughing faces poked round the green and white flowered cotton panels and I couldn't help but join in with their mirth as I realised how foolish I must have looked.

Always ready for a new challenge, I tried my hand at writing. Reading was of course the source of my inspiration, providing me with the material for my narrative. I sacrificed one of my school exercise books, writing my name on the cover, and the subject, My Story.

The story took place in England, a country I ached to visit. It centred on a schoolgirl who became a member of a secret society. She was drawn into all sorts of adventures with her fellow members, as they solved various mysteries in their neighbourhood. Food and drink flowed; beautiful clothes were worn. She lived in a village in the suburbs of London in a pretty thatched cottage with a latched gate to its driveway. Her fellow detectives hung about chatting by the gate. The front garden was filled with sweet-smelling roses, which her father bent over with pruners in his hand. An aproned, rosy-cheeked and buxom mother stood by the doorway inviting everyone in to a table groaning with plates of dainty sandwiches, jam-filled sponge cake, chocolate biscuits and tea in china cups. I revelled in the fact that I shared my story with no one. I could give free rein to my imagination, basking in it to my heart's content, but no one else was allowed into this imaginary world.

I tried my hand at composing poetry too but my endeavours were pathetic. I came up with four lines that caused endless sibling guffaws when used to accompany skipping and hopscotch jumps:

'My name is Lily
I am very silly
I went to Delhi
I bought a chilli...'

The expectation was that we would pursue careers that would bring in much-needed cash for the family. Indian families strongly believe that entering the professions was the only path to take. Professionals were guaranteed high earners, commanding respect from everyone and providing one with a good quality of life. I grew up with this traditional outlook and, wanting to do well for the family, it was a natural progression to set my sights on becoming a doctor. So I channelled all my energies into my studies rather than my writing. An early ambition to follow in the footsteps of Enid Blyton had to be shelved. Dad's ambition for me took precedence, and his aspirations became mine.

23

'Nature's bounty gatherer...'

Home Remedies

'Marie, Theresa and her family are coming to live with us. Our son-in-law has had a transfer to Kuala Lumpur to work in the registration department.'

I followed Dad into the kitchen, where Mum was busy frying tinned sardine with chopped green chillies, hand squashed tomatoes, sliced onions and garlic to serve as part of our evening meal. Holding the ladle, dripping with the thick rich red sauce, she turned round and treated us to her rare smile.

'He must have had a promotion then. We had better get the back room prepared for them.'

It was more than three years since our beloved eldest sister, Theresa, had left home and we so looked forward to her return. She came with three added bonuses: cute little curly-haired Charles, now two years old (he had miraculously been spared from contracting my smallpox), plus her one-year-old daughter Mally and baby Winston. Initially Theresa blossomed in the company of her siblings. The house was bursting with people and children scuttled everywhere. My youngest brothers, six-year-old Chandra and two-year-old Benny, had new playmates whilst Charlie and I, at seven and nine, were expected to be their responsible elders. I learnt to master the art of mixing bottle feeds for baby Winston.

'*Akka*, show me how to wind him; he is going to be sick.'

Nappy-changing and rocking the baby to sleep became part of my daily routine. Anna had reached marriageable age at eighteen but there was no knight in shining armour to whisk her away; instead, her responsibilities increased with many more mouths to cook for, clean and wash. Sibling rivalry between the two older sisters started to emerge and the tight-knit fabric of family life began to reveal holes and gaps that my mother desperately kept trying to fill.

I sensed a tense atmosphere within the household. I caught Anna whispering to Mum and they swiftly changed the subject as I approached. I was shooed away. Theresa seemed unusually quiet too, but I was too young to be caught up in household politics. My schoolwork kept me occupied; the rest of the time was spent in the youngsters' enjoyable company.

Our evening meal times adopted a new pattern, becoming more hierarchical. There were two sittings at the dining table: the men were served first followed by the women and children. Typical of large families, the children's food usually consisted of an amalgamation of what had been cooked. A large aluminium bowl would be filled with rice, gravy and vegetables mixed together, which was then shaped into individual balls.

'Line up everybody and put your hands out.'

With cupped hands held out the children stood in line to receive their food whilst the younger ones were hand-fed. A portion of rice and gravy was fed into their open mouths with the right hand whilst the left, cupped underneath, caught any spills. Then a deft sweep of the hand wiped the mouth clean, catching up any food that clung to it. I was willing to feed others but never to be fed myself in this way. I could never bear to have my food handled by anyone else.

'You are so strange, Lily, why have you got to be so different?'

I shrugged my shoulders. 'I just don't like my food to be all squidged up. I can eat from my own plate, thank you.'

With more mouths to feed, foraging took on added importance. The frequent thunderstorms, especially during the night, provided a harvest for the next day: I knew what daybreak would bring. Although I enjoyed the end product I rather resented being placed in charge of gathering it. After thunderstorms there were always plenty of succulent wild mushrooms in two particular areas. One was within our boundary to the back of the house, and so within easy reach, but the second, on the embankment, lay just outside our bougainvillea hedge. Sleepily and with a great deal of coaxing, Charlie and I rolled out of bed and picked up the rattan baskets that Mum held out to us, then set off to do her bidding. Charlie was all for creeping back to the house and getting back into bed, so I had to shout at him and give him a nudge now and again to wake him up.

'Come on you lazy lump! We have to be quick or other people will pick them first.'

I was growing up now, a young lady of nine going on ten, and had begun to take an interest in my appearance. As I bent to pick the mushrooms, I felt conspicuous in my crumpled, hand-me-down dress, the waist too high and the hem lengthened by a couple of inches. I passed my hand over the creases desperate to smooth them out. The early morning workers walked and cycled past us on the narrow path as we bent over our task. I finger-combed the top of my rumpled hair and patted the knotted single plait that hung down my back, conscious that it had not seen a comb at such an early hour in the morning.

I worked hurriedly, eyes focused on the ground, trying to ignore the passers-by and willing myself into invisibility. The fresh damp smell of the mushrooms hit my nostrils. Charlie continued to protest and somehow contrived to pick the least: my cheeky brother always seemed to get the better of me.

A clear stream ran at the bottom of our grandfather's estate, and Mum sent us to gather a special type of snail that could be found in the shallow stream. So I trotted off to Chocolate *thaatha*'s plantation with my brothers. I loved walking barefoot in the cool clear water, scanning for the grey-shelled snails, then dropping them carefully into an aluminium pail with a few inches of water in the bottom. Sometimes I sat at the water's edge under the dappled shade cast by the casuarina tree and daydreamed while my brothers splashed about in the water. The white washed pebbles twinkled in the morning sun. Turquoise dragonflies hovered over the shallow crystal clear water. My brother's excited shrieks brought me back to earth. Gathering up the boys and the snails we had picked, we walked back along the dirt track and proudly presented Mum with our bounty. I watched fascinated as she cooked the snails in the hot embers of our clay stove, using a large safety pin to prise the succulent flesh from the shells before smothering them in a fragrant garlicky sauce for dinner.

Ritually at the end of the meal Dad and his soul-mate, my brother-in-law, settled into their chairs, rubbing their hands together as though they had arrived at a gathering where their political prowess was going to be tested. They came alive during their political discussions, regardless of whether the topic covered was local, global or Indian. A peculiarity of their relationship was that they never addressed one another directly or formally, as a mark of respect. No names were used.

The Indian custom was to use a complicated system to identify relationships within their families. One always knew the relationship, by family titles. We used respectful terms to address our siblings: *Akka* was 'older sister'; *Annan* meant older brother; *Thanggachi*, younger sister; and *Thambi*, younger brother. We also had various words for aunts and uncles: Mother's family used different terms to father's – *Maamma* and *Athhai* as opposed to *Chitappa* and *Chinammah*. To complicate matters, first names were avoided as far as possible when addressing an elder or anyone who warranted special respect. Everyone else was just called Auntie or Uncle.

At social and family gatherings, the men tended to gather in groups in the sitting room, while the women gravitated to the dining area and exchanged family news and jokes. There was therefore a distinct division between the sexes. Any decision-making was – outwardly at least – made by the men; women tended to blend into the background, letting the men speak. Mum never spoke directly to her son-in-law. Instead, she used intermediaries to relay her conversations, provoking no end of teasing from the family. Arokiasamy respected her adherence to the traditional rules. Mum always made a special effort for him on his visits during the early years of his marriage, preparing tasty meals that she knew he especially enjoyed. He in turn expressed his compliments to her via his wife.

In view of all these conventions, much throat-clearing preceded the regular conversations between my father and my brother-in-law. They instinctively seemed to know when a comment was directed at them.

'Did you listen to the All India News today? The Prime Minister has just announced he is going to tackle corruption in India.'

'Yes, yes. It is about time someone took the initiative, and those chaps in the government offices are too much, you know. They need to be controlled. Throw them into jail, for goodness' sake. No excuses! You throw one fellow in and the others will behave; otherwise, they will carry on and on.'

Both Dad and my brother-in-law enjoyed their hours of political discussions as they put the world to rights. Dad drummed the table initially as he spoke but soon took to tapping on it more emphatically to emphasise his points. Occasionally he banged the table with his fist to emphasise a particularly passionate message. Dad thrived on political argument. If he was the encyclopaedia of Indian politics, speaking at breakneck speed, my brother-in-law was the dictionary. He was the younger gentler version of Dad; he broadened Dad's knowledge and gave his views context. Almost without exception the two of them were in agreement with each other's point of view. At family gatherings they often fell into political conversation the moment they sat down at the table, exchanging news and views about their beloved motherland.

When Indian men were introduced to one another, the first questions asked were invariably as follows:

222

'Which village do you came from?'

'Are you married?'

'Are your wife and children with you, or still in India?'

These then led to exchanges about the families they were mutually acquainted with as they explored the invisible bonds that linked people to one another, through their caste, village, country of origin and dialects.

When Dad could afford it, he subscribed to the Indian weekly paper, scanning it from cover to cover. He sat up with sudden indignation.

'Listen to this!' he exclaimed, setting off another discussion.

He was a true patriot and held the Nehru family and the Mahatma in high regard, needing little persuasion to join the Indian National Army during the war years. Meanwhile Mum was just happy to be surrounded by her beloved grandchildren, ideal playmates for her own younger children. Her tuneful hymn-singing seemed to rise a notch as she went about her daily tasks.

'How about rubber balls? Anyone want to come with me to the rubber plantation?'

Chandra and I took up Charlie's offer. Our natural surroundings provided us with hours of free entertainment – for example we made the most of our proximity to the rubber plantations. Treading on a carpet of dead leaves and low-growing ferns, we stood on tiptoe to reach the ends of the sour and rancid-smelling latex strings, twisting them round our index fingers and pulling them down. These strings were the residues left behind after the precious early morning harvest had been collected. Rolling them into tight balls, we wandered from tree to tree: the more we collected, the bigger the balls and the higher the bounce.

With the aid of a stick we also unearthed the seeds that had popped from their pods, rubbing one side of each seed against some sharp grit to flatten it. Then they made ideal counters for board games. Five of these polished seeds were shaken inside a cupped fist and, on the count of three, deftly flicked onto the cement floor so that they spread apart when they landed. Throwing one seed up into the air, we had to swiftly gather the rest. The player to gather the most seeds in one go was declared the winner.

Another pastime entailed making homemade plaster sine, water mixed with the plentiful clay soil that surrounded our house. Playing about with the squidgy clay, we fashioned miniature pots, pans, plates and cups and then laid them out to dry in the baking sun. We created our own miniature cooking utensils to play 'house' with our visiting cousins during our school holidays and our neighbour's children,

Moorthy and Parameswari. The adults by now seemed to have settled their differences. They were on nodding terms and we certainly held no grudges against our playmates. Moorthy was always good fun despite having acquired some of his mother's feistiness, always wanting to be the leader. Standing there proudly, clad in his khaki shorts, his bare chest would swell as he announced 'I'm going to be a lawyer when I grow up'. His ambition was no surprise. My heart skipped a beat as I gazed up at him. He was known to be an exceptional student. Standing next to him, Parameswari – or Parames as we addressed her – was a quiet little mouse, happy to take orders. Perhaps she had inherited her father's traits.

Multi-coloured rubber bands decorated our arms as we lined up to play another favoured game. Rubber bands were thrown from measured distances and when the bands landed overlapping one another we were able to claim the overlapped bands thus swelling the colourful bands on our arms.

Most evenings Moorthy and Parameswari called out from their side of the fence.

'Charlie, Chandra, want to play "counta-county"?'

Counta-county was just a matter of using two sticks of unequal length. The shorter of the two was placed over a burrow dug into the ground, then the longer stick was used to lever the smaller one out, flicking it as far as one could. I followed Chandra's efforts as the smaller of his sticks made a wide arc against the shimmering heat of the evening sun before landing just a few inches short of Charlie's winning spot. The owner of the stick that landed the furthest distance from the hole was pronounced the overall winner. Two sticks salvaged from the garden thus provided a huge amount of entertainment and much chortling laughter, as our shining bodies dripped with sweat.

Life would have been plain sailing if it had all been fun and games. But every now and again, to maintain our general wellbeing, we were forced to endure barbaric but necessary ordeals. A lack of affordable footwear forced us children to run around the grounds of the house barefoot, so we picked up parasites with ease. Amongst those that thrived in the gut was the dreaded long worm. A purging ritual occurred every six weeks. In nervous flight mode we stood in line while Mum and Dad waited at the ready with the purging medication: there was no escape. The medicine was a concoction of sorts mixed with castor oil. The stomach-churning smell hit the nostrils. Noses were pinched, mouths forcibly opened. The smallest children were held down on the ground, their mouths pinched open between thumb and index finger, and amidst much spluttering and flailing arms and legs, the revolting liquid was poured down their throats. The copious amounts of water we were then forced to drink produced the desired results: the familiar stomach cramps and rumblings heralded the beginnings.

We sprinted to the toilet. Those who couldn't make it in time, especially the little ones, squatted over the open drain at the back of the house. Mum and Anna then undertook the unenviable task of checking the faeces for round worms. Wriggling fat worms, half in and half out, almost making one faint, had to be tugged free by hand.

Theresa could never stomach this job. Of delicate constitution, she had a tendency to heave and always kept well away from any mess. Depending on the severity of the infestation, the unlucky ones had to undergo a further purge the following week. This process was often quite severe, leaving us totally drained of energy, but it was a necessary evil. The treatment did improve our general health and we always developed healthy appetites after our de-worming sessions. I am now a keen gardener but the sight of a wriggling worm still sends shudders down my spine and makes the tips of my fingers tingle. How our childhood memories shape our adult behaviour.

Funds permitting, the equally dreaded daily intake of cod liver oil had to be tolerated. The cream-coloured viscous liquid was contained in a large bottle, sticky with drips, smelling very strongly of fish. Arms held behind my back, tongue out and eyes shut tightly, I would swallow the spoonful as swiftly as I could but the resulting burps tasted and smelt strongly of fish. The effect would last all morning; faces were turned away and noses pinched as we left a strong fishy smell in our wake.

Common illnesses were cured with a combination of ancient Indian Ayurvedic principles and those of Chinese medicine, where the emphasis lay on restoring the body's balance. Illnesses were divided into hot and cold types, similar to hot and cold foods. 'Hot' illnesses were treated with a cold intake of food and vice versa. To this end weekly oil baths, considered body coolers, were undertaken by the older generation and (thankfully for me) meted out only to the boys as well. A cooling paste of soaked green beans was massaged into their reluctant scalps while fragrant oil was rubbed into their wriggling torsos. Theresa, with her *sari* tucked away from her lower legs, bent over her sons and poured sun-warmed water over their bodies to the accompaniment of squeals of protest. My younger brothers and nephews stepped out slick from their oil baths, desperately trying to clear their eyes of green pea skin, whilst I gleefully stood a respectful distance away, arms folded, thankful not to have to endure yet another ritual myself.

The number of children was growing fast. My mother had added the tenth child to our family with the arrival of Irene, whilst Theresa's brood now included Arthur, born in 1958. A house full of children was never dull.

'Mum, Charles is being selfish; he doesn't want to let me play with him.'

'Lily Aunty, can you tell Mally *akka* to share her sweets with me?'

'I didn't break it, Uncle Charlie did.'

Everyone blamed one another for any misdeeds. Squeals of laughter mingled with cries of frustration and annoyance. Innocent Winston, although very endearing with his wide forehead and wavy hair that refused to stay down, developed an extremely irritating habit of pushing himself forward whenever we gathered in a group, demanding centre stage. Charles had mastered some tricks making intricate designs using rubber bands. He hooked his fingers together and expanded the very elastic rubber band. Everyone ringed round Charles to watch his performance.

'Winston, stop pushing dah, look you have stepped on Arthur's toes, now he is crying. Why don't you stand back like everyone else? Go, go and join the circle.'

When the group disbanded, Winston performed his party piece: he could turn his eyelids inside out so that all one could see was pink veined flesh.

'Look, I have pink eyes.'

'No you haven't, you silly, if you don't stop messing around with your eyes you will go blind.' Seldom was a truer word uttered and one that was immensely regretted.

We hung our heads in shame and guilt when we found out why Winston had this habit of pushing himself forward. One day he arrived home with a letter from his teacher.

'Mummy, I was told to give you this letter by my teacher.'

Expecting it to be a letter of complaint relating to Winston's awkward behaviour, Theresa opened it, and read its contents silently. Her eyes filled with tears. She put her arms round her perplexed son.

'I am so sorry, none of us knew. Why didn't you tell us?'

He continued to gaze up at his mother with a quizzical expression.

'Why didn't you say that you cannot see properly? Why didn't you tell your teacher that you couldn't read what was written on the blackboard?'

He flashed his familiar grin. 'I managed to read what was written on the blackboard by walking up to it, so I didn't need to tell anyone.'

This explained Winston's peculiar behaviour. Suitably chastened, we apologised to him, but dear stoical Winston did not set great store by what had happened and laughingly retorted, 'It doesn't matter *lah*, really!'

Winston's thick-rimmed glasses transformed his little eyes into those of a startled owl, the pupils thrown into surprised focus. His vulnerability was emphasised tenfold. Without exception, we had unfairly treated a trusting and thoroughly lovable little boy. Those thick lenses through which his innocent eyes now peered did little to appease my guilt. But my bond with my sister's children strengthened. I was 'older sister' to cousin Charles, just six years my junior. The children would search me out if grit lodged in their eyes whilst out playing and I would prise apart their lower and upper lids and blow into their eyes until the offending particle was dislodged. When Theresa and her husband enjoyed a night out at the cinema it was Aunty Lily who made up the formula, fed baby Arthur, burped him, and rocked him to sleep. I became adept at dispensing Woodward's gripe-water from a metal conch (a shell-shaped container), pinching his nose while tipping the contents drop by drop down his protesting gullet. I was drawn into my mothering role quite naturally.

Ample nooks and crannies for heart pounding games of hide and seek abounded in the large grounds surrounding our house. Well covered Charlie and skinny Chandra, opposites in temperament too, quarrelled more than most. Brawn was pitted against brain. Charlie was often outwitted by Chandra, thin as a bean, left weakened by an early grapple with whooping cough. Chandra incited Charlie's wrath so much that he sometimes resorted to pursuing his younger brother with a sharp knife, a *parang*. Quick-witted Chandra fell to the ground in a faint. Shouts of help from a frightened Charlie drew Theresa and me to a rigid and still Chandra, while a petrified Charlie stood by, *parang* in hand, pupils dilated in fear.

'*Akka, akka*, I think Chandra is dead! I have killed him!' Tears coursed down his face. He knelt at Chandra's side, desperately trying to revive him. 'Wake up Chandra, hey come on *dah*.'

Theresa and I positioned us, ready to move Chandra with a log roll. Just as our hands touched his body, a faint sigh rose from his lips and his body rolled over gently and his eyes opened slowly as though from a deep sleep. 'Where am I? What happened?'

He was clearly shamming. Guilt-ridden Charlie looked terrified: sweat broke out from his frowning forehead and his eyes pleaded for forgiveness.

'Well, you went too far, didn't you?' said Theresa, winking at me and pursing her lips to stop herself from laughing out loud. I had to turn my face away to hide my own amusement.

'I didn't mean to hurt him, just frighten him; I wanted to teach him a lesson.'

'All right, get up Chan. Lily; give him a drink of water. Behave yourselves, the both of you. If *appa* had been here you would both be in a lot of trouble.'

Theresa's remarks were directed at both her brothers as she wagged her index finger at them, though she flashed a quick smile at naughty Chandra. We played along with his deception, determined to curb Charlie's tendency to play with dangerous knives. A quick drink of water seemed to restore Chan, who was anxious not to overplay his hand, and the brothers shook hands. Promises were extracted from both to indulge in harmless games in the future. A repentant Charlie was subdued around Chan, giving in easily to his demands. The younger boy was quick to take advantage of the situation, much to the family's amusement.

A sturdy four-poster bed, a legacy from a British family, took pride of place in our back room. Two sheets of sawn plywood were nailed in place instead of a mattress. My younger brothers' bodies uttered no protest. A thin cotton sheet, torn into three equal pieces with rolled and hemmed edges, and three half-size pillows were sufficient for their night-time comfort. Bedtime was strictly at 8 p.m. for my younger brothers. They were too energetic to fall asleep immediately so against a backdrop of cotton sheets rigged up to the frame of the four-poster bed, Chan commenced a pantomime performance to entertain his brothers. His voice would dip and rise, taking on mysterious cadences to imitate women engaged in fights in the marketplace 'like fighting fisherwomen'. Hurriedly stifled shrieks of laughter from gullible Charlie landed him in predictable trouble. Accomplished actor Chan feigned sleep if Peter ventured into the bedroom to investigate. But Chan's luck ran out quickly. After a few nights of Charlie's giggles, Peter was determined to discover the real culprit, so he changed tactics and stealthily peered over the partition wall. Chandra was caught in the act, in every sense.

'So, you are the real culprit, and Charlie is the innocent party. You had us all fooled Chan.'

Thus Chan's night-time theatrics came to an abrupt halt, though he still continued to hold daytime shows to amuse the whole family.

Baby sister Irene, the protected youngest child, was not to be left out, and provided her own repertoire. Her tiny feet shoved into our shoes, she tottered round the house, displaying her triumphant smile and undeterred by frequent falls. She was the darling of the house, a living and kicking doll, who won our admiration and indulgence. Irene was everywhere: she often positioned herself in her favourite niche between Peter's parted knees and swung on his V-shaped *sarong*. Peter swayed his knees rhythmically creating a swinging movement, much to our little sister's squeals of delight. Then he would jig his knees up and down and move his head from side to side, his lips moving in time to a song in his head. When Irene demanded even more attention, Peter would place her on his lap and uncurl her spine gently over his knees and down to his toes.

'Down, down, down you go!'

Then he would tickle her stomach to the sound of her electrifying squeals and chuckles.

Irene's favourite pastime however was kneeling in front of the altar, her head covered with a screwed-up handkerchief, hands clasped and head bent forward. Then she uttered a series of unintelligible words, mimicking our family prayers. She repeated the grown-ups' after prayers greeting. Having tested out the phrase, Irene then rose to her feet and faced her bemused audience. She held the palms of her hands together and bowed, greeting us in Tamil: '*Theetham 'pa, theetham 'ma.*' (This should have been: *Thostram appa, Thostram ammah.*) We hugged one-year-old Irene with pride, and loved her yet more fiercely for her childish earnestness and determined attempts to impress us.

Chocolate *thaatha*'s house and land was eventually bought by his younger brother. Our *Chinna thaatha*'s (younger grandfather's) eldest daughter had moved into the big house with her family. The estate was only a fifteen-minute walk away, allowing me to spend whole days at weekends and during the holidays in the welcome presence of cousins Archie, Rita and their baby brother Anthony. I looked forward to their young Uncle Iggie's (my reading companion) visits. The grounds reverberated with our squeals as we played cops and robbers, eyes shut to the end of a count to ten. Like trained retrievers, we galloped to unearth the robbers who had found safety within the large grounds, making sure that we avoided the area around the lethal durian tree.

Appetites were always whetted by these energetic games. My cousins and I spurned home cooked curry and rice for lunch and made for the dell that was a safe distance away from the durian tree. The other fruit trees were quickly scaled by means of young limbs and the spoils gathered. A huge bowl was soon full of chopped up fruit – bananas, guavas, pineapples, succulent pear-shaped pink water *jambus* – all soaked in salty soy sauce, with chopped red chillies to add heat and spoonful's of sugar to add a subtle sweetness. We dipped our fingers into the bowl, relishing the flavour of the sauce-coated fruit, and licked our fingers clean as they tingled with the chilli heat. Mmm-mm.

24

'Ties to Hinduism...'

Thaipusam

Following Christmas in December and noisy Chinese New Year, we looked forward to exotic February and *Thaipusam*. This Hindu festival, attended by all denominations, was celebrated in carnival style in one of Kuala Lumpur's main tourist sites. The great attraction for us was shouting and waving all day at the overflowing trainloads of revellers as they travelled past on the tracks behind our house. Our throats and hands seemed not to tire as we stood on upturned buckets and borrowed stools as the trains tootled and trundled past every half an hour or so, shifting the crowds to and fro. The masses made a pilgrimage to Batu Caves, enormous, cavernous opening situated three-quarters of the way up the broad side of a range of limestone hills that framed the horizon a few miles west of Sentul.

Our family friend Grace's invitation led to my first visit to Batu Caves. At the age of eleven I was still a novice in terms of exciting days out. Grace had gained my mother's permission for me to accompany her on her family outing. Grace was an attractive, fair- skinned, round-faced seventeen-year-old Indian girl, who seemed to utter every sentence at breakneck speed and complete it with a chuckle. An attempt had been made to tame her abundance of wavy black hair into two plaits that tapped her back in time to her hurried steps. Not two days passed without the sight of Grace's cheeky face peering round our front door, followed by her tinkling laughter. The family suspected Grace of having a crush on Peter but to our disappointment, Peter offered no signs of reciprocation. Despite this gentle rebuff Grace maintained her spontaneity, open curiosity and an endearing innate innocence. I was intrigued by her ability to laugh at any situation, a warm honest love shone from her and I regarded her as yet another older sister. It was her house I passed on my visits to my friend Andrea's house.

Grace *akka*'s mother, eldest brother Daniel and his Eurasian girlfriend had planned a day out to celebrate *Thaipusam*. The thought of my going on an outing – me! – made my heart race with excitement. Very early the next morning Grace's family arrived to collect me, as our house was on the way to the railway station where we were to board our train for our journey. We trod the same path I took on my holiday trips to Uncle Leo's.

As we walked, our numbers swelled; Indian families were out in force. We walked in the wake of the scents produced by fragrant jasmine flowers tucked into strands of the women's hair. Red vermilion spots adorned the middle of the foreheads of married ladies whilst the unmarried girls sported elaborately designed sticky-backed paper ones. Everyone talked and laughed, as an undercurrent of excitement gripped us. Having set off early, at eight o'clock, we were surprised to see crowds of people already forming long queues at the ticket counters.

Women, both young and old, added to the magic of the day with their extravagant coloured *saris*. Swathed in the clashing richness of vermilion red, saffron yellow, intense turquoise, electric blues and interwoven gold threads, the women shimmered in the early heat of the sun. The air was heavy with anticipation. Voluble shouts at children, reminders to stay close and stop their squabbling, rang in my ears. The crowds felt the heat. Women fanned themselves with the flappy ends of their *saris*. We joined the queue, and then fought for standing room space on the train as it chug-chugged its way to Batu Caves. As the train passed the back of our house, where the railway track was on raised ground, I waved frantically at the blobs of heads. I could just make out my young brothers waving randomly at everyone. Balanced on wooden stools they peered over our bougainvillea fence. Had they seen me or not? I would have been lost in the general blur of faces, but I was excited to have spotted them.

All along the few miles of the journey we waved constantly to people gathered in their gardens. The momentum of the train decreased as we neared our destination and my heart thumped loudly as I caught a glimpse of the thronging mass ahead. I could see the crowd snaking its way along four abreast where there was barely space for three, as everyone fought their way to the exit. The train came to a shuddering halt and I was thrown against the lady next to me and inhaled the heady perfume of the jasmine flowers that bedecked her head. Everyone made a dash for the doors. Grace, who was responsible for me, held on to my arm tightly and smiled at me as we made our way on to the platform and into the heart of the festivities. 'Keep close to me Lily; I don't want to lose you. There are too many people here.

I promised your mother I would take you back to her safely.'

I was totally overawed by the scene all around me. Street stalls sold every imaginable type of food. Stands overflowed with local handicrafts. Multi-coloured and shaped balloons and colourful kites glittered and shimmered as their tails flapped in the gentle breeze. Sticky-faced children wandered about grasping tightly on to bamboo sticks covered with baby-pink clouds of spun sugar. I looked on longingly at the excited little children as they brandished their treats with satisfied smiles. Kind-hearted Grace sacrificed some of her precious spending money and treated me to a magic pink soft cloud. My fingers shook as I gripped the stick and bit into the surprisingly sweet fluff that melted on my tongue. I took tiny bites to prolong the magic.

Engrossed in this pleasurable activity I nearly choked when we suddenly came across a group of drummers who were beating a rhythm on their drums and chanting their victory cry – *Vel Vel Vetri Vel*! They were heading straight towards us and following close behind were some ghostly-looking men. They were strewn liberally with ash and carried heavily decorated wooden frames, hooked into their flesh by dozens of metal rods. Dressed only in loincloths, their bodies were spiked all over with sharp spears and hooks. They walked one behind the other with glazed, vacant eyes, staring straight ahead.

'Gracie *akka*, who are these people? *Aiey-yo*, look at those spears in their bodies! How come they are not bleeding? I don't want to look, it looks so painful.'

'They don't feel any pain, Lily, they are possessed by God.'

'Really? Oh, I recognise that uncle there, that man, carrying that thing on his head decorated with peacock feathers. There is a spear going through the sides of his mouth – oh look, the spear is going through his tongue as well!'

I was amazed that the man's face showed no signs of pain and there was no sign of blood. I felt sick and repulsed at the same time and clung tightly to Grace's hand.

'He lives in Sentul. We know him.'

'These are people whose prayers have been answered and now they are fulfilling their vows. Don't look like that Lily they feel no pain I promise.' She gave my hand a reassuring squeeze followed by her uplifting tinkle of a laugh. 'They have to be holy and fast for a whole month before they can take part in the procession carrying those *kavadis*.'

I wondered what that uncle had prayed for; whatever it was, he must have had his prayers answered. I watched him but he was oblivious to my scrutiny. Eventually the crowd ahead swallowed him up.

Although I found it frightening to witness the devotees in their various states of what appeared to be extreme torture, I was mesmerised, unable to peel my eyes away from the colours of the rainbow as they twirled on the devotees' shoulders. The procession danced its way past us, the bare feet of the participants raising dust as they thudded them down on the hard-caked dry earth. They were making for the 272 steps that ascended a hundred metres up the limestone hills. The hills consisted of chalky white slopes split by fissures and crevices thick with vegetation: the rents in the tangled curtain of greenery exposed the white of the limestone in horizontal, jagged streaks. Colourful butterflies fluttered about in the bushy undergrowth but monkeys, disturbed by the closeness of the teeming crowd, fled in chattering retreat to the safety of tall, umbrella-shaped tropical trees.

The group of *kavadi* carriers headed straight for the steps, the crowds parting respectfully to let them through. The climb was precarious, with only swaying ropes on each side to grip onto for balance. Grace *akka*'s elderly mother rested against the roundness of a casuarina tree, enjoying its shade and wisely refraining from negotiating the steps. The rest of us followed the crowds who pushed ahead. The knotted handkerchiefs that kept the blazing sun off shiny heads bobbed along in front. Halfway up, curiosity got the better of me and I twisted round to glance down. My head spun dizzily as I looked at the shimmering waves of colour as the crowd behind us inched upwards. The ground fell away. I seemed to be suspended in mid-air and lost my bearings completely. I felt the colour drain from my face. My head felt light and I gasped for air. Sensing that I was about to keel over, Grace *akka* reached out and grabbed me round the waist, holding me to her so that I could sag against her. I broke out in a cold sweat and my knees started to give way but Grace's firm grip round hooked me up.

She guided me to the side, away from the main mass of the climbing crowd; I was unable to grab the swaying rope and let my full weight rest against my saviour. Aware that my underarms were wet, I winced in embarrassment.

Grace *akka* whispered in my ear, 'Don't worry, Lily, take a few deep breaths and when you are ready we will start climbing again. But no more looking down, okay?'

I nodded in agreement, unable to find my voice. My embarrassment deepened in the knowledge that Grace's brother and his girlfriend were stranded behind us – especially as I harboured a heart-stopping admiration for her handsome brother. Grace shooed them on. 'Go on, we will catch you up.'

To my further embarrassment the couple insisted on waiting, as they did not want to lose us among the teeming masses. After resting for a few minutes, I told Grace *akka* that I was ready to climb again. We did not rush but just let the crowds flow past us as we slowly resumed our climb. Once on the move again I took an interest in my surroundings. There were some shadowy caves on our left, from which an overpowering and foul smell wafted across. The smell even overrode that of the perspiring bodies all around us. Noticing my wince, Grace *akka* laughed out loud and then explained patiently that they were bat caves.

'The smell is from the bat shit, the Chinese gather it from time to time and use it to feed their vegetable plantations.'

'Yuck! We buy and eat those vegetables!' I exclaimed in horror.

I was not old enough at that stage to understand the usefulness of organic manure. (On another occasion, after discovering from my Uncle Anthony that human excrement was also used by the Chinese to fertilise their growing vegetables, I vowed secretly never again to eat Pak Choy or Kangkong Keerai, both used commonly in Chinese cuisine, but it was impossible to avoid such commonly used vegetables and I soon forgot my abhorrence.)

As we neared the entrance to the caves, I watched an elderly lady take the last few steps one at a time. She was panting hard and had to place a hand on each thigh in turn as she climbed and rested between steps. She was not giving up; her devotion was driving her and her marathon effort put me to shame.

On entering the cavernous opening I heaved a sigh of relief. I released my grip on Grace *akka*'s hand as she gave one of her tuneful laughs, like a peal of bells finishing on a high note. 'I thought I was going to have my hand wrenched from me! Never mind Lily, you are safe now. It will be easier going down, just keep your eyes on those steps.'

With thumping heart I followed the others deeper into the gloom, my legs stiff from the climb. The magic of the caves soon weaved its spell. On raised platforms against walls freshly painted in saffron yellows and pale blues stood brightly painted statues of Hindu gods and goddesses: Lord Ganesh with an elephant's head, the blue god with his flute performing a balancing act; and Lord Shiva, with his four hands stretched out, two on either side. Colourfully adorned statues decorated every limestone nook, their kohl-lined elongated eyes mesmerising and following us tantalisingly. They were truly mystical with their foreheads streaked with yellow sandalwood paste and their necks draped with elaborate gold and jasmine garlands. Brahman priests, clad in white cotton *veshties*, the holy string ropes looped across their bodies, rang little shiny brass bells and called the devotees to prayers. They dispensed offerings of sweet rice and sweetmeats to the visitors. I soon forgot my earlier fears and became totally immersed in the surreal atmosphere.

The caves themselves had high ceilings and trailing vegetation drooped from protuberances both blunt and sharp that covered the high vaults. Our voices echoed in a ghostly way in their vastness. The flickering candlelight cast strange shadows on the white indented limestone walls. I was very careful as I negotiated my way along the uneven ground. Numerous narrow corridors honeycombed away from the central area. Natural openings in the caves' ceilings allowed shafts of shimmering light through, which brought with them a welcome cooling breeze that made the hair on my arms stand up. The fresh draughts mingled with the air on the ground, heavy with the perfume of incense. I walked between the cool and sultry areas, attempting to avoid the press of the heaving crowds and their braceleted arms by holding both my arms out in front of me to make some space. My arms became sticky as the sweat of the upward journey dried. I was both happy and relieved when we finished the tour of the caves and headed back down the steps, strictly following the advice I had been given to resist the temptation of looking down at the heads of the descending crowds below.

The rest of the day continued in similar fashion; we were surrounded by noise and laughter, an array of colours and exotic scents that vied with the odour of sweat from the crowds. We were watching, fascinated, as some live performers took part in a fire-eating demonstration, when suddenly one of the onlookers keeled over. His whole body shook and then his limbs jerked and went into spasms. Foaming at the mouth followed these contorted movements. The crowds parted as the poor man's feet kicked at the dried grass, sending clouds of dust into the air. I flinched, concluding that this was another devotee going into a trance, but Gracie *akka* put me right. 'Vaa Lily, the poor man is having a fit: come, let's go away from here.'

However, curiosity got the better of me as we walked away and I threw a surreptitious glance or two over my shoulder at the victim. I was relieved to see that the man had stopped his shakes. A few minutes later he dragged himself into a sitting position and leant against a wall, looking dazed and groggy. Chalking this incident up as another new experience, I gave myself a shake and followed Grace once more.

The day passed all too quickly. Exhausted both mentally and physically, we set off on our return journey at twilight having had a magical experience. There had been much to see, plenty to eat, and lots to relate to my family. The day was etched in my memory for a very long time.

25

'Whooping cough and Bed-wetting...'

Sibling Rivalry

Peter's friend Jo arrived one evening armed with a guitar. Protocol did not allow young ladies to be present in the vicinity of young males, particularly non-relatives. However my sisters and I had devised our own strategy: we disappeared into the main bedroom, and took up our positions, eyes glued to peepholes. Confident of their privacy in the sitting room, Jo strummed on his guitar whilst Peter's deep baritone voice boomed out.

'What are they practising for, *akka*?'

'They are taking part in the church concert.'

Peter was a member of our church choir and participated in many church activities. The youth were encouraged to display their talents and a church concert had been organised: this evening's recital was a practice run for two of its participants. I closed my eyes, momentarily visualising the two men on stage performing to an appreciative audience, drawing thunderous clapping and rapturous demands for an encore. I was brought back to the present when Anna and Rosie, whose bodies were pressed close together, stumbled against me as I crouched to the lowest peephole. Listening to the men play was a welcome distraction from our usually uneventful day.

Peter and Jo belted out Harry Belafonte's hit song of 1957, 'Island in the Sun'. Then they discussed how best to stage a dramatic entrance: Peter was to stand on the stage while Jo made his entrance at the run, strumming on his guitar as he did so. Next they practised this idea. Peter sung out the first lines of the song as Jo made his speedy entrance, theoretically coming to a stop on one knee – but instead of arriving at a neat stop, his bent knee hit the puddle that baby sister Irene had created earlier. He slipped and fell sideways with an almighty thud. The stunned look on both the men's faces was so comical that the three of us burst into uncontrollable giggles, leading to even more embarrassment as we had now exposed our presence. Rags were loudly called for and a sheepish Anna, desperately trying to rearrange her expression into one of sympathy, ventured forward to mop up. The rehearsal was abandoned. Jo made a quick getaway and we faced Peter's wrath. But even he could not sustain his irritation for long. We all succumbed to fits of laughter while the real culprit lay cocooned in her cradle. However, Peter did take his revenge. Future visits from his friends remained behind closed doors in his bedroom. Our peepholes were plugged: 'You are not embarrassing me in front of my friends again.'

The older children in large families became natural carers to their younger siblings in addition to being roped in to help with household chores. The extended family also required help at times. Anna, having terminated her education at a young age, was an ideal candidate to help at home and in our relatives' houses too. Theresa had fulfilled the surrogate mother's role before she married but Anna, although glad to help certain relatives, understandably resented being sent to others who had not been too kind to her. She found herself in an unenviable situation. She yearned to get married, gain her independence and set up her own family life. The full extent of her dreams came to light with the accidental discovery of her self-collected trousseau, hidden in a battered old suitcase under the bed.

At three months old, our younger brother Chandra contracted whooping cough, a killer disease of the times. Each time he inhaled, the hollows near his collarbones grew deeper and tinged with blue, fluttering as if a butterfly was trapped under the skin. He struggled to squeeze air into his little lungs, and coughed constantly. Mum checked his phlegm. 'It is not yellow, it is as I feared,' she said, worry furrowing her brow. 'I think your brother has whooping cough,' she declared, with a sad shake of her head.

As a remedy, Mum used a green-leafed creeper, *kaipra valli*, which was used extensively as a cure for colds. The leaves were pounded and the resulting juice fed to the patient. *Kuppa mani*, another green-leaved plant, was pounded and mixed with either honey to soothe coughs or salt as an expectorant for chest congestion.

Mum, Anna and Rosie took turns to sit up with baby Chandra. I had to be dragged off to bed where I suffered nightmares, aware of the gravity of my brother's illness. I did not want to be deprived of another sibling. Prayers were constantly offered. Chan's bouts of coughing fits were paroxysmal; he was nursed upright to prevent him from choking. My heart ached for him, as he grew thin and emaciated.

He constantly turned blue and smelt permanently of Tiger Balm. I sat by his bedside, letting him curl his little finger round my index finger and watching his attempts at a weak smile in between his struggles with the coughing fits. Three anxious months later he pulled through to everyone's great relief, but Chan's limbs refused to fatten. As he grew older his spindly legs developed knock knees and the heels of his canvas school shoes wore away on the insides as his feet sloped in towards each other. It was a small price to pay for his life.

I was seven when baby brother Ben made his appearance and I became an accomplished dhobi. A huge stone boulder stationed by the well served as our scrubbing board. Squares of carbolic soap were lathered into the clothes; the clothes were then bashed against the stone boulder, worn smooth with constant use, to loosen the dirt before being rinsed with water drawn from our well.

Inventive Peter devised a new method of drawing the water up. A thick jute rope was threaded through a pulley, weighted by six bricks fixed to an oblong plank at one end and knotted to a bucket at the other. A certain degree of deftness was required to work this primitive contraption. One drawback to having a well that was situated close to the house was the constant danger it posed to the younger children. They were under strict instructions to avoid the area unless supervised. A heavy wooden cover was always kept in place when the well was not in use. One day, six-year-old Charlie, anxious to impress his younger brothers, climbed on to the lip of the well, managed to grab the rope that the bucket was attached to, manoeuvred himself on to the rim of the bucket and then let go of the rope.

'Look, no hands!' he yelled. Fortunately he just managed to grab the rope again as he fell off the bucket and into the well.

'Charlie! Charlie has fallen into the well! Come quickly!'

Hysterical screams from the horrified onlookers immediately attracted Peter's attention. Our quick-witted brother managed to rescue Charlie by telling him to cling tightly to the rope as he slowly and carefully dragged it in, bringing Charlie up to the surface. The family's complacency had received a real shake. To prevent further mishaps the well was filled in and Peter installed a water pump. It was an expensive outlay but magical while it lasted: the youngsters swung on the pump handle, put their heads under the flow, and drank straight from it. They worked their mouths like fishes then almost choked. Their bare feet squelched in the resulting mud around the pump, but their sport was short-lived. The humidity and heat soon rusted the workings, so the pump seized up and not a trickle could be coaxed out of it. A new well was dug and a bathroom erected in the front garden, and from then on water had to be fetched and stored for use in the kitchen.

Ben was particularly inconsolable one morning. I took my turn to pacify him. I hoisted him onto my left hip and with a shift of my weight placed him in a comfortable position, balancing him and gripping his left arm with my right. His legs splayed on either side of me, feet kicking in the air. Looking for a source of distraction, I spied some movement outside and ventured towards the jackfruit tree. The changing shapes of sunlight as the leaves were rocked gently in a light breeze lighted the circle of bare earth at the foot of the tree. The light also picked out platoons of red ants busily engaged in carrying the carefully sculptured leaves back to their nest. When Ben wriggled unexpectedly I stumbled into the ants' pathway. We had now become a distraction that the ants hadn't bargained for: we had stopped their important work and they took action. The frightened hordes of two-centimetre-long red ants took their revenge – 'get out of our way or we will leave our mark on you, see how you like that!' Like armed troops they swiftly clambered all over me, their sharp pincers striking my exposed skin. As I hopped about in my efforts to shake them off, I let slip my brother, who fell straight into the middle of the heaving nest. Petrified, unable to move, I started to scream:

'*Ammah, ammah, akka*! Quick, quick!'

Thankfully Mum came running, and made a dash for Ben. Working quickly she brushed the ants from Ben's body and ran indoors with the screaming baby, closely followed by me, his tearful, distraught sister. His screams didn't stop until Mum had covered his legs with soothing honey. I, on the other hand, endured a justifiable telling-off whilst receiving similar treatment.

'*Aiyyo*, don't you ever go near that ant hill again. Your poor brother, just look at the bites on his little body.'

I was let off pretty lightly because Mum felt sorry for me too; I must have presented a thoroughly dejected picture. The bites stung and the honey treatment took effect only slowly. I was mortified at having caused my little brother so much pain, however unintentionally. I cooed at him and tickled him, to make him chuckle and to distract him.

Anna was a constant presence in the background of our family life, like an anxious guardian. Sometimes she got things right but at other times drastically wrong. She devised all sorts of ploys to enlist our help with her chores. For example, she enticed us with treats from the grocery shop and make-believe play when she wanted our help to keep our garden clear of fallen leaves.

'Come children, now, you are all *maadus* (cattle). You have to eat grass so pretend to eat the grass, but the grass is actually the leaves that have fallen on the ground. If you are good *maadus* and eat up all your grass, then I will buy you all *kueh kueh*,' (cakes) 'from the Kakka shop.'

Initially we bought into this charade and pretended to be grazing cattle, competing with one another to gather the most grass, down on our hands and knees. But we soon tired of this silly game, particularly when we realised that the rewards did not justify the effort. Anna tried various other ways to enlist our cooperation but in the end she despaired of us and was forced to bend her own back to the task alone. I relented and tried to help her from time to time but my brothers did not.

'No thank you; I don't want your *kueh kueh*. You are so stingy you are cheating us. Five and ten cents' worth is not enough to go round.'

They failed to appreciate that Anna was using her own meagre pocket money to treat us, and that it was hard for her to come by this too.

In the hierarchy of shared housework I was deemed old enough to be given weekend household chores. Stained kitchen utensils required backbreaking scrubbing. The underside of used pots and pans were covered in black soot, a deposit from the burning of firewood. The humid weather also tarnished our brass water pitchers. To remove this, an initial covering of a salt and tamarind pulp concoction was applied and left to dry for a few minutes, then scrubbed off vigorously and the pitchers washed with copious amounts of water to restore their original gleam. It was hard but rewarding work. A row of gleaming brass churns graced the kitchen, bearing witness to my endeavours. The aluminium pots, however, needed even more vigorous scrubbing with harsh wire wool and crude soap. Calluses appeared on my childish palms. The undersides of my close-trimmed nails were coated with black lines. At bath-time, I scrubbed them with soap until my fingers resembled the pickled prunes that I loved to purchase at the Chinese store on my way to school.

Another weekly task was to soap and then rinse our newly purchased, plastic-coated sky-blue three-piece suite. Afterwards it would be leant up against the wall to drip dry, whilst the cement floor in the sitting room dried to a clean shine from its weekly bath.

Fancying a lie-in, I chose to attend the eight-thirty mass on Sundays, which meant I had to stoke the first fire of the day to make porridge for breakfast for all the family. I used scrunched up newspaper tucked among the firewood for the initial start, then blew into the embers to kindle the flames using a blowpipe. The blowpipe consisted of a copper pipe about eight to ten inches long and one and a quarter inches in diameter. Every household possessed a *uuthan golai* to use as bellows.

When the initial flames of the burnt newspaper died down, I blew on the embers until flames were coaxed once more into dancing shapes. When the ash settled, I emerged a grey figure, out of puff and coughing to clear my throat.

On Saturday mornings I could be seen squatting by the cement square round the well to do the laundry. Bars of carbolic soap mixed with water drawn from the well produced soap bubbles that made rainbows in the early morning light. Vigorous scrubbing ensued with coconut fibre brushes – slapping, rinsing, starching and wringing, accompanied with plenty of panting was the norm. Everything was hand washed, hand wrung and hung out to dry in the sun. Peter strung a length of thick jute rope between sturdy wooden posts to act as a washing line. I folded the clothes over the line and the drips from them soon evaporated in the hot sun. Later the dry clothes were sorted into piles, some for ironing, whilst the rest were smoothed flat by hand, folded neatly and stacked into our *almari* on our allocated shelves amongst the mothballs that perfumed our clothes.

Dad's engine-greased work clothes were boiled in large empty kerosene oil tins with sawn-off lengths of wood nailed into the sides for handles. Odd bits of wood gathered from the compound were used to set fires in pits in the open ground to heat up the tins. Scoops of caustic soda in the water loosened the grease. The boiled whites were lifted out on sticks in a haze of steam. A pinch of Reckitt's blue was added with great care to the whites' final rinse to brighten them; a heavy hand would result in a pile of blue clothes.

Our outdoors and school clothes had their creases ironed out with a small, heavy iron box. The box had a cavity that contained small pieces of charcoal. These were lit and more charcoal gradually added, the embers being fanned carefully to control the heat thus provided. I took in deep gulps of burning charcoal fumes as I passed the sole of the iron over the dampened shirts, making the creases vanish and leaving a smooth surface in its wake. A sprinkling of water dampened the clothes to prevent burns. The crinkling sound of burning cloth that accompanied a momentary loss of concentration and the justifiable scolding that followed had to be endured unless I managed to hide the item in the rubbish tip before detection. When we could afford it, our Sunday bests were deposited with our Chinese *dhobi* (commercial washerwoman or man).

As siblings will, Charlie and I often fell out. My mother despaired of our quarrels and we often ignored her pleas to stop. One of Mum's speciality lunches was her pork stew. The gravy in itself was delicious but the lumps of pork meat attached to a layer of pork fat swimming on the surface, to my mind resembling rubbery blubber, sent shivers of repulsion down my back. I dampened my rice with the milky liquid, carefully avoiding the meat, and topped up my lunch with a ladleful of fried vegetables. Fully aware of my squeamishness, Charlie developed a strategy to ensure that my portion of pork became his second helping. He parked himself directly opposite me and deliberately slurped loudly on his piece of meat, sucking the same piece in and out of his mouth repeatedly. I fell for his goading every time. He rolled about with laughter whilst I fled the table retching, yelling abuse at him as I went. Mum shook her head in exasperation, asking us when we two were ever going to get on with one another.

I had the last laugh though. We were sitting in the lounge one afternoon; I was immersed in my book as usual and answering Charlie's questions in monosyllables. Charlie was messing around with a newly acquired catapult whilst Mum was stretched out on the settee, her eyes closed for her afternoon nap. Out of the corner of my eye I detected a movement on the ledge that ran across the room just below the roof. Charlie had spied it too: it was a rat.

'Quick, get it with your catapult!' I said urgently.

Charlie took a pot shot, but missed by miles, giving the rat a chance to turn round and make good its escape.

'Butter fingers!' I shouted at him, collapsing in mock tears.

'All that boasting, you were just telling me you could shoot a bird from a hundred yards; you can't even get a rat that is just a few feet away!' By now my 'tears' had turned to laughter, and I slapped my thighs in amusement as I enjoyed Charlie's discomfort. He protested that the rat was a moving object and that it was impossible to shoot something on the move.

At this point Mum came to, rubbing her eyes as she awoke. I took great pleasure in embroidering the tale of the rat and its easy escape. Very familiar with Charlie's boastful claims, Mum broke into an amused smile. By now pretty peeved, Charlie snatched up his new toy and marched off into the courtyard. But a couple of minutes later he returned laughing helplessly and this time we all enjoyed the story together, collapsing in a heap of mirth. Throughout the day we succumbed to sudden bursts of uncontrollable laughter and the tale was repeated countless times to anyone who would listen.

There was a soft side to Charlie that my macho brother endeavoured to hide. He would sometimes buy my favourite pink Chinese steamed cakes and fried *you char kway* – two pieces of sweet yeast dough, deep-fried in fragrant oil and often dunked into black coffee. He placed them tantalisingly on the kitchen table and disappeared off to repair the fence. He expressed mock anger when on his return his purchases had dwindled in number.

'Who has taken my breakfast, which thief has stolen from me?'

The only response was my giggling. Mum's head shook in exasperation. 'You two! You will drive me crazy between you.'

Despite our constant bickering there was an unspoken understanding between Charlie and me. We were great companions; we missed one another if the other wasn't around but sparks flew when we were together even at a very early age.

One day when I was about eleven I carefully hid my own clothes in the centre of the dhobi's special pile. Charlie's curiosity had been aroused and he was one step ahead of me. He rummaged around until he unearthed my clothes and left them in a pile in the middle of the hall before carting the rest off to the dhobi.

'Somebody cunningly hid their clothes in the middle of the pile. Luckily I saw them,' he said. He ignored my tears. I wiped them away furiously and vowed vengeance.

'You wait, Charlie, I will get my own back on you.'

'You cannot, you are only a girl and I am smarter than you.'

I resolved to learn to ride a bicycle. Charlie had already mastered the art and I was determined to learn so that I too could cycle to the dhobi and take my dirty washing that Charlie had refused.

'I'll show my little brother. If he can master it, so can I. It can't be that difficult.'

The only available bicycle was Dad's heavy Raleigh bike. Charlie spent hours tinkering with it, dismantling it and putting it back together, then applied green-tinged grease to the bicycle chain that Dad had brought from work. Charlie had inherited Dad's gift of total concentration on any job in hand and was usually to be found at weekends in the front yard tinkering with the bicycle instead of knuckling down to his homework.

The original paint had faded with sun exposure, so Charlie used rescued scraps of sandpaper to remove all traces of the rusty old paint, using the sandpaper again and again until it was in tatters. The bike was then lovingly restored using the bright green paint so familiar from the railway engines. That's right, the paint was obtained courtesy of Sentul Railways. Charlie's real love, motorbikes, was unattainable, therefore he used Dad's bicycle as a substitute to fulfil his dreams. Norton was a popular brand of motorbike at the time and Charlie used bright red paint to write this brand name on the central bar.

Despite Charlie's attempts to claim sole rights to the bike I was aware of my rights too: after all, the bike belonged to Dad. Lowering the saddle as far as it would go, I then tilted the bike towards me by the handlebars so that I could swing my leg over. To begin with one foot hit the ground frequently as I steadied myself but eventually some semblance of balance was achieved. I practised on the dirt path then moved on to the grass, riding in circles and squeezing the brakes hard. My fingers grew welts as wide as our clothesline. Despite falling off over and over again and collecting countless grazes, I refused to give in. By the end of the day I triumphed: I had mastered it. The rush of adrenaline made me keen to show off.

The very next day I offered to take the dirty laundry to the Chinese dhobi and set off with the bundle balanced across the handlebars. Placing my hand between my thighs to hold my skirt down, I swung my right leg over the waist-high central bar, taking a few minutes to regain my newly learnt balance. I needed all my strength to work the pedals at the start, as it was an uphill journey. The bicycle tyres crackled over the quarry stones embedded in the clay track and rewarded me with a bumpy ride. The weight of the heavy men's bicycle worked against me but I was determined. I refused to be beaten. Calling on all my strength, I forced every muscle in my body to work. Triumphant and elated but hot, bothered and exhausted, twenty minutes later I rattled to a stop in front of the dhobi's house and delivered the bundle. My elation undiminished, I set off on the return journey. I grew wings on my feet on level ground but was unprepared for the steep downhill slope towards the end of my journey.

Kakka's store was at the bottom of the hill. One half of the shop was open while the planks that were used to board up the frontage of the shop were stacked up against the closed half. I had not yet mastered the art of applying the brakes effectively. Careering down the hill at a fast pace made me panic: I planned to step off the bike nimbly and run alongside it in an attempt to bring it to a halt but instead I went crashing into the closed section of the shop. Both bike and I clattered into the shop front, and the pile of planks scattered everywhere. The bike and I were not spared either. A devilish grin wreathed the shopkeeper's face as he stood, hands on hips, observing my humiliation. A shudder went through me as I swiftly looked away. Adding insult to my injured pride, who should come out of our gate at that very moment but brother Charlie, who stood howling with laughter. Mortified, I struggled home with my bruises.

My wonderful, caring brother had swiftly spread the news. The whole family was gathered by the front door. I limped towards them, dragging the bicycle with me, the front wheel buckled.

'Don't all come out to help me then,' I said bitterly, near to tears.

Luckily the family were more concerned about my welfare than the damaged bike and that helped to ease my injured pride. I refused to let the tumble prevent me from getting back on the bike the following day, once everything had been manipulated back into shape by my understanding Dad.

Dad helped with the household chores, which was quite unusual for men of that era; he redoubled his efforts during Mum's numerous pregnancies. Sitting cross-legged, he ground rice and green peas in the stone mortar, deftly pushing the soaked rice and peas into the hole in the stone, grinding until the correct consistency was reached. The grainy, milky mixture was then left fermenting overnight to produce a light pancake mix to make spongy *dosais*, cooked on a flat iron griddle. Dad also ground spices into masala for curries. There was a knack to mastering this task, usually performed by experienced women, but Dad proved to be a dab hand. He gripped the rounded ends of the stone firmly and dragged it back and forth across the flat slab, adding chopped onions, soaked dried red chillies, coriander seeds and turmeric root until he produced a thick curry paste.

We loved him for his thoughtfulness when he purchased treats for our pregnant Mum. Orangey-red persimmon fruits, Mum's particular favourites, and a magenta-coloured bunch of grapes were tucked away in the top shelf of our *almari*. Peter and Anna were charged to retrieve these for Mum when prying eyes were closed in sleep.

Dad's accusatory finger pointed at me. 'I have asked you already, and this time I want you to tell me the truth. Did you eat your *ammah*'s fruit?'

My thumping heart raced: I was not the culprit, yet I felt as if I was.

Anna's eyes did not flinch as she declared, 'I saw her with my own eyes, she climbed up on the stool to get it.'

I gave way to loud sobs. 'Please *appa*, I didn't, I didn't. I swear I didn't!' Unable to accuse my sister, all I could do was to protest my innocence. My heart was in my mouth; it flooded with saliva and then went dry. My whole body stiffened as I anticipated the feel of Dad's rattan on my skin.

Dad looked at me long and hard and then glanced again at Anna. She didn't flinch. He shook his head sadly.

'I don't know which one of you is telling a lie: I cannot prove anything. Whoever is lying, you know who you are. But I have to punish you *ma*. Anna, get me the *rothan*.'

He is going to punish me after all, even though I am telling the

245

truth! I thought. I was appalled at the injustice. Couldn't he see that I wasn't lying? How could my own sister call me a liar? I could only surmise that Anna must have eaten the fruit and pinned the blame on me. The dread of her skin burning from the sting of the cane would have prompted Anna's subterfuge; although sympathetic to her predicament I was mortified to be sacrificed. Charlie and Anna had felt the cane often unlike me, whose escape from such punishment was due in part to my favourable academic achievements but also to my knack of self-effacement. Hidden in my inner sanctum, reading on my own, I seldom had the chance to invite trouble like the others. Mischievous Anna had plenty of opportunities and had often suffered Dad's wrath while hot-tempered Charlie endured constant punishments, through his academic under-achievement too. Dad sometimes hit him so hard that weal's covered Charlie's legs; I would cringe during the administration of these punishments. Soft-hearted Theresa's response was usually more dramatic – the thud of her body on the cement floor as she lost consciousness brought proceedings to an abrupt stop when Dad's concern for his eldest daughter took precedence and Charlie escaped further punishment.

Now it was my turn: I was to be at the receiving end. Dad raised the cane just once. The sting of it on my leg was more than a physical pain. My pride was deeply hurt by the fact that my father believed I could lie. Physical pain I could bear but emotional hurt lay buried deep within.

When news of the incident reached Peter's ears, he had his suspicions but couldn't voice them. Instead, he pressed ten cents into my palm to buy myself a treat. There was a knowing look in his eyes that went some way to salve my wounded pride. Even Dad did not refer to the incident again and was extra gentle when he next spoke to me. Surely, I thought, Dad cannot love me as much as before, not if he believes that I am a liar. The wound was deep and the scar would last forever. Anna couldn't bring herself to say sorry to me. No one referred to the incident again but my sparkle diminished a little and I became Mum's shadow when not immersed in my book.

The harshness of our lifestyle began to have its impact on Mum ageing her before her time. Along the line of her jaw a fold of flesh hinted at jowls to come. Around the corners of her eyes and mouth a fine filigree of lines formed. Her hair began to thin. Before silver streaks crept in, she collected her falling hairs and twisted them together to fashion a tight black bun that grew to the size of a tennis ball. When she changed into her outdoor clothes, the ball, held in a soft, black net, was pinned to the nape of her neck, her now silver-streaked hair fanned over it, and the ends tucked in expertly. Finally she spiked a decorative pin through the bun, the semi-precious stone embedded in the blunt end twinkling in the sunlight. When not in use, the bun sat safely on a shelf in her bedroom, next to a bunch of *keeha* pins.

Mum's preparations before she left the house weren't complete until she had applied her matrimonial mark to her forehead. Picking up the twenty-cent-sized tin, she carefully prised open the lid. She licked the tip of her index finger, pressed it into the red *Kumkum* powder and applied it to her deeply bronzed forehead in a perfect round, wiping off the few grains that fell on the bridge of her nose with the tip of her *sari*. Now, she was ready to visit relatives or attend church.

My mother's last two pregnancies were particularly difficult times for her. She fell pregnant for the tenth time with my sister Irene in 1956. Her distress was palpable. We all rallied round but it was Peter who provided much-needed moral support to Mum. He introduced an element of fun to her pregnancy, cutting out photographs of all sorts of beautiful babies from magazines and attaching them to my parent's bedroom wall with thumb-tacks.

'*Ammah*, make sure you look at the babies' photographs when you first open your eyes in the morning. The new baby will be fair and beautiful just like the ones in the pictures.' This was a popular myth believed by many. So, Irene, you have Peter to thank for your good looks!

In January 1957, when Mum was five months pregnant with Irene, the Malayan Railways sent Dad on a six-month course in engineering. His destination? England – the land of my dreams. This might once have seemed an impossible achievement for Dad, who was a late learner. His gratitude to his father-in-law, who enabled him to study by paying for his adult evening classes, never abated but he could never have dreamt of one day studying in England. Everyone expressed their admiration. 'Well done Anthony, what an achievement. England, eh?'

No family member had ever set foot in the all-powerful colonial motherland. Dad's impending trip was the talk amongst all the families. We all gave him a grand send-off at Sungei Besi airport where Dad was to board the BOAC aeroplane with half a dozen colleagues from work. Decked out in a suit specially tailored for the occasion he cut a dashing figure. Tears mingled with our pride. Young Benny created a really emotional scene; sensing the impending separation, he clutched Dad's legs and would not let go. His heart-rending screams reduced everyone to tears. His fingers had to be prised off one by one, and his sobs suppressed on Peter's shoulder.

For weeks afterwards Ben's pathetic little figure ran out of the house every time an aeroplane flew overhead. Pitiable cries rang out:

'My *appa* is on that plane; my *appa* is on that plane! Please *appa*, come back *appa*.'

We missed our Dad with every fibre of our beings. Mum, who had never before experienced separation from Dad, was especially vulnerable during her pregnancy. Peter came into his own as the man of the house. At just twenty-two years of age he performed his role with unquestioning love and understanding, taking enormous care of Mum.

Whilst Dad was away, Peter embarked on a grandiose project. One evening we had just finished our evening meal. This tenth pregnancy was having its effect on Mum and Peter fussed around her.

'Stay where you are and I will fetch a pillow for your back.'

I prepared myself for some exciting news, as Peter had been unusually quiet during the meal, mulling over whatever was on his mind. His bottom slid to the edge of his chair, his neck now resting on the hard wooden edge. His flexed his arms and raised them to the back of his head and, fingers entwined, cradled his head in his hands. He raised his eyes to the ceiling in contemplation and then emitted several deep sighs. He straightened up again and crossed his feet. What gem was he going to come up with this time?

'*Ammah*, I am going to build a new house with plenty of bedrooms. I have been planning it for some time. Wait till I show you the plans that I have been working on.'

He returned with a large sheet of scaled paper. 'Look, we will have a veranda to the front. Behind that our sitting room, then a dining room, behind that two bedrooms. There, this is a corridor in the centre and on the other side of the corridor we will have three bedrooms then the kitchen. The bathroom will go to the back.'

'This looks so big, where are we going to get the money?'

'I have plans for that too. I have been saving money from my pay. You will all have to help me though. We'll do all the work ourselves. The only professional help I will need is when we erect the roof. If you have any spare money I will need it to pay the contractors for the roof. We can do it, *ammah*. *Appa* will have a big surprise when he comes home in August!'

'But where are we going to live while you break this house down to start on the new one?'

'Ah-ha, I have a clever plan for that.' His eyes flashed with excitement.

'I will build the new house around our present house. No one has ever done this before, *ammah*. Everything, the walls, window frames, doors, all can be built first. Once the roof goes up, we can start taking this house down and then the inside building can go up. I know it is going to be a lot of hard work and inconvenience but if we tackle it together we can have a lovely big house for all of us. I have been dreaming about this *ammah*, I know we can do it.'

Mum could never say no to her favourite son and so it was that three months of upheaval commenced with all hands on deck.

'First of all our old mango tree must come down,' said Peter. 'The branches are mostly rotten anyway and it has given us plenty of fruit for long enough. Now that *paatie* is dead we can cut it down without feeling guilty.'

'Yes, I suppose you are right.'

It was eleven years since we had moved in to this house: eleven years since I had been born and then grown up under the shade of our bountiful tree, now to be sacrificed to erect our new house. The sound of ripping, sawing, crashing and later the crackling of bonfires soon surrounded us. Some of our coconut trees and two of our three rambutan trees were felled as well. Our chickens had long gone.

Wood was extensively used in house building as it was relatively inexpensive and readily available. Bullock-cartloads of freshly cut planks trundled in to our property, raising circles of sawdust, and the unplaned planks were stacked in piles on timber supports. The building became a family project. Scaffolding was erected with various family members shouldering the weight. Peter, with bent head, stomach muscles contoured and hard, glistening with sweat, held the nails in the corners of his mouth. He pounded them into the planks of wood held in place by willing young hands.

Despite her pregnancy, Mum insisted on helping too. She worked her way through the pile, stacking the now smooth-planed planks against the wall and reaching out for the next piece of hair-covered wood. Her back straight, her rounded tummy on show, her hands stretched and flexed as she passed the plane back and forth. She paused to push stray curls of hair out of the way, tucking them under the taut, combed hair of the bun that rested on the nape of her neck. Her skin glistened with sweat. The air smelt of wood and a fine film of sawdust covered every surface like brick dust. It settled on our sweat-soaked faces and hands, in our hair and on our clothes. No sooner had we showered than a fresh coating settled on us, as the breeze whipped up the sawdust from every corner. We sneezed violently to clear our nostrils. Despite the discomforts, we watched the progress with excitement, the promise of a big house with all those extra rooms turning us into willing helpers. It was truly an Anthonysamy family project, involving the whole clan.

Peter hired some reputable Chinese contractors to erect the

roof supports and amazingly they completed the job within a day. Mimicking my brother, I constructed a table and stools utilising some of the offcuts. They lasted for a remarkably long time. I covered the table with a remnant cloth and then arranged my books on my handiwork. Unfortunately my 'chairs' could never bear my weight properly as the legs buckled once my full weight was rested on them: bonfire fodder!

Peter kept to his original plan. The new house grew around the old, ensuring a roof over our heads at all times. Once the walls and roof were secured the old house was methodically dismantled. The sound of his hammering echoed dully in the evening air. The house itself was completed in a few months but we could not afford to paint it. Odd items of furniture that had seen better days after constant use now became material for the bonfire.

It was during this busy period in our lives that Mum found a miracle cure for the bed-wetting problem that still afflicted me. A Chinese vegetable vendor at the market supplied my mother with a remedy. According to ancient Chinese medicine, at least this particular aunty swore by it, my body was lacking in a certain chemical. By consuming the entire urinary tract organs of a pig – genitals, bladder and kidneys – for three consecutive days, this missing link would be replaced and a miracle cure would be the result. I was so desperate for a cure, having tried various concoctions over the years from self-styled medicine men and women that I devoured everything placed on my plate. The addition of spices disguised the taste of the meat and I fought the urge to throw up with all my might as I chewed on the leathery strips.

Who knows whether this was indeed a miracle cure or whether the bed-wetting was naturally coming to an end. I was just so grateful that such a humiliating aspect of my life had come to an end: I was on cloud nine. My faithful wooden door bed was added to the bonfire. A cheer leapt out of my mouth from the depths of my stomach. I was the princess who had found the hard pea from underneath the mountains of mattresses. I had redeemed myself. By now Peter had finished building our new house and I took proud possession of my very own room. There would be no more taunts, no more sniffing myself, no more dabbing copious handfuls of Cuticura powder on my freshly scrubbed body every morning before donning my school uniform. I could sit next to my classmates and rub shoulders with them without wondering if they would take a step back because of the whiff of staleness that clung to me, despite my taking a stiff brown brush to my skin in the shower. The most liberating change was that our relatives' doors were finally open to me. Now I could spend school holidays with them, no more 'you cannot go, Lily, they cannot be dealing with your bed-wetting habits'. I felt human again.

A private maternity clinic in Ipoh Road on the outskirts of Sentul became Mum's home during the last two weeks of her pregnancy. Fears for her safety were heightened as she had developed pre-eclampsia. Her blood pressure had risen to dangerous levels and she leaked protein in her urine. Total bed rest was advised. Dad's response had been swift. 'Admit your *ammah* to the private clinic in Ipoh Road; make sure she and the baby are given the best care; no expense is to be spared for either of them. When I come home I will settle the bills.'

We placed our trust in God's hands and the clinic's expertise, which came highly recommended. Fear spread to all members of the family. Candles were lit and invocations to every saint were made. The food provided by the clinic was not to Mum's taste and every effort was made to provide her with nutritious food to tempt her taste buds. I took a bus to the start of dusty Ipoh Road and then walked along it to reach the clinic, gripping the tiffin carrier filled with food. Mum's smiling face was reward enough for my long journey. Anxious times followed until we received news that we had been blessed with a baby sister and mother and child were doing well. The long-awaited news was swiftly sent off to Dad in a telegram.

In his next letter Dad described his colleagues' reaction. He had an inscribed medal – 'Superdad' – hung round his neck and then photographs were taken and speeches made to thunderous applause. Modern England was clearly unaccustomed to such large families. Dad proudly displayed his medal in our sitting room on his return in August of that year. At last he was able to say hello to his three-month-old daughter and he was also just in time to celebrate Merdeka, the day Malaya gained its independence from England on 31 August.

Peter had achieved his goal too: he won both Dad's approval and his admiration for all his hard work. Dad was anxious to add his own contribution to the new house. The workers in Sentul workshop were habitual pilferers. They were often stopped and searched but they took their chances and Dad was no exception. He took a flask to work every day, supposedly filled with tea. The bulky inner core of the insulated flask had been loosened and discarded and the empty space was now filled with green paint. Slowly, painstakingly, our house took on the colour of Malayan engines. The cloying smell of paint seemed to hang around for months, as a flaskful a day covered only a limited area. Our hands and feet became flecked with green paint that refused to come off at bath times. Many of the houses in our area were painted the same colour.

Dad brought back with him a record of his time in England – an album filled with black and white photographs. In one he could be seen standing between a young English couple in Brighton, Brian and Irene. Irene's pale hair was windswept by sea breezes whilst a debonair Brian was wreathed in smiles. Dad's arms were draped over the young couple's shoulders, their pose promising an easy camaraderie. Dad also posed with Big Ben at the Houses of Parliament in Westminster, at Piccadilly Circus and outside Buckingham Palace. These were places that had previously only taken shape in my dreams. Dad also told us jaw-dropping stories of a strange phenomenon, an underground train tunnel! This made his listeners draw deep breaths of disbelief. By comparison life in Sentul seemed akin to living in the Stone Age.

Our tenth sibling had been named after Dad's English friend Irene at his request. The following Christmas a parcel arrived from England, causing a ripple of excitement as the postman proudly handed it over with a flourish as though he was handling mail from royalty. The contents drew oohs and aahs: miniature squares of chocolates were revealed, each wrapper depicting scenes of a snow-covered English countryside. I saved all the wrappers, flattening each one out carefully, and stored them like pressed flowers in a heavy book. Periodically I lifted them out and laid them end-to-end, gazing at them with longing before returning them to the book and shutting it with a sigh of resignation. Dad maintained a correspondence with Brian and Irene for years to come, but to his regret the young couple never made it to Malaya.

I was convinced that the latest addition to our family would be a boy. Irene's arrival usurped my status as the youngest daughter, but my disappointment didn't last long. My little sister captivated me, all six pounds of her. I stroked the back of her little hand and traced the dimples between her fingers. Her fingers curled round my index finger tightly; and gripped my heart simultaneously. I was lost in love. I hurried home after school to mother my baby sister.

Irene was barely a week old when she was rushed to surgery. She had developed a cyst on her right buttock that required lancing. Her baptism was brought forward as a precaution but she proved to be a little fighter and suffered no long-term ill effects. I cradled Irene in my folded arms as I took her for walks round the house and fed and burped her. After she had emptied her bottle of formula, her satin smooth stomach rose taut in a gentle dome. I pressed my mouth to

Irene's stomach and blew on it, making her chuckle loudly as she waved her creamy palms and soles. As I changed her muslin nappy, she smelt of milk. Her eyelids grew heavy with sleep. Toilet training commenced relatively early, when she reached her ninth month. Having watched Mum and my older sisters train my younger brothers, I copied them. I balanced Irene between my feet, her soft belly pressed against my lower legs. Then I firmly gripped her wrists and willed her to pee on the concrete bathroom floor, making encouraging shh, shh, shh noises until she obliged. A pat on her rounded buttock and 'clever girl, Irene, well done' produced a rewarding smile.

Soon after Irene's arrival, my Chocolate *thaatha* developed diabetes and had to be hospitalised. His daughters and daughters-in-law took turns to provide twenty-four-hour care. Mum's recent confinement limited her time with him but the others kindly offered to take her turns. During her precious last moments with him, Chocolate *thaatha* held Mum's hand in his and predicted a prosperous future for Irene. A tenth child in the family was a rare gift from God.

'Don't worry, *Puth-aavathu Paakiavathi*. The tenth child will be a blessing for you. You deserve some good fortune in your life after what you have been through and now through the birth of your tenth child there will be a turnaround in your fortunes.'

A tear-stained Mum thanked her dying father. When Uncle James arrived with news of grandfather's peaceful death, Mum's shoulders shook with grief.

The wake was held at Leo's house. We had all been fond of our silver-haired grandfather. His seven children and their respective families gathered in force to say their last farewell. Grandfather's eau-de-cologne splashed body was laid out in the narrow sitting room. The air was heavy with the cloying smell. Professional, breast-beating mourners, who interspersed their wailings with a recital of the rosary, ringed his coffin. It was a bizarre scene of theatricality mixed with genuine grief. As was customary in Malaysia we children attended his funeral and were caught up in the drama of it all. Thankfully we could not see the actual lowering of the coffin into the ground as the adults in the front rows formed an impenetrable barrier. A generation of our family had come to an end.

26

'Changing Terrain – Exotic Penang?'

Second Wedding

In 1958 Anna's prayers were finally answered. She was twenty-two and more than ready for marriage. A tall dark handsome man from the exotic island of Penang was the knight in shining armour who would sweep her away from a life of drudgery. The semi-arranged marriage suited both the bride and the groom. Their wedding was attended by only my parents, baby Irene and Ben. No amount of tears would change our parents' decision: 'You cannot take a break from your classes.'

Peter, the responsible adult of the family, was already in employment and, apart from public holidays, individual holiday requests were only met according to seniority. Peter in employment was also required to stay at home to oversee us minors. As a boarder at the convent in Seremban, Rosie was out of the picture. I wasn't happy though.

'Why can't I go, it's not fair. Everything good that happens I cannot enjoy, it is always school, school, school. I am fed up with school!'

'But you must look after your brothers and take them to school, they can't miss school either. It will only be for two days. No means no. You have to stay behind. We will all be back soon and have a big feast when we get back. Who is going to cook and feed your brothers? Your *annan* has to go to work and you have to cook for him too, so stop crying and do as you are told. *Chee chee*, what a cry-baby you are.'

Chastised by Dad, sobs combined with my tears, as he very rarely directed his displeasure at me. Out of pique, I hid when the wedding party left for Penang the following day. I failed to understand that my parents had been left with little choice, for the addition of three more children to the travelling party would have incurred all sorts of worries about both supervision and accommodation. Feeling hard done by, I knuckled down to my tasks while Charlie and Chandra kept out of my way until I had calmed down.

The next morning I made sure I woke up in time to prepare breakfast. Lunch was a simple affair of fried rice but for supper I was spurred on to become more adventurous. A sour soup, *rasam*, was a family favourite and I had prepared it under Mum's supervision in the past. A simple sardine *sambal* and an omelette flavoured with chopped chillies and onions, accompanied by some fluffy rice, was all devoured with appreciation by my companions. A 'well done Lily' from Peter warmed my cheeks and the disappointment of being left behind diminished a fraction. With renewed enthusiasm, I began to plan the next day's menu. Perhaps I could make a dhal curry and fry some vegetables for supper tomorrow?

The two days at home without the rest of the family did seem to drag a little but the anticipation of having them all home on the third day, and the promise of my new brother-in-law, Soosai, for company helped to raise my spirits.

The wedding party arrived home as planned amidst a flurry of excitement. Soosai's sister Roseamah and her husband were also residents of Sentul. They had played a part in the match-making process and had now been invited for a post-wedding feast. I was shy around Soosai, another Malayan railway employee, but with his easy smiles and twinkling eyes he soon won me over. Soosai also met with my parents' approval and became a welcome addition to our expanding family.

With a sister settled in Penang, my holiday destinations ranged further afield. The second long train journey since that early memorable trip with my Dad was a solitary affair. Dad's ticket allowance came in very handy. I chose a seat that did not have stuffing pushing through the seams and tucks. The speed of the trains hadn't changed; those melodious sounds still went round and round in my head. I carried a bag full of snacks, *meehoon* and a flask of tea, bananas and the ubiquitous hard-boiled eggs. The smell of appetite-whetting spices permeated the carriages.

There was a sudden lurch as the train pulled away from mid-way stationed Ipoh and a carelessly placed item of luggage pitched forward. The owner, a Malay lady, reached up and pushed it back into place, smiling at me apologetically. She offered me some *kueh lapis*, a layered cake, which I gratefully accepted. We made small talk to pass the time; she was also making for the same destination, '*Balik Kampong*' as she put it, meaning going back home. The train rattled on, lurching a little from side to side as I sat in my window seat and watched the landscape pass by rapidly.

The terrain was very varied, from cultivated to the thick of the jungle. Here and there tall trees soared above the usual level of the forest. Lush creepers covered their foliage from branch to branch. The jungle was vibrant, pulsating with life but with an impenetrable and threatening air of abandonment about it.

The track curved sharply in places. As the train snaked its way along, it glided from shadow into sunlight. A cooling breeze blew through the open window. I tilted my face away from the sun and into the wind, letting it caress my face. At times we meandered close to water the colour of milky coffee, in which the lime green spikes of transplanted rice seedlings could be seen. Mud ridges divided the seedlings into sections. The workers, conical sun hats made from bamboo anchored under their chins with jute strings, bent double as they planted the seedlings. The women straightened up and shielded their eyes silently as they watched the speeding train go past. Sometimes a hand was raised in a wave, occasionally rewarded with a brief acknowledgement from someone on the train. Gazing at the workers, admiring the scene, I started humming the verse of a catchy song that I had been taught in primary school:

> *Planting rice is never fun*
> *Bent from morn till set of sun*
> *Cannot stand cannot sit*
> *Cannot rest a little bit*
> *When the early sunbeams break*
> *You will wonder as you wake*
> *In what muddy neighbourhood*
> *There is work and pleasant food*

My lazy gaze took in water buffaloes trying to keep cool as they basked in the mud under the intense heat of the sun. The Malay village houses typically stood on stilts some six feet off the ground. Some had utilised the space beneath as dining areas, others as storage for a myriad of gardening tools, or for spare and broken furniture awaiting repair, all stacked against one another. The majority of house owners had put up penned-off areas made of chicken wire in which to keep hens and roosters whilst goats were tethered to timber posts. Lines of washing dried in the hot sun. The wind that whipped past in the train's wake lifted the pegged-out clothes on the line like a wave. Quacking ducks scratched for food in the cool shade under the houses. A whistle from the engine with an accompanying puff of smoke drew barks from excited dogs. Weather-beaten workers toiled on the train tracks in the scorching sun and waved to us as our carriages passed by.

The train stopped at every major train station, not only to pick up more passengers but also to fill up the thirsty engine with water. It tooted appreciatively when it was full. The train guards unloaded round rattan cages housing cackling chickens for housewives with babies fixed on their hips. Proud stationmasters kept whitewashed wooden fencing on either side of the train platforms in pristine condition. Potted plants, supported by coconut fibre ropes, hung from the beams of low wooden buildings while magenta flowers spilled in profusion from the bougainvillea shrubs that lined the narrow platforms. Exuberant signalmen waved their triangular red and green flags, one to stop it and the other to start the train off again on its onward journey. Every time the train navigated a bend, a gust of smoke entered the compartment.

At the end of the journey, when the train pulled into the final station on mainland Prai, my brother-in-law waited to greet me and accompany me to the island of Penang. My sister was anxiously waiting my arrival at his parents' house. Soosai was standing on the platform scanning the coaches as they squealed to a halt. He waved to me when he caught sight of my anxious face.

'Lily, over here! Come, come,' he said, as he relieved me of my trunk. 'Did you have a good journey?'

'Yes thank you,' I answered, head bowed and feet turned inwards. I was shy again; this man was still relatively unknown to me.

'You must be tired after so many hours on the train. Food and an early night will help. You will be fine by tomorrow.' He flashed a row of shiny, white, even teeth, which highlighted his ebony skin. At six-foot one he towered over me; I came up to just above his waist. His lopsided, welcoming smile warmed me. My brother-in-law was a good man but I couldn't wait to see my sister.

'Who is this young lady with you?' shouted out a short, stocky comrade from across the platform.

'The wife's sister, come for her school holidays.'

The man waved. 'Enjoy yourself, girl' he replied as he continued on his way.

Penang was a fascinating island. Europeans had visited the island since the fifteenth century but it was Sir Francis Light, an English naval officer, trading between India and Malaya who had obtained the trading rights and established Penang as a port. A sum of one thousand five hundred pounds secured the trading rights for the British East India Company and Penang became a tax-free port, a status it enjoyed until 1969. The island was an impenetrable jungle and immigrants were allowed to claim whatever land they could clear. Malays, Sumatrans and Indians, all of whom worked in the ports, as well as a large number of Chinese traders, soon settled on the island and there was a roaring trade in tea, spice, china and cloths.

We boarded the ferry at Prai on the mainland to go across to the island. The port was a bustling hive of activity; rickshaws plied their busy trade for a few cents, a plentiful and cheap mode of transport. As the ferry moored, the foul fishy smell from the waters below hit my nostrils. Moored fishing boats bobbed and creaked while further along the grey mud glistened with a coating of oil and grease in the fierce sunshine.

We soon reached George Town, the capital city, named after George IV. Imposing colonial buildings such as the city hall, the town hall and the court house all stood testament to former British rule. Road signs were in English – Gurney Drive, Union Street and Light Street for example. Balconies and terraces with balustrades crowned shops whose displays of goods overflowed on to the pavements. Rickshaws looped in and out of the traffic on crowded streets. Shops with peeling lime wash were interspersed with freshly painted frontages. The façades of an ornate church and Chinese temples broke the line of shops.

My brother-in-law's family, the Mariasoosais, lived in a terraced wooden house in Jelutong, a small village by the beach. Our bus trundled over a bridge and as we crossed the broad, brown, foul-smelling River, an all-pervading smell of decaying fish hit me full in the face, travelling down my throat and making me heave. Although I covered my nose with both hands it failed to stem the smell, which seemed to cling to my clothes and hair. Produced by a combination of the filthy water and the reek of fish, the terrible stench was a distinctive feature of Jelutong.

The house was the last in a row of low, wooden, terraced houses. We stepped into a four- by six-foot sitting room with a central corridor that ran from it. Two bedrooms were situated to the right of the corridor, utilised by my brother-in-law's family. The first of the two had been offered to the newlyweds while the rest of the household shared the second bedroom. The man of the house slept on the veranda. Two rented out rooms, each housing a family of four, lay to the left and the end of the corridor opened out into a large communal kitchen.

Two little children with runny noses, dressed in nothing but little cotton vests, gazed at us with their huge, black, curious eyes. We heard children's cries in the background. Their mother's admonishing tones rose shrilly from the back of the kitchen, but the crying stopped abruptly when we appeared in the doorway. A *saronged* housewife with a baby resting on her hip was stirring the contents of a pot on the stove. She smiled shyly as I made my way in and asked for directions to the toilet. I was conscious of the noise I was making as I squatted to pee on the concrete floor of the crudely constructed bathroom, which was situated at the right hand corner of the kitchen. Anna had not made a great change to her life: from like to like, maybe, though worse in that there was no privacy. Too many families lived under the same roof.

I heard the crashing of the waves from the kitchen and went out to investigate. A bucket system toilet was sited directly in front of the back door, ruining the view. Mariasoosai's younger brothers, Jevamallai and Arrputha, were keen to show me round. Their feet were shod in mud-caked Japanese slippers and their sun-bronzed bodies clothed in sleeveless white singlets and khaki shorts.

'What are those big holes, what hides in them?' I asked, pointing to some holes along the shoreline.

'I'll show you something,' volunteered Jevamalai, the older and brasher of the two brothers.

He kicked off his slippers, ran along the muddy beach in search of a piece of driftwood and poked the end of it into one of the holes. We waited to see what happened, but the crabs that lived in them must have sensed us and did not emerge. Jevamalai's chest expanded as he recounted his exploits with his mates, his neighbours, who would use the technique he had just demonstrated to catch the succulent crabs. Then they would light a driftwood fire for an instant barbecue, feasting on their fresh catch.

'At weekends, we have beach parties,' he grinned, his coal-black eyes flashing and his pearly white teeth on show as he recounted these evocative tales.

Penang, a tax-free port, was a big draw for everyone, particularly for those ladies always on the lookout for the latest *sari* styles and materials. Every new Indian film advertised and dictated the latest fashion.

'Have you seen Padmini wearing that beautiful *sari* in the film Vanjikottai Vaaliban?'

'Yes, it was beautiful; I want to buy one of those to wear to my sister's wedding. Where do you think we can buy them?'

'In jual murah' (a cheap sale) 'they are selling beautiful *sari*s including the one that Saroja Devi is wearing in the movie Palum Pazhamum.'

'My sister lives in Penang, so I will ask her to buy two, one for you and one for me. It is much cheaper to buy them there.'

Often, the shopkeepers were asked to display a particular *sari* that a particular actress was wearing in a particular film: such was the commercial power of the big screen. To smuggle the bargain *saris* across to the mainland successfully, the ladies employed ingenious tricks. Despite the threat of a heavy fine if caught, everyone took his or her chances. A popular method was to wrap the length of the folded *sari* just below the waistline so that the ladies could pass themselves off as being pregnant. This made for scores of 'pregnant' ladies waddling across the platform that led from the ferry to the jetty. If luck was in your favour, you might well escape the scrutiny of the customs officers. Sometimes, though, bribes had to be offered in exchange for an official's cooperation. The regular passengers knew which of the officers could be bribed and which had to be avoided at all costs. Thanks to my brother-in-law's relatives who lived on mainland Prai, I was able to return home with *saris* and *sarongs* for all my family.

'Hey, Rosie *akka* is coming home for good!'

One sister had just left home and now it was time for another to return. Rosie's presence had been missed for years, although a few fleeting holiday visits had been made to see her whenever possible – given the distance that had to be travelled and the bus fares that had to be paid. When I was younger and accompanied either Mum or Dad to Seremban I was always overjoyed to be reunited with my beloved sister. These trips were also particularly memorable for the meals, as my aunt, Sister Raphael, fed us strange but tasty European food. Mashed potatoes, peas, chops, chips and battered fish were all new tastes for me but daily fare for boarder Rosie. I was shown round the convent and proudly introduced to her new friends. I saw them engaged in what to me were unfamiliar sports, such as rounder's and hockey, in the large enclosed gardens surrounded by high brick walls.

'I cannot take you into a dormitory but there they are,' said Rosie, pointing to a row of brick-built, two-storey buildings with corridors that ran their length and that overlooked the beautifully tended gardens.

'Wow.'

Some of Rosie stories were equally exotic. Handsome Hindi actor and producer Shashi Kapoor, married to British actress Jennifer Kendal, had both been part of a travelling Shakespeare troupe that had given a performance at the convent. 'I shook hands with them,' Rosie told us proudly.

I imagined a slim, tall, blonde, blue-eyed goddess, gliding across the stage, trailing diaphanous swirls of fabric, with a dashing young man at her feet. I knew nothing about *Kiss Me Kate* but I looked forward to exploring such new and exciting territories. I was humbled by Rosie's experience of life in what was to us an exalted society. Sleeping in dormitories, bedtime cocoa, picnics at the seaside, pork chops and mashed potatoes – all elements of a privileged world far removed from life in mundane Sentul. Envy crept into my thoughts but Rosie was older than me and therefore commanded my respect and obedience.

Worryingly, Rosie had developed an unexplained illness whilst she was away, her skin breaking out in blotches that miraculously disappeared during her visits home. These bouts had been increasing in frequency of late. The cure seemed to be a permanent return to the family: Rosie could not complete her education. She returned to us as a self-assured young lady but the years of separation had built an invisible wall between us. A stranger had re-joined the family.

Now that she was home, she described her real experiences in great detail.

'I did not stay with the regular boarders because *appa* couldn't afford the fees; instead, I had to sleep with the orphans. I hated that, like I had no parents. There were so many of us sharing the dormitory. The girls were noisy and I had to help look after the younger girls. To make some money they let me teach Tamil to the primary class girls. My life improved after that; things got a bit better.'

Reading between the lines of what she said, I got some inkling of how she must have felt: apparently abandoned by her family, she felt unloved. Mistakenly I had envied her, but Rosie had resented being sent away and concluded that her parents did not love her as much as they loved the rest of us.

Our leisure time with Rosie and her freedom was short-lived, as with more mouths to feed Rosie was once again forced to earn her keep. Jobs were difficult to come by especially for young girls. Every opportunity had to be exploited. Eventually she found employment at a local shop, which paid a pittance for backbreaking work. Housed in a ten feet by six feet wooden building, topped with a corrugated zinc roof, the shop stood on a patch of green diagonally opposite our Kitchi's provision shop.

Bypassing my usual short cut home via the rubber plantation despite the intense heat, I took the longer route from school to stop for a chat with my sister. The mid-afternoon heat shimmered in the air as it rose from the asphalt road. I cupped my hand over my eyes to shelter them from the glare, my school bag clasped over my shoulder as I trudged along.

As I drew closer, my heart ached with both pride and pain as I caught sight of Rosie's bowed head. Yards of colourful, see-through, crepe de chine *sari* material were draped over her knees as she attached colourful sequins to the pre-drawn patterns. Stacks of completed *saris* stood on sagging shelves, the sequins glinting in the rays of filtered sunlight. Further stacks of *saris*, their ends and borders embroidered in a myriad of silk threads and all sewn to order, were arranged in glass-fronted cabinets. Rosie's fellow worker was a Eurasian girl called Janet, whose lively chatter and infectious laughter lightened their spirits in the cramped, workhouse-like conditions. A tall, pleasant-looking Indian nodded in greeting. He was Rosie's boss and was busy in the background creating more work for his employees by tracing the elaborate patterns onto the fabric of the *saris*. Pattern books stood open on the narrow wooden table. Acutely aware of Rosie's work deadlines, I spent a few treasured moments with my beloved sister before reluctantly saying my goodbyes. I continued my journey home with a heavy heart.

Eventually Rosie obtained a much sought-after sales position in Handlooms, a store owned by the Indian government, which sold quality Indian clothing – silks, gold-embroidered *saris*, men's traditional outfits in raw silk and an array of beautiful handcrafted giftware. She was much happier now.

27

'A penitent's plea...'

The English Girl Develops

A promotion enabled Anna and her husband to move into government quarters in mainland Prai, the busy, smelly port where the ferries docked from the island of Penang. Prai was also home to the family of our brother-in-law's late older sister. Mariasoosai was devoted to his sister's seven children and maintained a close friendship with their widower father. The two families were mutually beneficial to one another and usually attended church services together. It was the week before Christmas; I had been invited to stay during my holidays and we made ready to attend mass. The heat of the sun slowly gave way to a balmy twilight as we made our way to the tributary that flowed inland from the sea, as the quickest way to reach the local church was to cross the inlet by sampan.

The sampans were narrow, flat-bottomed wooden boats that could carry a maximum of ten people. They worked the seawater locally, skirting the roots of the mangrove swamps with great care. The wizened, Chinese skipper, was bent double, his skin battered and beaten like the driftwood on the beach; he had drawn the sampan up onto the beach so that it was half in and half out of the water. We picked up our sandals and climbed in gingerly to avoid the boat rocking dangerously. As we stepped into the boat one by one, the hull was pushed deeper into the water until the muddy waters seemed to my apprehensive eyes to reach almost to the rim of the boat. No one seemed bothered, least of all the Chinese man, as his oar sliced through the salty water, sending spray into the air and over the human cargo. The still warm sun dried the salty splashes on my arms into miniature diamonds that glittered in the sunlight.

I sat still, stiff with apprehension, trying not to unbalance the boat, as I was well aware that it could tip over and I had no skill in swimming.

Once we got under way, a host of jellyfish, soft, deceptively innocent white balls, floated to the surface in greeting. I had heard many tales of jellyfish stings that were not only unpleasant but also sometimes dangerous. I sat tensely until the fifteen-minute ride was over.

A narrow pathway led to a quaint Old Catholic church set in large grounds. Frangipani trees scented the evening air with their distinctive, sweet, evocative perfume. People milled everywhere. The joyous sound of children's laughter rang out as they gathered round a raised, purpose-built platform. They were all dressed up to take part in the nativity play. Proud and anxious parents were cajoling timid little angels, 'come on or we will be late', 'don't worry, you will be fine'.

A festive atmosphere swirled in the air. To the sound of encouraging applause, the play took off with great aplomb. The children put on a marvellous show; there were a few tears and a few forgotten lines but this did not diminish its spirit. As it came to an end, everyone hurried to claim a little corner in which to attend the main attraction – mass. The country church did not seem large enough to house the crowd milling about in the grounds. Joyous peals of bells rang out and mass commenced: the church was packed to overflowing. The priest's voice, despite the help of a loudspeaker, failed to reach me properly but I caught the echoes. I was squashed up against a pillar, not quite tall enough at thirteen to peer over the adult heads to catch a glimpse of the priest.

Head down, eyes closed, hands clasped in prayer, I felt a tap on my shoulder. I looked up quickly and found myself gazing into a pair of intense blue eyes. A young, unshaven, blond man, a scattering of freckles on his flushed cheeks, was trying to gain my attention. My mouth dropped open in surprise. He beckoned with his index finger and I instinctively moved closer. He looked to be in his early twenties. Sporting a creased white cotton shirt, unbuttoned at the top, and knee-length shorts that matched the colour of his eyes, his dishevelled blond hair was a little too long for convention and unruly strands fell tantalisingly across his slightly grimy forehead. He pushed them back with a dirty-nailed hand. A desperate pleading shone out from his mesmeric eyes and a melancholy smile played around his mouth.

He lowered his head to my ear and whispered earnestly, urgently, 'I am a poor sinner; please, please pray for me.'

Pressing some coins into my hand, and before I could react, he moved away and I lost sight of him in the crowd. There was no mistaking his distress; his eyes told all and his pain was palpable. Despite the heat of the packed church, a chill emerged from deep within me. I gained Anna's attention by tugging at her arm.

'*Akka, a vellakaran* just gave me this money and told me to pray for him. What do I do? He said he was a sinner.'

Anna's bowed head moved sideways towards me so that she could reply.

'Pray for him then. I don't know why he picked you, but do as he asked. *Paavam* (poor man). Yes, he certainly deserves our sympathy.'

'What do I do with this money?'

'Put it in the *oondeial* when it comes round.'

I did as directed, although I battled with the temptation to keep the money. He had given it to me, hadn't he? Surely he must have wanted me to keep it. I could have spent it in so many ways. But I overcame the temptation and reluctantly parted with the coins, fingering each one as it disappeared into the cavernous opening of the collection bag. Those intense, sorrowful eyes had affected me though. I felt strangely disturbed and sad, heavy of heart, and had a feeling of great pain that I couldn't account for. I burned with shame at my earlier temptation and asked God's forgiveness.

What sin could such a nice-looking man have committed that he felt he needed a young girl to pray on his behalf? Why did he choose me when he could so easily have picked another? Was it my demeanour? Did I look like someone God would listen to? After all, didn't Christ gather little children to him? I remained distracted until the end of the service and kept my eyes peeled for another glimpse of the dishevelled Englishman.

Detaching myself from the pillar I walked up the aisle after offertory to join the queue of ladies who had veiled their heads with a fold of their *saris*. On bended knees we devoutly slid the tips of our tongues forward to receive the body of Christ from the priest, the Communion wafers held between his finger and thumb. I offered a silent prayer for the young man. After mass I scrutinised the crowd but the mysterious stranger seemed to have evaporated into thin air. He had disappeared as quickly as he had appeared in the first place. I could not get him out of my mind, wondering where he was and what had happened to him. I wished I could have helped him but decided that God would look after him in answer to my prayers. Questions to which there were no answers went round and round in my head.

Mariasoosai was a well-respected overseer of the railway coolies who laid and repaired railway tracks. Having successfully fulfilled this task he was posted to pastures new, to Kuala Kerai on the balmy northeast coast of Malaya. The family's semi-detached house faced a river. An exceptionally heavy downpour had caused the river to flood, causing extensive damage to their property.

'I was more upset at losing my photo albums. Furniture can always be replaced.'

Anna, the ever-practical hoarder, had collected all the family photos together and kept them with her. She must have squirrelled them away in the battered suitcase under the bed, which she had transported to her marital home. None of us were aware of this or even missed the photos. But my Christmas visit seemed to lift her spirits and Anna was proud to show off her little sister who had obtained good grades in her exams.

'Come, I will take you to my tailor. Aminah makes all my *sari* blouses and she sews them for me cheaply. We have become good friends. I always take something for her and she gives me some of her lovely Malay *kuehs*. I got some *kebaya* material for you, it will go with the *sarongs* I bought for you at the market stalls.'

As we walked through the railway quarters, many friendly hands were raised in greeting. Anna had blossomed after her marriage; married life suited her and she seemed to have made lots of friends. Escaping her drudge of a life at home seemed to have liberated her. Aminah's wooden terrace house lay on the outskirts of the railway quarters, close to town, and we trudged down countless lanes and passed several rows of houses before we finally reached our destination. The doorway was low; Anna had to bend her head as we entered.

'No one shuts their front doors here – it is not like Sentul. Aminah, I have brought my younger sister from Kuala Lumpur. Can you sew her some *kebayas* from this material?'

'*Boleh lah*.' (Yes of course.) Aminah chattered away to us in Malay. Her east coast Malay was slower, more long drawn out and I couldn't understand some of the words but followed the general drift. Once my measurements were taken and cakes had been duly exchanged we took our leave.

'We will come back in three days time. *Terimah kaseh* (thank you) Aminah.'

Back at Anna's, it was just like old times in Sentul. She coaxed me: 'You are very good at washing pots. You can always make them shine much better than I can.'

For once I didn't mind being used. Anna was kind really, and hadn't she just asked the tailor to sew all those blouses for me? What was a little bit of scrubbing by comparison? Anyway, my pans do shine, she was right there. During the course of the morning she managed to sweet-talk me into scrubbing her entire set. We both stood back to admire my handiwork. The pans shone brightly as they caught the sun as they dried in the open yard. My nails had been blackened in the process but a handful of coarse salt mixed with a few drops of oil soon scrubbed them clean.

I then made the mistake of regaling her with tales of my recently acquired skills at art classes. Purchases were hurriedly made; a set of white bed linen was duly stencilled with colourful flowers and butterflies and Anna's neighbours were brought in for a viewing.

'Look what my clever sister has made!' In return for my efforts Anna, a skilled cook, tutored me in the art of creating my favourite dish, fried *meehoon*.

'First fry the crushed garlic, and you must put plenty in otherwise it won't give the right taste. Now, add the soaked dried shrimps and the *belachan* (shrimp paste). Next add the chilli paste and a little bit of brown sugar and fry everything well. Where is the chopped pak choi, add it now, you don't have to cook it for too long. Put in the soaked *meehoon* (rice vermicelli) and stir well, don't let it catch. Sprinkle over the thick soy sauce and the thin soy sauce and a little fish sauce and mix everything again. Taste and see if it is salty enough, if not add some more thin soy sauce. It is ready now – you can put the *meehoon* into a bowl. Now just wipe the *quali* (wok), put some more oil in and pour the beaten eggs in to make an omelette. Fold the omelette over to make a pancake and then cut the pancake into strips to decorate the top of the *meehoon*. Chop some spring onions and scatter those over the *meehoon* too. There, see, you have cooked your own *meehoon*! Happy?'

I was certainly happy to serve my successful first dish of *meehoon* to my appreciative brother-in-law.

Anna returned home to Sentul for both her confinements. Grace was born in 1959 when I was a gangly thirteen-year-old. I was enchanted with her; she was beautiful, with jet-black curls that framed her fair-complexioned face. An angel in repose, her tiny fingers and toes responded to my caresses with involuntary movements.

Cecelia, Grace's younger sister, also arrived in Sentul, in August 1961, four months before my mother and brother left for India. When Cis was born I was at home. The midwife, our trusted friend Margie *ammah* had arrived earlier and disappeared into the back bedroom, her enormous black bag swinging by her side.

'I have the baby in my bag. If you all pray hard enough and are good children, it will be a boy, if not it will be a girl.'

Obviously we children didn't pray hard enough, as a second girl eventually made her appearance. Before this the bloodcurdling screams of the birth process sent a chill down my spine. We youngsters offered prayers and were then banished out of earshot to play by the front gate. Thirteen-year-old Charlie was in charge of the young gang but I was told to stay in the house in case I was required for fetching and carrying. Two-year-old Grace was happy to play in the corner of the sitting room. With no idea as to what was going on behind the closed door, all I could do was offer my prayers at the altar. 'Please God, look after my sister, and don't let her suffer.' Hearing a sob behind me I turned round to see that the little ones, tired of their games, had returned. Their eyes were the size of saucers, shining in terror. I shooed them out. 'Go, go on all of you, go back out and play.'

The boys went out again reluctantly but seven-year-old Mally clung to my hand and four-year-old Irene's face was all screwed up, her lower lip trembling. To drown out my sister's cries, which seemed to be increasing in intensity, I encouraged the girls to pray aloud with me. I concentrated as hard as I could, my eyes tightly shut, and entreated God to keep Anna safe. A shrill cry on a totally different note announced the arrival of baby Cis. She certainly made her presence felt – feisty young Cis was a different kettle of fish from her older sister Grace, but was a welcome addition to the family just the same.

28

'Society's prejudices…'

Womanhood

I floated around for the most part in a state of self-absorption, sealed inside my private world. Whenever I could I sought out a corner where no one was likely to find me. I could be a bit of a loner within the cramped confines of my family life but in Sentul itself there was no escape: crammed church, smelly markets, labouring bullock carts and large groups of people forever thronged the streets. Overfilled buses spewed out black oily fumes as they dodged the few private cars, drawing envious stares from those on foot. Ice cream sellers called out loudly, their portable iceboxes strapped to the back of bicycles. Bronzed bodies, with what appeared to be the contents of a whole shop on their backs, struggled along on their bicycles, their bent, spindly legs straining on the pedals.

Until Irene came along I had some status at home. Self-deluding it may have been, but I could push my chest out with pride as 'the youngest girl in the family', an epithet that earned an affectionate pat on the head. Suddenly I was relegated to insignificance, the child in the middle who faded into the background – until a rude awakening one morning.

'What's this, blood on my panties?'

A little perturbed, I went in search of Mum, who was busy in the kitchen as usual.

'Ammah, just now when I went to the bathroom, I noticed blood on my panties. I think I must have a sore down below.'

Bent over the task at hand, Mum half raised herself.

'Go and see your *Peria akka*, tell her what you just told me, she will tell you what to do.'

That was no explanation. Mystified, I wondered what my eldest sister was going to tell me that my mother couldn't.

My sister's response was equally puzzling. She disappeared into the bedroom and I heard the sound of ripping cloth. I went in when summoned. Over Theresa's left arm were draped long strips torn from an old *sari*. With her right hand she held one of them out to me.

'Hold this first, I have to twist it into a rope so that you can tie it round your waist.' She did this, and then instructed: 'Tie this round your waist like a belt and make a tight knot.'

She triple-folded another strip into a long piece.

'Take off your panties. Tuck one end of this piece into the belt at the front, then pass it between your legs and tuck the other end in at the back.'

I did as I was told. 'Now, when this cloth gets wet, you need to replace it with a fresh cloth; see, I have stacked them on the bottom shelf of the almari. You mustn't leave this wet cloth where anyone can see it. You must wash it well with soap and water and hang it to dry where no one else will see it. Now put your panties back on to keep everything in place. Don't forget to check it, and change the cloth. Okay?'

I nodded, unsure about the need for all this secrecy.

'What has happened? Have I caught a dreadful disease that I have to hide from the rest of my family?' I asked nervously. Sensing my confusion Theresa softened.

'Don't worry, this will happen every month. Just do as I say and you will be fine.'

When I waddled back into the kitchen, feeling the wad of material chaff between my legs, nothing in her voice indicated anything untoward when Mum addressed me.

'Did your sister tell you what to do?'

'Yes, *Ammmah*, she did.' Mum turned away and carried on with her cooking. Thus dismissed I made my way to my bedroom to escape once more into my private world. Thankfully there was no rush of blood, just a trickle that dried up after three days. A month later a friend at school, Lily Grace, enlightened me. In preparation for PE we were changing into our white blouses and pulling on our pale blue shorts when I caught sight of the outline of a bra under Lily Grace's blouse.

'How come you are wearing a bra already?'

'Haven't you got your period yet?'

'Period, what period?'

'You know, when you get blood flow from below.'

'Oh, yes, but it was only just little bit of blood, after three days it disappeared.'

'Mine wasn't like that. I was sitting on the veranda reading when suddenly I was drenched in blood and I bled for nearly a week. My mother told me that it was normal for all girls to get a monthly blood flow. I have become a woman and now I have to behave like one! You wait, your blood flow will get more after the first month, then you too will be needing to wear a bra like me.'

So I had attained womanhood: at thirteen my childhood days were over. Only a few years down the line the dreaded marriage proposals would loom. Marriage spelled separation. I would have to leave and return home as a mere visitor. A desperate sense of loneliness sprang from the pit of my stomach. I would not belong to myself any more – instead a man would own me, a stranger. He would have earned the right to rip me away from my beloved family, from my very existence. I did not want to grow up. The memory of Theresa's reluctance when she had had to walk into the room with a tray of drinks when a stranger came returned to me with clarity. I too would be propelled forcefully into what seemed to be a brick wall: my independence was going to be smashed to smithereens. But with the adaptability of youth this shocking realisation soon became a reluctant resignation. The inevitability of life's circle had to be ridden.

I was now plagued with a fresh menace. With the onset of womanhood I had also gained frequent migraines. A dazzle of lights, like fireflies on the prowl at dusk, grew in the line of my vision. A heaviness spread across the top of my head, its tentacles gripping my temples in what felt like a vice, squeezing until my eyes bulged. The sockets of my eyes ached permanently. My eyelids felt like heavy shutters and I sought the comfort of a darkened room. Bed-wetting had given way to periodic migraines. No Chinese wisdom achieved a magic cure this time. A trip to the optician resulted in a period of wearing spectacles but they made no real improvement, so an expensive purchase was abandoned in favour of the darkened room, which proved to be more effective.

Rosie turned heads; she was attractive and vivacious and employed in a job she loved. People gravitated towards her. Rosie could afford tickets to the cinema and she treated cash-strapped Theresa and her husband. I, on the other hand, was a scholar. An interest in cinema was thought to be detrimental to my studies. I suffered the unfairness of this judgement like steam under a tight lid. I was forced to hide my feelings of resentment. The six-year gap between Rosie and me was too wide. I was not mature enough to be her friend and I had to content myself with making friends of my younger brothers: but the gender difference meant that I could not share my girlie thoughts with them.

Rosie and Theresa enjoyed an intimacy that excluded others. My eldest brother-in-law was equally fond of Rosie and the trio were inseparable. I fought my resentment because I loved them too; my siblings were my flesh and blood and my pulse quickened if they were hurt in any way. There was such a tangle of emotions to unravel and to understand, such as envy, guilt, reverence and respect for older people, as well as the inevitable self-pity.

My academic ability alienated me from other members of the family; end of school year results were a mixed blessing. My grades, when compared with those of my cousins, did not endear me to them. Thankfully my siblings accepted my prowess and were proud of me, but my success could be divisive too.

Our relatives loved children. They were happy to have them around, but did not always realise that little ears were sharp and that we, like elephants, never forgot. One example of this was the remark: 'what does he think he is doing? He keeps on producing children when he cannot afford to feed them.' My Dad was being criticised and it hurt me. In my view they had no right to talk about him like that. 'Why are they so nice to my father to his face, but say bad things about him when he is not around to defend himself?' I grew hot with indignation on my father's behalf when they berated him like that, but with strict rules about respecting our elders, I had no choice but to be civil.

I was fiercely protective of my parents. My mother had been criticised too for the same reason, which is why she avoided seeking financial help if she possibly could; she always strove so hard to live within our means. I owe my wonderful Mum so much, for her courage, her loyalty to my Dad and her justifiable pride in her family, and above all for her tenacity in overcoming hardships. She avoided any criticism of Dad in front of us; my parents' disagreements were kept within their bedroom walls. A subdued demeanour, an unwillingness to answer Dad directly or my mother kneeling at the family altar was the only indications of a personal disagreement. Every problem was offered to God, and Mum's unwavering faith was her strength.

At times I resented the segregation between the sexes. The kitchen was usually the exclusive domain of the female sex where men did not tread. One day Mum sliced her right thumb with her super-sharp knife, sharpened just that morning. Deep red blood dribbled onto the cement floor. Squeamish Theresa was of no help and she left the kitchen, retching.

'Oh God, Mum, are you all right?' I dashed across. Feeling faint, Mum slipped to the floor and leant against the wall.

'Quick, scrape some soot from the *quali* and put it on my cut.'

I thought this a strange request, but did not argue. No wonder we never washed the underside of the wok. In fact the firewood that we burnt in our clay stove held healing properties. Undaunted by the spill of blood, I applied a teaspoonful of black soot to the cut and bandaged the thumb with a torn-off piece of old *sari* material. I took over Mum's job, slicing the purple-edged shallot slices. Then I made a start on the cooling accompaniment to the already cooked beef *rendang* (Malay-style beef curry). I was bent over my task – rubbing the thick, frothy bitterness out of a short fat cucumber ready for it to be sliced thinly and mixed with chopped green chillies and sliced shallots, all to be stirred into thick natural yoghurt – when Charlie walked in with a mischievous grin. He reached out for a chapatti, tore off a hunk with his teeth and then helped himself to a piece of beef. Mum slapped the back of his hand and shooed him away, but he had got away with a tasty morsel. As he ran out he cast a triumphant backward glance over his shoulder.

Charlie was not expected to share in the chores. I bristled with the unfairness of our society. Charlie could tinker with his bicycle outside whilst I was stuck in the kitchen: unfair, unfair, I thought. Why couldn't men wash their own plates after eating? Had they lost the use of their arms? The privileges enjoyed by my brothers as a result of their gender represented an imbalance that irked me. Our lives were bound by such cultural protocols. Sometimes I questioned them but observed the rules and resented them only covertly.

'Now, now, Lily *ma*, you know the kitchen is a woman's place. Men go out to work to provide for us and it is our job to feed them.'

It was accepted that it was in men's nature to grapple with the outside world, while women had to be protected from it.

'But Dad does things for you.'

'Your dad is different. I only give him jobs that need muscle power, or when I am not well or pregnant. When you get married I hope we choose someone like your dad for you.'

Without a doubt we lived in a male chauvinist society. We had grown up with a set of rules, which we defied at our peril. Anything domestic was a woman's domain, as was the kitchen itself. Don't look, and definitely do not speak, to boys who are not family members. Respect your elders at all times; they know better. Follow the Ten Commandments and you won't go far wrong. Men were acclaimed as superior beings, whilst the prudence and hard work of their womenfolk took second place.

When it came to my attitude to marriage, I knew I was on thin ice if I questioned our traditions. With a resigned sigh I set to work again in the kitchen, muttering under my breath. I was screaming inside, 'I don't want to marry a man who has been chosen for me.' My sisters had been right in their assessment of me at a young age. We may have been members of the same family, but you would think that we had been born into different ones. I belonged to our family but sometimes felt very distant from it. I tried to blend into the background, to become an unobtrusive part of the landscape. The world in which I lived was almost wholly attainable through the books that I read. They were my refuge and I felt safe in them.

29

'New blood new promises...'

Sister-in-law

A stranger entered our sitting room, followed closely by Peter. This handsome fellow, whose name was Guy, sported a pencil moustache above his full-lipped, sensuous mouth. He spoke with a slight lilt in his voice. I was mesmerised by his arresting good looks and his smart appearance: he sported a pair of tailored beige trousers with sharp creases down the fronts of the legs and a white cotton shirt with sleeves rolled up to mid-arm. The top two buttons of his shirt were unbuttoned and wisps of curly black hair peeped seductively through. Curious, I peeped round the corner and felt my face flush. My heartbeat quickened as he caught me out; he smiled at me, and winked provocatively. Swiftly I drew back and dashed back to the kitchen, highly aware of the stranger's magnetism.

It transpired that he was an old school friend of Peter's, Guy Pathmaraj, who had moved to India with his widowed mother and older sister. They lived in the former French seaside colony of Pondicherry. Guy was on holiday in Malaysia and had decided to look up his old friend. Curiosity got the better of me and I crept back to the sitting room, taking care to keep hidden behind the partition so that I could eavesdrop.

'It is always good to meet Peter's friends. Stay for dinner, son. How do you like living in India and what is Pondicherry like?' asked Dad.

'It is a good place, Uncle, unlike most parts of South India. It used to be a French state so everybody speaks French. It is pleasant to live in a seaside town. My mother and sister love it there; my sister was married but her marriage failed and she is back living with us. I was just asking Peter why he wasn't married yet and he tells me he hasn't found the right type of girl who would fit in with his family.

I explained to Peter that there are some very good Catholic families in India with marriageable daughters. I am sure my mother will find a suitable girl for him. The families like to marry their daughters off to overseas bridegrooms. Indian girls make very good wives; they will fit in with your family very well.'

Suddenly I heard Dad call.

'Lily, can you make some tea for us?'

Oh no, now I would have to come face to face with Guy! I did as I was told, taking care this time not to look into those all-knowing eyes, even though I desperately wanted to gauge his reaction.

'Thank you.' He looked at me and I grew hot. I nodded acknowledgement of his thanks and turned on my heel, aware of his amused eyes on me as I scuttled out of the room. I stole the odd glance through the doorway when I thought it was safe and my heart was beating with the daring of such teenage romantic illusions. I was relieved when the visit came to an end.

By the time Guy did leave, my brother was sold on the idea of taking an Indian bride. It would suit the family well. A wife was expected to become a part of the family and a help to her mother-in-law, while the live-in son's wage would be a welcome addition.

'We are such a large family *ammah*, a Malayan girl might break up our family, but a girl from India might be the answer. What do you think?'

Everyone agreed that the idea was worth pursuing and Guy was given the go-ahead. 'Don't worry Peter, I will start the ball rolling and we will find a great girl for you.'

Previously there had been marriage proposals for Peter from our relatives in Malaya, but Peter was not keen and the matter had been dropped. Now excitement set in as we awaited news from India, every pile of letters from the postman scoured for the familiar blue airmail envelope. In due course a fat blue envelope did arrive, enclosing photographs of a possible bride for Peter. Eager to catch a glimpse of our proposed future sister-in-law, we crowded round for a good look.

'Oh, she looks very pretty *annan*. She looks as if she is pale-skinned and such long black hair! What an unusual name – Letitia? It must be French.'

I could not read Peter's face as he turned away quickly, taking one of the photographs into the privacy of his room while we pored over the others with Mum, who warned us to be careful how we handled them. I giggled nervously, aware that a change in our family was imminent: our beloved brother was going to be married. What changes that would bring I could not imagine but I was eager to welcome a newcomer to our family. After all, it could be fun to have someone new to make friends with.

We were all caught up in the romance of the situation. No ordinary, bossy Malayan girl for our brother, but a dutiful, shy bride, bringing with her the promise of Indian culture. She was bound to be in awe of progressive Malaya we thought and we would be able to shower her with love and welcome her into our close-knit family. We all loved Peter so much and his wife would share that love. The future looked distinctly rosy.

Letters were exchanged between Guy and Peter. As the Pathmaraj family were the marriage brokers, they were given the green light to make the necessary proposals to the bride's family. Due to financial constraints only my mother was to accompany Peter for his forthcoming nuptials. Travel arrangements were made and Mum's diamond earrings and ring were taken to the jewellers for a professional clean. Our family goldsmith's assistance was sought once more and a solid gold heart was strung to Mum's necklace, to be melted down and fashioned into whatever the new bride-to-be fancied. The bottle green metal suitcase was packed to the brim. Mum and Peter left by boat, the *State Of Madras*, on 19 November 1961 on a journey that would took five days to reach India.Once again, Theresa undertook the mother's role at home. My newly married brother returned home in early January. The entire family gathered in the lounge when Mum and the travellers approached. Theresa was on hand to perform the official welcoming ceremony. A silver tray had been procured on which liquid turmeric floated. Halved lemons were placed in the liquid next to a pyramid of opaque squares of camphor. The camphor was lit and Theresa rotated the tray in a circular motion in front of the couple to ward off the evil eye. When the couple entered the house, as tradition dictated the bride placed her right, gold-toe-ringed foot down first, to entice prosperity and luck to her new family.

What seemed like a never-ending line of large tins was brought in and to our delight they were filled with delicious Indian sweets and savoury titbits that Dad used to treat us to on our rare outings with him. Large bottles of lime and mango pickles and the very special Indian ghee, highly priced in Malaya, were carefully stacked on the wooden shelves in the open area near the kitchen. Mum's family heirloom diamond earrings and ring sparkled on fair Letitia's ears and finger.

Her own jewellery and expensive *sari*s, apart from the sweetmeats and the ever-silver kitchen utensils she had brought, screamed wealth. The photographs taken during the three-day wedding feasts, when the local poor were fed on the third day, stunned us. Why had someone from such a rich family married into ours? Surely they knew of our circumstances? My grandiose idea that my future sister-in-law would be impressed with our Malayan life was trodden into the ground. I was now in total awe of Letitia.

I was only eleven months younger, but Letitia's married status elevated her position. Initially I was shy around her. She was not very talkative. The picture I had visualised before my brother went to India to bring home his Indian bride and the reality when he returned with her bore no comparison with each other. It was a difficult time for both the family and Letitia. Adjustments to the new situation had to be made. Our brother was not totally at our disposal any longer. He was a husband now, responsible for the wellbeing of his wife. The atmosphere of our house was subdued. Peter took to spending his evenings with his wife in the sanctuary of their bedroom. The dynamics of the family had changed, however subtly. 'What did you expect, you silly girl? He is married now for goodness sake!' said Mum.

However Letitia and I soon became comrades: the closeness in age helped. Over time we learnt of her family history. She was the eldest of three girls and her father had died when the girls were still young, but there was a sort of step-dad, a Muslim who was a family friend, who helped in their upbringing. There was wealth in the family but the mother was anxious for her eldest to be married, sacrificing Letitia's education in the process. Ambitious Letitia's love of learning was brought to an abrupt halt with the proposal from overseas: traditions had to be upheld and personal sacrifices forced. The sixteen-year-old promising French student Letitia became the bride of a man who was not only ten years her senior but whose six feet and three inches towered over her four-foot-eleven-inch person.

At the time I had little realisation of Letitia's ordeal and homesickness. Proud Letitia, no doubt schooled in the protocols of a daughter-in-law, was not communicative, hiding herself in the bedroom to seek privacy from what could only have felt like a menagerie. Peter blew a fuse when Letitia, used to riding side-saddle in India, refused to sit astride on Peter's Lambretta. Much coaxing from Mum was required, with an explanation of Malayan customs, before Letitia complied, as the Anthonysamys could certainly not afford a car. Mum tried to tempt her daughter-in-law with her favourite dishes but Letitia continued to eat like a bird. It seemed that all Mum's efforts were fruitless and she was finding it increasingly difficult to build bridges. Our lives were poles apart and we walked around in hushed silence; there was an increasing awkwardness in the atmosphere that no one could remedy.

Mum's presence at the altar increased. All Peter's aspirations, of bringing home a wife to be Mum's future helper when his sisters married and left the family home and his hopes for a companion for his siblings, were coming to nothing. Letitia's expectations of marrying an exotic foreigner and living an exotic life were a miserable failure too. It seemed to be a total disaster all round and you could almost touch and smell the tension.

The hot, spicy, lime pickles in the large emptied-out sweetie jars, arranged temptingly on the shelves, became addictive. I was in and out of the room surreptitiously consuming ladle after ladle of a seemingly never-ending supply. A couple of weeks later I woke up one morning feeling so weak that I found it impossible to get ready for school. Realising that I did not have the strength to walk there, I turned to Mum. Peter was standing in his bedroom doorway. He was not a happy man. I was expecting my dear brother's sympathy but unexpectedly he turned on me.

'I am sure you are all right; there is no excuse for not going to school. Come on, pick up your bag and go.'

I was never one to play truant because I loved school too much. Mum stood silently by, unable to intervene. Peter's word was law, but I could see her eyes cloud over and her mouth set as she looked away. Peter's unusually harsh words brought ready tears to my eyes. My brother's attitude confused me. *annan* did not believe me but he would have believed me in the past. What had happened to him? With a heavy heart, copious tears blurring my vision, I dragged myself off to school. Every step needed a supreme effort. The lessons that morning did not register; I fought a desperate urge to lay my head on my desk. This I did during recess, and then realised that someone was shaking me.

'Here, it is Lily isn't it?'

I turned my throbbing, leaden head sideways. The kindly face of Sister Bernadette peered at me over the rim of her glasses.

'Why did you come to school today? You don't look well at all. The whites of your eyes are all yellow. You had better go home straight away and ask your mother to take you to the doctor. Will you be all right to go home by yourself?'

I assured her I was. No one could accuse me of lying now because my teacher was sending me home. I was vindicated. My return journey took twice as long as usual. My legs kept giving way and my school bag seemed to weigh a ton. When I eventually dragged myself in, my mother's face changed immediately, registering alarm.

'*Saysuve*, sweet Jesus, sorry *ma*, I should have listened to you this morning. You should not have gone to school at all. Come, I will take you to Dr Arasu.'

We walked slowly along the dirt road to the bus stop. Mum's soft but steady hand gripped mine tightly. We had to stop periodically for me to get my breath back. Mum threw anxious glances at me all the way to the doctor's surgery. Dr Arasu diagnosed jaundice, an unfamiliar term to me, but apparently it involved my liver. It was serious and I was to be taken home and put to bed. I suffered the sharp pain of a jab; I didn't have the strength to protest. A jab emphasised the seriousness of an illness; it was a stamp of approval.

'No spicy food for her, only rice porridge and plenty of water to drink and she must rest.' The stress was on rest.

'How long will it take before she gets better?' asked poor Mum.

'It will take weeks, maybe six or seven. Don't let anyone go near her. She must be in a room on her own, this could be contagious.'

When we got home I took my shoes off in my usual way, easing one off with the toe of the other, then using my bare foot to push down on the heel of the remaining shoe. Even this simple process made me breathless.

This was the second time in my life I had been isolated due to illness. My body flopped as though the bones in my arms and legs had dissolved. The illness seemed to have emptied me. My jelly-like limbs lay useless on the bed. I slept for long spells that day, occasionally being woken up for broth and glasses of water. In the evening, I heard Peter's Lambretta pull up. Fresh tears oozed from my eyes and I pushed my face into the pillow and sobbed quietly. I heard footsteps coming up to the doorway but I couldn't face him. I feigned sleep and he crept away. He popped his head round the door the next evening and I was ready for him then.

'So, you really are ill, aren't you? Sorry I didn't believe you. I cannot come in. You rest now, okay?'

There was a lump in my throat, and I couldn't answer. I turned away and shed a few more tears.

I spent a lot of time sleeping. Progress was slow. While I was physically weak, I was content to spend my days in bed just lying there and sleeping, but as my health improved, when I caught the whiff of spices wafted through during lunch and dinner preparations, I drooled. In my mind's eye I saw a plate of hot fried potatoes, rich with chilli, red and yellow turmeric, and studded with charcoal-black popped mustard seeds and crispy fried onions. Fragrant curry leaves might be tucked between the cubes of soft curry encrusted potatoes too. But nothing like this came my way.

I lay listening to every footfall, the chirping of birds outside, the sounds of conversation and laughter that floated from within and outside the house. The quarrels of the younger children, which I would once have shooed to silence, now quickened my pulse. The sound of night creatures that punctuated the still air outside reignited my childhood fears, quelled only by the sounds of sleep emerging from the surrounding bedrooms to keep me company. I longed for companionship. Everyone was rightly following instructions and keeping away from me. There were no library books that I could borrow to read. It was an agonisingly long month.

Once again, I survived a major illness. Letitia was kind to me, maintaining a safe distance but talking to me from the doorway of my bedroom. From the little she divulged I began to understand the effects of the upheaval in her life caused by her marriage to Peter. She had enjoyed school, winning awards in every subject; she was the top student of her class, brilliant at maths. Her dreams of a university education had been cruelly dashed to fulfil the traditions of family life and her own life sacrificed to increase the marriage prospects of her two younger sisters.

30

'A change in fortunes...'

Family Fragments

In 1960 Theresa had added Frank, her fifth child, to our ever-expanding family and the following year Peter had brought home his wife. It became obvious that our family had to fragment as space was being stretched to its limits. Sensing the need for change, good old family stalwart Margie ammah, keen to repay us for our kindness to her son, offered the best she had. For a nominal rent she offered what can only be described as a lean-to adjacent to the back of her house. It faced the last few feet of our local market. An open stream, from which market smells were much in evidence, ran alongside the barbed wire fencing that formed the boundary to Margie *ammah*'s house. Theresa and her family took up the offer.

The sitting room was a narrow eight feet by four, just long enough to house two chairs, two three-legged stools and a narrow wooden table. Its width could accommodate three abreast. The kitchen, which jutted out from the main building, was decked out with narrow shelves from floor to ceiling on one side. Two people in the kitchen made a crowd. A variety of odd-sized tins held the provisions that house-proud Theresa arranged in order of height. A raised wooden bench across the back housed single clay stove. A tap protruded from the corner, a dented aluminium bowl underneath it.

At one end of the narrow sitting room, a wooden step led to a raised, enclosed windowless single bedroom, where seven bodies slept on mats, which were rolled up and stacked against the wall during the day. An almari stood in the corner; the mirror, spotted with age, had enough life left in it for my sister to use it to adjust her *sari*. Sheets of rusty zinc enclosed the open-air bathroom and a wooden bucket system latrine, adjacent to the bathroom, was shared with Margie *ammah*'s family to complete their living accommodation. Her son David had married his sweetheart, while daughter Stephanie had fled her own house one night and arrived at David's. Margie *ammah*'s entire family made for good neighbours.

Living with Mum and Dad had assured that no one went hungry in Theresa's family but setting up home on their own was proving impossible. Debts began to mount and Theresa was forced to seek employment. The Hindustan theatre in the centre of town became her employer: she sat in her little cubbyhole selling tickets to the theatregoers who queued up to see the latest Tamil and Hindi films. The job was full-time, taking up every evening and including matinees at weekends as well. To add to the number of bodies sharing the bedroom, without even a ceiling fan to stir the humid air, a twelve-year-old live-in Tamil girl from Serdang estate was brought in to help with the chores whilst I attended school in the mornings. School was but a short distance from my sister's house and I was happy to live within my sister's household for the next few months.

At weekends I travelled by bus to deliver Theresa's packed lunch, hoping that my luck might be in. Sometimes, she managed to wangle a seat for me when a particularly good movie deemed suitable for my viewing was screened. Her manager, a Mr Murugasan, a short, fat man with a kindly face, would smile at me genially.

'So, your sister tells me you would like to see this film, eh?'

I smiled timidly and nodded my head, excited at the prospect but mindful that the only reason I was being admitted was as a result of our poverty. If only I could have afforded to pay proudly for a ticket.

'Go on then, before I change my mind. Go, go, tell the lady at the door that I said it was okay for you to go in,' he smiled, followed by a conspiratorial wink.

'Thank you, sir.'

I slipped into the back row of the darkened theatre, feeling the folded-up seat with the back of my leg and reaching behind me to pull it down as I joined the fee-paying crowd of enthralled viewers. These treats averaged out at one every six to seven weeks, so as not to abuse my sister's employment status. I would cough and splutter through the clouds of cigarette smoke that swirled around me, my head would throb and when I stumbled out into the light after the show, the fresh air would hit me making me retch. Despite this, I never failed to take up the offer of a free viewing: for entry into the magical world of films and film stars I would have put up with anything.

One day I was on my haunches leaning against the doorway, the hem of my dress tucked between my legs and resting my back against the ledge, engrossed in my book. A pathetic whimper drew my attention to a stray dog that stood on the far side of the barbed wire fence. His soft brown eyes were beseeching. Bits of hair clung to his emaciated body and his ribs stuck out; open sores, yellow with pus, were clearly visible, and fat black fleas were clinging to the bare bits of leathery skin. I was unable to drag my eyes away as his soulful eyes followed my every movement. His scrawny tail wagged in anticipation. My thoughts flew back to the doleful eyes of another dog, one that had been my companion and saviour only a few months earlier.

During the lonely days when my mother and Peter were in India and the other adults had gone out to the cinema, my childhood fear of the dark tormented me once more. I would crank up the volume of the radio in the corner of the sitting room, in an attempt to distract myself from the stillness of the night as my vivid imagination ran riot. Every creak of the window was a thief desperately trying to gain access to the house; the scuttle of night creatures on the gravel were undoubtedly the stealthy steps of burglars. But the reassuring tones of the announcer – 'Good evening, you are listening to this week's top ten hits' – followed by Cliff Richard's voice blaring out '"cos You're my Theme for a Dream, yes you are" did little to stem my shivers. Dad was often out, attending either a union meeting or a political meeting with the Malayan Indian Congress, leaving the fifteen-year-old me as the only semi-adult at home.

After the arson attack on our kitchen and before sister Theresa's wedding, Dad had decided that we needed a guard dog to give us advance warning of any imminent danger. He knew that Peter's good friend, Thomas, was a dog breeder, so had asked Peter to mention this to him. Vera, my favourite, was a golden Alsatian, presented to us by Thomas; he was the latest in a long line of guard dogs. The others had been mainly mongrels but Vera was the king. His height was intimidating at first but he soon won us over with his doleful eyes and winning ways. Vera's protective presence was such a comfort as I waited for the return of my sisters and brother-in-law, often late into the night. The soulful brown eyes of this poor stray outside Margie *ammah*'s fence reminded me strongly of Vera's unwavering and devoted gaze.

With pounding heart I located a small hole in the barbed wire fence, widening it with my fingers to allow the grateful dog room to squeeze through. He didn't seem to mind the red weal's as a couple of the barbs scratched his back. I had started something that I should not have done, knowing full well that I would be in for a good telling-off. An overwhelming sense of protectiveness gripped me and, paying no heed to the consequences, I proceeded to wash and dry him with a faded old towel peppered with holes that Theresa had placed on the kitchen shelf, as a rag to grip the hot pots and pans. I felt proud of my handiwork, as my nephews and nieces gathered round. Oohs and aahs followed my every move as they watched, fascinated. Scraping out the lunch remains from the pot I gathered enough food onto a battered old enamel plate and watched with growing satisfaction as the dog lapped up every last grain of curried rice. My new playmate gave a gentle twitch of his hairless tail as he whined his thanks.

I shrugged off the expected and well-deserved scolding from my sister and brother-in-law, as everyone, including Margie *ammah*'s family, began fattening him up with scraps from their plates, elevating his position from pariah to family pet. Brownie, now sporting a chocolate brown body and a white-tipped patchy face, became my faithful shadow.

With promotions coming his way, my eldest brother-in-law finally qualified for government quarters and after nine months of cramped living, Theresa and her family settled in Kampong Pandan, a leafy suburb of Kuala Lumpur, two bus rides away from Sentul. Rows of government brick-built semis were set well back on either side of a narrow tarmac road. A range of dwarf coconut trees, with clusters of tantalising green coconuts hanging at arms' length, tall *neem* trees and hibiscus bushes covered in a profusion of blood-red flowers lined the road. A well-trodden pathway on the grass frontage of the houses led to each semi. A veranda ran across the front, the exposed brickwork of their veranda painted an eye-catching red. The house boasted two upstairs bedrooms and a bathroom. The front door opened into a large living room, with a doorway into a dining room. A small but functional kitchen lay to the right, opposite a useful storage alcove under the stairs. From the back of the living room and adjacent to the kitchen, another doorway led to a walled, cement outdoor area. There was no necessity for the family to traipse hundreds of yards to an outside toilet as a brick-built, bucket system toilet was housed in the right hand corner within the concreted outdoor area.

The contrast with their previous accommodation could not be greater. A valuable strip of land to the side of the house already had my green-fingered brother-in-law making plans. Before any furniture was installed, moving-in ceremonies were performed to invite prosperity. A stove was placed strategically in the centre of the living room, to represent the centre of the house, and fresh milk was brought to the boil on it until the milk almost frothed over but not quite, to mimic the prosperity that they wished to flow into the house. This milk was shared with the gathering. The sound of an approaching Lambretta scooter had everyone rushing to the veranda, as the local parish priest dismounted. My brother-in-law dutifully rushed forward to park the scooter on the hard standing between the edge of the wall and the open drain that ran round the outside of the house.

'Welcome, welcome father, thank you for coming,' he said, as he led the priest in.

Prayers were offered in front of the newly erected altar. Father Munro walked through the entire house muttering prayers. With his index finger he drew the sign of the cross in every corner, to rid the house of any resident evil spirits. The house was now deemed ready for occupation.

Theresa's family soon settled in but I did not get to spend time with them in their new home, as my life was about to change direction. Just five months into her marriage, Letitia fell pregnant. Her isolation from the rest of the family increased as she often took to her room with extreme fatigue. Morning sickness took its hold and she developed a craving for spicy food. A *sambal* made with sour tamarind pulp, mixed with soaked and ground dry chillies and onions, and became her favourite. It was too spicy for me but Letitia relished it, helping herself to thumb-sized pieces daily. I felt sorry for Letitia and offered to pound the ingredients for her but when Peter smelt the brown concoction that she had hidden in a covered bowl in a corner of their bedroom, he threw it away ruthlessly, pronouncing it to be too spicy for pregnant women. He faced his wife with a mixture of concern and exasperation. 'Why do you insist on eating this foul-smelling rubbish? It cannot be good for you or the baby.' Stoic as usual, Letitia bore the deprivation for a few days before succumbing once more to her craving. I became complicit and ground up small amounts of the *sambal* periodically for her. No one else was any the wiser.

One Saturday afternoon I heard a scream from my brother's bedroom and a red-faced, dishevelled Letitia emerged in great distress. A grass snake had found its way in but thankfully Peter was on hand to deal with it. Snakes were a bad omen for pregnant women. If they were not killed immediately and instead allowed to escape, the baby would be born with a tongue too long for its mouth, a risk not worth taking.

Not long after this particularly disturbing episode Peter was clearing undergrowth in the grounds of the house. I was sitting on the veranda with my book, my usual evening habit, whilst the dull thud of Peter's chankol echoed in the background as the sharp-bladed flat piece of iron sliced into the clay soil. Peter's back glistened with sweat as he placed his bare right foot on the shoulder of the spade and forced it into the soft clay soil. I looked up suddenly when the thud was replaced by a shrill, sharp squeal. He kicked out sideways and bent over to move a large stone; with lightning speed and great force he brought the spade down.

'It was either him or me!' he shouted.

Bending down, he reached to pick up a thick grey rope that was still wriggling frantically. Peter had uncovered a viper, curled up under the boulder. With repeated blows he managed to kill it. Shuddering, I made my getaway pretty quickly. I had an instinctive abhorrence of the slithering rope. Ever since an early encounter with a snake I had felt like this – perhaps it was the beginning of a phobia? The first time I had been frightened by one had been soon after I had started at school. Walking home along the path beside our fence, I detected a movement on the path; I lifted my foot just in time. Frozen for a few seconds, I saw the tail of a snake disappearing into the bougainvillea bush that formed our boundary. Shivering from head to toe I was thankful for my narrow escape. My feet grew wings, as I ran the rest of the way home; I arrived sweating profusely and with a thumping heart. I was barely able to speak.

'*Ammah*, I nearly stepped on a snake on the path,' I squeaked.

'Where, which path?'

'There *ammah*,' I replied, pointing with a shaky finger at our bougainvillea, 'just on the other side. I could easily have stepped on it. I just caught a movement, as I was about to put my foot down. I saw it disappear into our bushes. It might still be there.'

'I am sure it has gone by now, but I will go and look.'

'You go. I am not coming. I am going to stay indoors.'

After a while, Mum came back into the house. 'I couldn't see anything; it must have gone somewhere else. I am sure it was a harmless grass snake.'

The second time I saw one was again in close proximity to our house. Sand had been delivered for one of Peter's building projects. It was piled up near the hedge close to the entrance by the gate. I was enjoying my five o'clock read on the veranda when I sensed a movement. I looked up to see a snake on the crest of the pile, slowly zigzagging its way down. I froze; the hair on my arms stood on end, my mouth dried and my throat constricted. Vera, our lovely dog, was playing dead in the shade, but he barked furiously at the intruder, which loosened my tongue and I let out a piercing scream. Our combined voices sent the snake slithering back into the hedge, leaving me shaking.

'What happened, why are you screaming?' asked my mother.

'Snake, snake! I saw a huge snake coming down the sand heap!'
I shouted wildly.

'I can't see anything now; you must have frightened it away.'

I had nightmares that night. There were snakes all around. I woke up drenched in sweat and reached out for my cover, pulling it tight round me to leave no gap where a snake could creep through. Letitia seemed to share my fears.

Changes were afoot not only in our household but in the country as a whole. My childhood in Malaya was drawing to a close. The British policy of rule by division segregated the peoples. Malaya belonged to the Malays; those people of other races, some of whom had lived there for centuries, and some, who had been imported into the country by the British, were deemed to be temporary residents. The belief was that having made their fortunes, the non-Malays would return to their respective motherlands. During the 1950s, anxiety among the other races, particularly after Malaya became independent in 1957, increased. The British government were facing economic problems back home in England. After the enormous costs of the Second World War, they were only too ready to give up their rule in Malaya.

Malay was declared to be the official language of the country. Malays' education and economic development was to be encouraged, and subsidised to bring their economic status into line with that produced by the astute business acumen of the immigrants. As a concession, Chinese and Indians were to have proportionate representation in the cabinet, but Parliament would run those states where Malays were in the majority. The Education Act of 1961 decreed that Malay and English would be taught in secondary schools, but in state primary schools only Malay would be the language of education. All these changes sent out alarm signals to the non-Malays. It was at this point that I fully understood why my Dad had volunteered to join the Indian National Army. Indians' experience of living in Malaya as second-class citizens caused them to perceive a link between that status and the treatment they received in the so-called 'land of gold'. Dad announced that those of Indian ancestry some of them who were his relatives were leaving the country and Dad decided that our future lay in his motherland too.

Our family had retained its ties with India. Grandpa's widow and my father's now married stepsister lived in Cuddalore, a bus drive away from Pondicherry. The land in Kumulanguli was let to contractors and the family house was rented out. My Grandpa's property, according to Indian tradition, had been bequeathed to Dad as the eldest son, whilst his widow, with Dad's blessing, was to enjoy the revenue from it during her lifetime.

Dad was unwilling to stay in Malaya and gamble with the future of his school age children. His aspirations were for an English education for them. Since the political situation was becoming unstable, Mum and Dad decided to make sacrifices for their children. Mum was to make a new life in India indefinitely. Soon the whole family would break apart; family ties would dissolve and its members scatter. Sentul Palace was no more the heart of the family. Ironically, an eye to the future and the need to ensure our family's prosperity had prompted Dad to leave India for Malaya in the first place: now we were returning to India for the sake of our education.

31

'Vomit, filth and opulence...'

India

Letitia was seven months pregnant and, as was the custom in Indian families, she was due to travel to her maternal home in India for her baby's birth. Rural Kumulanguli was deemed an unsuitable place to live for those of school age so what better place for us to put down roots than Pondicherry, where we now had ready-made relatives via the connection with Letitia's family. Surely this was the answer to our prayers?

Our household in Sentul became a hive of activity. Preparations for our epic journey to India were in full swing. Shopping trips were frequent, large trunks were crammed with piles of new clothes, sat upon and strapped shut; our names were stencilled on the lids in white. Dad the breadwinner was to remain working in Malaya to finance our living in India. The exchange rate was favourable assuring us to maintain a reasonable standard of living in India. Charlie refused to accompany us choosing instead to live with his beloved older sister Theresa.

Finally, on 10 November, 1962, my sister-in-law, mother, brothers Chandra and Benny, our youngest sister Irene and I set off on the five-day voyage to our ancestors' birthplace. There were only two ships that regularly journeyed to India from Malaya: one was the *State of Madras* and the other named *Rajula*. We were on the former; a vessel crewed entirely by Indians.

The excitement we felt at the novelty of a long journey by sea was soon quelled as we rapidly realised exactly what third-class passage – the only level of travel that we could afford – entailed. Nervously, we witnessed the scramble to book sleeping quarters by our fellow travellers as they rushed to spread their sleeping mats in an open area on the lower deck. Thankfully, because we were travelling with my obviously pregnant sister-in-law and with youngsters in tow, we were helped by our fellow passengers and were able to claim our own little patch with relative ease. A young married couple were particularly helpful, spreading out our mats for us.

The mats were placed right next to each other, with only a pencil's width between them. Soon the lower deck was covered with mats of every colour and description, with every available space taken apart from the narrow gaps left for people to walk past. Makeshift partitions of triple-folded cotton *saris* were erected, the thin material offering little more than a nod to privacy. An overpowering smell of sweaty bodies hung in the air.

In an attempt to distract Irene, I took hold of chunks of hair from either side of her head and started to fold them into a single plait at the back, securing the end with a rubber band that I always wore on my wrist. She smiled her thanks and then followed my brothers for a walk on deck. When the ship hit choppy waters people were sick all around. The vomit welled back and forth along the deck with the rolling of the ship. Relatives of the seasick splashed seawater to get rid of as much of the foul-smelling gunk as possible, but the smell clung tenaciously. The fresh sea breeze that came sweeping through the open doorways failed miserably to sweeten the air. Pregnant Letitia must have had a horrendous journey but she remained quiet and uncomplaining, silently counting the days until she would be reunited with her dear family again.

My resourceful mother managed to negotiate a special deal with the ship's purser: we could shower in the bathrooms designated for second-class passengers. We waited for the signal from the anxious purser, aware of the reprisals for him and for us if caught.

'Come quickly,' he would hiss at us, nervously. 'You don't have very much time.'

We gathered up a fresh change of clothes and hurried along to our very welcome showers.

At mealtimes we tagged on to a long queue of third-class passengers all eager to get there first for the best pickings. Generally the food consisted of dhal curry and fried vegetables, with the occasional treat of fried fish. Gazing out to sea as we queued, I sometimes caught a glimpse amongst the tumultuous waves of a fish arrowing through the water. Such delightful scenes helped me face the biggest trial – the ever-present stench of vomit.

When the skyline of the city of Madras at last appeared on the horizon we joined the excited crowd on the top deck, necks craning, hands gripping the rails as the ship finally creaked into port. We walked down the swaying gangplank with the smell of the ship still clinging to us. We scanned the waiting crowd anxiously and were relieved when my sister-in-law's family were spotted. The porters helped us with our heavy metal trunks and after the customs officials had questioned us – thankfully without the rigmarole of having to open up our trunks, unlike some other unfortunate passengers – we followed our new relatives, led by Letitia's stepfather, Mr Kadar, to the bustling city outside. The youngest sister was pale-skinned Gandhi; her face brimmed with laughter and her eyes twinkled like the shiny bracelets on her arms, while large earrings tinkled on her delicate earlobes, hanging just short of her shoulders. Her whole demeanour promised a subtle naughtiness. She clung to her pregnant sister's hand chattering excitedly, pausing only to offer us her beaming smiles.

My first impression of India was the prevalence and public display of poverty. Although we had experienced poverty in Malaya, it wasn't on this scale. Beggars lined the streets. Our relatives strode on ahead and their eyes never wavered; they seemed oblivious to what was all around us. There appeared to be no semblance of hygiene either. The roadsides, right next to open drains, were piled high with food. The scent of heady spices fought against the stench of the open sewers. And everywhere, everywhere, were teeming masses of people.

There was so much to take in. Lean-to shop fronts were filled with open gunnysacks, their tops rolled down to display their contents – chillies, pulses, flour and rice. Crowds milled around, haggling noisily with the shopkeepers. Luscious varieties of sweet-scented mangoes were piled up on the pavements. The smells of decomposing food and excrement vied with the wonderful aroma of ripe fruits, and spices, all fighting for dominance, as did the contrasting impressions made by the opulent rich, the emaciated poor and the suppurating beggars.

Vendors of varying degrees of poverty, revealed by the quality of the clothes they wore, tried to entice passers-by with brownish water proffered in glasses that looked sorely in need of a good wash. Others beckoned to us, beaming: '*Vanga, vanga*. Come, come.' Waving us to sit on rickety wooden stools by the roadside, they encouraged us to partake of strong tea, coffee and pyramids of *jelabies* (pastries soaked in sugar syrup) and balls of sweet *laddus* studded with roasted cashews, both local delicacies. Craftsmen on every street corner whittled away at little keepsakes, carving intricate designs from ordinary pieces of wood at incredible speed.

Vibrant colours were everywhere: those in rich silk *saris* embroidered with gold thread rubbed shoulders on the street with the cotton *saris* of the less well-off. Men were equally resplendent in traditional garments, some gold-edged and others in plain cotton *veshtis*, like those worn by Mahatma Gandhi. The poorest men were draped in threadbare loincloths that in some cases barely covered their modesty. I looked away.

Animals roamed freely. Mangy-looking dogs nosed for scraps of food around the stalls. Cows sedately wandered the roads, their foreheads adorned with vibrant coloured powder, trailing garlands from their necks; no one shooed these kings of the streets away as the people and the traffic carefully skirted round them. Children ran around everywhere, little girls dressed in beautiful long skirts and blouses with shawls slung across their shoulders in a fashion peculiar to the South Indians. Shiny black oiled and plaited hair was tied at the ends with flowing ribbons, and strings of sweet-smelling jasmine flowers, some fully open and others still in bud, bounced at the napes of their necks, held in place by a strand of hair.

Our family seemed to have been thrust into a great big open-air theatre. We were surrounded by the blast of Tamil songs from the latest blockbuster movies that blared from every shop, complemented by massive posters glued to the pock-marked walls. Large mobile placards also advertised the movies, progressing slowly forwards by pedal and bullock power. Life was in full, rambunctious flow, and my eardrums rang with the incessant blasts on the horn and the yells of the pedestrians; the frenetic movement of the throng of rickshaws, bicycles and overflowing buses was overwhelming.

The excited anticipation of our new life was now tempered by a sense of vulnerability and fear; thankfully the calming presence of our mother and sister-in-law helped to reassure us.

I watched, fascinated, as the rickshaw-wallahs, scrawny, leathery-skinned men, strained to pull the full weight of the people sitting in their buggies as they threaded their way deftly through the impossible crowds, utilising every available nook and cranny on the road. They jostled with cars that crawled along, and people who walked bicycles with the ends of their *veshties* tucked into their waistbands. We could see men hanging off the sides of the overcrowded buses as Mum, Chandra Irene and I travelled along in style in the second of Mr Kadar's cars, taking in all the sights and sounds; we were goggle-eyed at first, but slowly became weary and settled back into our seats.

A bullock cart trundled along the main road out of Madras. The honking of our car's horn made little impact on the ebony-skinned man perched precariously on the edge of the wooden ledge that served as a seat, slapping his whip against the cud-chewing cow to hurry its pace. Only when he was ready, clearly resenting the rich owners of cars, did he draw the cart to the side of the road, raising plenty of dust in the process. The driver deftly overtook the cart, muttering softly under his breath.

After a long three hours that felt more like six, we entered the state of Pondicherry. One hundred and fifty kilometres to the south of Madras on the Bay of Bengal, Pondicherry had been ruled by the French between 1814 and 1954, thereby avoiding the restrictions of Indian rule until relatively recently. There was a noticeable difference in the environment: French spellings were daubed on signboards, the streets had French names and all the streets were aligned at right angles in the preferred style of French architects – they criss-crossed like lines in a book keeper's ledger. Everything here looked fresher and greener.

The cars pulled up in front of a substantial brick detached house, with a colonnaded portico surrounded by a walled garden, accessed via a padlocked grille gate. As we piled out of the car, a welcome breeze soothed our flushed, travel-weary faces.

Servants came rushing out to meet us and orders were shouted for our luggage to be carried indoors. A big, buxom lady, pale-skinned and with arresting good looks, came towards us, wreathed in welcoming smiles and fragrant with the perfume of flowers. Her abundant, wavy black hair was tied in a chic chignon that rested on the nape of her neck, a profusion of jasmine flowers anchored around the base. Her short neck was adorned with a gold necklace and a roped chain as thick as my little finger hung almost down to her waist; equally intricately patterned gold bangles jangled at both wrists. The keys of the household, tucked into her waistband, jingled when she walked. I was struck dumb: Letitia's mother looked truly majestic in the surroundings of her equally majestic house. The middle daughter, more modestly clad, dripped with gold jewellery nonetheless. Dimple-cheeked Rajathi, her skin a milky coffee colour, was shy and demure with a serene face; she was equally welcoming.

A short flight of stairs with pillars on either side led to the veranda, from where we were ushered into the main part of the house. Again, the architecture was striking, with intricate carvings and elaborate cornices; in the centre of the house a pillared quadrangle with a double-height ceiling reached the top of the first floor, where slatted glass windows let light and air into the central seating area. The lounge had corridors running from all four sides leading to bedrooms on three of them and a dining room on the fourth. From here, cool concrete flooring led to a courtyard and an outdoor kitchen. Totally overawed and somewhat subdued, we dutifully followed the servant into the back bedroom, which housed a very visible iron safe.

'Good God, what a house,' I whispered to my siblings. 'These people are very rich – look at the safe. I wonder how much jewellery and money is locked up in that thing?'

The scale of the family's wealth, the stately building and its solid dark furniture intimidated us. My thoughts flew back to when my sister-in-law had set foot in our household for the first time. Her reaction when she saw our wooden house in Sentul in comparison to this grand palace had given nothing away. Her face had been inscrutable. Why hadn't she given us any indication regarding her background? Suddenly she had become a stranger. Every bridge that I had tried to build was shattered. Our home seemed a long way away now and homesickness hit me hard. What on earth were we doing in India? How were we ever going to fit in with Letitia's family? Looking at her pretty sisters, I couldn't imagine what they must be making of me: I'm not pretty; I'm plain and dark. I had never felt more alone. I could only guess at what my two younger brothers and sister were feeling.

After a much-needed bath and a change of clothes, we were invited into the dining room for a feast. Exhausted after the long journey, I tried to muster a few smiles from the storm of my confused feelings. My siblings, too, were unusually subdued, and we were all thankful when the meal was over and we stretched our aching bodies on the mats spread out for us in the back room. I drifted into a fitful sleep; my head still keeping time to the sway of the ship.

The following morning the sounds of activity all around prompted an early start. We ventured out shyly, our feet dragging. A young woman whose creased face did not match her years was vigorously scrubbing brass pots in the courtyard with the very same mixture of tamarind pulp and salt that I had used in our Sentul house. She cupped her hand and filled it with water, then washed the residue off the pots to reveal a brilliant shine. The lady was not wearing a *choli*, but covered her body with her *sari* draped round her shoulders and tucked in at her waist. A boy of about two, runny-nosed and tearful and dressed in nothing but a thick black string with a brass leaf threaded through it to strategically cover his modesty, was tugging at his mother, vying for her attention.

'Shoo, wait until I finish my work. *ammah* is busy now.'

She glanced at us shyly and I wondered what was running through her mind as she observed the visitors from overseas.

At the corner of the back garden, the milkman had walked in his cow via a gated entrance and tethered it to a pole. A young, bald-headed servant girl of ten or twelve stood by the side of the cow with a stainless steel bucket, into which the cowherd was squirting the frothy milk.

I later discovered that the servant girl was called *mottai*, a reference to her baldhead, which struck me as a little cruel though the girl did not seem to mind. A lively young child, she called us over for breakfast, taking care to stoop slightly in deference and deftly avoid any forbidden physical contact with us, as she placed freshly prepared, smoking *iddli* (domed steamed rice cakes) and *dosais* (flat pancakes also made with ground rice), accompanied by generous helpings of aromatic coconut *sambal* (chutney) with a swirl of popped black mustard seeds, onto gleaming, rimmed, stainless steel platters. Seconds were soon offered too, a wave of a hand over our plates required to stop the steady flow. Hot, rich coffee was poured into stainless steel tumblers. The coffee had been prepared with fresh milk sweetened with sugar; globules of fat skirted the rim of each cup. As I swallowed the tasty skin at the top of my coffee I decided that I was going to like living in India after all.

We spent the morning quietly, our relaxation interrupted only by a flurry of excitement when visitors arrived to pay their respects to the newcomers. Mr Khader's Muslim wife, covered in a white cotton cloak, and their family shuffled in, their heads inclining towards the ground as they entered; as soon as they crossed the threshold, they shook off their outer cloaks to reveal sumptuous *saris* and bodies adorned with sparkling gold jewellery. They greeted Mum warmly, having met her at Peter's wedding celebrations.

Mr Khader was an engaging man, big and broad, with an infectious smile and a booming voice. His belly jumped in time with his frequent laughter. Nothing was too much trouble. He was solicitous of our welfare and we warmed to him quickly.

In due course we discovered that he was more than an ordinary family friend. My mother explained that after Letitia's father died, Mr Khader, already a close and wealthy friend and married with a family of his own, had offered his protection to the new widow and her three daughters. He helped to collect the rents from the various properties and land owned by his now departed friend. A story circulated that Mr Khader had actually exchanged vows with Letitia's mother to formalise their relationship and fulfilled a father figure role in the three girls' lives. This most unusual situation, especially for a Catholic family, was particularly difficult for the local community to accept. They tried to accommodate the family in their own way, and even though the Catholic Church had officially excommunicated the mother, she and her children were still allowed to attend mass and participate in all church activities bar the receiving of Holy Communion.

Mum did not encourage discussion of this delicate situation and accepted the status quo. Equally, Mr Khadar's Muslim family treated

Letitia's mother and siblings as part of their extended family; they were caring and polite, cooing over my pregnant sister-in-law and pressing lavish presents on her. Once pleasantries had been exchanged and we had been given the once-over, they took their leave.

Soon after their departure, we were taken to view our house: rented accommodation in Thambu Naiker Street, fifteen-minute rickshaws ride away. This was clearly downtown Pondicherry. The broad roads narrowed into smaller alleys. I drew a sharp breath of disappointment as I watched the opulent houses become smaller and drabber, panels of palm fronds topping the rooftops instead of slate. Wooden posts replaced the grand pillars. We passed through a labyrinth of roads of terraced houses that led off the main street.

The pavements were home to vagrants. Rolled up, ragged-looking sleeping mats leaned against the pitted walls festooned with peeling cinema posters. The smiling faces of mega-stars looked down on the homeless. Rickshaws and cars raised a dry dust that settled into open clay cooking pots. Water flowed from the crowded municipal standpipes; the children filled dented aluminium vessels while a few women were engaged with their laundry, hiking up their tattered *saris*, brandishing the dripping clothes over their heads and then bringing them down hard against strategically placed rocks, oblivious as to who was getting wet around them. I saw boiled rice, worked into a paste, being tucked into the corner of a naked child's mouth, while further down the road another mother was spit-washing dirty streaks from her child's cheeks with the free end of her *sari*. The vacant eyes of the homeless reflected nothing but the passing traffic.

Our rickshaws turned into a narrow side street where open drains ran along either side, carrying the debris of life. Lean-to shops on street corners served the local rows of houses. Our future home was a ground floor apartment in a terraced building. Two steps up, a narrow porch-cum-public-footpath led to the main heavy wooden door. On entering the doorway, a flight of steps to our left led to the flat above. Facing us at the end of a short dim tunnel was a set of doors, the top third grilled and the lower part was solid, this was the entrance to our one-bedroom flat. Halfway down the tunnel and to the left, an alcove housed a standpipe on a lipped cement square with a drainpipe in one corner. I made a mental note. Peter *annan* will have to duck to enter our flat, an observation that further dampened my spirits.

Our front door was split into two halves. The right was latched and the left opened with a key that my sister-in-law's mother produced from a cloth bag secured at her waist. A dried sacred palm tucked into the back of a framed picture of the crucifixion hanging over the doorway would have comforted Mum, but I struggled desperately not to show my disappointment with our new living quarters. Our benevolent guide waved her hand theatrically as she beamed at us, pointing out the layout of our new abode.

'See? This is the sitting room and through here is your bedroom.'

A single bedroom leading off the corner of the sitting room lay to the front of the house, about six feet wide and ten foot long. When we unlatched the top half of the single grilled stable window, the dappled light that streamed in failed to reach the length of the bedroom, the grille cast ghostly shadows on the cemented floor. The sitting room had an open area to the left supported by four pillars and a one-step-down lower square. I could cover the open square in three moderate strides; I gazed into the hot blue-sky overhead. Despite its valuable contribution of air and light, the area encroached onto the seating space, which was a wide, bare unfurnished five foot corridor that narrowed on two sides. Excitedly, Chandra and Ben rushed past me to open the two wooden cupboard doors that lay flush to the wall; their faces fell. A couple of narrow, foot wide warped shelves, wide enough only to house a few knick-knacks, were revealed. The edges of the shelves were cracked and the flat edges rose, having drawn in the humidity. It would be impossible to balance any item on them. A strong smell of fresh lime wash invaded the house. An altar built into an alcove in the middle of the wall proved the only real saving grace, bringing a satisfied smile to Mum's face.

The dining area was no more than a walk-through leading to a tiny, dark kitchen with a raised cement shelf on which stood a clay stove, with vents above to let in fresh air and dilute the cooking smells that could otherwise suffocate the cook in the tiny rectangular space. Another grilled window, like that of a prison cell, set high up into the back wall.

Through the kitchen doorway we stepped into a six-foot square concrete courtyard. Against its wall a few branches of forgotten stripped *saukai*, topped by a couple of dried cowpats, were resting. I shuddered when I noticed a centipede scuttle from its wooden hidey-hole. I resisted the urge to stamp it realising I was bare-foot, and averted my gaze to the opposite left-hand corner of the yard, where I caught a glimpse of brown, leathery hands, with veins raised in exertion, drawing water from a raised well. Panels of woven palm fenced off each backyard from its neighbours, offering scant privacy between the three houses. The panels were placed in such a manner that the neighbours to the left and behind us shared our well. The unmistakable sounds of someone bathing on the other side of the wall reached everyone's ears. In the open air, heavily flavoured with heady spices, came the strains of the latest Tamil song.

Our new abode could not provide a starker contrast to the opulence of my sister-in-law's home. Ours was a doll's house in comparison, minus even the miniature furniture that might have made it feel homely. Letitia's mother's final words rang fatefully in my ears: 'I hope you settle down in your new home,' as if our comfort was assured in this tiny one-bedroomed house. But my mother seemed content with the arrangements and the rent was affordable. Our landlords were two teachers who lived a few streets away in a similar terraced house: a polite, middle-aged, childless couple of few words who were happy to let their property to fellow Catholics. We moved into the house the following day and that is where Mum, Chandra, Benny, Irene and I lived for the next three and a half years, with my fifteen-year-old brother Charlie joining us in 1963.

Our neighbours were friendly and took an added interest when they learnt of our Malayan roots. Most families had or knew of someone working and living in France, as the French recognised the rights of the colonial citizens of Pondicherry to settle there if they wished. The expats could then send much-needed cash back to their families in India. Malaya was less well known, viewed as an exotic and rich country, well out of reach. So having us for neighbours was a novelty: 'They are from Malaya, you know!'

A brief glance out of the bedroom window offered a view of a boy of three or four squatting on his haunches, dimpled buttocks suspended over the edge, defecating directly into the open drain that flanked the main road. A bare-chested man, his paunch hanging over his bunched-up *veshtie*, leant against a wooden support and spat *paan*-coloured liquid in an arch that landed a few feet away from the squatting boy. The whole picture blurred as passing rickshaws honked their way through the crowds of hurrying human figures.

A shuddering realisation of our future life flashed across my mind. My heart grew heavy and my eyes yearned for the leafy surroundings of our home in Sentul. I lay on my mat imagining the gentle swaying of the coconut palm fronds and the dodging, zooming bats that stirred the evening air. I missed the creak of our gate and the clang of the heavy chain being dragged through as my family members traipsed in and out leaving for work, returning home, the children leaving for and returning from school. I missed the variety of food, for there were no plates of spicy *meehoon* or soy-sauce-covered noodles. No spoken Malay or Chinese could be heard.

I was grateful for the privacy afforded by our tiny, dark squatting toilet, adjacent to an equally tiny shower room, but the open drain into which the water flowed was home to cockroaches that would scuttle for shelter when I flicked the light switch on. The dim light cast by the single forty-watt bulb on a length of flex dusted with cobwebs barely reached the corners of the tiny space. Help, was that a scorpion with its tail poised to strike? Heart pounding, I would make a quick exit, mentally making a note to use the standpipe in the backyard for my ablutions. When night drew in the light bulb seemed even dimmer and, our eyes narrowed until they adjusted to the ghostly gloom. Our own gloom matched that of the room.

A couple of days later an elderly lady, who lived two doors down, knocked on our front door, her face pressed to the steel bars of the top third. She was quick to introduce herself as a family friend of our newly acquired relatives by marriage. The dimensions of the house allowed for every conversation to be heard throughout.

'Let the lady in, Chandra.' Mum's soft voice floated from the kitchen.

A rotund, grey-haired lady, dressed in the white cotton *sari* of widowhood, sidled in. Her *sari* was draped round her bare top, covering her sagging breasts. Her teeth were stained a rusty red from chewing *vethelali*. Her sunburnt skin was slack and wrinkled like the hide of an elephant, whilst the backs of her bare, splayed feet displayed cracks and crevices like the sides of a limestone hill. She advanced into our lounge deferentially at first, eyes downcast, and avoided the brand new green rattan chairs with diamond shapes plaited on the head rests, which had been delivered just that morning. She lowered herself to the floor, her back against the white washed bedroom wall, and sat modestly, with one leg placed across and the other tucked behind her. Her eyes darted everywhere, angling her head to get a better look, quickly taking in the cheap rattan furniture: there was no opulent sandalwood furniture here. Swiftly the expression on her face changed and a knowing glint appeared in her eyes – 'they may be from Malaya, but there is certainly no evidence of wealth in this household'. Her lips curled, as she looked me up and down.

As Mum entered the room, the self-invited visitor's manner changed as she became more confident. Clearly she felt she was talking to an equal now. She had the measure of us, or so she thought, and quickly worked out how she could use us to her advantage. She assumed a proprietorial interest in our family, claiming unjustified privileges as she cited her links with our relatives. Her furtive demeanour did not endear her to us, quite the reverse in fact, as we unanimously decided not to accept any 'help' she offered. Our instincts were spot on, as 'the spy', our nickname for our new 'friend', contributed to the future trials that were to end in tears for both Mum and me.

Complicated tales, involving lying and embroidering the truth (traits that were alien to our strictly Catholic upbringing), began to rear their ugly heads. She oozed concern but exaggerations and untruths rolled off her poisonous tongue. With hindsight we later realised that this lady was practising a survival exercise. She had found refuge in her son's household, but her son's family, his wife and two young children, had only his meagre wages as an office peon to live on. Our 'spy' thought that if she could ingratiate herself with some rich people, feeding them with juicy contrived gossip, she hoped to be looked on favourably and to obtain food and clothing for herself and her son's family.

During her frequent uninvited visits, the complaints against her shy young daughter-in-law never ceased.

'My son is a good-for-nothing, he always takes his wife's side, never gives me any spending money, I have to eat their leftovers and he knows I am not very well. Look at my torn *sari*, I cannot even afford a blouse.'

Mum would listen silently, her retort as always.

'All we can do is pray to God, and ask Him to take care of you.'

With that she fetched one of her own cotton *saris*, which was swiftly grabbed and tucked out of sight in the folds of the old woman's garb. Her apparently failing health did not diminish her appetite, as she made short work of any food or drink placed before her, her arm-fat swinging as she tipped the food into her gaping gullet causing the folds of her neck to move like a concertina. I vowed not to engage in conversation with her unless it was strictly necessary.

The biggest disappointment about our move to India was the change in my sister-in-law. Back in the comfort of her own home, in the bosom of her beloved family and with servants at her beck and call to fulfil her every need, the eleven months that Letitia had spent in Malaya can only have been a nightmare by comparison. She had been ill prepared for such a total change in circumstances at the tender age of sixteen. Our presence in India was a cruel reminder of a period in her life that she no doubt wanted to forget. Consequently her visits to us became fewer and fewer and finally ground to a halt. Pregnancy's hormonal changes fuelled the fires.

We felt abandoned and the scars ran deep for me. I had considered myself a friend of hers and I had made great efforts to be so in Sentul. It was Letitia's family ties that had brought us to Pondicherry; Dad might have chosen another part of India for our new home, perhaps a city closer to his own village and family. Our life in Pondicherry was akin to having taken a step backwards in time. There was a light at the end of the tunnel though, a visitor whose presence we anticipated excitedly: our beloved brother Peter was due to arrive for the birth of his first-born. He was someone we could connect with, a familiar face who would bring a breath of Malaya with him. We were totally unprepared for Peter's apparent change of outlook when he did arrive. Without fail, my mother was reduced to tears after his visits.

A chain of criticisms followed. 'Don't you know how to behave yourselves in other people's houses? Chandra, Benny, why did you jump up and down on the swing seat and run around making a lot of noise? *Tchh, ammah*, Lily, why didn't you control the children's behaviour?' He was working himself up into a rage and it was all so familiar. We were reminded of his challenging teenage exchanges with Dad.

'Lily, who is this girl who comes to visit you on her bicycle wearing shorts? So, she is your classmate? She lives in the *ashram* and was brought up in Kenya. You should not be associating with girls like her.'

The final humiliation was his radical change of opinion regarding women's education: education that was of such paramount importance to Dad, and the very reason why we had been shipped off to India. I was hurt and totally bewildered when Peter turned on our silent Mum during one of his now dreaded visits. 'Why are you educating Lily? After all, she is just a girl, and she will get married and leave the family soon. It is a waste of money.'

Was this really my brother's view? I leaned on the wall at the bedroom doorway, listening in dismayed silence as tears welled in my eyes. My scholarly life was now deemed unimportant, irrelevant even, to a young woman of marriageable age. Peter had become a frightening stranger. Silently I cried out for Dad; I missed his reassuring presence, his compassion and the benevolent twinkle in his eyes. Where was Peter getting these ideas? How was it possible for him to change his opinions so radically? Why had his mind clouded over, a veil seemingly drawn over his usually sharp analytical mind? Millions in India echoed the sentiments he had just expressed, which may have appeared laudable on the surface but which were fundamentally flawed.

Peter hadn't finished.

'How are you ever going to find a groom for Lily? And why are you both always crying? It is a bad omen for the family.'

Mum sat, head bowed, on the rattan chair. Her hand rested on six-year-old Irene's puzzled head. No reply was necessary. Mum began weeping silently. Chandra and Benny stood in the kitchen doorway, frightened into silence.

Stamping his foot in disgust, Peter made his exit into the bosom of his new family, leaving behind a cowed, dejected and helpless group. Peter's cruel words were crushing. They were weighted with ignorance, arrogance, small-mindedness and cultural backwardness, falling into the very pit out of which our Dad had climbed. He had held out his enlightened hands to his offspring and pushed them forward, encouraging them to enjoy the freedom that a good education promised. Dad's all-encompassing passion and his hope was that each and every one of his children, regardless of their gender, should have equal opportunities. My dearest beloved brother was expressing sentiments that ran completely counter to Dad's sacred beliefs.

Alphonse, my nephew, arrived on the 21 January, 1963, just under two months after our arrival in India; two months that had felt like two years. Letitia had produced a much-coveted male first grandchild and now drew even more of her family's attention and admiration. After our initial visit to the maternity unit we kept our distance.

Peter and Letitia left for Malaya when the baby was a couple of months old and life for us returned to some semblance of normality, though our initial expectations of enjoying any benefit from our newly acquired relatives remained a pipe dream. We missed Peter despite the fact that his visits were often tear filled. He remained our much-respected and beloved older brother. This had to be a temporary lapse, he was bound to come to his senses once he returned home. No one back in Malaya was wise to our situation. Our daily life continued. We practised one of Mum's ten commandments: '*Dushtherai parrthaal dhura poh.*' This roughly translated as 'keep your distance from troublemakers'.

32

'A storm at sea and at home...'

Charlie

A year had passed and we had settled into a routine. We were becoming used to the narrow streets of the city, populated by a constantly ebbing and flowing sea of human beings. The routines of school, church and home formed the pattern of our lives. Then another of our siblings joined us. Meanwhile Malaya as we had left it was now known as Malaysia. On the 16th of September 1963 Singapore (between 1963-1965) Sarawak and Sabah joined Malaya to become Malaysia. We had now become Malaysians.

Charlie's studies had taken a bit of a nosedive and in desperation Dad packed him off to India, hoping that Mum's influence might succeed where his and Theresa's had failed. We were on countdown now, because two months before his fifteenth birthday Charlie had boarded the *State of Madras*, the same ship that had carried Mum and Peter in 1961 and us in 1962. But unlike us, Charlie was travelling alone. I could only imagine what Charlie was experiencing. I wondered if he was seasick, if there had been anyone Dad could introduce him to, someone to keep an eye on him? Every day brought its own fresh anxieties but these were mixed with excitement. In the grey evening light our ghostly figures knelt before the altar beseeching Our Lord for Charlie's safety. Mum's rosary beads were fingered constantly.

Two days before Charlie was due to arrive, preparations began in earnest. Mum was offered a safe escort to Madras by Periavur. Our stalwart neighbour could not have been more than fifty, but his lined face appeared to carry the weight of the whole world. His face had aged prematurely. His generous eyebrows shadowed deep-set eyes; the whites were flecked with brown age spots. His aristocratic nose was the shape of a perpendicular triangle. His measured speech indicated great suffering. We learned that his wife had died in childbirth, and, contrary to tradition, he had decided against marrying again to provide a mother for his young children. He chose instead to take responsibility for the upbringing of his daughter and baby son Guna single-handedly, earning the respect of the local community in the process. He carried himself with dignity. His soft, caring face showed concentration as he listened. He could be relied upon to say and do the right thing, and was a universal friend when in need but a formidable foe if provoked. Affectionately known as Periavur, meaning big in knowledge and age, the name was a sign of respect as if he was a village elder. His big-boned, tall frame meant he had to dip his head to enter our tiny sitting room where his size became accentuated. Painful echoes of my Dad's role in his local community were prompted by his presence.

Mum and our neighbour were to stay overnight at Periavur's friends' house before meeting Charlie's ship when it docked in Madras the next day. We were strangely restless the night before they were due to leave. There was an eerie stillness in the air, as we tossed and turned on our mats. A huge clap of thunder and a howling wind outside our bedroom window in the early hours of the morning rudely awakened everybody. The ferocity of the torrential rain that soon followed rendered our speech inaudible. Peel upon peel of thunder preceded startling bolts of lightning. The streets were thrown into pitch darkness as the lights went out. We groped about by feel. Urging us to remain calm, Mum managed to make her way into the sitting room and locate the candle and matches on the altar. She did not light the candle until she had re-entered the bedroom and shut the door firmly against the ferocious wind that was moving our furniture around in the sitting room. Silently, whilst we huddled together in bewilderment, Mum mouthed her prayers, fingering her rosary beads with a bent head.

The dreaded monsoon had arrived at exactly the wrong time for us. There was no respite from the relentless rain and a raging torrent of water mixed with debris soon replaced the street outside. Mum's planned trip was impossible. Periavur fought his way in, shaking his head with exasperation.

'So sorry, there is no transport anywhere. The trains and buses have all stopped. Floods are everywhere. We will have to wait for the rain to stop and the buses to start running again. I hear that the monsoon is raging in Madras too.'

Our hearts sank deeper and deeper into despair as dark as the murky flood waters that kept on rising. Water seeped under the main door and filled the narrow corridor that led to our front door like water spilling over the lip of an overflowing drum. But thankfully it rose no further. The sunken forecourt adjacent to the open drain was

305

under water but our lounge and bedroom and kitchen area escaped, assuring us of our food supply and a dry floor to sleep on.

We seemed to age in the next two days of helplessness. Had the ship managed to dock? Had it and all its passengers perished in the storms? If it had managed to make it by some miracle, what was Charlie's plight? As ever Mum's unswerving faith was our lifeline. Finally the waters started to abate and everybody engaged in a mass clear-up operation. Ever in our thoughts, though, was our brother; we had no inclination to chat.

Our neighbours informed us that a skeleton train service was about to begin. Mum hurried to prepare once more for her interrupted trip. Chandra and Benny had disappeared. An hour later their excited shouts echoed in the narrow corridor. My back was bent over as I snapped Mum's suitcase shut: I turned to the sound of a whistle and nearly tripped over the nearest rattan chair. There stood Charlie, Chandra and Benny in his wake with wide grins fixed on their faces, eyes shining with unshed tears. They had won the biggest trophy of their lives.

'Praise the Lord! How, how, *how*, did you manage to make your way here?'

We were hysterical, crying with relief, crowding round Charlie and touching him. Our mother faced the altar and uttered a silent prayer of gratitude. Charlie's inscrutable gaze was fixed on no one in particular. He prised the white canvas shoes from his feet without untying them and flicked them into the corner. He swaggered about, his eyes raised to the ceiling at our reaction, as though he couldn't understand what all the fuss was about. Typically, Charlie hid his true feelings and made light of his experiences, only telling us the bare facts as my imagination ran riot. I pictured a young lad getting off the ship after a lonely five days in the horrible conditions that we had all experienced. Searching anxiously for a friendly face among a sea of people. His worried face would have searched in vain and despair would have slowly settled in, as time passed with no relative in sight.

But these were only my imaginings: Charlie's answers to our questions were mere one-liners, which we had to join together to come up with the real story. The ship's welfare officer had accompanied Charlie to a basic hostel where he had spent two nights. As soon as the trains started operating again the officer then escorted Charlie to the station, making sure he knew about the need to change trains in Villapuram, a local village on the way up. On arrival in Pondicherry, Charlie had been on the point of getting into a rickshaw when Chandra and Benny, who had been hanging about at the station and hoping against hope, spotted their travel-weary brother. As there was room for only two passengers in the rickshaw and Charlie's luggage occupied the vacant space by his side, an over-excited Chandra and a grinning Benny had followed in a second one. Now here they all were, and after three days of continuous fear, everyone could breathe easily again. The dread of never seeing my brother again had been so strong that the feeling of relief made me break down. But Charlie kept us all at arm's length.

'What is the matter with you all? *Chee, chee*! Look, I am fine. I know how to take care of myself. Stop being so silly, stop crying.'

I could not comprehend the new Charlie who had joined us: it seemed that a hostile stranger had arrived. The year apart had wrought changes in him that were inexplicable. He continued to distance himself from us, which was exasperating. He showed no inclination to study and he lacked any academic prowess. Under duress, and after a few lectures on the importance of education for a young man who would be expected to support a family, Charlie reluctantly followed me to Petit Seminarie. The plan was that he would join his brothers, but Charlie's academic levels were such as to place him with his younger brother Chandra. Our father had had to face a similar situation years before when he originally left India and arrived in Malaysia. Charlie was hugely insulted by the prospect of sharing a classroom with those much younger than he was, and refused to accept it. He decided against school altogether. Our hopes for his future were clothed in grey clouds. Mum and I pleaded our case, desperately trying to get through to him, but he remained steadfast, defiant.

'I told you; I don't want to go to school. I will find a way to make money. You don't need an education, there are other ways; besides, I want to start work now, not in a few years time.'

'What can you do now, who is going to give you a job?' we asked.

Optimism surged through his young veins.

'I have already spoken to Murugan's brother. He owns a bicycle repair shop and he said I can work for him, so I am starting work tomorrow.'

A teenage girl called Pitchamma lived in one of the terraced properties that faced us. Her house lacked running water as the water supply came from a communal well. She paid regular visits, a highly polished brass pitcher balanced at her waist that lit up the gloom of the corridor when she came to collect drinking water. When the standpipe under the stairs in the hall was turned on, I listened to the sharp sound of the water hitting the bottom of the empty vessel, a sound that gradually become duller as the pitcher filled. Any moment now her grinning face would be pressed against the grille, her finger-combed hair pulled into a loose bun sitting on the nape of her jewellery-free neck. At a nod from me, Pitchamma would wrench open the door and skip in. Her feet were bare but her ankles were circled with tinkling, silver-covered patterned anklets. Her sparkling eyes searched for Charlie and her cheeks turned pink when he walked in with his exaggerated swagger. Her timing was impeccable as always. Her gaze hit the floor demurely for a second but returned to Charlie immediately as she gave a little laugh. I watched the pantomime with an indulgent acceptance, thinking that no harm was being done, that they were young and this was just a small romantic interlude in their adolescent lives. Mindful that her family were awaiting her return with the water, she reluctantly turned to leave, after eliciting a shopping list from me and throwing more sidelong glances at Charlie. Protocol prevented her from mustering the courage to speak directly to my brother. Her long single plait hit her pert little bottom as she turned on her heel, casting a last glance over her shoulder.

I accompanied her to the door. I was sympathetic to her girlish, romantic yearnings; I understood her feelings for Charlie. Her glass bracelets tinkled as she embraced the belly of the water pitcher with one arm and grasped the lip with the other hand, deftly lifting the filled container with one swift move and balancing it at her waist. Returning home, she spilled splashes of water along the way as she almost skipped along in her excitement. In return for this water, for which we paid, Pitchamma ran some errands for us.

We were introduced to the rest of her family. Her father was long dead and her elderly mother had been responsible for her upbringing, though her older brother and his wife, Kani *ammah*, kept a watchful eye on the teenager as they raised their own son. The second brother, a skinny young bachelor called Vijayan, was a shy fellow with an almost self-deprecating smile. He was always busy on his old foot-pedalled Singer sewing machine. He made many a *sari* blouse for Mum and me, using our old ones as templates, as well as dresses for Irene and clothes for my brothers. All these garments were sewn expertly and cheaply in the two-by-six-feet pavement store on Periavur's premises. Another older brother, also very shy, was Muga, who owned the bicycle shop a few streets away where Charlie was going to work.

Murugan, the last of Pitchamma's brothers, worked as a mill hand. His lower lip didn't quite close in his square face. He looked like an old man but Murugan was only eighteen. His gums were prominent when he smiled and a childhood accident at a game of marbles had left him blind in one eye. His one good eye roved all over the house, his whole head moving with his eye as his sight was limited; it bounced from side to side like that of an excited child. It made me feel quite dizzy until I got used to it. Charlie and Murugan became firm friends.

Mum and I eventually admitted defeat in the face of the fifteen-year-old Charlie's determined plans, and bowed to his wishes. It was strangely reassuring to hear his early morning whistle as he readied himself for work. He returned late in the evening, tired and filthy, but his contented smile was our reward.

After two years of toil, having learnt all he was going to, Charlie grew defensive when questioned about his future career path. Dad resigned himself to the fact that Charlie was against any further education in whatever shape or form, and was persuaded that he should return to Malaysia, leaving the five of us in India. Without educational qualifications, Charlie could not find employment alongside Dad in the railways. Instead, he started work in a provision shop in Petaling Jaya, a new town that was developing fast on the outskirts of Kuala Lumpur.

33

'Beggars and Kolums…'

Indian Traditions

Pondicherry's proximity to the Coromandel Coast allowed sea breezes to wash over the coastline, maintaining a pleasant, even temperature. Communication was mostly in Tamil. In Malaysia, every sentence was interspersed with words adopted from our colonial masters' language; similarly, in this part of India, Tamil sentences were peppered with French. With the aid of French primary school books and a French dictionary, I soon learnt to mimic the locals. I chose the Indian national language of Hindi as my second language at school, a choice I unfortunately lived to regret.

Periodically, Dad would dispatch parcels of goodies to us via various visiting relatives and friends. One day I unpacked two nylon *sari*s, all the rage back home, in orange with green flock embroidery clearly meant for me whilst Mum's was more sedate beige with chocolate brown. Each came with detachable, matching *sari* blouse pieces, ready for Vijayan's expert fingers. Four pairs of Japanese slippers, blues and greens for the boys and pink for Irene, were also unwrapped. Malaysia had come to me in the package. I perused the Malayan *Straits Times* newspaper wrapping, inhaling the smell of it as I read. The familiar tears were never far away as I devoured every item of news, however insignificant.

Impatient to show off the slippers, Charlie, Chandra, Benny and Irene marched off to the beach to dispel their high energy. Their feet kicked into their new Japanese slippers as they dashed out of the door and shot down the narrow corridor.

On a whim, they decided to bury the slippers in the soft sand of the beach. Young Irene was entrusted to stand guard over the spot, as the boys were enticed away by their friends' games. But bored Irene left her station to join in. Engrossed in their play, no one realised the implications until it was time to return home. Having spent fruitless hours looking for the buried slippers, my subdued siblings returned home totally crestfallen. Their feet were blackened and grazed and Irene's hair had broken loose from its plait, the ribbons hanging in twists.

'We told Irene to stay where the slippers were buried, but she left them and moved from the spot,' said Charlie.

'You didn't remind me though when I came to play with you – you were happy for me to join you,' she sobbed.

'Never mind, Irene, don't cry, it was our fault. We should have known better.'

Mum and I could not chastise them; losing the valued slippers was punishment enough. We caught one another's eye and suppressed our smiles. Every time the story about the loss of their brand new slippers was recounted it drew a heartfelt sigh from the quartet.

India teemed with the visible poor. Their homes were the filthy pavements, where rodents, eight to ten inches long, scratched about for pickings. Flyblown garbage littered the streets. A string of familiar beggars frequented our local streets, recognisable by their signature songs, which were surprisingly tuneful and entertaining. One middle-aged woman, dressed scantily in rags, appeared every few weeks with streaks of dried blood down her legs. Was this a genuine lack of a suitable cloth to stem the flow of menstruation, or a ploy to get our sympathy? She accompanied her supplicant stance with a particularly heart-rending song that never failed to move us. Despite us presenting her with an old *sari* to cover her modesty, she regularly appeared in her familiar rags. Mum shrugged her shoulders with resignation, aware that the cunning lady had got the better of us. We continued to offer her lunch, neatly packaged in a banana leaf, which she accepted with gratitude from Kamachi our maid, casting audible blessings for the residents of the house.

It was almost a daily occurrence to witness youngsters of eight or so years old with suppurating sores, oozing in thick rivulets down their blood-streaked, emaciated, dusty, bluebottle-covered legs. Barefoot and with blackened toenails, they dragged makeshift wooden carts along, into which a parent was crammed. The parent's claw-like hands rendered them incapable of grasping anything; their faces were deformed, with holes for noses and ears and their stumpy limbs rubbing against the rough wooden sides of the cart. Leprosy affected their nerve-endings so the individuals experienced no pain as they were bumped around on the uneven roads. The furnace-like temperatures scorched their skins and the dry dust reached deep into their lungs.

Our neighbours discouraged generosity to beggars of any type; they were not swayed by their emotions as their own lives were governed by poverty. They clicked their tongues at us in disapproval.

'You shouldn't be encouraging them; they are lazy people, not willing to work. The more you give them they more lazy they become. You are a soft touch. They can sense you are foreigners – see how they linger by your doorway but bypass ours? They are crafty, that's what.'

There may have been an element of truth in this view, but there was no way of distinguishing between individual cases. Our generosity was their lifeline. The uneven distribution of wealth was there for all to see: the colossal houses that lined every smart street bore witness to the obscene wealth of some. Tall iron railings guarded households where large amounts of money and gold were held in steel safes. Our sister-in-law's house held three such safes and I knew that this was true of my rich classmates' families too. Ghee-soaked-biryani-fattened men and women heaved themselves into human-powered rickshaws. The scrawny rickshaw-pullers strained their backs and the wheels creaked as they dodged the traffic.

The location of our house brought us into close proximity with all aspects of life. Diagonally opposite our house was a long stretch of pock-marked wall, ending at the junction with the main road. On the dusty patch of land by the weathered wall, a cow was tethered to iron rings cemented into it. She could be seen from our bedroom window. The lower half of the window was kept shut for privacy, but the boys craned their necks out of the higher section and round to the left for a good view. Irene, balanced on the ledge on tiptoe, called out to me excitedly.

'*Akka*, come and see! Something is happening to that cow, its eyes are rolling, and it is moving about from side to side.'

With little knowledge of nature's life cycle, I could not throw any light on what we were witnessing.

'I don't know what is going on; it does look strange, doesn't it?'

My head stood out above the rest of the children as we peered curiously through the steel bars.

'Look, look! Something is coming out from its behind, *aiey-yo*, something all slimy and wet. The cow is all shaky now. Look, look the thing is falling!'

The cow stood next to a steaming mound of her own dung, and a pool of yellow urine was trickling down to the road. She was in a lather of sweat, frothing at the mouth. Her bulging eyes rolled. I realised, too late, that I should have sent my brothers and sister away from the bedroom window. The mother licked the glutinous membrane that encased her baby, gently pulling it off to free the calf. We watched, wide-eyed, as the calf first attempted to get up onto its forelegs, then fell, too weak to stand at first. With repeated efforts it eventually stood up and started suckling from its mother. Show over, we moved away from the window and back to our interrupted chores, a little wiser to nature's wonders.

The trumpeting of elephants would make every household member dash outside. Richly adorned, garlanded elephants came as part of a religious procession with equally decorated statues of Hindu gods balanced on the palanquin strapped to the elephants back. Other times they came singly with a loincloth-clad *mahoot* balanced on the elephant's neck. This was a chance the *mahoot* took to earn a few extra pennies from devotees, and there was never a shortage of them. Mothers offered their children, including babies, to be held against the smelly elephant's head for blessings. Others pressed coins into the grasping hands of the master, which swiftly found a home in the waistband of his loincloth. After a brief glance, I lifted my finger to my nose and drew back indoors.

Smoking dung piles, dropped by the cows that roamed freely on the streets, were deftly collected by bare, nut-brown hands, mixed with straw, shaped into pancakes, and used to decorate the sun-warmed walls of the houses. Housewives sold the cakes for profit, or used them in their houses as kindling to start a fire in their clay *adupus* – stoves. Everything was turned into a commercial product. The firewood for cooking was sold on the streets, bullock carts piled high with the very same saukai that was cultivated in my father's land in Trichi. The resulting ash made a powerful soap for washing the soot off cooking pots. Women balanced bundles of kindling sticks on their heads; one hand holding the bundle while the other gripped their child, as they pounded the streets with their wares.

The welfare of my siblings naturally fell to me, the eldest of the present household. I was responsible for their behaviour. My mother was vulnerable and I was aware of her reliance on me. We were ultimately still foreigners attempting to fit into a restrictive culture. I tutored my siblings, overseeing their schoolwork, and generally exercised discipline. My mother's firm belief was that God had the answer to all her problems, but my faith was not as strong as hers. I cultivated a more realistic attitude.

A problem seemed to be developing with Chan's shower routine. Had he been frightened by the ever-present rodent, or by a scorpion or a centipede? Gentle reminders were being ignored, so drastic measures had to be employed. My will to be obeyed was strong. I walked with purpose to the bathroom, turned on the shower, and dragged a reluctant Chan, fully clothed, into the bathroom, and shut the door with a bang. I listened out for the sound of the bolt being shot home in the door but it did not happen. The entire family sat on their rattan chairs in the sitting area watching the scene. I flounced back to them, huffing and puffing, and took my own seat with the words; 'You are not coming out of there until you've had your shower!'

There was total silence from the audience. The sound of water hitting the concrete floor lasted for a few minutes. I lifted an eyebrow at Mum, but she busied herself tightening a loose button on Charlie's shirt. I scanned the pages of my book without taking it in. Charlie continued to tighten the nut on the lid of a saucepan that had worked loose. Irene attempted to memorise some lines of poetry set for her homework. My attention returned to the shut bathroom door as I contemplated what to do next.

An almighty sound reverberated round the room. The door had given way to a kick, and it flew open on its hinges. The still-clothed, crane-like figure of Chan, his spine erect, arms held stiffly at his sides, stormed towards the front door. Darkened by the water, his short shorts emphasised his spindly legs. He was dripping water everywhere, and it made a pool on the cement floor.

Our mouths gaped open as Chan's figure disappeared from sight into the street. We turned to one another wide-eyed, shocked at first, but then collapsed into laughter, shoulders shaking, bent over our stomachs, tears running down our faces. We laughed until our ribs hurt. An audible chuckle and smile even emerged from Mum, who rarely laughed out loud. Clearly I had lost and I admitted defeat. Chan's rebellious adolescent streak, rarely exhibited, had won the day.

He returned an hour later with his clothes crinkle-dried. No one made any reference to the incident for days, silenced by the sheer unexpectedness of the scene made by the usually placid Chan. My misjudged action had however paid off: Chan required no further reminders about his shower. A week later he returned from school with a book in his hand. He had been shopping, spending his pocket money.

'Here *akka*, I was passing by the *ashram* shop, they had the latest book in the series you read. I bought it for you.'

'Thanks Chan, I will pay you back for it.'

'No, don't, I can afford it. I am sorry for last week. I know you were only doing the right thing and I was at fault.'

'Don't mention it Chan. It is forgotten.'

It certainly wasn't forgotten though. Every now and again we collapsed with laughter as we recalled the scene and dear Chan was forced to join in. Despite the frustration on both sides, the roots of our affection went deep enough for true forgiveness. Chan's way of expressing his guilt was so eloquent and I was humbled by his generosity. I wished I had shown equal consideration and not cornered him. I made a mental note not to make my siblings do anything they were really unwilling to do, even if in my opinion it was in their own interests.

I was content to succumb to the ways of Indian culture, to practise the traditional way of life, but I drew the line at Indian marriage customs. Girls married early. Marriages were arranged for the convenience of their families, anxious to retain their own wealth and land. When male visitors came to our house, particularly those who were not family members, I stood respectfully in the doorway to our bedroom, head bowed in deference, as custom demanded. But I resented being put on display when elderly ladies arrived. I was expected to prepare drinks for our visitors and then serve these to them. All my movements were scrutinised, approval or disapproval acknowledged by a nod or a shake of the head. I could read their minds – 'she would make a good wife, I must talk to my son when I get back'.

Thankfully such visits were few and far between. I accepted the Indian lifestyle at face value and our family's good name had to be preserved at all costs. On this one matter I stood firm: I had no plans to accept any proposals that came our family's way.

Dutifully I observed the customs of a young Indian girl. My neighbours and in-laws did not know the Malaysian me, just the person I had become as I willingly embraced the local way of life. Draped in *saris*, long skirts and *cholis* we walked in the street with bent heads. Every evening, housewives and young ladies gathered at their respective doorways, a practice made socially acceptable by the presence of my mother and siblings. Everyone would exchange pleasantries whilst the children played on the streets, dodging cycle rickshaws as the drivers tooted their horns or rang their bells shrilly. We conversed with our female neighbours as the setting sun reduced the air temperature a degree or two and then the street lights gradually stuttered into life as dusk fell. Under our families' protection, we furtively eyed the steady stream of people who passed by. Young men cast appreciative glances at shy young girls dressed in their colourful evening finery, freshly showered, powdered and bedecked with flowers. With racing hearts and suppressed giggles, young girls threw furtive sideways glances at the would-be Lotharios as they cycled slowly past, repeating witty, provocative lines from the latest movies and songs.

Always game for a challenge, I knuckled down to another tradition performed by the maidens of every family. Before the lord and master left the house, and even before the morning sun had peeled away the shadows cast by the dim street lights, with angry gnats brushing against the exposed bulbs, ghostly figures of barefoot teenage girls, still warm from their mats, slipped out into the semi-darkness. We balanced highly polished brass containers on our hips, filled with water. Cupping our hands and dipping them into the pots, we proceeded to sprinkle the water onto the street that faced our houses and swept the road clean with palm-frond brooms. Then in relative silence we set to work. Ground rice was mixed with water to form a paste, and with this we created elaborate patterns on the freshly prepared roads. Furtive glances were cast around to judge the most intricate and novel pattern. My bosom swelled with pride when my latest creation drew appreciative remarks; I positively glowed at such an honour.

'Can I copy your pattern?'

'Yes of course. I will lend you my pattern book.'

'So what pattern are you drawing tomorrow then?'

'Wait and see. I created a new design last night, so I hope it turns out well.'

Just as I joined up the last two dots, my opposite neighbour ambled out of his front door. He ignored his daughter bent over her design and stretched his legs by squatting briefly to the ground, let out a loud yawn, stood up, cracked his elbows and with clenched fists stretched his arms out and struck the air.

'Lazy git,' I muttered furiously under my breath. 'He won't step out on to the road until his daughter has sanctified it for him.'

The emerging sun gave life to the *attap* roofs. Its groping fingers found raised verandas and woke sleeping figures stretched out on their mats. I turned my back on the waking bodies and returned to our house. I was quick to embrace the way of life in India, complying with restrictive local customs, and I was content to contribute to the colourful canvas of a vibrant, pulsing community.

My brothers and five-year-old Irene enjoyed far more freedom than I did, but in the background an element of romance was entering my life. Dashing young Guna, the only son of Periavur, our neighbour and community leader, provided a welcome diversion. Safe in the knowledge that there could be no future for the two of us because of our religious differences, I indulged in harmless daydreams about him. My pulse raced when I saw him cross the road, dressed in a short cotton *veshtie* that sat above his knees and was tied to his slim waist. His fair, muscular body glistened in the sunshine. He pushed back his wavy, jet-black hair from his high forehead and his gaze was steady behind his spectacles. He called out authoritatively to his young cousins as they played by the roadside. There was a certain swagger to his walk, as if he expected everyone to know whose son he was. I was never quite sure if this daily strut-around was in my honour, because I was convinced he was aware of my scrutiny from the sanctuary of our bedroom.

A medical student enrolled at the Pondicherry Medical College, he was instrumental in acquiring a place for me there, provided that I could fulfil the necessary entry requirements. Siva and I shared another common interest: we were avid readers. In pride of place in our little sitting room was a gate-legged square table placed against the wall. It had been lovingly covered with a green baize cloth, and on it my collection of books was arranged by height in ascending order. A couple of bricks at either end served as bookends. I fingered my books with pride on my way to the kitchen or the bathroom. Guna took note of my neat arrangement during one of his rare visits with his father.

'I see you love reading too. I have some books that you might be interested in; maybe we could exchange reading material?'

Our go-between was Irene, and via her we swapped our books backwards and forwards until we had exhausted our stock. Siva's novels mainly concerned the world of American cowboys, a new subject for me to explore, though I did so without much enthusiasm. Cowboy language did not strike a chord with me.

My mother missed Peter's presence terribly. In a way Siva became a substitute for Peter, once Mum discovered that Siva's mother had lost her life giving birth to him, her second child. Siva had grown up deprived of motherly love, which aroused Mum's maternal instincts. She prepared tasty meals for his family that Irene and Chandra were entrusted to deliver, meals that were gratefully received. Mum's culinary talents were practised to the full. Meat cooked to succulent tenderness with Malaysian-influenced spices, garnished with golden cashews fried in rich and fragrant *vanaspati* ghee and the green of fresh coriander strands, was Guna's favourite. Malaysian food was a definite winner as far as he was concerned. 'Tell your mother her food is delicious.' In her eyes he was still a young, motherless boy. Mum accepted his compliments with her customary humility.

Guna's best friend was the brother of my classmate Gita. Their father was a respected local doctor, a near-neighbour of my sister-in-law's family. Gita had just turned seventeen when her parents arranged a suitable marriage for her. The bridegroom, a much older man from the southern town of Madurai, was a graduate. The well-to-do bride's family provided a suitable dowry.

I attended the wedding by invitation, aware throughout the ceremony of Guna's very visible presence, as he shadowed his best friend and helped to guide the guests to their seats. I sensed furtive glances thrown in my direction. We both took great care not to acknowledge one another, unwilling to provide the gossipmongers with any leverage, in a house full of wedding guests. Two days later, aware of Gita's impending departure to her husband's household, I arrived by rickshaw.

'Hello aunty, I wanted to say good bye to Gita before she went away.'

'Gita and her husband are enjoying a siesta. I cannot disturb them but I will let her know you called,' her answer delivered in hushed tones.

With that I was politely shown the door. The family were unwilling to upset the new bridegroom in any way, and the sound of conversation from the sitting room might wake the sleeping couple from their afternoon slumber. After all, Gita was now the property of her husband and he was her first priority. All ties to her former life were relegated to second place. I hung my head in embarrassment, feeling suitably admonished and belittled. I had intruded into my friend's new life and I should have known better. A heavy heart accompanied my rickshaw ride home.

Well, well, poor Gita, I thought; I wonder what her married life is going to be like. She was such a fun-loving person, with a permanent smile on her face and a mischievous glint in her eyes. A sigh of resignation escaped my lips as I wondered if I would ever see her again.

My hand reached for the knob on the radio as I walked through the sitting room on the way to my early morning ablutions. To me, life without the gentle sound of music was like walking in the desert with an empty water bottle. The lyrics, cleverly constructed, described the nuances of love, of deep forbidden longings, of the forced separation of lovers, through familial expectations and loyalties. Jubilant lovers celebrated their union; a mother's lullaby comforted a hungry baby; the searing anguish of loved ones was captured as they bade farewell, or the laments of women in mourning. Voices were raised in unison as men and women worked the caked soils with calloused hands. Music nourished the soul, as did trips to the cinema, the nation's favourite pastime. Thanks to my early education I was able to decipher the

Tamil film credits. The radio repeatedly broadcast the songs from the latest film releases and I could also read the flimsy songbooks bought for a few *annas* and follow the Tamil lyrics.

Films were churned out at breakneck pace. To miss any film featuring our screen idol, Shivaji, would be unthinkable. He was unquestionably the darling of the South Indian people as he breathed life into every role, often reducing the audience to tears. His films had a high moral tone, where personal happiness was sacrificed for the good of the family and the possession of money led to a rich but corrupt life. His screen songs were full of fervour, the unforgettable lyrics rich with parables, and they were immediate hits.

We debated endlessly about which scene, in which movie, had produced a particular song. What was the character's name? Which actor had played the part and sung that song? Was it Gemini Ganesan? He was another handsome hero of the time; his wavy black hair had a seductive curl that fell forward onto his broad forehead, and he was the man who invaded many maidens' dreams.

There were five 'talkies', or cinemas, spaced out around the relatively small town of Pondicherry. Each screened a selection of South Indian Tamil and North Indian Hindi movies. Every show was packed. Chandra, our family cinema buff, was armed with in-depth knowledge of all the latest film releases and unerringly knew which cinema was going to screen which films. Mum entrusted him with the money to purchase our tickets – first-class tickets, booked in advance, ensuring us comfortable seats. Those who purchased the cheaper tickets were in the majority, forming a swelling crowd. They occupied rows and rows of hard, backless, wooden benches, arranged at the front of the cinema. People hopped from one bench to another, amidst excited chatter before the film commenced, in their efforts to obtain the best view and the greatest proximity to the screen. Excitement flowed through the waiting crowd as everyone anticipated a couple of hours of escapism. We joined the merry throng as we approached the jasmine-scented sweetness of the first-class seats.

The very air around us seemed to be draped in a cloak of romance. Young married couples occupied a large number of the seats nearby: the educated, rich, city couples linked arms, whilst others chose a chaste mode of behaviour. The wife, decked out in her brand new *sari*, its folds still visible, no doubt chosen from her dowry package, walked two steps behind her betrothed. Once seated, the proprietorial bridegrooms reached out a hand to their bashful brides, fresh from the intimacy of their bridal bed. The sound of the jangle and clink of multi-coloured glass bangles knocking together jostled with the shouts of vendors, who balanced trays of drinks in their hands. 'Soda, colour (milk coloured pink with sweet sherbet a herbal root boiled in a sugar solution), tea,' they called, as they picked up a bunch of three or four glasses at a time with the ends of their fingers, nails embedded with black dirt, and exchanged them for a few Pisa's offered by the well-dressed ladies. The lack of hygiene was stomach-churning. I refused to be tempted, even if my tongue was sticking to the roof of my mouth with thirst.

Raucous laughter at some of the provocative scenes made the young ladies squirm in their seats. Swords-fights were common, as well as physical fights with plenty of blood and guts, hugely appealing to the male members of the audience. These violent scenes were a must for the baying crowds, while the romantic scenes had the ladies lowering their heads coyly. MGR, an ageing actor, was a favourite hero, often engaging in love scenes with ladies young enough to be his granddaughters.

Sex was always implied, though not even a chaste kiss was actually exchanged on screen. The scene might shift from a couple seated on a bench, where the man gently lifted the girl's chin to his eye level while she coyly closed her eyes, to two birds sitting on a bough, pecking affectionately at each other. P Susheela and AM Raja, favourite background singers, beautifully expressed the romantic songs with their dulcet voices and lifted all the spectators into heights of ecstasy.

Sometimes Mum and I would decide to walk home after a show. The nights were languorous and spicy, with cooling winds from the sea funnelling through the maze of streets and picking up the scattered debris, swirling it about madly. The romance of the film lingered as we walked with light hearts and we were kept amused by the young men who followed us at a discreet distance on their bicycles. They weaved their way through the traffic, singing a verse or two of a song from the film we had just seen. Warmth spread through me as I blushed a little, embarrassed at the implications of the lines. I could see the boys without moving my head. Mum was amused and a soft smile accompanied the twinkle in her eye. I was at peace. I felt very close to Mum as I caught her smiles.

Closer to home another innocent thrill awaited, a cat and mouse game that Mum was well aware of but refrained from discussing. My heart missed a beat and my breath quickened and shallowed. I nervously scanned our neighbour's veranda and felt vindicated when a man's figure could be seen, leaning on the rail, outlined against the dim light from the bedroom behind. He withdrew quickly into the shadows but Guna was not quick enough. Mum cleared her throat in acknowledgement, but nothing further needed to be said.

Pondicherry beaches, famed for their fine white sand, were a draw too difficult to resist. We set off along the narrow streets that led down to the wind-whipped sea front. The raised stone verandas of the houses we passed held rolled up mats leant against their walls ready to be unrolled for the night. String beds stood with bedding balanced at one end. Elderly men and women passed the time by exchanging gossip as they sat cross-legged or dangled their feet over the edge, chewing *paan*, and periodically spitting out the vermilion liquid into the open drain. They acknowledged us with a smile and a nod or a clearing of the throat as we walked past. The sea breeze mingled with the stale smell from the open drains as they snaked their way through the narrow streets. Putrid dregs caught in the grooves of the open drains on either side of the roads; they were littered with the remnants of children's faeces, caught in the kinks in the drains, decomposing and mixing with the stench of urine. We kept to the middle of the road to avoid the splash of the spittle and gave as wide a berth as we could to the debris. We hurried through the congested streets to reach the sweeter, cooling air from the sea front. The breeze pasted the thick folds of my *sari* between my legs. We filled our lungs with deep gulps, eager to feel the gentle caress of the air on our warm cheeks. As we drew closer, Chandra and Ben broke into a trot while the rest of us kept up an easy pace.

Having reached the crowded Beach Road, we strolled along at the edge of the water, letting the waves curl and eddy round our toes to cool them. The pearly white, soft sand felt like satin, every grain freshly cleaned by the gently lapping waters. Parked on the edge of the road, vendors sold fragrant fried chickpeas, glistening in a coating of coconut oil and flecked with specks of dried chillies, black mustard seeds and fragrant curry leaves. These treats were piled high into newspaper cones and cost only a few Pisa's. My own weakness was peanuts fried in oil, their delicate brown skins still clinging to them but easily removed by gently rubbing between the palms of the hands, the tiny wafer-thin wisps then whisked away by the cooling breeze.

Performing monkeys drew admiring crowds, earning supper for their masters. Flies that gathered round the vendors were deftly swatted with palm fans. Seagulls swooped round the children as they played and then settled on the railings that encircled the monument to Gandhi on the beachfront. Bits of paper rode the air currents in corkscrew motions as they were hurled this way and that in the breeze. A row of ships could be seen anchored far out in the deeper waters, flags flying gaily in the breeze.

The hustle and bustle of the beach scene was enriched with young girls parading along, dressed in all their finery. They glanced coyly at the groups of boys as they walked past them, who responded by quoting provocative lines from Tamil films and songs. The seemingly embarrassed smiles that played round the lips of the dark beauties were not convincing. These daily pantomimes were a tribute to the amazing hold that the film industry had on the everyday lives of the Indian peoples.

We often walked home via Barathi Gardens, brushing past the bougainvillea bushes. Only the previous week I had witnessed a coy female film star dancing around one of these same bushes while the entranced male lead looked on, hands folded and feet apart. The camera crew had tried very hard to keep their focus and ignore the crowds gathered on the periphery, desperate for a glimpse of one of their heroes or heroines.

At weekends I indulged in my love for baking, trying my hand at making Western cakes, biscuits and, yes, I even attempted to make chocolate. At Christmas our neighbours were treated to my creations and we in turn enjoyed their offerings during their festivities. We lived safely in the knowledge that our neighbours could always be relied upon when we needed them. They kept a watchful and sometimes not-so-welcome intrusive eye on us.

Grandma paid an unexpected visit. She travelled by bus from her village, laden with goodies she had made with her own hands from produce gathered in the village. Her serene face radiated love and humility. She opened the top of a gunnysack into which she had lovingly transported peanut balls, amongst other things: these are delicious treats – peanuts cemented together with a syrup of palm sugar and then coated in toasted sesame seeds, fragrant with crushed cardamom seeds. Another gift was yoghurt-soaked chillies, dried to a crisp in the sunshine and when deep-fried produced a spicy crunch in the mouth. A frugal population wasted nothing: leftover cooked rice was squashed together with crushed dried chilli flakes and fragrant seeds, then pinches of the mixture again dried in the midday sun and deep-fried to a crisp tasty treat to accompany a simple meal. Grandma also produced a few kilos of precious tamarind pulp wrapped in newspaper.

'This is from our plantations. I gathered the pods and dried them myself. You can keep this for a long time if you store it in an earthenware pot.'

Bestowing her gentle smile on us, her deep brown eyes full of emotion, Grandma handed the parcel to Mum. Despite being our father's stepmother, as opposed to his own mother, she was everything a grandmother should be. She took pleasure from rubbing cooling tamarind pulp into my hair, massaging my scalp gently but thoroughly to revitalise every pore before pouring cupfuls of water over it to cleanse my hair. As she did this she squatted easily by my side in our outdoor bathroom in the yard, tucking her *sari* between her legs and above her knees. She towelled my hair dry and then combed out the knots, letting the hair dry naturally by fanning it out on my back. Unfortunately this memorable stay with us was short-lived, as her pregnant daughter in Cuddalore required her services.

34

'From hope to disappointment...'

Mum's Recuperation

Dad's letter arrived with the long-awaited news. A fourth wedding in the family had been successfully arranged. Rosie had moved in with her soul-mate, sister Theresa and her family in Kampong Pandan, whilst we were in India. Theresa's marriage brokerage efforts and blessings from Dad brought about sister Rosie's nuptials. Theresa's former neighbour from Serdang, whose mother's medicinal knowledge was sought when I took my first bath after recovering from smallpox, was about to become a formal relative. The prospective bridegroom, Arulsamy, was the eldest son of the elderly lady and brother to my sister's former neighbour. The beauty of the family married Arulsamy in March 1964.

Financial restraints once again prevented our return to Malaysia to join in the celebrations. Seven months' pregnant Theresa, expecting her youngest child Betty, fulfilled Mum's role.

'What a pity we cannot go to Rosie *akka*'s wedding!' I exclaimed.

'It cannot be helped *ma*. We can only pray to God and hope that everything goes well.'

'It's not fair: another family wedding we cannot attend.'

Despite Mum's reassuring presence, we missed the physical presence of the rest of the family. During the bleakest hours of homesickness I curled up with a book and attempted to lose myself but memories always seeped through to distract me. I did not belong to my 'home'. India did not feel like my true home despite all my efforts to fit into its society. I was forced to exist within myself.

Rosie's wedding day became just another day in our lives. Our week-old letters held stale news. Dad confirmed that Rosie continued to work in Handlooms and travelled daily to and from Serdang. The newly married couple had been allocated government quarters and became next-door neighbours to Arulsamy's family, a coincidence that worked out to the advantage of both families.

It was not until May 1964 that we obtained first-hand news of Rosie's wedding. Rosie's father-in-law had reached the same conclusion as our Dad about education. His youngest son, thirteen-year-old Kolandasamy, was yet another young man who, for the purposes of education, was to share the same fate as us. Father and son had travelled to the same village from which my Dad had originated. Busy with affairs of his own concerning property and land deals, Mr Thoppian entrusted his son to his nephew, yet another young man named Anthonysamy. This Anthonysamy had returned to his village whilst on holiday from his job as a lecturer at Vellore University and was happy to offer his services to his uncle from Malaysia, so he accompanied Thoppian's son young Kolandasamy to Pondicherry.

Anthonysamy was a tall man, ducking at the door to enter our sitting room. For reasons of propriety I did not appear fully before him but stood half in and half out against the doorway to the bedroom and listened politely to the conversation between him and Mum. He endeared himself to me when he asked for my help.

'I was told to ask you to help me procure a place at Petit Seminaire for Kolandasamy, as you know Father Peter well. I hope you don't mind if I accompany you as I would like to meet Father Peter for myself.'

I broke into a sweat, finding myself in such close proximity to this handsome young man. As he explained the purpose of his visit, I gave only monosyllabic replies to his questions, a simple 'yes' or 'no', and kept my head bowed in deference.

Teenager Kolandasamy was a brash, good-looking lad. His smart white shorts and short-sleeved shirt emphasised the almost blue darkness of his skin. A ready smile flashed often, and he was confident for his years. He unpacked his trunk to show us a few wedding photographs. Memories of my eldest sister's wedding flashed across my mind. I was imagining past family rejoicings when Kolandasamy cut in. 'Two goats were killed for the feast and the whole village turned up.' He was full of admiration for my sister, Rosie, but now she had become his sister-in-law. I felt the loss of another sister: she had entered Kolandasamy's family and left ours. 'We all like our *un-nee* very much; she is very good to me.'

It was a hard act to follow my sister's example. But I accepted the challenge, determined not to let the side down, as I prepared to display my special relationship with Father Peter, the principal of my younger brothers' school. Father Peter was an ascetic man. Gentle brown eyes smiled out from his smooth, handsome face, but there was knowledge in those gentle eyes and his probing look could see into your very soul. A boarder slipped out from a door on our right and Father Peter's demeanour changed instantly as he admonished the skinny young boy, who could not have been more than ten years old.

'Johnny, shouldn't you be in your Latin class? What have you been doing in your dormitory?'

'Sorry Father, I forgot my Latin book. I just went to my dormitory to get it Father.' He scuttled away as fast as his little legs could carry him.

This gentle-looking man was nobody's fool. His eyes and ears seemed to cover three hundred and sixty degrees and woe betides anyone who tried to hoodwink him. My respect for Father Peter was palpable and I flushed with pride at his solicitous attitude towards me. 'Hello Lily, what can I do for you?' he asked.

'Good morning, Father. I have brought my relatives with me. This is Kolandasamy from Malaysia; he is my brother-in-law's youngest brother. His parents would like to enrol him as a boarder in your school.'

Having acknowledged them and ascertained which village they came from, Father Peter smiled at us. 'I don't see why not. Go and see my secretary. I assume you have brought your school reports with you? If they are all in order I see no reason why we can't offer the boy a place in our school. Just tell my secretary that you have seen me, Lily. He will work out all the details. Nice to see you again: give my regards to your mother. How is she, is she okay?'

'Yes Father, she is fine and thank you, Father.'

'That's okay Lily, anything for your family. You look after yourself. Tell those brothers of yours I am keeping an eye on them.'

Seemingly with very little effort, I had obtained a place at a prestigious school for my latest little relative. My return footsteps were winged. Anthonysamy politely offered his thanks. 'It is nothing much,' I answered self-deprecatingly, as the blood rushed to my face.

To my surprise but not to Mum's, soon after Anthonysamy returned to his village a marriage proposal was put forward. Had there been more than one reason that Anthonysamy had been chosen to accompany Kolandasamy to Pondicherry? Thankfully, as I was still in education, I was able to turn down this proposal. I had no particular objections to the man himself and I was sure he would have been a great catch for a number of girls, but I cherished my own hopes and aspirations. I needed to fulfil my ambition to qualify as a doctor and crucially my plans included a need to get to know my future husband, and to be allowed to make a personal choice. Thankfully my parents respected my wishes and no coercion was exercised.

News of Rosie's first pregnancy followed and she became a mother to Anita in the February of 1965. This was a cause for celebration indeed but Mum missed not being there in person and this cast a shadow over her happiness. Her health began to suffer with the emotional stress of developing a relationship with our new relatives, as she was forced to scrutinise our every move in case it could be interpreted as improper behaviour. It was taking its toll on our long-suffering Mum. I observed her almost daily decline with dismay. The weight of middle age that had padded her face and the flabby ring that used to be folded over beneath her blouse when she sat down was fast diminishing. The half-moons under Mum's eyes were beginning to crinkle and speckle with age. Her moles became a shade darker than her ebony tint and too many deep sighs emerged from her. Drastic action was called for. My next aerogramme to Dad was a plea to him to invite Mum to Malaysia for a much-needed holiday, together with reassurances of my capability to care for my siblings. Preserving Mum's sanity took priority over everything.

Every month Dad deposited funds with his friend in Kuala Lumpur and this man's colleague in Pondicherry then paid a visit to our house bearing fat envelopes full of rupees. This month Dad sent the extra money required to purchase a ticket for Mum's return to Malaysia. The extent of her unhappiness could be measured by her willingness to take a couple of months break and to leave me to take charge of the family. She left for Malaysia in April 1965. I was eighteen years old and full of confidence.

The tenants who rented the apartment above us moved out a week before my mother's departure, which heightened her anxiety for our safety.

'Are you children going to be all right? It may take a while before new tenants move in and you will be all on your own. I know that Periavur will keep an eye on you but you will still have to sleep at night without anyone living above you.'

Unwilling to exacerbate her already fragile state I attempted to reassure her.

'*Ammah*, I am sure we will be fine. You never know, somebody might move in very soon. Don't worry about us. Our neighbours will keep an eye on us.'

Mum insisted on obtaining the neighbours' reassurances and reluctantly left for the port, accompanied by Periavur. We crowded round the doorway with mixed feelings as we waved our goodbyes.

During Mum's absence I kept scrupulous accounts of all the money

I spent in my little beige and brown tortoiseshell notebook. I sorted the bills into piles – paid, unpaid, and to be paid. Everything was recorded in my little book. Family members' birthdays, wedding days and recordings of important events were also carefully noted in my diary. I budgeted for everything, marked envelopes being filled with the exact notes and coins, and every bill was accounted for. Charlie broke into an amused chuckle as I placed the stack of envelopes in between the folds of my clean *saris* for safekeeping but I earned his respect when I thrust some money into Chandra's hand to purchase suitable material to be sewn into shirts for the boys and a couple of dresses for Irene. All were completed within a few days by our local tailor, Pitchamma's brother, and excitedly appreciated by the recipients.

Our bank balance had swelled by two hundred rupees by the time Mum returned, earning her admiration and respect. Chandra, my faithful, reliable and willing errand-boy was sent to the *ashram* shop, clutching a list of my much-coveted storybooks. I rewarded him with a rupee and encouraged him to spend it on books for himself. Dutifully he purchased a comic book, which prompted him to start his own collection and he developed a reading habit of his own that he gratefully attributed to me, his older sister. I was delighted that my collection of books was growing too.

Meanwhile I sat for my final matriculation exams. Reliable Chandra came to my rescue by overseeing the domestic duties. Breakfast was purchased from Pitchamma's aged grandmother, hunched through years of bending over the stove to maintain her morning pavement kitchen, earning her *annas*. Her spongy *dosais* and rich *apam* rice cakes, with thin crisp edges and fat middles, glazed with sweetened coconut milk, were mouth-wateringly good but she specialised in *puttu* – alternate layers of rice flour, grated coconut and brown sugar fitted into a hollow bamboo tube and then steamed. The resulting dryish but delicious mix of flavours required copious amounts of milky coffee to wash it down.

Chan traipsed round the markets for bargains and with the aid of a cookery book I had purchased for him managed to produce some very appetising meals. Occasionally he was dispatched for take-away biryanis. He sourced the best restaurants, returning home with spicy curries to accompany our biryanis. Once exams were over I relieved Chan from cooking duties but having made his contacts at the markets he continued to supply me with fresh vegetables and meat.

Soon after Mum departed, a heat wave made for uncomfortable nights of sleep in our fan-less bedroom. We vacated our bedroom, instead stacking the furniture against the walls and spreading ourselves out in the lounge. Guilt prompted our daily prayers, kneeling in front of the statue of the Blessed Virgin Mary with whom we were intimately familiar. A well-loved face offered us security, blessings and peace. I drew the sign of the cross at the four corners and blessed the area we were to occupy whilst we slept, and enlisted God's protection. No evil spirit could break through the ring protected by the signs of the cross, and if it did the flames from hell would burn it. One night I woke to a noise that originated from the flat above: it was the unmistakable sound of water gushing from an open tap. The apartment upstairs was still unoccupied. I woke my brother.

'Charlie, Charlie wake up, I can hear some noises upstairs. Listen, can you hear it too?'

Charlie stirred groggily as I pushed and prodded him insistently. I had woken Chandra in the process and both brothers were fully awake now. We remained quiet, straining our ears. We checked the open drain in the lounge for signs of water flowing from the flat above. The drain remained bone dry. We couldn't account for the noise.

'Let's creep up the stairs and look through the door,' suggested Charlie.

'Are you sure? I'm afraid.'

'There's nothing to be frightened about. If we see anybody, we can all start shouting and the thief will run away. Our neighbours will come to help us when they hear us. Come on just follow me. We will all go together.'

Our chatter had woken Irene. She looked bewildered. Rubbing sleep from her eyes she brought up the rear as we crept up the stairs in single file as quietly as we could, our hearts beating fast and our hands clammy.

'What if we see somebody? We wouldn't be able to fight them.'

The slatted front door allowed us to peer into the lounge: no sign of anyone. The noise of water running disappeared once we were on the move but as soon as we got back to our sleeping quarters it resumed. We lay awake for a while, stiff with fear and huddled together for security, refusing to allow our heavy eyelids to close. Eventually the noises petered out and sleep overtook us. Irene was the first to succumb, followed by my brothers, and then my tired eyes closed too. These strange noises continued night after night. Sometimes it sounded as though someone was engaged in grinding spices on a flat grinding stone with a stone roller, other times we heard the sound of an electric fan at full blast coupled with the slam of bedroom doors.

Baffled but not unduly worried, we related these incidents to our next-door neighbours. I detected a strange look on their faces. They assured us that there was nothing for us to worry about. As Catholics no harm would come to us but they advised us to move back into our bedroom. We followed their advice and latched the bedroom door firmly, at the same time drawing a protective blanket of faith around us to give ourselves the strength to ignore the strange sounds coming from above. New tenants moved into the flat a week before our mother was due home and the noises came to an abrupt halt.

Not wishing to alarm the younger ones, Mum later spoke to me in confidence. She had repeated our story to our Hindu neighbours and they had offered her their own explanation. The previous tenants were known devotees of the goddess Kali, the goddess of destruction. Once the tenants had vacated the flat with no one to appease her, the angry goddess Kali had displayed her displeasure. Mum and I remained sceptical, unwilling to give credence to this entertaining explanation, but unable to come up with a rational one of our own we let the matter rest. However we had to re-evaluate our beliefs when we acquired a Hindu servant.

One day a soft-spoken lady, unusually tall at about five foot eight and dressed in a white cotton *sari*, arrived on our doorstep. Her arms were folded respectfully together as she stood on our lowest step to explain her willingness to trade her work for food. Her bare brown feet, devoid of the customary toe rings of matrimony, were scrupulously clean. Her oiled hair was parted severely in the middle and coiled into a bun at the nape of her neck. We were accustomed to impoverished strangers knocking on our doorstep, willing to split wood for our fires for a bowlful of rice, but there was a quality in this lady's face that appealed to both my mother and me. Her half smile, her slightly bowed head and the closed lips that hid her slightly protruding teeth all contributed in some way to her trustworthy appearance. But there were shadows too; her face harboured some sadness that remained unexplained. 'I don't want any money, just some old clothes, food and a corner to sleep in.'

Mum decided to take her on a trial basis and offered her accommodation in the tiny little space, the so-called dining area, between the lounge and the kitchen. A single mat and pillow was all that was required. We did not regret our decision. The latest addition to our household soon became irreplaceable. Kamachi was always grateful for any little kindness shown to her. Initially she found it strange that we addressed her in respectful terms, in words normally used to address our elders, but soon she grew to accept our ways and took to spoiling us.

Irene became the daughter she didn't have. Every morning she oiled Irene's hair, plaited it, threaded it with white ribbons and looped it over her ears. She pushed shiny plastic clips that she had purchased at the market stalls on either side of Irene's middle parting. Irene moved her head from side to side to make the loops swing, laughing merrily. The newcomer managed most of our marketing and cooked under my mother's guidance. Spontaneously she would purchase little treats for us: for example jasmine flowers to loop into my hair. She delighted in oiling my long hair, combing and plaiting it and then securing her gift of flowers to complete the style. 'There, you look nice now.'

Kamachi's livelihood depended entirely on the competence of the care she gave us. She was deferential and glad to be of use, alert to our every need. She guarded us as faithfully as our dog Vera, my teenage companion, had done, and was fiercely protective. She growled at strangers who came begging and soon spotted imposters. A month after her arrival, now well settled with us, Kamachi ventured to ask a favour.

'My younger sister her husband and their son want to travel from their village to spend a couple of days in Pondicherry. They don't have anywhere to stay *ammah*. Can they sleep in the dining area? They won't be any trouble: I will see to that.'

'That's all right. Sure, ask them to come.'

They duly arrived and as promised were courteous, undemanding and self-effacing, grateful for their shelter. They left the house during the day for sightseeing and returned at nightfall for sleep. No complaints were made at their cramped conditions. Kamachi stretched herself out in our sitting room. Having witnessed the camaraderie between the sisters it came as a shock when Kamachi eventually plucked up the courage to confess some devastating news. With no wish to jeopardise her sister's visit, the shrewd lady told us her story after their departure.

The sisters were orphans. Kamachi was left bereft when her husband died tragically in an accident a few years into their marriage. The young widow had sought shelter at her only sibling's house, with her younger sister. She had settled down gratefully, enjoying her sister's company and playing auntie to her nephew. But her newfound security had come to a horrific end. Under the influence of drink, her brother-in-law took advantage of Kamachi's vulnerability and raped her. The result was an unwanted pregnancy. Kamachi was unwilling to break up her younger sister's family unit so decided to take drastic action. With no specific place in mind, she left the temporary haven that had evolved into such a nightmare, hoped to earn a living somehow. She had not been on the road too long when she found refuge with us. Mum's nurturing spirit was kindled by this poor woman's plight. She offered her support but left the desperate lady to decide for herself on

331

the destiny of the baby when it arrived. Mother Nature, however, had her own plans for the budding life.

A few months into Kamachi's pregnancy, Mum woke to find our devoted servant rattling at the front door and trying to get out. 'There is a girl out there, look, she is calling to me!'

'There is no one there. You must have been dreaming, go back to bed.'

The following night Kamachi managed to unlatch the door and was on the point of walking into the road when Mum, a light sleeper, again intervened.

The whole saga culminated in tragedy when poor Kamachi woke up again later, screaming with pain. 'This child is jumping on my tummy! Get her off, somebody!'

She was writhing on the floor as she cried out. Resourceful Mum managed to enlist the help of a sleeping trishaw man at the corner of the road, and accompanied the distraught woman to hospital. Mum left her there and returned home to her still sleeping family, none of us any the wiser.

Mum recounted the night's drama to a silent and perplexed group the next morning.

'Why did you not wake me up *ammah*?' I asked.

'I knew there was nothing you could have done – and besides you all have school today and cannot afford to lose any sleep.'

When we returned home after school we were shocked to see an exhausted, subdued maid slumped in her usual corner with her back against the wall. In hushed tones Mum explained that Kamachi had lost her baby. Her nightmares did not abate though. Eventually her coping mechanism kicked in and she apportioned the blame for her miscarriage to the intervention of evil spirits. This seemed to tie in with the neighbours' tales of a resident and unappeased evil spirit.

Poor Kamachi's sleepless nights continued. Sleeping in the vicinity of the altar did not seem to improve the situation. In desperation Mum invited her to sleep between the two of us in our bedroom. The desired effect was finally achieved and peace reigned once again. Whichever spirit had terrorised our beloved servant gave up its cruel games. Was the miscarriage really the work of evil spirits? The answer remained an enigma.

35

'Scholarship days revisited...'

Cluny

The caretaker opened the wooden gates to the main entrance and ushered Mum, Irene, Benny and me inside. The gates were set into high surrounding walls. In fact the school was enclosed on all sides but two roadways divided the buildings into three separate areas. We stepped into the white flag-stoned quadrangle. In its centre the branches of a mature tree rose majestically upwards, spreading out in a natural umbrella shape to provide some much-needed shade. It reminded me of our mango tree back home in Sentul. To our right, a single-storeyed building housed the primary school children. The girls wore sky-blue pinafores and white blouses whilst the boys were in pale blue shorts and white shirts; all were at their desks. A few smiled and waved, eliciting a response from the irrepressible Ben, but others merely stared curiously at the visitors in the yard. Cluny was a co-ed school for the first two years, after which the boys had to leave and find another school. Cluny then reverted to being a single sex school from Standard Two onwards: a peculiar practice for which there was no obvious explanation.

A narrow pathway straight ahead of us led to a basketball court. Behind it we glimpsed a white, two-storeyed building with a balcony that ran its length. A head bobbed up and down along it. Arches lipped with narrow ledges were cut into the outer walls of the balcony. The directions from the caretaker were to branch off to the left and follow the signs to the office. The flagstones came to an end and we walked on fine sand before stepping up to an open veranda. Two identical doors stood at either end of the building, outside which signboards hung on wrought-iron hooks: 'Office' was written in bold letters on one, and 'Principal-Reverend Mother Peter' on the other. A rosy-faced nun in a full white habit emerged from this door and then turned back to lock it with a big black key. Round her neck hung a large, beaded, black rosary, weighed down by a silver crucifix. Mum was of average height but Reverend Mother was a good few inches taller and radiated authority. Mum nudged my brothers and sister, nodding her head in the direction of the nun as a gentle reminder of our manners.

'Good morning, Reverend Mother,' we chorused as one.

'Good morning everyone. Are you here to see anyone in particular? Can I help?'

She cocked her head to one side quizzically; her mouth widened into a smile that reached her light blue eyes, creased at the corners with soft crow's feet. Mum returned her smile but I was the one who replied, aware that Mum would rather I conduct all the negotiations.

'We have come to register for school, Reverend Mother.'

'Well, you have come to the right place. Where are you from? You don't sound as if you are from around here.'

'From Malaya, Reverend Mother,' I answered.

My baby sister Irene gazed up curiously at this grand figure, nervously twirling the ends of her two pigtails with her fingers. Mum moved closer to her and placed her hand on Irene's head, pressing her close as though to protect her.

Reverend Mother Peter quickly became acquainted with our family history. My sister-in-law's connection to the French section of Cluny Convent was the reason that we had arrived in Pondicherry, and we also touched on Chandra's enrolment at Petit Seminarie.

'Yes, it is a coincidence that both of us principals share the same name, and we are good friends too,' she chuckled.

Her enchanting smile had us eating out of her hand. Having ascertained our current levels of education she took us to the office and instructed the school clerk to take good care of us. As she took her leave she threw a final remark and a wink at her three new recruits:

'I shall be looking out for you.'

With a nod and a quick wave of her hand at little Irene and Ben, she turned and went on her busy way. Her stockinged feet in open sandals were soundless on the soft sand.

Once the formalities were complete, the clerk permitted us to wander round the buildings provided we were quiet, because classes were in progress.

Behind the office, the bulk of the secondary school was housed on two floors. A large quadrangle at ground level, worn and scuffed by hundreds of feet, formed the assembly area. A winding wrought-iron staircase from one corner of it stopped at an open doorway and led to the secondary classrooms. Windows with iron bars across them were wide open, allowing us a glimpse of pupils' heads on the floors above.

We left the sculptured white buildings, crossed the roadway and entered the grounds beyond more high walls, where a large, open-sided, porticoed school hall was situated. Stacked seats lined the edges. The south-facing end led to a flight of wide cement steps and a raised wooden stage. We then came to the buildings shared by both the English and French medium schools. A pathway led through immaculately maintained gardens, bordered by a small but colourful chapel with stained glass windows. The French school where my sister-in-law had been educated lay beyond this building – but we had seen enough by now. The whitewashed walls and well-kept surroundings spoke of discipline, careful maintenance and high standards. This was no ordinary secondary school: it oozed history and opulence. In a bit of a daze we made our way home. Our rickshaws creaked past the surrounding palatial houses. An abundance of crimson and rich purple bougainvillea made a vivid colour contrast as they clung to the high white walls that provided security and guarded the privacy of its wealthy residents.

The crash of the nearby waves and the squeal of the rusty wheels of rickshaws were the only sounds in this neighbourhood of the rich, educated and expatriate communities. The beach road was lined with government buildings. We craned our necks as we tried to take in all the magnificent architecture. Most of the buildings near the beach were painted a virgin white. The cool, clean air gradually grew thicker with pollution, the smells of rot, dirt and human waste, as we returned to the centre of Pondicherry.

Pondicherrians were very proud of their French heritage. This was represented in the architecture and the street layout. Straight roads crossed one another at right angles and opened out into numerous quadrangles. Many official buildings sported French names. We are off to *l'hôpital, ammah* is not feeling too well, or the children are at *l'école première* were phrases that easily rolled off the tongues of our acquaintances. In 1963, a year after our arrival, a buzz of excitement prevailed as several thousand people opted to take French nationality. At least one working member of a majority of families was making preparations to immigrate to France, mostly to the capital city. In Paris, French-speaking professionals could procure jobs.

Despite some initial misgivings, I settled into Cluny Convent with ease. It was during my first year there in 1963 that I was privileged to gaze upon a much-admired figure, a living legend: Pondicherry was preparing for a visit by Pandit Jawaharlal Nehru. He was a man revered by millions, including my Dad; with Mahatma Gandhi, he had played a vital role in bringing about the independence of India in 1947.

We Cluny students took up our designated places amongst the welcoming crowds who lined the road that ran through the Botanical Gardens of Pondicherry. We joined thousands of other schoolchildren, all waving miniature flags of India, whilst bunting made of similar flags had been looped between the street lamps, fluttering merrily in the incoming breeze from the nearby seaside. The importance of the occasion could not be overstated as we paid homage to one of India's greatest sons. Cheers preceded the open car that transported Mr Nehru. A knot tightened in my stomach as my eyes followed the handsome silver head topped with his very distinctive white Nehru hat. His sensitive and gentle face smiled broadly, his trademark red rose protruding from his lapel as he waved to the joyful, cheering crowd. Patriotism coursed through me as I imagined Dad's excitement: I tried to share the moment with him, to view the venerated man as if through Dad's eyes.

A chip off the old block and inspired by the great man, I volunteered to join the Indian National Cadets as part of my extracurricular activities at school. An hour's early start once a week to attend the training parades in our playground proved to be no deterrent. I was fired up with a sense of patriotism. The training was tough. Luckily it made no difference that I did not have an Indian passport. 'Your commitment is all that is required.' With great pride I took part in school parades, marching past our teachers and Reverend Mother Peter during official events.

An aerogramme filled with the news of Pondicherry's extremely special visitor winged its way to Dad the very next day. I could just hear him proudly making his announcement to anyone who cared to listen: 'Guess who Lily saw!'

When the great man died in May 1964, we listened to the news live on the radio with tears coursing down our cheeks, as we shared the grief that the world was experiencing.

Alka was hunched over her desk, the very first one as you entered the classroom. She did not look up with curiosity like the rest. She was enveloped in an air of concentration, offering only monosyllabic answers to the questions posed by the teachers. Her gaze returned immediately to the open book on the desk. Her knee-length skirt was a contrast to the ankle-length ones worn by her classmates. Her short, light brown hair was drawn into a ponytail, again a contrast to the style of her fellow pupils, most of whom had long hair left loose or neatly plaited into single or double plaits and finished off with colourful ribbons. Alka's light brown, short-sighted eyes were flecked with gold. Her gold-rimmed glasses were pushed into place every few minutes with a finger. Her high forehead was set on a broad face and her full lips parted to show a set of evenly spaced teeth. Her very silence during class roused my curiosity. There was no spark about her, giving an impression that almost bordered on boredom; she was there because she had to be. Her shoulders were always hunched as she bent to her tasks, tasks that seemed well within her scope. She doesn't look as if she is from Pondicherry. I wonder where she is from? She looks just as foreign as me. She fascinated me.

'Hello, I am Lily. I am from Malaya. My family and I have not long been in Pondicherry.'

'I'm Alka. We used to live in Kenya. I was born in Kenya and spent most of my life there. We moved to Pondicherry last year.'

'There is something different about you, are your parents Indian?'

'My father is from Maharashtra and my mother from Rajasthan.'

We carried on our conversation, both answering and asking questions. Maharashtra and Rajasthan are North Indian states. Alka's parents were both professional teachers and had emigrated to Kenya after their two older daughters had been born. Alka and her younger brother had both been born in Kenya.

'I miss my life in Kenya. I miss all those little girls with tight curly hair, so soft. It looked like fine wire wool, but was really soft when you touched it.'

'I miss Malaya too. India seems to have so many rules that restrict the behaviour of girls and I am used to more freedom.'

'My mother joined the *ashram* after my father died. She didn't want to stay on in Kenya as a widow. She missed him too much and decided that a change in her life was what she needed. She researched the *ashram* and decided that she would be happy to live within its spiritual community.'

She was a woman of means and could afford to part with the funds required in return for the *ashram*'s protection. The *ashram* was a large organisation; it ran its own schools, health care and support network. Alka's younger brother attended one of these schools.

'My mother decided that my older sister and I would be better off at the convent, so we are both here. Our eldest sister is married and lives in Bombay now. She trained to be a nurse in England but did not want to marry there. She met a Sikh, fell in love and married him.'

'Well I now live in India with my mother, two brothers and my youngest sister Irene. My father and the rest of my family live back home.'

'Where do you live? I could come and visit you in the evening after school. I find it difficult to relate to the local girls. They don't understand me they think I am strange. I dress strangely, and speak strangely, in fact they positively avoid me.'

'No Alka, I don't think they look on you like that. If that is true than we must both appear strange to them.'

'No,' she insisted. 'People seem to like you, they talk to you, and it is me they don't like.'

I was sorry for her and tried to reassure her: 'I am sure that is not true.' Yes, she was different, but I had not picked up on any particular undercurrents amongst our peers. She broke into one of her soft smiles; she appreciated my efforts to be kind.

The two of us slipped into an easy intimacy. We were two lost souls, thousands of miles away from our birth nations and the cultures that had shaped us; we were separated from our friends, the companions of our childhoods. Despite our Indian ethnicity we were different from the locals. There was an ache in our hearts that we each recognised and we gravitated towards one another as if to an oasis.

Indulging our passionate interest in books, we shared a deep chair in the library, sitting back-to-back with our legs draped over the sides. We slipped into a companionable silence. Alka nibbled on the soft skin of her thumb and forefinger, while I twirled round an escaped tendril of my hair, each of us totally engrossed in our chosen books. The Chalet School series by Elinor Brent-Dyer, set in the Austrian Alps, was devoured at breakneck speed. Wouldn't it be fantastic to visit Austria? Hmm! It certainly would. Wouldn't it be marvellous if the school really existed? Inevitably we caught the attention of both teachers and pupils, and they often wondered what 'the twins' were up to now.

Cluny Convent was run very much along the lines of Western schools. At the end of term our teachers, Miss Thomas and Miss Gowrie, had great plans for a special show for the school. They threw down the gauntlet to the whole class.

'We want the whole school to be impressed by you. Now, see if you can come up with something spectacular that we can perform. Lily, Alka, you two bookworms, we expect great things from both of you, so get your thinking caps on. Maybe you can write a play and the class can participate in it?'

Fired with enthusiasm, I took up the challenge. My play was based partly on the experiences of my early school days in Malaya, where Geraldine's antics were a particular inspiration, and partly on the capers of the Chalet School series. The play concentrated on the teacher-pupil relationship in a classroom full of rowdy children. I drew on all the quirks and foibles exhibited by our teachers, but tried to tone down the characterisations to an acceptable level. For example Miss Gowrie, our English teacher, was a Hindu lady, mild-mannered and with a soft round face: she had a slightly crooked nose that was somewhat endearing but easy to caricature. In the middle of her forehead a vermilion spot added to her femininity, as did her abundant hair, which she brushed until it shone. Sometimes she brought it forward and draped it over one shoulder but at other times she left it loose in a single plait, again draped over one shoulder. She never raised her voice but she conveyed a steely determination that meant business. I included some of her favourite expressions in the play.

Roman Catholic Mrs Thomas was particularly feisty and strict. Of average height, she was slim with a slightly pock-marked face; her sharp, aquiline nose had a raised bump on the upper third. Her sharp black eyes never missed a trick and her direct gaze could make anyone's knees quake. Her black wavy hair was pinned back severely into a bun that was swept into the nape of her neck, whilst a short, gold chain with a crucifix sat in the hollow below her throat. She did not suffer fools gladly or tolerate misbehaviour of any sort. Her response to naughtiness was to strike a pose, her left index finger on her lower lip, the chalk held in her right: then she would take aim. Her accuracy was legendary. The chalk always landed on the culprit engaged in chat with her neighbour. Sometimes a book replaced the chalk, as whatever Mrs Thomas had in her hand became her missile.

My play was full of people's eccentricities, whether teacher or pupil. Alka helped with the fine-tuning. Many of the lines were hilarious to those who recognised the inspiration for them, and I took great pains to match the actors to their parts. The play was performed on open ground, the basketball court opposite the teachers' living quarters. The senior students were particularly entertained as they all recognised the traits of the teachers portrayed in the actors' dialogue and their actions. I glanced sideways at Miss Thomas surreptitiously; had I gone too far, I wondered? But the rapturous reaction from the audience could not be ignored. Miss Thomas kept her face inscrutable, accepting the indirect teasing gracefully. The expressions on her fellow teachers' faces were a picture though, which was satisfaction enough for me: the play was pronounced a great success. Some of the teachers were well aware that I had 'got away with it', that I had taken liberties. The play was talked about for days afterwards amidst smothered sniggers but Reverend Mother Peter was impressed apparently and the popularity of our class was sealed.

The school prided itself on an impressive level of performance at the annual concert. Entire families attended and took great pride in their children's accomplishments. Alka and I landed parts in a Shakespeare play, *The Taming of the Shrew*. The normally docile Alka was coaxed into strutting around as Petruchio, a gentleman who comes to Padua in search of a wife. I was cast in the role of Katherine, a headstrong, obdurate shrew, whom Petruchio has to tame. He marries her and then deploys various physical and psychological torments to manipulate Katherine into becoming an obedient wife. As best friends, a great deal of fun was guaranteed during our rehearsals. In the end our version of the play was voted the best amongst all the performances and earned us a slot on All India Radio. A reluctant Alka and a rather more jubilant me travelled to Madras with the rest of our classmates.

I told my brother, 'Hey Chan, Alka and I are going to be on All India Radio. We are going to perform our play.'

Chan was overjoyed and clapped his hands. 'Wow, wait till I tell my classmates.'

Then he had a brainwave, as he saw it a chance to show off to all his classmates.

'You know what, I will tell Father Peter and I am sure he will let us all listen to the show.'

Despite stage fright, or more correctly, radio fright, as we were well aware of the huge audiences that All India Radio attracted, we delivered our performance with aplomb. We had done it. Thousands, maybe millions, had tuned in to listen to us. We received good reviews from other schools, especially that of my brothers. 'That is our sister,' they said proudly. This small claim to fame had been appreciated.

Miss Thomas and Miss Gowrie, our two Malayalee spinster teachers, never failed to amaze me. The guinea pigs for their latest scheme were again chosen to be Alka and Lily. To introduce a sense of fun to our curriculum, the duo were keen to hold a proper election to select a head girl for the school – in true 'Chalet School' style. Everyone was encouraged to take part in the process. Alka and I were rather reluctant participants as we did not want to be opponents, but we had no choice. Banners were posted in strategic locations, proclaiming in big bold letters 'Vote for Alka' or 'Vote for Lily'. But it felt incongruous because Cluny Convent was not The Chalet School and we cringed with embarrassment. The teachers worked hard to make the event a success though, and school rules had to be obeyed. I did not want to be the cause of Reverend Mother's disappointment, especially when faced with her enthusiastic support for the elections.

I geed Alka along. 'Come on, I know neither of us wants to do this but we have to show some enthusiasm.' However Alka was a realist. She had already worked out what I in my naïvety had failed to do.

'You know what the outcome of the elections is going to be: you are going to win hands down. It just seems a farce pitting my name against yours. Don't get me wrong; I will be voting for you myself. I could not do the job and I know you will be good at it. No hard feelings, Lily.' She pressed my hand when my face registered my embarrassment.

It seemed a pyrrhic victory when I stood on the podium and made my winner's speech. Despite Alka's brave stance I felt for her. No one relished losing, even to his or her best friend. Typically, Alka put aside her defeat with a toss of her pigtail and stood next to me with a smile on her face, joining in the enthusiastic applause.

My soprano voice stood me in good stead in our school choir. I was beginning to get carried away with my popularity at school. Pride certainly goes before a fall. I disgraced myself in spectacular style at a major school concert, proudly attended by my entire family. My mind went completely blank during a solo and I required very obvious and heavy prompting to complete my part. I stammered and stuttered throughout and my heart pounded, resonating in my ears. My hands grew clammy and I felt light-headed. As we filed out at the end of our piece the cement floor rose up to meet me. My head brushed against a pillar as I fell to the ground with a dull thud, all colour, sight and sound drained away to blackness. A sort of fog filled my entire being and a chill reached right to the tips of my fingers and toes. When I came to, the fog cleared and my eyes focused. Alka's anxious eyes peered down at me and helpful hands lifted me into a sitting position. I stood up on shaky legs but realisation kicked in and I was stunned into humiliated silence. I had made a spectacle of myself in front of a large and important gathering. With the aid of my family and Alka and her mother I made a quick exit and hid my head in shame within the enclosure of the rickshaw's hood. I was doubly embarrassed the following day when understanding students offered their sympathy.

Devoid of support from my sister-in-law's family, I felt cocooned by Alka's love and attention. Both her and her mother's concern for my wellbeing was honey to a fresh wound. The fainting episode had clearly shaken Alka. She cycled round to our house most evenings, the woven basket fastened across the centre of the handlebars brimming with gifts: chunks of chocolate, plump tasty tomatoes or paper bags filled with whole almonds. The instructions from her mother were delivered with great conviction: if I soaked the almonds overnight and then ground them, mixed them with milk into a nutritious drink and consumed this on an empty stomach, the migraines that had plagued my life ever since I attained womanhood would be cured. Mum approved of Alka, aware that this friendship filled a void in my life. She stood firm when my brother Peter disapproved of it.

During my second year at Cluny Mum shared her financial worries with me. Unavoidable circumstances prevented Dad from sending sufficient funds for an indefinite period. Faced with her distress I volunteered to move to the state-run, free education system. I went to see the headmistress of a local school that my neighbour attended. A place was offered and accepted. With a heavy heart I handed in my notice to Cluny. During lunch I was summoned to an audience with Reverend Mother Peter in her inner sanctum. A solid wooden crucifix on the wall dominated the room. Against the same wall a highly polished piano stood with its lid open. The ivory keys gleamed in the slanting sunlight. I had occasionally heard the sound of the piano being played when I passed Reverend Mother's office, but now her concerned face drew my roving gaze. She opened the conversation by asking me what had happened.

Hesitantly I explained our temporary situation and my need to help the family. Reverend Mother brushed my worries aside with a sweep of her hand. She smiled. 'Well is that all? I thought something unpleasant had happened to make you want to leave. There is no need for you to leave Cluny. We offer scholarships to promising students. Your youngest brother has left to join Petit Seminaire so that leaves just you and your sister Irene. I will grant you and your sister scholarships, so no more of talk of leaving. You are both welcome to continue your studies here.' She brushed aside my attempts to thank her.

Still determined to make a contribution, I decided to give up the costly rickshaw rides to school and resort to pedal power. Irene could easily ride pillion on the luggage rack behind the seat. With Mum's blessing I persuaded Charlie to purchase a second-hand bicycle for me, using his influence at the bicycle store. Charlie bought me a lady's bicycle, a contrast to the heavy metal Norton with a bar across that I had first practised on, Charlie's childhood pride and joy in Sentul. Following a bit of initial nervousness and learning to hold the folds of my long skirt between my legs, I worked the pedals on my bike quite easily and began to feel confident. Our books were tied together with string and held securely in the green wire basket that hung in front of the handlebars. The first week passed safely. Irene, wide-eyed, perched sideways on the carrier behind the saddle, holding her legs out a little to avoid the rotating wheels. One hand gripped the metal support under my seat, exposed by the fact that the saddle had been lifted slightly for my comfort.

The early morning traffic was heavier than usual one day. I approached a crossroads, looked to left and right to assess the flowing traffic and back-peddled a little to slow our speed. Seeing a gap, I nudged forward, but was unprepared for a car that suddenly crossed my path. I panicked and applied the brakes hard. With a sinking heart I jack-knifed into the car's boot. A crowed gathered immediately and willing hands lifted the buckled bicycle. I was unhurt, with just a few grazes to my elbow, and my concern was reserved for little Irene. She had nimbly jumped off her seat and stood there unconcerned. To add insult to injury our unfortunate accident had taken place at the junction outside the lean-to bicycle shop where Charlie worked. The commotion had roused the workers and Charlie and his boss rushed over.

I winced, reliving a previous incident when Charlie's raucous laughter had echoed in my ears. Bless him, he realised I was close to tears with embarrassment; he took control of the situation and shooed the crowd away. With downcast eyes I assured Charlie that no physical harm had been done. My pride had suffered more. Eager to get away from the scene of shame I allowed him to hail a rickshaw and Irene and I continued on to school. The mangled bicycle was returned to the very shop it had left in fine shape just a week ago, and that was the last time I rode one.

Mistakenly, I had chosen to study Hindi, the national language, as my compulsory second language of the school curriculum. A grand total of two students took up Hindi. The rest chose French. The two of us sat in a gloomy room downstairs with our Hindi teacher, a traditionally proportioned, grandmother-like figure – a merry widow in white cotton.

'I follow Gandji's teachings.' Our enthusiastic teacher believed in instilling patriotism. 'Hindi is an ancient language derived from Sanskrit. You must be proud of your heritage and you are doing the right thing choosing Hindi rather than a foreign language.'

Mastering the alphabet did not come easily as we were starting at a relatively late age. The letters hung on a bar drawn from left to right. My name, spelled with a single letter of the alphabet, proved most amusing. A single L was the shape of an upside-down walking stick, the hook pointed to the left. A double measure of the letter, one on top of the other, emphasised the sound of the middle letter, and the same upside-down walking stick, this time hooked to the right, completed my name. Despite my language teacher's enthusiasm and my own diligence I only just managed to scrape through in the exams.

During our final year, more confident now and ready to brush off any anticipated criticism, I accompanied Alka after school. She walked her bicycle along the main road and we passed the boys' French secondary school.

'I read this book last night. It was on my mother's book shelf and it was all about a homosexual who was having problems being himself in his community.'

'Who is a homosexual?' I asked Alka.

'What, don't you know?' She raised her eyebrows in surprise.

'No, I don't. Who is a homosexual – something to do with sex I suppose?'

Alka giggled. 'Sometimes, Lily, you are so naïve. Homosexuals are men who love other men. They have sex with them.'

'How is that possible? What do they do?'

'I don't know really, I need to find out for myself. Do you not know about lesbians then, you know, female lovers?'

'No, I definitely do not. Yuk!' I hunched my shoulders in disgust.

I was intrigued but had no urge to find out any more about 'sexual deviants' as I categorised them. We continued to discuss other books we had both read recently as we walked. A group of boys were gathered by the gateway to the boys' school, their bicycles leaning against the wall. Their laughter increased in volume as we approached and became quite raucous as we walked past them. I looked sideways in mock anger but quickly turned my face away.

'Hey, that is Hassan, a cousin of my sister-in-law. Handsome fellow, isn't he? Too bad he has seen us. I hope the family do not come to hear of us sauntering along this road.'

'You worry too much, Lily; you will get one of your headaches. I bet he won't. Boys don't gossip like girls.'

We made plans to meet up the following evening: Alka was to come over to our house as a fair was to be held on the green, near the junction of Bussey Street. 'It will be fun,' she said, 'we might bump into some handsome fellows.'

I giggled. 'Alka, you are so much fun, unlike the rest of our goody-goody classmates.'

Alka arrived by rickshaw the following evening, draped in a sky-blue *sari* with a matching sleeveless blouse that sported a wide neckline at both front and back, showing off her flawless creamy skin. The blouse daringly exposed her midriff. Her normally pony-tailed hair was brushed out and sat softly on her shoulders. A light touch of lipstick outlined her full lips. She looked stunning and drew a few appreciative looks, this gorgeous creature who had befriended plain nondescript me. My stature increased as I proudly walked alongside her in my mid-sleeved blouse draped in a new very prettily embroidered nylon *sari* that had just arrived from Malaysia.

'Wow, Alka, I have never seen you in a *sari* before, you look great.'

'You look fantastic too, Lily. Let's see if we can turn some heads!' she replied, a wicked glint in her eyes that made the gold flecks take on extra depth. I chuckled nervously. In some strange way I felt as if I was playing truant, but Mum's blessing was the only seal of approval I required to enjoy the evening. It was delicious. Then a wicked thought popped into my head: I wondered what my brother Peter would say if he could see the way Alka was dressed and his little sister boldly walking alongside her. I enjoyed my forbidden treat all the more. The fair was teeming with young men and women dressed to impress. We received our fair share of wolf-whistles and appreciative comments as we wandered from stall to stall, returning home that evening with our heads in the clouds.

All too soon my school career drew to a close, and with that a parting of the ways for Alka and me loomed ominously. Alka planned to travel to England to train as a nurse, following in her eldest sister's footsteps. Matriculation level in India was not a sufficient qualification for entry into an English nursing school so a further year of studies in a secondary school in England was required. Alka's mother could afford the necessary fees and arrangements were in progress for her departure. My friend dreaded our parting just as much as I did; she used every argument she could to persuade me to accompany her. 'My mother could lend you the money, you wouldn't have to pay it back straightaway.'

As tempting as it sounded, I knew that going to England to study would be an expensive option that our family could not afford. Mum was in Malaysia during this difficult time and there was no way I could approach the family with such a proposal, although it had always been my dream. Alka was lucky to be able to go but I did not begrudge my best friend her good luck.

How could we mark the end of our schooldays? We came up with an idea that we hoped would be a first for our school friends: an English-style farewell party. Alka undertook to supply the food. I wrote out the invitations and helped to decorate Alka's dining room with balloons and festoons.

On the 10 April 1965, eighteen of us partook of dainty cucumber sandwiches, a wobbling jelly rabbit, a sponge cake sandwiched with jam and my contribution – biscuits I had baked. All of this was washed down with homemade limeade and we made no apologies for including lashings of ice cream *Kulfi*, a delicate green from crushed pistachios, provided courtesy of the *ashram*. Our classmates were profuse in their thanks and amid much hand-wringing, a few tears were shed in sympathy for our imminent separation. 'We know you two are going to miss one another terribly after being such good friends. Don't forget to come and visit us once Alka leaves.'

On Mum's return, omitting to tell her about Mrs Shah's generous offer, I approached her tentatively with the idea of my study nursing in England. Bless her; she did not immediately dismiss the idea as I was convinced she would. Instead, she sought Periavur's advice. His advice was sound and I couldn't argue with it. If I were keen to pursue a career in nursing the cheaper option would be to train in Pondicherry. Devastated, I laid my impossible dream to rest; I shut it in an imaginary drawer, turned a key in the lock and then discarded the key. My communication with Alka petered out on my return to Malaysia. My emotional state was too fragile. I forced myself to leave my memories behind.

36

'Unsolicited romance...'

Pre-University

Dad's aspirations for me were now attainable; my grades were more than good enough for a place at Tagore Arts College. Good grades in science in particular would then assure me of a place at Jawaharlal Institute of Postgraduate Medical Education, where our neighbour Siva was a second year medical student. When Periavur was made aware of our plan his offer of help was much appreciated. 'I will ask Siva to put in a word for her,' he assured Mum.

My future was now clear. I had to dedicate one year to serious study and no distractions would be allowed. Dad's reaction was suitably predictable; he gave Mum assurances that he would find the money to fund me through university. With the memory of Charlie's failure in his studies still fresh in my mind, I acknowledged my obligations to fulfil the family's dream. Effortlessly I procured a place for pre-university studies at Tagore Arts College, reading Chemistry, Physics, Biology, English and the compulsory second language. Having previously studied Hindi at the Convent and obtaining a pass with the minimum pass mark, I was aware of my Achilles' heel. Studying Hindi at pre-university level was going to test my abilities to the full but I was left with no other choice.

During enrolment I was informed of a thriving Cadet branch and as my previous involvement emerged I was encouraged to enlist. I obliged reluctantly, convincing myself that weekly attendances could easily be endured. I had progressed from the all-white cadet attire to khaki uniform; this offered a certain status that could prove useful in the future.

In July 1965 I entered the white gates of Tagore Arts College, a ten minutes rickshaw ride away from home, as a student. I joined thousands of enthusiastic book-clutching young men and women. The university was built round an open quadrangle. Mounting the steps to the arched entrance I took note of the principal's office, administrative offices and lecturers' offices. To the left of the main entrance were the doors to the female students' locker room where an oblong wooden table in the centre provided a place for students to eat their lunch. A round, smiling face peeped out curiously from the doorway, her body well concealed behind the door. The owner of the wide smile ushered me in, pointing out the lockers that were available for our use. She chattered non-stop, university gossip interspersed with useful information, and continued to greet the returning students by name. Then she rushed headlong into introductions: within a few minutes everyone knew my background – 'Lily is from Malaysia you know!'

A large, well-stocked library ran along the length of the right-hand side of the ground floor. A four foot wide balcony on two floors carried the weight of an army of giggling and jostling students as they rushed to the lecture theatres situated on the first floor and on both wings that radiated outwards from the sides of the building.

Female students represented just twenty per cent of the overall numbers. They kept a low profile while the vociferous male students dominated the classes. The female students occupied the first two rows in the lecture halls whilst everyone else made their overwhelming presence known by much scraping of chairs and chants of bravado. Two sisters from the Untouchable caste took great care to distance them from the rest of us. When I introduced myself they cast their eyes down to the floor and deferentially made their apologies: 'You are aware that we are from the Untouchable caste, aren't you?' I told them that this made no difference to me, as I briefly cast my mind back to the status of the night soil gatherers in Malaysia.

I had hoped that a change in legislation would also bring about a change in society. I was unaware of the girls' private narrative. To categorise members of society as Untouchables was derogatory; they should make no apology for their temerity in attending college. Why were they attempting to make themselves almost invisible? They smiled shyly when I not only acknowledged them but also included them in our group discussions: the look of adoration and gratitude in their eyes was uncomfortable to endure. The situation was difficult to handle. Thankfully even the Brahmin student, Janaki, with more rights than most to treat the sisters as inferior, made no reference to their caste. I was proud of my colleagues. They were a good bunch. I was going to be comfortable.

At the end of a long day of lectures we strolled to the entrance ready for home. Two official-looking senior students sporting armbands authoritatively directed us to the central square. Pushed and shoved, we did as we were directed. Loudspeakers blared.

'Everybody listen! We are going to join the protest march which has been officially organised by the citizens of Pondicherry.'

'What official protest? I don't want to take part in any march. I need to go home. I don't like the look of this – it seems like trouble to me. Surely the men can attend this rally? Whatever it is, they can leave the girls out, surely?' I said.

The girls around me echoed these sentiments. Fearful looks were exchanged. What were we getting involved in?

'You are aware that the central government has declared that Hindi is now the official language of India. We in South India want nothing to do with that. We are proud of our mother tongue and will not tolerate central government's dictatorship. We want English and Tamil to be our official languages. If we give in to this then we will become subordinate to the North and lose our identity and culture. We have to make a stand: show Delhi that we will not be dictated to. We will leave the college building in an orderly fashion and join the main body of protesters in the town.'

Dad was not around to keep me informed on politics. I had no interest in the subject myself. I had been unaware of the impending changes or the strength of feeling of the general populace. But I could see no escape from this proposed march. A few senior female students joined in the persuasion. 'We have to support the boys. This ruling affects all of us and our future job prospects, so come on girls, join us in our just fight.'

The men displayed black armbands but female students were spared from that, much to my relief, but the relief was short-lived. We filed into the main street to the sound of a battle cry and an atmosphere of fervent, desperate anger filled the air. I became a reluctant participant. All my childhood fears of intimidatory situations were aroused. I wished myself anywhere but in the central square. Fear gripped my heart, squeezing it tight. The humid air thinned leaving me breathless. I turned in desperation; Janaki, sensing my discomfort, squeezed my hand reassuringly. 'Don't worry Lily, we will be all right, just stay close. We will stick together.'

The organisers were well prepared. Large numbers of Indian flags were passed from hand to hand down the lines. Placards were positioned and carriers nominated. Like sheep to the slaughter we obeyed orders and followed the main mass of protesters out of the college to join the main demonstration. Chants of "Tamil Nadu for Tamilians" and "Down with Delhi, we will not be subdued" echoed all around. As the crowds gathered strength the chants grew in intensity and some of the protesters became hysterical. Panic surged through me; I looked desperately for a way out but was unable to find one. The odour from the sweaty crowd assailed my nostrils. Harsh voices echoed out of the numerous loudspeakers. I moved onwards, battling along with the beat of the crowd as I joined in involuntarily with the chants. Our voices rose as one as the fanatical leaders herded us along, instructing us to shout out and wave our flags. The streets were lined with sympathetic crowds.

All the time I was thinking of my family back at home, wondering where I was. It was way past my normal return time. Rumours of the street protests would have reached them by now and they were probably listening to the sounds of the procession as we marched through the nearby streets.

Finally I managed to manoeuvre myself to the edge of the crowd and when we passed close to my street I swiftly peeled off and made my way home, much to the relief of the family. They were standing by the front door, scanning the crowds. Mum's rosary was hanging from her hand, her mouth moving in prayer.

'What happened? Why did you join the march?'

'I had no choice *ammah*, the college students surrounded us and we were ordered to march.'

'Praise the Lord you are all right. We were worried, you know.' My face must have registered my anxiety. 'Never mind, come in. Come and have something to eat. You must be exhausted.'

News of the marches and unrest dominated the news agenda for the next few weeks but thankfully we did not have to participate in further demonstrations. I would have stayed at home if more protests had been planned. The newspapers and radio were full of dramatic stories. Martyrs set light to themselves in public places. Railway carriages were burnt in protest and stores looted. Fists were clenched and slogans were repeated in strident voices: variations on the theme 'we will not be dictated to by Delhi'. The Prime Minister had to react to the sometimes violent and escalating protests, and in the end issued a proclamation that English and Tamil would both be retained as official languages for the time being.

Eventually everything quietened down. I had experienced at first-hand the extremes to which patriotism could be taken and hoped never to be involved in a repetition. Thankfully, college life continued without further interruption.

I often stayed up late into the night to study and woke early, surviving on only a few hours sleep. This pattern was set for the rest of the year and I spent hours poring over my biology notes. My illustrations of the cross-sections of plants and animals were drawn in minute detail, outlined with constantly sharpened B4 pencils.

One day I was sitting on the bench in the common room, tucking into my lunch with a group of students both junior and senior, when a discussion developed.

'Hey girls, what do you think of Clement? Isn't he gorgeous?'

'He certainly is a catch.'

'I hear that he fell in love with one of the students.'

'Yes,' piped up our all-knowing cleaner. 'Her name was Lily, same name as you Lily,' as she wagged a finger in my direction. 'Anyway, apparently at first she was all over him then later changed her mind. Yes, poor Professor Clement, he was so heartbroken; I had seen him with that Lily at the beach sometimes. They held hands and took walks together. I don't know what happened but I never liked the girl anyway. She was very proud and never talked to the likes of us. Cleaners were beneath Our Lady. She had her nose in the air, that one.' Flicking her single plait back, the cleaner turned her attention to me. 'Not like you Lily, you come from Malaysia and yet you don't look down on me.'

The need to live up to the standards expected of me made me a bit uneasy. I had to do Malaysia proud. My every movement was under scrutiny. Thankfully a diversion took the focus off me – one of my fellow students was curious to know the outcome of the cleaner's story. 'So, what happened? Was Clement all right?'

'No.' She shook her head from side to side sympathetically. Her eyes clouded over. 'Ever since then he has become a recluse. He doesn't look at girls any more. All the other professors feel sorry for him. They like him a lot, you know, and they feel protective of him, so don't play the fool as far as he is concerned or the others will be after you.'

The focus returned to me once more as I was put on the spot.

'Hey Lily, do you like him? He is so dishy.'

'I suppose so. I do like him but I am sure he won't look at any of us, so there is no point in hoping, is there?'

'Don't say that, Lily! I have seen him look at you when you walk down to the parade ground. It is your sexy walk you know. I have noticed him stand in the corner and watch you when he thought no one was looking but I am a nobody, no one notices a cleaner, but we cleaners know everyone's business.' She chuckled.

'Don't be silly Saro, he won't be interested in me at all. It is all in your mind: you are imagining things. You said yourself that he is not interested in girls any more.'

'Ah, but that was before you came. Since you started here I have seen him change.'

Nervously I brushed her remarks aside, unable to control the deep flush of heat that rose up and spread to the tips of my limbs. The cleaner was fantasising; with nothing better to do she was making things up. She was such a gossip anyway and I didn't believe a word. She was just showing off, wanting us to acknowledge that she knew everything that was going on at the college.

Clement was originally from the South Indian capital city of Madras. He was Anglo-Indian by birth and in his early thirties. A slight man, he was wiry with a sweep of wavy, dark brown hair, longer than normal for a professor in a prestigious university. Occasionally his hair flopped across his forehead, adding to his boyish charm. His pale skin accentuated his indoor complexion. His soft, light brown eyes were lively behind silver-rimmed glasses. Prominent cheekbones above shallow dimpled cheeks led the eye down to a rather becoming stubbled chin. Curly dark hair peeked from the top of his shirt. His shoulders, though, seemed permanently hunched forward. He was definitely someone out of the ordinary.

Clement's particular charm was his command of English. He spoke in a surprisingly deep voice for his slight frame; it was both educated and cultured without any trace of the Indian accents that surrounded me. He was often to be seen walking the corridors clutching a small pile of books with his long, smooth, sensitive fingers, his head bowed in concentration. He knew his subject well and was passionate about English literature, my favourite subject. He displayed his romantic nature during his lectures; he loved Dickens's novels and his particular favourite was *A Tale of Two Cities*.

An impertinent student asked him why. His slender, rather feminine hand gripped his copy of the book as his eyes rolled upwards, an exultant smile extending across his face as though he was reliving a particularly romantic moment. His other hand gently swept across his chin as he momentarily slipped away into a reverie. Then he pushed his round-rimmed glasses further up his nose with his index finger, the rims meeting his bushy eyebrows that resembled the curve of a hairy caterpillar.

'Well, I have great admiration for Sydney Carton, who sacrificed his life for love. Lucie's French husband was about to be executed and Sydney made the ultimate sacrifice that any lover can make. He took the place of her aristocratic husband, Charles Darnay, who had been condemned to the guillotine during the French Revolution. What greater sign of love can a man make?'

I was impressed. What a profound man; it was unusual to come across someone like him in India, where most men are quite macho. He was certainly interesting to listen to but not very realistic. I was certain that I would not be sacrificing my life for love: or was I?

At first I was unaware of Clement's interest in me but found myself singled out to read aloud when the occasion called for it. When he threw a question out to his audience his gaze often rested on me in expectation. I had been drawing comfort from belonging to a group of 'admirers of Clement', with safety in numbers, but panic set in when it became obvious that I was being singled out for attention. I sat at the end of the first row of girls. A second row was behind me with the rest of the lecture hall being made up of male students. Head down, I was busy writing away during one of our exams when I ran out of ink. Inwardly cursing I looked up into the intense brown eyes of Clement. A smile stretched across his face as he peered over his spectacles before settling them on the bridge of his nose with one finger, its polished nail gleaming. With the other hand he held out his pen to me. 'Here, have mine. Take my pen. Yours has clearly run out of ink.'

My hand shook as I reached out to take it, conscious of his close proximity. I realised that he must have been scrutinising me closely and I bit my lip, acutely conscious of my exposed situation. The whole class had witnessed the incident. Clement had openly displayed his interest in me. What would everyone say! I didn't know how I was going to finish my exam. A warm flush spread through me and I broke out in a sweat, my heart palpitating. I could not remember finishing my paper. I stumbled out of the lecture theatre and tried to put some distance between us. I tripped as I hurried out. I felt trapped.

'Serves you right,' I scolded myself. 'You thought it was all a bit of a giggle, joining in with everyone.'

It was one thing to admire someone from afar but daunting to find that that person was obviously interested in me. What should I do now? How do I handle this situation for the best? So far, like every young girl, I had fantasised about boys falling in love with me but my yearnings were the product of novels; this was no novel but stark reality. I had no experience in how to handle the situation. Some people might call me a tease. But was I really a tease – had I actually invited his attentions? I couldn't recall that I had. I preferred to be in the shadows and admire people from afar. Maybe if I ignored it, the situation would go away.

I shook myself.

'Don't be silly. He was just being kind, offering his pen when yours ran dry. Don't read too much into it.'

Having thus consoled myself, I heaved a sigh of relief. I was clearly wrong. 'Stupid girl, do you think that someone like Clement is going to find you attractive?'

I began to feel a bit foolish about my worries but also felt stronger as I returned home that evening. I contemplated confiding in my mother but decided against it. After all what could I tell her? 'By the way, Mum, you know that professor I told you about? Well I think he fancies me.'

'And what makes you think that?'

'Well, the cleaner said he did. Apparently he watches me at college and today...' No, I definitely wasn't going to go down that route.

I wasn't going to get away that easily either. I seemed to bump into Clement constantly: was he stalking me? Hiding out in the library became a no-no. When I arrived early for my cadet practices I would find Clement heading in the direction of the English department; he would cast a quick smile and a wave of his hand in my direction. I made up numerous excuses to myself for his presence. He must be coming in early to make a start on his work, I told myself, aware that he was a committed teacher who took pride in his work.

However I could not ignore the rumours that were circulating, that Clement was in love again. Apparently his fellow lecturers were happy for him. Maybe it is someone else I thought, sighing in relief. You stupid girl, that is the answer; it must be some other student. There were plenty of beautiful girls at college, girls who would give their eye-teeth to catch Clement.

Clement's appearance went through a change. Now he sported snazzy clothes, his shirt tucked in smartly, and there was a spring in his step. There were no more hunched shoulders. He was clean-shaven and there was an extra sparkle in his eyes, as well as a constant smile on his face. I had played along with the rest of the girls in showing an interest in Clement initially but I knew that I could not afford a scandal. My behaviour would reflect on my family. No hint of the stories being circulated must reach my sister-in-law's family.

'Look, *ammah*, look! See who is in that pew there. Quick, let's get out of here before he comes over to say hello.' I became a bit panicky, hurrying my family along. 'Let's go, let's go, come on boys, Irene, come on I tell you. Get going.' I had caught sight of Clement as we tumbled out of the cathedral; the cathedral was situated within the school grounds of Petit Seminaire.

'What on earth is the matter with you?' asked Mum.

Finally I poured out my suspicions to her. 'I thought it was some other girl but *ammah*, it has to be me. I was told that Clement stopped going to church after his disastrous affair but he is now in the same church as we are!' Away from the grandeur of the university, Clement seemed to be a normal part of the human race, to be just part of the crowd. Dressed in grey trousers and a white, long-sleeved cotton shirt, he did not particularly stand out but his eyes constantly scanned the crowd, his head moving up and down and from side to side as if he was searching for someone. Aware that that was probably me, I urged my family to move quickly away from any proximity to Clement. Chandra, who had been eavesdropping, piped up.

'Father Peter was talking to us about miracles that happen in people's lives. He told us about this man who had lost his faith because of a love affair that had gone wrong but this man's faith had been renewed as he had found love again. I thought it was strange that Father Peter kept looking at me when he was telling the story. You are right: it must have been you he was referring to, because I saw Father Peter talking to Clement near his office a couple of weeks ago.'

To avoid any more embarrassment, Mum agreed that we should attend a different church, located on the south side of town, for the following Sunday's service. I breathed a sigh of relief when there was no sign of my pursuer. However, the following Sunday we glimpsed the by now familiar figure once more. From a vantage point he stood scanning the crowd, but we beat him to it, hurrying into our rickshaw before he could approach us. Drastic measures were now called for so we tried a third church, which was at least half an hour's rickshaw ride away. It was a much smaller village church, situated on the periphery of Pondicherry. Thankfully these tactics paid off. After a few weeks we went back to our favoured cathedral and luckily there were no more unwelcome advances.

'*Savdhan* (Attention) Lily, Janaki, Vasantha, *Line Thod* (Fall Out) *Vishram* (stand at ease).'

We obeyed our sergeant's commands; the three of us fell out then relaxed, our hands behind our backs. None of us had noticed the Colonel's presence during our training that morning. Engrossed in our marching our eyes had been concentrating on looking straight ahead. The Colonel was a tall, slim, handsome man. He could easily have been mistaken for a European, apart from his dark hair and deep brown eyes. We stood expectantly in line. The Colonel had a friendly expression in his eyes; he smiled and his eyes twinkled as he stood in front of us, twirling his sturdy baton in his hand.

'Don't worry. I am not here to tell you off. I am on a mission and I would like the three of you to come to our head office. I won't tell you any more now, just that there might be some good news for you.'

Our sergeant refused to enlighten us. He suppressed a grin and asked us to be patient, saying that all would be revealed soon. We arrived at headquarters and pulled up on the curve of the sweeping driveway in our little jeep. We jumped out and followed our sergeant closely, glancing questioningly at one another with our eyebrows raised. We found the Colonel standing in the open quadrangle. At a nod from him, our sergeant marched us individually and then together. Then we stood together in a group, totally mystified. We wondered what the implications of the marching exercise were: was it a test and if so for what purpose? Why just the three of us? We did not have too long a wait to find out.

'Well girls,' he smiled, as though he was about to tell us that we had won the lottery.

'You three are very lucky. You have been chosen to represent the state of Pondicherry at the Republic Day parade in Delhi. I am impressed with your performance. You still have a lot of training to do but I am sure your sergeant here,' with a nod at the beaming sergeant, flushed with pride at his protégées' success, 'will be able to polish your performance. I will leave him to explain the details of the trip to you. Good luck and well done.'

With a nod and a salute, he left us to face the jubilant sergeant.

'I will talk to you about the details whilst we are travelling back to the university.' Once we were safely seated again in the speeding jeep, he filled us in with all the details. We had already been successful in the first selection process but now we were to leave for Madras for two weeks of intensive training, after which a final selection would be made. The chosen candidates would then travel to New Delhi to spend another two weeks camping with representatives from all the states of India, and the finale would be to attend the Republic Day Parade on 26 January.

Regardless of the immense honour of being selected I was reluctant to accept the offer. I was fully committed to my studies and had no wish to jeopardise my future career. The cadet corps was an extracurricular activity not intended to be pursued seriously, so in the end I did decide to decline, much to the astonishment of our sergeant. Unable to persuade me to change my mind, he referred me to the principal. I was subjected to a strong lecture about the privilege of being chosen to represent the state. But once the principal ascertained the reason for my reluctance he was unexpectedly accommodating: he made me a promise that all the missed lecture notes would be delivered to me on my return by the relevant lecturers. I was unwilling to appear churlish and was also mindful of the implication of ingratitude if I refused the principal's generous gesture, so I was forced to accept it. Janaki and I teamed up with Vasantha, a first year BSc student. Heads together, we were walking along the first floor corridor discussing our forthcoming trip when a familiar voice cut in from behind.

'I hear that you three ladies are representing Pondicherry in Delhi. Congratulations: you have done well. When do you leave?'

What does that matter to you? I wanted to shriek in irritation; instead I remained silent, my head bowed, annoyed at being cornered.

Janaki answered for the three of us. 'We leave for training in Madras in a couple of weeks. Then they will make the final choice and if we are lucky we will be leaving for New Delhi in the New Year.'

My heart sank as Janaki gave Clement all the details of our trip.

'I will be in Madras for the Christmas holidays. Give me the address and I will come and visit you,' continued Clement.

Oh my God: disaster, I thought. I could sense his gaze on me but refused to acknowledge it. Nervously I cleared my throat. I was furious with Janaki. My hands were sticky with perspiration and my mouth dry. I rounded on Janaki once Clement was out of earshot. 'Why did you promise to give him the address? You know he is going to come and visit us now. How could you do that?'

She threw her hands up in the air. 'What could I do? He would have found out somehow. Anyway, it will be nice to see a friendly face when we are in Madras.' She winked at Vasantha, who tittered in response.

I had to let the matter drop because it was too late – the worst had already happened and the cat was out of the bag. Janaki was right; we could not have suppressed the information. Heaving a deep sigh of resignation, I followed my giggling companions along the corridor as they enjoyed a good laugh at my expense.

37

'A funeral, and a new leader takes the salute...'

New Delhi

'Anyone know where the Pondicherry girls are? They have a visitor in the reception room.'

Oh no! The others refused to leave me behind or make excuses for my absence. My body moved but my head was spinning. My heavy feet dragged along as I followed them. I tried to remain in their shadow.

'Hello girls, how are you? Is your training going well? I brought you some chocolates.' He pressed the generous-sized box into my hand; a broad smile lit up his face.

'Thank you, sir, I am sure we will enjoy them,' I replied automatically.

The rest of the encounter was a bit of a blur. I was conscious of my own deliberate silence whilst my two friends were forced to make all the conversation. We thanked Clement for his visit but we had to go, as it was time for our practice.

'I hope you have a good time in New Delhi – I shall be looking forward to hearing all about it when you return.'

'Thank you, sir, we will.'

We said our goodbyes in unison. I refused to play ball with their pathetic attempts to leave me behind for a tête-à-tête while they dashed ahead. My legs couldn't move fast enough. I endured playful taunts from both Janaki and Vasantha. 'You know that he didn't come to see us. He only had eyes for you!'

'Oh, shut up, it is not true. You are both such teases.'

I took refuge in the barracks and refused to be drawn into any banter. The girls were silenced when they realised that they were treading on sensitive ground. To myself, I was in denial. No, I thought, he was in Madras anyway and just decided to look up his students; it was completely understandable that he should. I should not read anything into his visit. I was no beauty: so wise up, get real and stop these sentimental fantasies, I told myself firmly.

We were surprised to learn that we were not the sole representatives of Pondicherry. We were introduced to three other cadets, young men from Petit Seminaire who were acquainted with my brothers, known as 'the boys from Malaysia'. More representatives from different areas of Southern India gathered, swelling the numbers at our training centre. During the day we were hard at work but the evenings buzzed with a true camp-style atmosphere. We let our hair down enthusiastically, as we had earned our entertainment. Songs like 'Kumbaya', 'She'll Be Coming Round the Mountain' and 'Waltzing Matilda' were belted out with gusto. The very air seemed to vibrate with energy. Every minute was made to count. Impromptu games and plays were organised by the more enterprising seniors and to add a bit of spice there was romance at the camp.

It seemed an unusual partnership but a short, full-figured, senior Eurasian cadet, her round freckled face framed by a mass of black ringlets, had chosen as her romantic partner a handsome, six-foot, blond guy with hazel eyes. Their romance flourished during the two-week training period. The two of them left the entertainment site simultaneously and reappeared, pink-cheeked, after a suitable interval. Other pairings were on the increase too, with the couples' absences being kept short to avoid detection. Their loyal friends closed ranks, colluding together to employ various distraction strategies, such as volunteering to perform a solo act. We fellow cadets were quick to spot such subterfuge and we nudged one another in the ribs when our young eyes witnessed a quick getaway. Meanwhile our instructors seemingly remained engrossed in the evening's entertainment.

As we had been warned, a second round of selections followed the two hard weeks of practice. A few tearful farewells were exchanged but all the Pondicherry cadets survived the process and preparations were soon in full swing for our train journey to Delhi.

I recalled the lines of my childhood poem: my name was Lily all right. Was I still silly? Maybe I was, by ignoring Clement's interest in me. I was certainly on my way to Delhi, but would I buy a chilli while I was there? Once I returned home I must remind my siblings of the lines I had written so long ago; they would surely laugh at them now, and Charlie and Chandra would recall their teasing of me at the time.

The train was really overcrowded but our status as military personnel guaranteed us allocated coaches. A three-day journey to

New Delhi commenced. The landscape changed from lush green to brown hills and plains. The climate became distinctly colder the further north we travelled. We peered at sleepy villagers huddled round open fires, which they fed with scraps of scavenged wood. At every station where we stopped, food vendors appeared with yoked baskets on their shoulders containing fried snacks. Others balanced woven trays on rounds of coiled cloth placed on their heads. The trays were piled high with dust-covered fruit and packaged chapattis smeared with dhal. Their shrill shouts advertised their wares as they brushed past the open carriage windows. Food was exchanged for rupees. Precariously balanced large trays were quite often borne by very young children. They made a pitiable sight with their pleading eyes and winning smiles, desperate for a sale. Our faithful boys in khaki from Pondicherry, our self-appointed bodyguards, were on hand to keep us supplied with bottles of water, chapattis and crunchy *murukus*. A welcome chai, tea with milk and sugar already mixed in, was served in crude clay cups, which could be discarded through the open windows. Ready smiles reached the eager, dark brown eyes of our guardians as they chivalrously declined our proffered rupees. 'No, no, you don't have to pay us back.'

We rewarded them with grateful smiles; it would have been impossible to manage the plethora of food vendors on our own. One of the cadets, slim and with a mop of shiny, wavy hair and earnest brown eyes was particularly attentive. He took great pains to seek me out, bestowing on me the most winning of smiles. My two companions were quick to notice.

'What is it with you? You seem to attract the attention of men so easily.'

'For goodness sake, just because he smiles at me it doesn't mean anything. He is just looking after the Pondicherry girls.' My heart missed a beat however. I was more than a little pleased to attract the attention of this young man. Maybe I was not an ugly duckling after all.

On the second day of travel we received news that called our whole journey into question. Lal Bahadur Shastri, the second Prime Minster of India, had died unexpectedly in Tashkent in Russia while on an official visit: 11 January 1966 was a day of mourning for India. Was there any reason to continue with our journey? Maybe there wasn't going to be a Republic Day parade after all. But the green light was given; we were still to go.

The train slowed and chugged into Delhi's train station. Hundreds of people tried to get off the train while determined hundreds more were trying simultaneously to get in. They pushed in all directions, bent on securing seats even before the carriages had been vacated. People shouted at one another in Hindi, Urdu, English and a whole host of other tongues. Shoving and elbowing was the order of the day. There were enough of us in our military uniforms to command a semblance of both curiosity and respect. Our private bodyguards appeared and two of them elbowed a way through for us whilst the third, the youngest of the three, protected us from behind. We made our way onto the platform, half-dragging our knapsacks towards the Major who was gesturing in our direction with a baton held high. He greeted us in English, directing us to file past him and make our way to the waiting army trucks. My arms were covered in goose pimples in the cold Delhi air. We quickly reached the rows of waiting army trucks; we shivered as we clambered in, helped up by the willing hands of the male cadets already on board, and set off for camp.

Having left the warm south we were ill prepared for the change and even less prepared for our accommodation. The trucks rolled through the camp gates, opened by guards armed with rifles. Barbed wire fencing curved away on either side of the gates as far as the eye could see, reminiscent of the prisoner of war camps we had seen recreated on celluloid screens. Two corrugated zinc covered buildings, heavily guarded, were stationed parallel to one another on our right. 'That is where those who play truant are imprisoned,' our driver announced, turning round to wink at us.

'I take it that none of you will be tempted to escape camp to visit the city at night?'

Where had we been sent to? Was it truly a training camp? Any glamour in the idea rapidly diminished as the trucks trundled along. The Madras and Pondicherry female tents were thankfully situated at the top end of the site. We jumped out on to orange soil, raising dust with our army boots. The grey tops of the rows of canvas tents had their sides rolled up and secured. They housed rope beds five abreast with narrow gaps between them. The tents stood in straight rows on either side of a wide main pathway. My heart grew heavy and any excitement abated abruptly. This was to be our accommodation for the next couple of weeks.

We arrived exhausted and jaded. After a meal of dhal, which lacked salt, and the ubiquitous chapattis that were to appear on every menu varied only by the vegetable accompaniments, we were ordered to get on our hands and knees and prepare the ground on which our tents were pitched. We occupied two tents, ten in each. Our task was a technique called 'lapoying'. Cold water was sprinkled on to the clay soil and with a sweeping motion our bare hands levelled and smoothed until not a toe-tripping protuberance was in sight. My eyes remained fixed to the floor momentarily, as I pictured my child self, sitting cross-legged on the lapoyed kitchen floor at Sentul waiting for my breakfast to be served. I missed the warm and reassuring presence of my Mum. Shaking myself free from the reverie I kept up with the task at hand to create the firm, smooth floor on which to rest the wooden legs of our rope beds.

In military style we laid our kit out on the beds. The open ends of our kit bags faced away from the entrance. We spit-shone our shoes to a high polish and paste-polished our brass buckles until they glittered in the daylight. Everything had to be laid out daily for inspection.

Night-time ablutions proved to be an endurance test. We were given one tumblerful of warm water, ladled out from copper cauldrons above wood-burning fires. The wiry serving women, heads covered by the ends of their *saris*, gesticulated that they were sorry; they could not give us any more. One tumblerful was deemed sufficient for swilling round our mouths after brushing our teeth.

We queued by the communal shower cubicles. The swing doors came up to shoulder level. Gripping the soap in one's cold hands was an art in itself. The brutal cold water cut into our skin like razors while our feet froze on the cold concrete floors. We returned to our tents shivering, teeth chattering and hair frozen stiff. Towelling merely skimmed off the surface water.

Our day began at five-thirty in the morning. We left the cosy warmth of our beds; the icy freshness of the air was akin to stepping into a fridge. We blew on our cupped hands and stamped our feet on the hard floor. Gratefully we applied soothing lip balm purchased from the campsite shop. The early morning march after a short truck ride warmed our bodies somewhat.

'You are in the army now. It makes no difference whether you are male or female. A soldier's life is a tough one, so stop complaining about the cold and carry on with the march. You will soon warm up.'

We were constantly reminded of our military role and eventually settled down to the routine. Stepping into my pressed trousers, pinching the creases to restore their edge, became a habit. Caps were set at a precise angle and feet thrust into solid boots.

The camp buzzed with a variety of dialects. I stared in amazement at the representatives from Kashmir, who were tall, blond and blue-eyed. That tall blond romancing soldier in Madras may not have been English after all – perhaps he hailed from Kashmir. Northern India embraced a colourful history, having been ruled by Turks, Afghans, Persians and Moguls who settled in India and married the locals. There were soldiers of all colours, sizes and shapes in the Indian Army, representing all the diverse cultures and groups. One day we attended a cultural show in the grounds adjacent to the Houses of Parliament. The show was a truly magnificent display of regional Indian dances, the like of which I had never witnessed before, not even in the celluloid world. The colourful attire and sheer energy of the dancers was toe-tappingly brilliant.

After the energetic show a leisurely stroll in the gardens of the Houses of Parliament followed. I inhaled deeply and my heart filled with pride. I was part of what I surveyed. This was my ancestral heritage: witnessing the breath-taking architecture of the building where history was created, India's Independence discussed and negotiated, was both humbling and exhilarating. My chest swelled and I imagined I stood in my Dad's shoes. His eyes would have shone in veneration had he been by my side. My eyes mirrored his as I gazed at the equally jaw-dropping gardens. The lawns were immaculately trimmed and sculptured trees were arranged in aesthetic lines surrounded by sweet-smelling flowerbeds and borders. I noticed a retinue of splendidly dressed guards patrolling the grounds. I might be in luck; a minister or even the Prime Minister might open one of those windows to take a peep into the garden. I scanned the windows in vain but they remained firmly shut. Consoling myself that this was an important moment in my life anyway, I mouthed my thanks to the college principal for having cajoled me into the trip.

More was to come. A day trip via a procession of coaches took us along dusty crowded roads with pavement stalls groaning with tourists' paraphernalia. Hands tugged at us the moment we stepped off the coaches, shoving trinkets into our faces and pleading for us to buy. Shaking myself free I found refuge among my friends, tucking myself into their midst. Our first stop was the Hindu temple in Mathura, which houses priceless art, mostly of Hindu deities. Still reeling from the splendour of the artwork at the temple we were taken to the magical Red Fort at Agra. It is built of red sandstone and is where the famous Peacock Throne, a source of great pride and Mughal supremacy had once stood, before being looted and taken to Iran. The renowned Kohinoor diamond, now ensconced in the Tower of London, once resided there too. But the best was yet to come.

We alighted by the banks of the River Yammun and it was a heart-stopping moment as I gazed at the real-life Taj Mahal, built of striking white marble. I had often admired miniature replicas perched on show on the shelves of acquaintances' homes. I had been humbled by its magnificent presence on the celluloid screen when young lovers danced coyly to the accompaniment of romantic songs along the main thoroughfare. But this sight of the real thing was beyond compare. It was a symbol of survival, and a representation of India's illustrious past. Shah Jahan, inconsolable when his third wife Mumtaz Mahal died in childbirth giving birth to their fourteenth child in 1631, engaged in building a tomb that was in construction for more than twenty-two years. It remains the grandest tomb in history.

We shadowed our guide, who kept up a running commentary.

'You know, all the precious stones were looted by the British in 1857? The master craftsman's hands were cut off so that he wouldn't be able to reproduce the design.'

How barbaric, I had been warming to the tale of this great lover but now repulsion replaced my admiration. Every step up the pathway led closer to the gigantic symbolic entrance. A little of my former admiration returned as we trooped in single file down the narrow, twisty stairway that led to the tomb of the worshipped queen. I was brought back to earth by quick fingers that dug into my buttock through my starched khaki uniform. Humiliated, I turned to confront the culprit and looked into the eyes of an equally enraged girlfriend.

'Some filthy idiot has just pinched my bottom!' I hissed.

'Mine too.'

'I am furious, the rotten whatsit.'

Unable to identify the culprit, I suggested my friend walked close to me and glanced backwards periodically to warn off anyone else who fancied his chances. It broke the spell somewhat. The voice of our guide had lost its magic as I nodded less enthusiastically when he pointed out the centrally situated tomb of Mumtaz Mahal, which took pride of place. The tomb had been lined up with the main entrance whilst Shah Jahan's tomb lay next to hers almost as an afterthought, spoiling the symmetry of the room. We posed for photographs at the base of one of the gigantic columns and posed again in the gardens together with our three guardians, our fellow Pondicherrian cadets. Where were you when I needed you? I sighed, but didn't voice the thought.

Flushed with pride when I penned my next aerogramme to Dad, I described all the excursions in great detail. I smiled to myself as I pictured him recounting everything to his friends and basking in reflected glory.

Once again I mouthed wordless thanks to our college principal when we were invited to attend the funeral of Prime Minister Lal Bahadur Shastri. We lined the streets of New Delhi, through which the open coffin of the Prime Minister was to be carried to its final destination, the funeral pyre. As we took our places I was very aware of my privileged position. Not only was I able to witness such an important moment in history, but also to play my own official role, however minor, in the running of the event. I stood proudly in my uniform alongside my companions, back straight, eyes straight ahead, my secret smile giving way to a solemn expression as we stood in silence at the edge of the road, awaiting the procession. Behind us, thousands upon thousands of the general public were packed into terraced wooden stands that had been wheeled onto the roads for the occasion. Many waved the Indian flag as a sign of their patriotism while the air resonated with shouts of '*Jai Hind*!' ('Hail India!') Others members of the crowd maintained a dignified silence. Many of the women were dressed from head to toe in white, the Hindu colour for mourning. Tears ran down their cheeks. An amalgamation of people of all classes jostled together, united in mourning for their leader.

The coffin appeared and we saluted formally as it was borne past in the motorcade. Police-escorted limousines followed, transporting various foreign dignitaries who had come to pay their respects. I noticed a number of white faces in the cars: European countries had sent their representatives too.

My battalion was stationed close to the funeral pyre. The Prime Minister's body was reverently placed on top of a huge pile of logs. The top of the pile was about level with my eyes, perhaps five feet high; I could just make out the uncovered head of the dead man. The rest of his body was draped in white cloth.

My first experience of a Hindu cremation both repulsed me and roused my curiosity as Shastri's eldest son lit the fire at strategic points all along the logs with a flaming torch. As the fire took hold, a great cry went up from the crowd. Prayers were chanted all around. I felt tears sting my own eyes as I too was caught up in the maelstrom of emotions of shock, grief and loss that surrounded me. During our return journey silence prevailed, everyone deep in thought; we were touched by the solemn atmosphere and reflected on the importance of the historic event that we had just witnessed.

The interim Prime Minster, Mrs Indira Gandhi, had already been sworn in. Soon after the funeral she visited our camp in order to wish us well in the forthcoming Republic Day parade. The campsite was a hive of activity. We carefully rolled up all four sides of our tents and secured them to the roof so that our living quarters were open to inspection. We stood in line outside our tents in the cold to wait for the arrival of our important guest.

The Major General of the Indian Army was the first to stride into view. With his stocky build and imperious manner, he cut an imposing figure and his immaculate uniform bristled with medals that shone fiercely in the afternoon sun. An entourage of army personnel shadowed the woman we were awaiting. Mrs Gandhi radiated even more importance than the combined authority of the uniformed men around her.

My father had worshipped Nehru and his family and I had been indoctrinated with his views. I took careful note as Mrs Gandhi approached, every movement etched in my memory. She was dressed simply in the widow's garb of a white cotton *sari*, the free end of which covered her head respectfully. As she drew near, we raised our hands simultaneously in a formal salute that she acknowledged with a slight incline of her head and a small upward movement of her clasped hands. She was at the start of her ministerial career. Her elevated position in one of the most populated and diverse countries of the world commanded respect; but the respect she showed to us, mere cadets, on that cold day in a New Delhi army camp ensured that I willingly gave her mine.

The march past on 26 January was the culmination of our weeks of training. Mrs Gandhi took the salute. That moment was worth the preceding four weeks of hard toil. I had accomplished what I had set out to do. After the formal march past a carnival atmosphere prevailed. A flying display performed overhead was breath-taking whilst on the ground a never-ending procession of lavishly decorated floats drew the crowd's appreciative claps and whistles.

I returned home elated. When my colleagues and I alighted at Pondicherry railway station a group of photographers and press lay in wait. Flashes blinded us as microphones were thrust under our noses for a response to the journalists' questions. Like the others I put my hand out to cover my face but nevertheless our photographs were soon splashed across the local papers. Much finger-pointing had to be endured for a few weeks as a result.

Not long afterwards a special ceremony took place when I was presented with the award for 'The Best Cadet from the state of Pondicherry', a trophy given by our very own Colonel. I received the honour with mixed feelings as it ruined my determination to shun the limelight – particularly on discovering that Clement's interest in me showed no sign of abatement.

38

'A wolf in sheep's clothing...'

Failure

Our principal kept his word and the notes on missed lectures were delivered to me but I found it difficult to catch up and maintain my current workload at the same time. Exams were fast approaching at the beginning of March. Memories of New Delhi rapidly faded into the background as I burnt the midnight oil. My place at medical college was already assured and I had an obligation to deliver, but fate had her own plans.

Our next-door neighbour, Periavur, had a younger brother who had become a frequent visitor during my university days. Unlike his good-looking older brother, this uncle was a bandy-legged man. He cut a sorry figure with his atrophied left ear and loose, creased flesh. He was blind in one eye but the remaining one was sharp and intrusive. His broad, fleshy nose was slightly off-centre in his face. Flared nostrils, *paan*-stained teeth and splayed feet that I had never seen covered were all part of his rather unattractive appearance. His almond-shaped head was sparsely covered with wavy silver hair. His face, pitted with the scars of a childhood fight with chicken pox, resembled dimpled pewter.

No one would have guessed the relationship between the two men. Chinnavur's wife and seven children occupied the ground floor of heir house whilst his brother and Siva lived above. He took to visiting us in the evenings for an hour or so. After the initial greetings, I retreated into the bedroom but Chinnavur seemed to take an interest in my studies. He made an aluminium shade for the bare bulb on the wall of our bedroom that doubled as my reading light. He popped his head through the bedroom doorway.

'Is your reading light all right? Are you getting sufficient light now?'
I nodded.

'Yes thanks, Uncle.'

Satisfied with my answer, he beamed his way to a rattan chair in the lounge and chatted to my mother. One evening, he arrived with some *ladoos* in his hand and insisted that I should eat them: in his view I was studying too hard and the sweetened *ladoos*, moist with ghee, would nourish me. Not wishing to offend him, I ate one under his watchful eye: a satisfied smile appeared on his face. Sometimes his shy, comely wife and daughters would drop in too.

'I have never known my father to take such a liking to any family before. He likes you just like a daughter, Lily *akka*,' said one.

The delivery of the sweetmeats was becoming a nightly occurrence. He ignored both my mother's and my protests. 'Nonsense, nonsense, you are a studying girl and you need all your strength.'

'You know, Chinnavur is keen for you to marry his nephew,' said Mum one day. 'He told me so last night.'

'Me marry Guna? Doesn't he realise that we are Catholics and that he is a Hindu? Besides, his brother will be looking for a suitably rich bride with a big dowry for a would-be doctor like Siva.'

I recognised the idea for what it was, just a pipe dream; Chinnavur could never pull it off although it did have its merits. I did not waste time dwelling on the possibility. Besides, I was still grappling with Clement's unreciprocated interest.

I had no respite from constant headaches at this time. Nothing could shift them. Periavur arranged for a consultation with an eye specialist at the General Hospital. X-rays were performed and glasses prescribed but the headaches persisted. Massaging my aching temples, I persisted with my studies. Chinnavur expressed great concern and promised my mother that he would make his own enquiries for a suitable remedy. Yes! He had found one. He came in that evening with a fistful of leaves and ordered Kamachi to pound them. He convinced my mother that the remedy had to be applied by him personally, as recommended by the medicine man.

I was instructed to lie down in our bedroom on the mat. Chinnavar came into the room, then walked over to the far end and shut the window. What on earth was he up to? Where was my Mum, or Kamachi? Why weren't they with him?

Then he proceeded to shut the bedroom door. I stiffened and drew my breath in sharply.

'I have to switch the light off,' he whispered. 'I have to apply this paste to your temples in the dark. Everything has to be very quiet and calm for this medicine to have its effect and it has to be applied by a male to the female. The strength passes from my hand to you.'

Not knowing what to expect, but aware that my mother had consented to this treatment, I lay still. My head was pounding. I so hoped that this treatment would be a magic cure, like the unconventional treatment that had cured me of my bed-wetting. In the darkened room he proceeded to apply the paste to my temples with one hand and with the other he was shoving a *ladoo* into my mouth.

'Eat. It is good, yes?'

Nausea started to overcome me. I could taste bitterness at the back of my throat as the sour flare of his curry-flavoured, spice-laden breath misted my face. I turned my face away but froze as he placed his hand on my chest, then nonchalantly undid the top button of my *sari* blouse and proceeded to rub the paste on the top part of my breasts. I spat the ladoo out onto the cement floor.

'Now, now, don't be like that, this is all part of the treatment. Lie still and let me finish, I am not going to hurt you. You have to have complete faith or the treatment won't work: the medicine man gave me instructions of exactly how I should apply the paste.'

I was a mere woman, totally vulnerable, and obliged to submit to male authority. I had no ready answer, numbed as I was by fear and revulsion. In a way I had reverted to childhood, I was completely helpless and revisiting my childhood nightmare – but this time my Mum was apparently complicit in what was happening to me. Why was I lying frozen? I should be hitting out at him, screaming, anything, rather than let him touch my skin with his rough, calloused hand. In the dim light I could make out his one eye fixed on me; his *paan* breath was hot on my face. Just as I forced my leaden hand to hit his hand away, we suddenly heard persistent rattling and banging on our front door and raised voices.

Chinnavur retracted his hand as though touched by a live wire. His wife's distinctive voice shrilled out:

'Open the door, I know my husband is here!'

His knees creaked as he rose to his feet; he opened the bedroom door and stepped out just as I heard my Mum slip the latch to the front door. I sobbed with relief and in a daze went through to the sitting room, anxious that his wife should see me with my forehead covered in the tell-tale green slime of the paste remedy.

I shuddered as she threw a venomous look at my Mum, hacking up her spit from the back of her throat and releasing it onto our floor.

'*Che, che,*' she chided.

She was breathing fire and her chest heaved in self-righteous anger. She was usually a mild-mannered lady with a ready smile, and when she accompanied her husband on his evening visits she bore her

369

baby daughter on her hip, to be fussed over by us. She turned on her husband in fury.

'What were you doing in their bedroom? Gereja's' (our neighbour opposite) 'mother came, and told me that she saw you at the window, shutting it. How do you think I felt? Such scandal in our family, being talked about by the neighbours!'

Chinnavar's muted voice mingled with my mother's.

'He was applying some medicine, that was all. He is like a father figure to us.'

'Huh! Father figure indeed, I have been hoodwinked by all of you. I trusted you and respected you, treated you like my own family. God knows what has been going on all this while.'

Chinnavur pushed his wife towards the door, denying any wrongdoing; it was all a misunderstanding. The door banged shut horribly loudly, striking a chord in my chest. The sound of raised voices floated back to us. Our entire neighbourhood had surely witnessed the drama. That busybody neighbour from opposite had stirred up trouble.

An uneasy stillness descended. I was shaking all over, my mouth dry. Kamachi stood in the kitchen doorway with her green-stained hand, her mouth wide open. My Mum, my poor dear Mum, walked over and sank into the nearest chair, pulling the end of her *sari* tightly across her chest in modesty. Her eyes reddened, and she clasped her hands in prayer as she turned towards the altar. The realisation that a sick old man had duped us was beginning to sink in. Irene and the boys huddled together in the corner, unable to make any sense of the scene that had just taken place. Mum made us all kneel in front of the altar and offer silent prayers.

'He didn't do anything to you, did he? Touch you anywhere?' she whispered.

'No Mum, he just applied the paste to my forehead.'

I was forced to lie to save my mother's face and salvage some dignity from the humiliating situation created by the evil intentions of a man who had wormed his way into our family as a trusted friend, a family surviving without the protection of an adult male. At whatever cost to myself, I had to suppress the true nature of the evil unleashed in the confines of our bedroom. The air was oppressive, heavy; I could hardly draw breath. I wished I could turn the clock back by just ten minutes. The thought 'if only, if only' kept buzzing round my head. It was a long, restless night, and a sleepless one.

Subdued, we set off for mass as usual the following morning. Gereja's mother stood by her doorway. She cleared her throat and spat into the drain, then turned her back on us as she disappeared indoors.

My legs turned to jelly. I forced myself to look straight ahead. My clammy hand searched for Irene's and I took her index finger in my tight fist. We walked along the road together and I felt comforted by the feel of her trusting finger. We walked to church in silence. Mum, rarely given to open demonstrations of affection, walked very close to me, as if to shelter me.

'We have done nothing wrong. God will look after us. Let's just go to church and pray. It has just been a terrible misunderstanding. I am sorry that I allowed the whole thing to happen. I was desperate to try any remedy to cure your headaches. I should have known better.'

I leant gratefully on my mother's strength. Periavur visited us later that afternoon, his forehead furrowed in embarrassment.

'I am sorry for the misunderstanding caused by my brother. He is a weak man; he has caused problems before with another family. I have had words with him and his family and they will not trouble you. I can only apologise for my brother's foolishness.'

At night, forgotten memories of childhood encounters once again emerged to haunt me. Why did such things happen to me? Did my behaviour invite them? Was I evil? Was there something about my face? My saviour in all this was my mother. I shared my fears and worries with Mum, my greatest friend; we drew even closer together in the face of this betrayal of what had seemed an innocent friendship. Men were evil, vile and cunning, out to cheat vulnerable women. How cleverly the web had been woven and how helpless we had been. We had followed our hearts and not our heads. What could we have done differently we wondered; why didn't we see this coming? Hindsight came too late. Nothing could wind back the clock and we had to face our adversity stoically and with courage, a quality in which I had been distinctly lacking for the past few months.

Whenever we walked past our neighbours' house now, whoever was standing by the doorway would quickly disappear inside. This included the children, with whom we had become good friends. The silent accusations, and in particular the children's reaction, were a bitter pill to swallow. The sound of the patter of little feet and bubbles of excited laughter had ceased. Gloom settled over both households, as though both Christmas and Diwali had been cancelled. Stalwart and upright Periavur, with his strong sense of justice and natural benevolence, continued to visit us whenever we required his help; this went a long way towards silencing the acid tongues of our neighbours opposite as they openly voiced their disapproval of us. Mercifully, the rest of our neighbours did not share their view and did not change their attitude to us. 'Don't worry,' they sympathised. 'That Gereja's mother is a troublemaker. We know what you and your family are like, we trust you.'

Meanwhile Clement's amorous advances were like grey clouds hanging over me, adding to my already grey vision of life. Gradually, insidiously, depression was taking root; as it grew, it seemed to suppress my desire for nourishment. So gradual was this process that I was unaware of my decline into what became a total abstinence from food.

As my food intake diminished, my stomach seemed to shrink. Even the freshly prepared tempting morsels that Kamachi traipsed over to college with every day failed to tempt my appetite. Listlessly, I dismantled the tiffin carrier in the students' sitting room during our lunch break. One held white fluffy grains of rice, glistening with rich curds of yoghurt and with Mum's favourite lime pickles tucked into one corner. The second contained fried chicken and the third, spinach and pureed dhal. At one time I would have polished them all off in five minutes, but now all I could do was to force down a few mouthfuls while the rest made me retch.

Around me clattered tiffin carriers being dismantled, followed by the slurping of curd-soaked rice and the crunch of poppadums.

'Try some of my *payasam* – it is really good, made with real ghee, my mother's special recipe,' failed to tempt me. My fellow students were concerned about me and tried their best to tempt me with tasty dishes but I declined gracefully. Kamachi's look of concern as she looped her fingers onto the handle of the still full tiffin carrier forced me to look away. She clicked her tongue in concern.

'It feels nearly as heavy as when I brought it to you.' I shrugged my shoulders. 'Sorry, I couldn't eat. No appetite. Tell *ammah* I am sorry.'

Mum persevered, as did Kamachi, who arrived daily with a tiffin carrier packed with freshly cooked food despite my continued failure to do its contents justice. I remained emotionally drained. Mum then tried to entice me with nourishing drinks instead. Tears gathered in her eyes as she knelt by my bedside with a tumbler in her hand. 'Lily *ma*, at least drink your milk. You are getting so thin; you won't have any strength left. I worry about you.'

A few sips at a time were all I could manage. With supreme patience, Mum bent over me, coaxing me to drink a mouthful at a time. I became exhausted with the effort of overcoming the gagging reflex in my throat. In the end I kept going on liquids alone, as I found solids impossible to swallow. I was consumed with the need to focus on my studies. During the few hours of sleep that I managed, apparently I took to sleep talking. It seemed that I recited chemical formulae and mathematical equations during my fitful and exhausted sleep. The family teased me about this relentlessly. In the end I did manage to sit my exams, albeit in a zombie-like state.

The celebrations for the end of the university year were soon to take place. Representatives from each year had formed a committee and all the students were encouraged to perform on stage. Jean-Claude, a fellow pre-university student, asked me to take part; he would not take no for an answer. Eventually he wore me down and I agreed to perform a rendition of a Malay song – but not before I had made some pertinent enquiries.

Did all the lecturers attend the function, I asked, and in particular, Clement? I was assured that the event was not his scene and that he had not put in an appearance at it for several years. Heaving a sigh of relief, I decided that there was no harm in performing. The due date arrived: Sunday, 13 March 1966. The evening commenced with a lavish spread, courtesy of the university. Tradition dictated that the pre-university students served their seniors. Chatting excitedly to my fellow servers as we approached the laden table, I took my place in the line; I picked up a tray full of food and approached the lines of seated lecturers and senior students. I was about to start serving from one end of one of the tables when I froze: my skin seemed to tighten and I almost dropped my tray in shock. There was Clement, seated a little apart from the rest of the assembled crowd.

I felt the blood rush to my face. My stricken gaze fixed on him in disbelief. His shoulders lifted a little as a smile lit up his face; his eyes grew wider behind his glasses as he tried to engage with mine. I bestowed on him the briefest of smiles in acknowledgement as I edged backwards and sideways towards the door I had just come out of, bumping into a knot of helpers in the process. I needed time to compose myself, to tell myself that I was perfectly in control, and that there was nothing untoward in seeing Clement sitting at the table. I composed my features carefully. Quick thinking was called for now and my wits did not fail me. I approached the other servers with an earnest plea:

'Can one of you change places with me?'

Janaki looked quizzically at me and was on the verge of mouthing 'Why?' when thankfully, sensing my distress, she volunteered herself. 'Okay Lily, you can join this group and I will take over yours.' I whispered my grateful thanks as the pounding in my ears drove everything else out. I became almost deaf and blind to my surroundings, mechanically continuing to serve the rest of the guests. What a narrow escape.

The emotions I felt were overwhelming. This highly revered professor really did seem to be interested in me. I could hardly believe it; it couldn't be true. What on earth was he doing turning up at such a public function and wearing his heart on his sleeve? I felt faint. I had been unable to meet his gaze properly as his smiling face shone radiantly at me, his eyes behind the thick-rimmed glasses soft and inviting: 'Yes, it is because of you that I came. Look at me, give me some encouragement.'

I was far from capable of doing that. Clement sat at his table, stirring his tea round and round with a foolish smile on his face that accentuated his dimples. Every now and again he whipped out his pristine white handkerchief and slowly mopped his forehead and neck as though he had all the time in the world; perhaps he imagined that his patience would pay off in the end.

By the time we had helped to clean up after the dinner, night had fallen; lowering itself like a curtain to offer me some much-needed cover. I moved about in the shadows. Feigning nerves, I begged my colleagues to let me off my solo performance but they were unwilling to make last minute changes.

'Everyone experiences nerves. Your name is on our list and a place has been allocated so you cannot back down now. You are the sole female representative of the pre-university students too.'

Worse was yet to come. The veranda served as the stage. A flight of steps led down to the main quadrangle where all the students and teachers were seated, waiting expectantly. I sat with a fellow classmate about halfway down. How the hell was I going to walk up those steps? I told myself to look at no one, to pretend that I didn't know whom Clement had come to see. Yes, I needed more proof that it was I who was the focus of his attention and not some other girl at college.

Having calmed myself down, I sat waiting to be called, totally unprepared for the next turn of events.

'Ladies and gentleman, we are truly honoured to have Professor Clement here to sing for us this evening. He has told us that he does not normally perform in public but this is a special occasion for him. So put your hands together for Professor Clement, who is going to sing a romantic song by Elvis Presley: "I Can't Help Falling in Love".'

Pandemonium ensued: a chorus of wolf-whistles and roars of encouragement were followed by huge applause. Clement's deep baritone voice rang true. Each line of the love song resounded in my pounding head and heart. His heart was certainly in tune with the lyrics. Heads seemed to turn towards me – or was my imagination playing games with me again?

My classmate Letchumi's hand suffered as I clutched it for support. The palms of my own hands were damp with sweat. I had barely had time to recover from Clement's performance when I heard my name over the tannoy. A squeeze of my hands and an insistent whisper in my ear from Letchumi, coupled with a steady clapping of hands, propelled me to the podium. Every step I took towards the microphone felt ridiculously heavy. My gaze ranged out above the gathered crowd; I was careful to look at no one in particular. My voice squeaked as my dry mouth failed to keep it in tune. But after a couple of attempts I gained confidence and finished my rendition in a daze. The appreciative clapping hardly registered as I stumbled towards my seat, nearly tripping over the last few steps. The blood beat in my ears beat loudly rendering me deaf to my surroundings.

The majority of the students seemed oblivious to my distress. This end of year event would be remembered for years to come, but not necessarily for the right reasons. I could feel the blood rush to my face and the ends of my fingers pricked. The knuckles of my right fist drove into the palm of my left hand. My throat was constricted, and my heart seemed to be stuck in my throat as it thumping furiously. I felt like a bird trapped in a cage for the entire world to gawp at, unable to fly away. None of the other performances registered. I was intent on making an escape as soon as possible, without drawing attention to myself. But perched halfway along the row of seats, escape was impossible. I was forced to wait before making my exit.

Clement was not ready to give up. He had arrived with an agenda, which he seemed determined to fulfil. He was firmly ensconced at the gateway, talking animatedly to all the students and shaking their hands as they filed past on their way out. 'Good night sir, enjoyed your singing sir.'

Even from a distance I could see the upturn of his mouth. I pictured his eyes fired with triumph. Hadn't he just confessed to the whole university that he was in love? Now he was waiting for his love to reciprocate his feelings.

I turned round and sought out my friend Letchumi, pleading with her in desperation.

'Please stay with me; I cannot leave yet. Look, there is Clement by the gate; he is talking to everyone who is leaving and not moving away. I know he is waiting for me to go past so that he can talk to me. Truly I cannot.'

'Look Lily, I cannot stay for long, my family will be waiting for me and become anxious if I am late. We have to get going soon.'

I sensed her patience was wearing thin. After all, this was not her problem. Her face was set, her mouth turned down in disapproval.

'Okay, okay,' I nodded dumbly. 'Just a few more minutes please, that is all I am asking. Help a fellow girl, who is getting desperate.'

I was wringing my hands in despair. Students kept passing us by. 'Mrs Clement' someone whispered, before dissolving into gleeful laughter. I turned away to talk to Letchumi, pretending not to have heard. Inwardly I seethed at Clement's obstinacy as he continued to stand firmly by the gate, casting searching glances around him. Letchumi and I approached him together. The light from the porch picked out his shining eyes. He stretched out his hand. I bent my head and focused hard on the small area that took in my feet and the ground right in front of them. The fine sand that covered every corner of Pondicherry felt gritty under my sweaty feet.

'Congratulations Lily, I didn't know you had such a beautiful voice.' There was a chuckle in his voice, an excitement maybe, but I was cruel: I could not offer him what he was obviously seeking, some sort of sign. Instead, I chose to ignore his outstretched hand. 'Thank you sir, sorry sir, I must go, our trishaw has been waiting for us and it is getting late.'

'Yes of course, of course; goodnight then girls, see you soon.' He bowed gallantly with a sweep of his hand; a broad smile was still stuck to his face, as though his wish had beens granted.

Not if I can help it, I thought to myself. Thank goodness term was over, as I wouldn't have to face him again. I followed my friend into the trishaw and sank into the seat with a deep sigh of relief.

The strain of Clement's unwanted and un-encouraged interest, the weeks of interrupted studies and the unwarranted sexual interest by our depraved neighbour had all taken their toll. Time dragged, and even my books failed to speed it up. On the 1 June 1966 the course of my life changed fundamentally for the second time. Chandra had been sent to purchase the regional newspaper and made his way into the sitting room with measured steps. I sensed a degree of hesitation as he handed it to me. Eager to see my results, I took scant notice. My heart in my mouth, my eyes eagerly locked on to Tagore Arts College and the pre-university results. In disbelief, I looked up slowly from the page; I could taste my bitter disappointment as bile regurgitated and hit the back of my throat. The tears flowed easily as my family's eager smiles faded before my eyes to be replaced by deep sympathy.

Stricken with grief, I sat staring at the wall. The open newspaper crackled in my unsteady hands and dropped neglected onto my lap. My heart thumped so loudly and quickly that my breath dried as I gulped air through my open mouth. I struggled to my feet and rushed to shut myself away in the bedroom, overcome by huge, racking sobs that were audible to everyone. But I was beyond caring as I indulged in the full flow of self-pity. I could feel that my eyes were swollen from crying as the hot tears seared my salted cheeks and dribbled into my open mouth. I covered my eyes with my arm, my favourite sleep position, and finally, exhausted and spent, I fell into a fitful sleep. I had failed both Hindi and Chemistry: how on earth had that happened? I could not have devoted any more hours to study.

When I eventually emerged the following day and flopped into a chair it was way past lunchtime. Kamachi sidled up to me, her face creased in sympathy. Silently she handed me a plate of rice and rich curds but for the first time ever she had failed to spot a dead fly that lay close to the pile of lime pickle. I stared at the fly; it seemed to represent all that was not right on that day. On the plate lay my shattered dreams, my father's ambitions, my mother's wasted prayers, and my siblings' unquestioned adoration. The newspaper swam before my eyes. I felt both physically and emotionally drained. I had never felt so low or so ashamed in my life. I had lost my way.

There was stillness in the house as if there had been a death in the family and we had just returned after the burial. I certainly wished myself dead. Better that than face the world as a failure. The air thickened with my frequent bouts of racking sobs. There was no daily music to lighten the atmosphere, no scraping of chairs; tones were hushed as everyone whispered. I emerged from the bedroom on the second day, still oblivious to my surroundings, until I was forced to look at two sombre faces: colleagues from the university had come to sympathise, the two sisters of the Untouchable caste. They refused to enter our lounge.

'No, no we cannot come in, we just wanted to come and see you.'

They stood by the doorway, demure in their *saris*; the ends pulled across and tucked in at the waist. Their centrally parted hair was combed severely down on either side and ended in two stiff, skinny plaits. The ribbon-ed ends turned upwards comically. I gave myself a shake: two concerned individuals stood before me and all I was noticing was their comical appearance.

'Please come in, it is all right for you to come in,' Mum invited them.

They cleared the doorway with a stoop of humility but politely declined a seat, maintaining their natural self-effacing attitude. They stood just inside the door. The bespectacled younger one was bolder than her older sibling. With bent head, and placing her hand over her mouth (a gesture that was meant to divert her polluted breath away from upper-class me), the skinny young girl faced me with genuine grief. Tears glistened in her eyes as she stuttered apologetically:

'*Akka*, we cannot believe it. How did we pass our exam and you didn't?' The emphasis was on 'we'. 'We are so upset for you. We always looked up to you; you are so clever. We had to come and see you, to let you know how we feel. Please re-sit; you won't have any trouble passing. We cannot be happy even though we passed. It is not fair *akka*. We will pray for you. You have got to be strong.'

This was a brave speech from my diminutive little friend; and strangely enough I did take some comfort from the sisters' genuine concern. For the first time in two days, I broke into a weak smile.

'Thank you so much for coming; I know it was very brave of you. I am sure given time I will be all right. Are you sure you don't want to stay for a drink?'

I might as well have offered them a grand dinner from their alarmed reaction.

'Oh no, no thank you. You have to rest now *akka*, become strong. Thank you for all your kindness. We will go now *akka*.' They left as quietly as they had arrived, but they had achieved a gentle lifting of the veil I had drawn round myself. Now I could stomach a drink of coffee, sitting hunched in one of the rattan chairs.

I so regretted the trip to Delhi and all the fuss afterwards, with my photograph splashed across the pages of the local newspaper; not to mention the ridiculous song I had sung in front of the whole university. I would willingly have exchanged all the attention for success in my exams. I sank deeper and deeper into depression. I refused to attend church. I was aware that I could re-sit my paper, but lacked the will. If I failed to do so then the doors to medical college would be closed for good and, if that were the case, the next option would be marriage – too humiliating for me to contemplate. I was not ready to make the sacrifice; I missed the rest of my family in Malaysia. For me the outside world ceased to exist. I was like a tortoise, withdrawing my head safe into my shell house, except that it wasn't really safe. I was plagued by constant raging headaches that not even copious amounts of Tiger Balm could alleviate. Periavur and Guna came round to visit. A pair of sandaled feet edged into my circle of vision.

I leant against the bedroom doorway, fixed my gaze on the floor and counted my toes, unable to face them directly. Directing his initial words to Mum, Guna expressed his sympathy and surprise. He had heard nothing but positive reports of my progress from the lecturers. I raised my head in surprise. How on earth did he know about my progress? Siva turned to me. 'My friend made enquiries. I hear that you failed the practical in your Chemistry exams. You can easily re-sit in January. Your place at medical college will still be waiting for you, you know.'

I shook my head, unable to reply for fear of collapsing disgracefully in front of them. Offering their sympathy and a few kind words, they took their leave. Even Guna's concern did nothing to raise my spirits; in fact it served only to reinforce my sense of failure. There was nothing more to be said. I did not relish the thought of another five months of intensive study with no guarantee of success at the end of it. Throughout the years I had earned my academic reputation through sustained success but this last year I had thrown absolutely everything I could into my studies. I had made many sacrifices and certainly not one novel's pages had been opened during that year. I went to the library for research purposes, not for pleasure. Surely my failure had not been through a lack of intelligence or diligence: why had God forsaken me when I had worked so consistently?

Crunched up on the chair, I flipped over the pages of my book. I had been playing around with my dinner when Mum cut into my thoughts.

'Lily, I just want to talk to you about something. Now don't get upset with me, just think about what I am going to say.'

Mum did not do serious talk, particularly when I was down in spirits, so I angled my face towards her to listen.

'Look *ma*, I know you are very sad at failing your exam. You know, it wasn't your fault really. You studied so hard. You shouldn't have gone to Delhi maybe, but never mind. What are you going to do now?'

Tears of self-pity welled up and I fished in my sleeve for my embroidered handkerchief. 'I don't know *ammah*; I really am so confused. I have no strength to do anything. I just want to go to sleep and wake up to find everything back to how it was before my exam results.'

'Why don't you want to get married? After all, you did like Clement before he started to follow you around; he is an intelligent man, and he has a good job. With his connections he can find university places for your brothers when they leave school. You did like him, didn't you, so why won't you think about marrying him? I am sure he is heartbroken. There he is, sad because you don't care for him, and here you are, sad because you failed your exam. The exam is not so important but your future is. So what do think?'

This was an unusually long speech for Mum. There was a speculative look in her eyes that I could not avoid. She had my best interests at heart and had been driven through desperation to speak to me in this way. She was never one to dictate and her dealings with me were always respectful but she failed to realise that the prospect of getting married was completely outside my comfort zone. I seemed to be in a state of suspended animation where nothing made sense – my body existed but I couldn't connect to it. So far my twenty years of existence were implicitly connected with studying and above average passes; I did not seem to exist beyond the realms of book knowledge. My physical being was of secondary importance to my academic achievements. I could not even contemplate such a sudden change of emphasis.

I dashed my mother's hopes with my reply. 'Sorry *ammah*, I cannot marry Clement. Imagine what our sister-in-law's family will say. I didn't encourage him you know. Yes, I do like him, there is nothing wrong with him; in fact I can see that all your arguments are good ones, but somehow my heart is not in it. I am weak, I feel disappointed with myself and I cannot even face anyone outside this house. I do not want to ruin our family's reputation. The gossipmongers will have a field day: "so, she went to college to enable her to go on to medical college, but what does she do? Fall in love with some Eurasian man." That might not be so bad but what if they go on to say that I seduced him? How could the family survive that sort of gossip? I don't want to take that chance *ammah*.'

A reputation once tainted was impossible to restore; like a flower, once plucked it loses its bloom forever. I sighed, conscious that every word I uttered would be hurting my mother but I had to stick to my principles.

I was guiltily aware that Mum's suggestion was an entirely reasonable one in the circumstances but a perverseness persisted in me. No man was going to claim me as his prize, to pin me down once the chase was over and domesticate me into housework and childbearing – the plight of the majority of women. I yearned for more time to discover the inner me. Who would be my ideal partner? Yes, my heart had fluttered a few times but my deepest feelings had not been stirred. So far no flash of certainty had hit me but deep within me lay the conviction that it would. A cauldron's contents had been warmed by knowledge gleaned from books, exactly as my sisters had predicted, but it would take a special someone to make the contents come to the boil. That intensity of feeling I had not yet experienced. Clement had come close and Siva had certainly touched the periphery but neither had jumped over the rim and entered the pot.

'All right *ma*, I just thought I would talk to you and see what you thought. Never mind, I won't say anything more.'

Mum's gentle face showed no emotion as she busied herself lighting the candles at the altar. I hoped that I had not spoilt her plans but couldn't help smiling at a silly thought that entered my mind at that precise moment. I visualised a thick elastic belt running from the altar and circling Mum's waist. She was drawn to the altar all her life, never straying far away from it.

Avoiding Mum's puzzled look, I retired to bed. A change of mood set in. I was sick of God; if there were one, I reasoned, he would not have been so unfair as to reward all my hard work with failure. I had no wish to challenge Mum's faith though. True to her word, she let the matter of my marriage drop, which was a testament to my parent's exceptional qualities. This was particularly true for the times we lived in, when arranged marriages were the norm. Suggestions were made but no force or manipulation was involved; children's preferences were respected but they were still expected to comply eventually.

I spent my days in a limbo of depression, lazing around and fingering books but unable to concentrate. My appetite had improved a little and when Kamachi returned with our daily marketing she continued to tempt me with sweetmeats or treats she had bought.

'Come, I got you this jasmine.'

Swinging a loop of threaded jasmine buds in her fingers, she hooked it into my hair. Listlessly I let her, but didn't bother to try to sniff the sweet scent, retiring to bed with the flowers still twined into my hair. I did not show any interest in accompanying Mum to the cinema either: the celluloid screen had lost its allure.

No chink of light showed me my future pathway; I would have welcomed a crossroads, with a two-way choice, but instead I was in no-man's-land. I missed my family in Malaysia and that pain was a constant one. Unbeknownst to me, Mum had been corresponding with Dad and this time it was she who was interceding with him.

'Look, your Dad has sent enough money for a fare for you.'

'What are you saying, Mum? You cannot mean that I am to go back to Malaysia? I was incredulous. 'What will happen to the rest of you? How can you stay here without my help?' Despite a genuine concern for their welfare, I could not disguise my elation – but I had always been by Mum's side, her confidant, her pillar of strength. I couldn't ask her to make such a sacrifice for me, but she was very persuasive.

'We will be fine. But before you go, do me one favour: go and see Father Peter, and arrange for your brothers to be accepted into the boarding house. I will see how I get on and if I cannot manage, Irene and I will return to Malaysia too.'

I did as I was bid for I certainly owed my mother that much. Father Peter was very solicitous. 'Are you sure you won't change your mind? It will be a sad loss for us. You showed so much promise, but I respect your wishes and will pray for you my child. God will look after you. I will check on your progress through your brothers. Don't worry about them, they will be well looked after.'

Mum was anxious for me to return to Malaysia immediately. Finally, I could see a way out too. I stood at my crossroads now and chose the signpost to Malaysia, saying good bye to India. Light-hearted at last, I felt able to take the short rickshaw ride to collect my exam certificates from college. It was mid-afternoon and the college should hopefully be deserted for the holiday season. I gripped the certificates firmly in my hand; the red letters 'failed' across Hindi and section B of the Chemistry practical renewed my sense of failure. Lost in self-pity, I turned to descend the steps that led towards the main gate and almost collided with Clement. He was carrying a pile of books under his arm.

'Sorry sir, I did not see you.' I cursed silently. Clement was the last person I wanted to bump into. Why did God desert me every time?

I faced him with mixed feelings. He looked so sad that the familiar stirrings of guilt surfaced; yet I was painfully aware that I was unable to ease his suffering. My mind was made up: I was returning home, going back to my extended family, hoping to be healed. Clement extended his hand in farewell.

'What are your future plans? Are you going to re-sit your paper in January?'

'No sir, I am leaving for Malaysia.' My response was immediate. I wanted to make sure he knew where he stood.

'Are you going for a holiday? You will be coming back, won't you?'

'No sir, I am returning there for good.'

His eyebrows knitted in incredulity. 'Are you sure? Surely you can re-sit and still continue with your studies in medicine?'

'No sir, I have made up my mind. I am returning home. Thank you for all your help.' This was ironic, as he certainly had not helped me, but social niceties had to be maintained. The deed was done. I took a deep breath. I had spelled out my future plans and quashed his hopes for good. He was bound to give up now.

He was a gentleman to the end. The palm of his hand was as soft as silk as I took it briefly. It would have been churlish to ignore it.

'Good luck, Lily, I know you have a bright future ahead. You will do well; have faith.'

'Thank you, sir,' I stammered, poignantly aware of the finality of our meeting.

I turned and made my way towards the gate, my leaden feet feeling heavy and awkward. I was conscious that his sad eyes were following my departing figure as he mouthed a silent goodbye. I was certainly not hardened to his despair. The sun failed to warm me and I fell chilled to the bone as I stepped into the rickshaw. That was an encounter that I would have chosen to avoid at all costs, but God seemed relentless in his punishment of me. Was it something I had done in a previous life? Was this pain my punishment for that? Hindus would certainly interpret my situation thus.

My passage had been booked but I had a few more weeks before my departure. The holidays were over and a new term had commenced. We had become acquainted with a family of the *Odayar* caste who had moved in just a couple of months before my departure, when it was still the school holidays. The younger two of their three sons often frequented our house. We passed our time playing card games. I was aware that Julian, the older of the two, was to attend Tagore Arts College. Following his first few days of attendance at the college he innocently related the university gossip. 'The whole college is talking about it.'

A familiar feeling of doom descended. I suspected what was coming next, but was curious to find out exactly what was being bandied about. Julian perched himself on the window ledge, his legs dangling as he kicked the air rhythmically and continued animatedly.

'They said that our English professor had fallen in love with a student!' My face was impassive as I fixed my eyes on him. 'She snubbed him apparently. Everybody feels very sorry for him. He is supposed to have gone back to his old ways, dressing up in his old clothes and wandering around looking dejected.'

Every word he uttered felt like a nailed boot stamping on a sore spot that was just beginning to grow a scab. I had no idea whether Julian knew that it was I who was the student. Was he waiting for my confession? The look on his face as he talked was open; his eyes sparkled. He was a genuine little storyteller enjoying a little light relief, and there was no sign that he knew who the student was who was implicated in the scandal. Breathing a sigh of relief I hurried to change the subject of our little chat.

'How about your subjects? Are you getting on all right with your professors and your fellow students? Has anyone from your school joined you?'

Successfully I encouraged him to concentrate on himself but I remained guilt-stricken, desperately trying to draw comfort from the fact that I had offered Clement no encouragement. I too had paid a price: my dreams of a medical career were in ruins. I had no clear idea of what the future held and I had ruined my parents' aspirations. My father had had to face his comrades and the humiliation of it all was just too much to contemplate.

I returned home to Malaysia in August 1966, just before my twentieth birthday. I had learnt the harsh realities of life throughout my teenage years in India. Heady with success when it came my way, I had been totally demoralised by failure and felt lost as I left the country. My future would surely be shaped by my failure.

39

'From proofreader to godmother...'

Maturity

As I sailed towards my oasis, I shook off the street dust, and left far behind the polluted open drains and the constant cries and extended arms of street beggars. My shaken self-belief required shelter and comfort. I yearned for the welcoming arms of my family but as I scanned the dockside I saw only Dad's lone waiting figure. I was convinced I fulfilled the role of an abandoned daughter as I staggered out on deck when the boat docked at the familiar port of Penang. Dad had travelled by train. His dear face had gained a few lines in the few years we had been apart, but it lit up with happiness as he greeted me. A few tears escaped his eyes to match mine.

'Don't cry *ma*, what has happened has happened.' Dad laid a comforting hand on my shoulder, his eyes soft with sympathy. His workman's rough hands, the nails ridged with age, cupped my face as he bent to bestow a kiss on the top of my head. I was able to supply him with first-hand news about Mum and my siblings in India, but was equally anxious to hear about my Malaysian family. However I could not stop myself from nodding off periodically throughout the train journey home.

I had endured bouts of seasickness throughout the voyage from India but thanks to Mum's forethought I was accommodated in a single sex cabin. Bunk beds riveted to the walls offered reasonable comfort for my weakened body. The kindly captain, a jovial, stocky man in his forties, kept a benevolent eye on me, dispensing paracetamol for my constant headaches and appointing a porter to tempt me with plates of nourishing food at mealtimes. I managed the drinks better than the solid food as the seasickness made me retch constantly. I was asleep more than I was awake. My fellow passengers were merely shadows that flitted in and out and the week passed in a haze. When the ship docked in Penang, the captain appeared. He doffed his hat and smiled at me, his white teeth gleaming under his straight, full moustache.

'Just making sure there is someone to meet you. Hello sir, you must be the father?'

Though I was surprised to be greeted in person by the captain of the ship, Dad responded with alacrity, and thanked him for his concern. After exchanging a few pleasantries, the captain took his leave to continue with his duties. My spirits lifted. A total stranger had cared for my safety: perhaps someone up there was looking out for me after all. Had Periavur intervened through his many contacts? I could only hazard a guess, as I lacked the courage to question such an authoritative figure.

We arrived in Kampong Pandan at Theresa's house. Memories of the housewarming ceremony came flooding back to me as my adoring nephews and nieces surrounded me. Mally had grown into a gangly twelve-year-old. Betty, the youngest, born when I was in India, was now a skinny little two-year-old; she was absolutely adorable, with short finger-curls sitting on her shoulders that I knew my sister Theresa had styled. She was dressed in a pretty embroidered dress and sucked her two middle fingers as she clung to her mother's *sari* and eyed me with curiosity. She pushed her face into her mother's *sari* but chuckled when I spoke to her and proceeded to play peek-a-boo. The boys had shot up in height and were less shy but it was Mally who spirited me up to the bedroom. 'Here, aunty, you can share my bed with me: the boys are going to sleep in Mummy and Daddy's room.'

I eyed the neatly made up double bed in the second of the two upstairs bedrooms. In true Theresa style, it had an elaborately embroidered bedspread with matching pillows and a sausage pillow in the centre that divided the sleeping area into two neat halves. It looked so inviting compared with the mats spread out on the cement floor that I had become used to in India. Hmm – civilisation! Our room opened onto a corner balcony where a cool breeze wafted through the day's washing. White washday! School uniforms, cotton shirts and shorts, all wrung out in a final starch rinse and tinted with the glow of Reckitt's blue, were pegged out to dry. We had been unable to purchase the familiar indigo blue cubes wrapped in muslin in India. The right amount dissolved in water gave a brilliant white to clothes. I smelt home as I brushed past the clean laundry but the fresh smell vied with a very strong, pungent one that rose from the well-scrubbed cement floor. My ever-sensitive nose had detected an unfamiliar odour that set me off into a sneezing fit.

'I know, I don't like the smell either, but Mummy uses Clorox'

(Mally pronounced it 'Clorax') 'to scrub the floor. She buys it from the Chinese ladies who bring it round every month. It really hurts your fingers if you don't use enough water to dilute it, but you know Mummy and her cleanliness! She puts it on neat, then uses a metal brush to scrub. If you look at her fingertips, you'll see they are eaten away, but she won't listen to Daddy's warnings.'

'No change there then,' I chuckled.

Theresa had always been fastidious about her cleaning. Her frantic 'I cannot stand dirt' attitude had led to more damaged clothes than anything else, as she washed coloured clothes with extra helpings of caustic soda, fading the colours and weakening the thread. But she would not be told. The family endured her fastidiousness with a shrug of their shoulders and laughed at her as she skirted cow dung or goat droppings on the road, pinching her nose and heaving until she had gone past it.

Ducking the clothes, Mally and I leant briefly over the balcony. A hand waved from the veranda opposite; the house was separated from ours by the two sets of grassed areas and the approach road that divided the two.

'That is Baby Aunty,' explained Mally. 'She has only got one daughter, Angeline. She will come over to meet you. Uncle Xavier and Daddy are good friends.'

'Why do you call her Baby Aunty?'

'I don't know, but everyone calls her that.'

'Who lives next door?'

'Oh, Aunty Saro Uncle Murugiah and their two children, Prema and Ganesh. Aunty Saro's two brothers also live there. We all love Mamma Uncle. He is nice to us. Mamma Uncle is the older one. He is a taxi driver and everyone here, when they need a taxi, use only him.'

What a lot of information in a short time! The boys did not leave us alone for long either. They thundered up the wooden steps and burst in on us, not wishing to be left out of the conversation. That enthusiasm was to set the trend for the rest of my stay. Indian music blared from Saro's house next door while more operatic Chinese songs floated over from the right. A Malay family occupied the other half of Baby Aunty's semi. Ramli and Razak, the two boys, were leaning over their balcony too; shy, chunky Razak, the eldest (a postman I was reliably informed), turned his head away but tall, skinny Ramli acknowledged the boys' wave. Their mother sent over mouth-watering beef *rending* – slow cooked meat in lashings of coconut milk and enriched with the unmistakable perfume of *daun pandan* and tongue-tingling aromatic spices – during their Hari Raya celebrations. Lorong

Jarret Dua was a mix of nationalities representative of Malaysia. I was happy in my sister's house.

Dad had divided our Sentul house into three parts, renting out two of them whilst Charlie and he occupied the third. They came over to Theresa's on frequent visits and kept up with my progress, or rather the lack of it. Having lazed around for a few weeks catching up with family gossip and picking up the ties with visiting relatives, now I needed to knuckle down to considering the serious business of my future. Theresa and my brother-in-law half hoped that I would change my mind regarding Clement.

'We can get in touch with him; I am sure he would be delighted to hear from us. We can tell him you have changed your mind, can't we? What do you think? He is a good catch, no? What about that other lecturer, Arulsamy's cousin, that Anthonysamy? We heard he was interested in you because Rosie told us. She would be happy if you said yes.'

All their suggestions received a firm shake of the head from me: no. But I was in a quandary: if I failed to find any worthwhile employment I would be faced with a string of marriage proposals. Various uncles and aunties with eligible sons paid mysterious visits. Appraising looks were cast up and down. My plans for the future were closely questioned. Even Thambi Raja, Margie Amah's son, who had been my playmate during my early years, visited in his soldier's uniform.

'He didn't come to see us, you know. He heard you were back, that's why he came.'

The gleams in both Theresa's and Rosie's eyes were impossible to ignore. Cornered, like a prize animal on show ready to be auctioned off to the highest bidder, I had to conjure up some sort of escape route. I decided that I would learn typing and shorthand and then look for a job. Swift action was called for.

Shaw's Secretarial School was only a bus ride away and it offered evening classes to older pupils. It became my refuge. I was soon banging out *The quick brown fox jumped over the lazy dog* on the old typewriter parked on a wooden table in Mally's bedroom, whilst listening to 'California Dreaming' sung by the Mamas and the Papas, 'Strangers in the Night' in the deep seductive tones of Frank Sinatra and the catchy 'Guantanamera' by The Sandpipers.

Our neighbour, Kitchi, was engaged in his favourite pastime. From my work desk I had full view of a footpath used by everyone as a short cut. Every evening, on cue, Saro's younger brother trod the path from the bus stop, sometimes accompanied by my brother-in-law as he too returned from work. My brother-in-law's time-keeping could vary though, as he was a workaholic. Kitchi's height resulted in him walking with a slight stoop. A permanent curl fell across his broad forehead. His head would be bowed downwards, his long strides hurriedly covering the ground, which was a ploy to avoid him having to acknowledge anyone lurking in his path, children and adults alike. Kitchi worked as a clerk in a government office, but he was a strange young chap. Not at all talkative, unlike his gregarious older sibling, he poured all his passion into music. For me this was a welcome accompaniment to mask the sound of my typewriter, and it livened the hours of finger-tapping practice. Music soothed my soul and sharpened my perceptions.

My diligence was rewarded; I had reached the level required to sit for the exams. I proudly proclaimed to my brother-in-law and my niece and nephews that I could type a hundred words a minute and take dictation efficiently in Pitman shorthand. Elated with success, I hunted for an office job.

Meanwhile, affairs in India had taken a downward turn. After my departure for Malaysia, my mother had lost the will to stay on: she missed the family too much. The boys were now at boarding school and Mum must have missed my companionship. I certainly missed hers; after all, she had been my constant companion for twenty years. I guess Dad missed her too. The decision was reached to send for Mum and Irene and they soon left India, arriving at the end of 1966 in time for our Christmas celebrations. I quizzed Mum closely about our neighbours and friends.

'What happened to Kamachi?'

'I hated leaving Kamachi behind. She was crying so much, and begged me to take her to Malaysia, but there was no way. She wouldn't have been allowed in – otherwise I would have done it.'

'Poor Kamachi, she was like an older sister to me you know, *ammah*.' My eyes misted over and Mum's gentle, smiling face swam before my eyes. I felt the loss keenly. Kamachi had been part of our family and I missed her shy smile and her mothering ways.

'Rotten politics, it messes up people's lives so much.' The Malaysian authorities would not have allowed Kamachi to take up residence in the country. I felt a hard knot of disappointment in the pit of my stomach, but our hands were tied and bureaucracy had won. Shrugging off the sadness, my mind leapt to my precious books.

'What did you do with all my books and my biology record books?' These had been my pride and joy: I had devoted many patient hours to reproducing exact drawings of cross-sections of flowers, seeds and dissections of animals, amidst much sharpening of 2D pencils.

My drawings had achieved much recognition and been displayed for public viewing by my personal tutor.

'I couldn't see the point of bringing them back with me, so I passed them on to Julian,' said Mum. Ah well, at least they didn't get thrown on the scrap heap; I would certainly have been upset about that.

I was overjoyed to have Mum's company again but missed my brothers – my film critic, my book purchaser and the dimpled, cheeky, lovable young Ben. But where were we going to make our home?

Peter came up with a solution. 'You can all stay with me; we have a spare room, and I am sure it can accommodate *ammah* and Lily too, if you would both like to come.'

It would have been churlish to turn down this invitation. Peter had moved into a relatively new block of flats in Brickfields. It was a three-bedroomed property, the middle bedroom being quite small and it served as their dining room. Peter's neighbour was Mum's younger sister Arul, my favourite aunty. Now widowed, having lost her beloved husband to cancer, she lived there with my cousins, Felix, Chandra and now married Alphonsia, plus her gem of a husband George, and my teenage cousin Mary. My very first visit to Gemas, my first train journey, was still vividly remembered. It would be exciting to live next door to the family and to pick up the threads of our friendship, as well as to acquaint myself with my youngest cousin. Mum looked forward to quality time with her lively younger sister.

I remained jobless but Peter had a number of influential friends. 'Lily, I have spoken to a friend of mine and he knows of a publishing firm who are looking for a proofreader with typing skills. Tomorrow I will drop you off at the office and you can go in for an interview. If you are successful, it will work out well because I can give you a lift in to work every morning. I have to drop off your sister *un-nie*' (sister-in-law) 'first, then I could drop you off as it is on my way to work.' I wondered what the next day would bring. I couldn't let my brother down. I had to land the job.

By now Letitia was a much-respected French translator at the French Embassy – her Pondicherry education had paid dividends. Mum now took care of their son, little Alphonse, while his parents were at work. Alphonse had just celebrated his fourth birthday. He would stand there on his sturdy, brown legs, his big, black eyes following my every move as I made his favourite sandwich of boiled and halved seasoned eggs encased in slices of buttered white bread, followed by his favourite glass of apple juice. His eyes would light up, his pearly white teeth on show, and proffer his thanks so graciously he melted our hearts.

Charlie and Dad rode their motorbikes to their respective jobs. Schoolgirl Irene was welcomed into Theresa's household. It was an enjoyable time in our lives. Our cousins and Aunty Arul's generous and loving nature and her irrepressible, childlike chuckles were a tonic to our souls. On Saturday nights we played poker when money was won and lost, but one weekend's loss was another weekend's gain; no one was out of pocket as play was kept to family members. We often played all night, wiping sleep from our eyes as our eyelids got heavier and heavier. Copious amounts of sweet tea and Milo were consumed. We cracked peanuts out of their shells too, the piles of pale brown husks growing bigger and bigger. We split salted watermelon seeds between our teeth too, and their husks grew into little black hillocks on the table. All this crunching failed to interrupt the concentration of the poker players but the grey of dawn and the first rays of sunshine that stole through the full-width glass windows signalled the end of play. We rose in unison, arms stretched upwards from the littered table, and made our way to our respective beds to enjoy a few hours of sleep before refreshing showers and a change into our Sunday best for mass. A sense of carefree gaiety prevailed.

My sister-in-law and I shared a passion for baking. Recently she had acquired a Christmas cake recipe. The only fruitcake available, everyone's treat, was a shop-bought, cellophane-wrapped slab of Big Sister fruitcake, jewelled with sticky, halved red cherries, the green of chopped angelica and the orange of candied mixed peel. We decided to put her recipe to the test. Peter was cajoled into driving us to M S Ali, a store famous for exotic food supplies. Armed with our list of ingredients we made our purchases; we were impatient to start baking. We followed the recipe's instructions to the letter, and after baking it we pricked the cake all over as we were told to do. Then we proceeded to feed the cake generously with brandy – what we had in stock was a VSOP Courvoisier. Flushed with pride at our success we wrapped and stored our cake. But the following day, Sunday, we gave in to temptation. After lunch, we cut ourselves a generous portion of the cake, parked ourselves in the lounge and consumed every scrap, licking our fingers as we went. We agreed that it had a very strong, unusual taste, but nevertheless we were determined to enjoy every morsel of our creation. Gradually our speech slurred and our eyelids grew heavy. 'Oh, I do feel funny! I feel a bit giddy. I can't get up and my legs are all shaky.'

The walls of the flat seemed to shift and a curious fuzziness seized our heads. I later woke up, having fallen into a deep sleep on the settee. Neither of us felt refreshed: on the contrary, we felt decidedly ill. No explanation occurred to us as to why we had simultaneously felt unwell. When Peter returned home later that afternoon we recounted our tale but his reaction annoyed us. 'What is there to laugh about? You don't know how ill we felt and we don't want to feel like that again,' I said.

'You silly girls, so you used my best brandy in your cake; it is extremely strong. Why didn't you didn't you ask me first? I would have told you not to use that. You were both drunk because you are not used to alcohol.'

We were mortified. We looked at one another sheepishly but then burst out laughing. We retired early that night, as sleep was the best cure. This story got hugely exaggerated of course and we endured plenty of name-calling; we became 'the drunkards' for a while.

On occasional Saturdays, after a visit to Central Market to purchase the week's provisions, Peter included me on his family jaunts to the Lake Gardens, where little Alphonse and I played hide and seek or Peter indulged in a kick about with his son. Passers-by would rescue the ball for my little nephew whilst Letitia and I took a stroll along the lake chatting about our work. Our experiences in India and its disenchantments had been laid to rest: I had no wish to rake up the past. I was concerned with more immediate matters, as my job was not living up to expectations.

My bosses were planning to move the business to Ipoh Road, which would have added miles to my journey. During the three months I had been employed, although I could manage the workload the tiny office space became claustrophobic. The job was repetitive and as the only employee I felt quite lonely. My two bosses flitted in and out, piled my daily tasks on the desk and then left me to my own devices. I felt disloyal to my brother who had procured the job for me but I was not happy with the work. The impending office move provided the ideal opportunity and I handed in my notice.

Unfortunately all good things come to an end. The strain of all seven of us living in two bedrooms was beginning to show. It wasn't long before everyone felt uncomfortable and tense. My parents missed their independence and planned a move back to Sentul. Our former home was being refurbished. It seemed logical that we should move into the first of the three parts and maintain the rentals on the remaining two. I was the first to move out whilst the rest of the family stayed with Peter until the improvements to the Sentul house were complete. Cousin Felix gave me a ride on his Lambretta scooter when I moved back to Kampong Pandan and further strengthened my bonds with my eldest sister's family. Theresa enjoyed a good social life. Her neighbours, Saro and family, Baby Aunty, Uncle Velu's family, Vijay's family and a host of others formed a tight-knit community and we enjoyed some great times together. Everyone looked after one another.

As I was now unemployed, I grabbed the opportunity to enjoy a couple of weeks with my sister Rosie in Serdang. By now she was mother to two girls: Anita, born in 1965 while I was living in India, and Caroline, who had arrived in August 1967. My sister Rosie bestowed on me the honour of becoming Caroline's godmother. I glowed with pride as I repeated my vows and accepted my responsibilities, earnestly promising to be a good role model and a guardian to my charge.

40

'Full Circle...'

CYMA College

Charlie, like Peter, had inherited both physical strength and enthusiasm from Dad. Father and younger son now joined forces at weekends, spending their time covered in sawdust and splashed with paint as they renovated the first of our terraced properties. With typical self-sacrifice, our parents were going to move into a stuffy back room whose single window opened out onto the concrete square where the well and open-air bathroom that served the occupants of all three houses was situated. Charlie had been allocated the slightly larger front room. It had a row of three windows secured with V-shaped wooden battens, which offered security whilst still allowing the light to flood in.

Irene's school year came to an end in December and she left Theresa's to be enrolled at Sentul Convent, my alma mater. Meanwhile I had been unsuccessful in finding employment. I might as well have held a match to my Indian matriculation certificate for all the recognition it received. If I had not moved to India and wasted all that time I would have sat for my senior Cambridge exams in 1964. Peter was the only one of my siblings who had reached that level of education. Much prestige was attached to this particular exam, as the question papers were set and marked in Cambridge in England. Unfortunately I was not in possession of this qualification, which would have opened many doors for me: instead I was bombarded with marriage proposals that were anathema to me.

My mother was missing my company.

'Why don't you come back to Sentul? You are not doing anything in your sister's house. Irene is joining us too, as she is going to Sentul Convent. The primary school has moved now; it is on the other side of Sentul Road not far from the main railway quarters. The school has grown Ma, Sentul has grown. The children from our rented houses, they all go to Sentul Convent so Irene will have company. Where you used to go is now just the secondary school.'

I returned with mixed feelings. There was a double bed in Charlie's room that I could share and there was sufficient room for a folding canvas bed in my parents' room for Irene. Tidy girl that she was, Irene stacked her bed against the plywood partition during the day. I had lived in Sentul, India, Kampong Pandan, Brickfields and now my life came full circle, as I returned to Sentul once more, at the age of twenty-one.

Our home had changed beyond recognition. The big house now divided into three bore scant resemblance to our previous palatial dwelling but our needs were modest and adjustments had to be made. During our exile in India the rent from these houses had provided the necessary funds for all of us. The move back to Sentul felt like a time-travel back to our childhood days. Children of all different ages were engaged in similar games on the very same grounds on which we had played. Instead of English and Tamil mixed sentences, the excited chatter was a mixture of English and Malayalam, the mother tongue of the two families who occupied both the middle and end two-bedroomed properties. Malayalees, who originated from the south-western coast of India, from the state of Kerala, were proud of their culture. Their dialect was somewhat similar to Tamil, but Tamils and Malayalees (according to my parents anyway) always vied for senior status and each considered their caste better than the other, but peace was generally maintained between them. Warnings were however aimed at marriageable daughters, discouraging them from forming liaisons with those of the other race: keep to your own kind and you will be safe.

A constant din emerged from the middle house. The bus conductor husband, employed by Sri Jaya Bus Company, and his wife – in her early thirties – had a large family. The timid, softly-spoken and long-suffering housewife was pregnant with her eighth child. The youngest children slept head to toe in the hallway, their night-time quarters. My Mum's soft heart was stirred once again; kindness was instinctive to her. Sister Raphael continued to offer her benevolence to her brother's family and occasionally, if surplus American rations were delivered to the convent, a tin or two of powdered milk and some donated clothing would be diverted to us. Mum shared this good fortune with our neighbours. A bus conductor's wages would barely stretch to feed so many mouths.

Through church attendance, I cultivated a friendship with a former Sentul Convent student two years my junior. Juliet was attending typing classes hoping to find employment on the strength of her senior Cambridge exam results. We had a lot of spare time on both our hands and spent it in one another's company. I was a welcome visitor at their two-bedroom rented property, which stood behind a row of newly constructed shops adjacent to the old Chinese photographer's, still flourishing under the management of the old man's son. Despite my further education in India I was the unemployable one of the two of us. It irked me but I did nothing to change the situation until Dad intervened and forced my hand.

Life changed fundamentally for me once I moved back to Sentul. The change began with an innocent friendship with the eldest of the seven children whose parents rented the end-of-terrace house. Soft-spoken, polite Mr Gabriel worked at the Turf Club, collecting money in exchange for the slips of paper that caused the punters to flush with hope. Titus, the eldest son, whilst studying at Peter's alma mater (St Johns in Kuala Lumpur) worked weekends at the Turf Club to supplement his father's income. He was eighteen and I was twenty-one. Titus was well-built and quite tall, about five foot ten. He was a member of the church choir and a popular guy with a host of friends. He had an engaging smile and showed genuine interest in my exploits in India. We used to chat whilst perched on a pile of logs under the shelter of a corrugated zinc lean-to that jutted away from my bedroom window.

Dad had cleverly moulded a piece of zinc to make an open drainpipe; one end sat close to the rim of the well while the other was pushed through a hole cut into the zinc wall of the bathroom so that it sat just above the lip of the concrete tub. When the freshly drawn water was tipped into the channel, the water flowed into the tub. The sound of the water falling into the empty concrete tub was loud initially but as it kept filling the sound became duller in stages until the person bent over the well knew exactly when to stop drawing. Titus was engaged in the afternoon ritual of filling the tub so that his siblings could bathe. I positioned myself on the logs with a book in my lap, admiring Titus as he flexed his shiny muscles. Sweat poured off him in the afternoon heat. We embarked on rather a stilted conversation until he had finished his work; then he called out to his siblings to begin their afternoon ablutions and sat close by me to continue our chitchat. Our mothers were equally occupied, away from our sight but within earshot. I had passed by them as I made my way to my favoured place in the shade.

After their day's work and a brief afternoon siesta both mothers enjoyed the delectable languor of the late afternoon. The fierce midday sun moved towards the horizon and cast welcome shadows under the rambutan tree. They swung their legs on the makeshift wooden bench, flicking their palm fans back and forth. Mum was clad in her home batik *sarong* and long white blouse, with sleeves that ended at her elbows; her velvety soft arm flesh dropped over her elbows in a slight bulge. Her listening face was full of sympathy for her fellow housewife as she nodded in agreement and made appropriate responses, moving her head from side to side.

Titus's mother – sharp-eyed and oval-faced, her sparse, frizzy, silver-streaked hair was centre-parted, combed severely and formed into a knot the size of an areca nut at the nape of her neck – was recalling her life in India. Her narratives were colourful and vivid, her eyes sparkled, and her tinkling, contagious laugh drew chuckles from Mum. Her index finger made lines along the exposed flesh above her breasts: every now and again she pinched off a fragment of loosened skin and flicked it to the floor. Mr and Mrs Gabriel had left their village on the suburb of the capital Trivandrum, on the south-west coast of India, with their baby boy Titus to seek their fortune in Malaya. Mrs Gabriel had a charming way of imparting the local gossip so skilfully as to avoid the label 'nosy parker'. Mum, never much of a one for gossip herself, was mesmerised by her entertaining neighbour.

The two ladies called a halt to their afternoon chat for their four o'clock cuppa. Mrs Gabriel dispatched one of her children on a shopping errand for cream crackers from the Kakka shop. She delved into her change, knotted into the waist of her *sarong*. Ever the careful housewife, she made every penny count. The eldest daughter took charge of mixing the strong brew of tea and Mrs Gabriel's strong, shrill voice rang out, instructing her children to stop their play and gather indoors. The family was shepherded into their sitting room for their evening cup of strong tea with cream crackers to dunk. Reluctantly, Titus dragged himself away from my company to obey his mother's call.

Titus and I whiled away many hours together. He seemed genuinely interested in my experiences and often chuckled when I amused him. I rarely opened up my soul to anyone but I felt comfortable with his sympathetic and understanding ear. When I divulged the saga of Professor Clement there was no judgements made. I had found my soul-mate my confidante. No one seemed to take any particular interest in us, despite a culture where every interaction between male and female was suspect. I comforted myself with the thought that Titus was just eighteen and I was twenty-one: there should be no harm in a sister-brother relationship. Titus initially addressed me as *akka* but gradually the 'older sister' term was dropped. He addressed me by name and that earned a reprimand from his mother. 'Hey Titus, she is your elder, have some respect.'

An attraction was growing between us that neither of us was willing to acknowledge. When he was late, I missed him. His eagerness to see me was obvious. I admonished myself, 'Don't be silly, he is only a young boy; he could be your younger brother for goodness' sake.'

One Sunday morning both families had left for church. I was intending to attend the later eight o'clock mass. There was a knock at the front door. I opened the door to Titus: an anxious look framed his usually jolly face.

'Hello, is anything the matter?'

He stood rooted to the spot and continued to gaze at me.

'If you want to come in, come in and sit down.'

He came in very quietly. 'Li, I need to tell you something. I don't know how to tell you. You might throw me out when I tell you.'

My heart was pounding. He was looking at me so strangely and he looked scared. My eyes locked with his deep brown ones. His dilated pupils were shining as he gazed back at me, his face full of earnestness. He was silently pleading with me to understand him.

'I think you know. I hope you know how I feel about you.'

That was it – he had said it. Now it was out in the open. I felt I was suffocating, caught in the web of our conversation and I was unable to free myself. Before I could really take in what I had just heard I blurted out, 'I feel the same way too.'

He was visibly shaken and weak, and flopped into the rattan chair. 'Oh my God, Li, I thought you were going to tell me off! To say that I was only a young boy and I didn't know what I was saying.'

I dissolved into tears. We were both overcome with emotion. The house suddenly felt cold. Just as I was basking in the sweet wonder of his declaration, the cold realisation of our families' likely reaction dampened my euphoria. Elation was followed by guilt but I brushed it aside. I knew full well what their reaction would be, their justified reaction, but right at that moment there was no stopping the joy I felt. Titus loved me; I had just witnessed the truth of that statement in his eyes.

'What are we going to do? Our parents will kill us!'

He took both my hands in one of his, then placed the other hand under my chin and tilted my face gently up towards his.

'You know we cannot let anyone know about this.' Before I could give voice to my own misgivings, this young man, younger in years but not in knowledge, had pre-empted me.

'Li, we cannot tell anyone about our feelings for one another.'

He was the younger yet he was making the decisions. I nodded in agreement. I could not hurt him or rebuff him in any way. 'We have to study hard and find good jobs and then when we are making enough money in a few years time we will get married. Until then we have to keep our love a secret.'

His face was so serious. He was speaking of marriage to validate our relationship, to anchor it. There were no doubts about our long-term commitment. The magic word marriage would ward off any objections that could be laid in our path. He gazed at me so seriously that I blinked to relieve the intensity. His arched eyebrows accentuated his ardour. Feeling for the chair with the backs of my legs, I fell into it. He squatted on the floor in front of me; his shorts rode up to expose his strong, muscular thighs, emphasising the contrast with my slight frame. I fought an overwhelming urge to melt into his embrace, but stilled myself.

My heart fluttered, my breathing was shallow. My head felt light as his rough, masculine hands touched my cheeks. I had handed him this right by confessing to my own feelings. My cheeks burned where the pads of his fingers rested firmly, caressingly. His chest almost visibly swelled. He took my hand and grasped it tightly, claimed ownership. We had limited time, as the rest of the family were due back from church shortly. I had not started on the Sunday porridge.

'Look, Li, I will write to you, from now on that is going to be our only way to communicate. I will whistle as I walk past when I go to the bathroom and I will leave my letter on your windowsill. Make sure you pick it up straight away or we will be in trouble.'

I agreed with his plan and let him out of the house. Than stared at the shut door after he had gone; that same door would soon be welcoming my returning family. A maelstrom of emotions fought within me. My life had changed and it was no longer my own – it had become tangled up with another. I was not the same Lily who had woken up that morning. My heart was racing. I had felt his naked hand on mine, I had responded to the gentle pressure of his caress; my whole body had reacted sharply to his touch. For a short time we had been enclosed in an intimate space of our own.

I was lost for words as my physical feelings made words redundant. Feelings had been unleashed in me that refused to be contained: being in love was to exist in a delicious state. Surges of emotion came over me in wave after wave. However the ecstasy of love that I was experiencing for the first time was overshadowed by the fear of discovery. The awakening of the sensual side of my nature made me feel vulnerable, like a quivering butterfly that had just broken out of its cocoon and now spread its wings to bask in the warm sun. I smoothed the hand that had been so swiftly and firmly appropriated, blushing as I did so, for my skin retained the memory of Titus's touch. Our situation as a couple was as insurmountable as Everest itself. But surely we could convince our parents that ours was a true love – perhaps we could gain their blessings and guarantee a happy-ever-after ending? Such a hope was naïve in the extreme!

Mechanically I walked into the kitchen: I had breakfast to prepare. Everyday chores beckoned. A sober feeling returned as I envisaged our parent's disappointment. The new flame that had been ignited in me so suddenly started to quiver in the cold breeze of reality.

I was surprised that no one appeared to detect the glow around me. I attended eight o'clock mass; I knelt on the kneeling board, head bent and hands together. I recited the 'Our Father' but the words became meaningless as thoughts of Titus invaded my mind. My head throbbed. Guilt, and images of my parents' likely reactions, prized open every cell. I shook involuntarily as even the hairs on my arms reacted to the shame I felt. I received Holy Communion and returned to my pew. Then I saw Titus walk up to receive the body of Christ. Did he look any different? Did he really say all those things to me just a short time ago?

That evening, Titus kept his promise. The first of numerous letters arrived. He whistled as he walked past our house on his way to draw water from the well, as he had said he would. I entered the bedroom that I shared with my brother Charlie. A neatly folded letter was tucked into the groove of the window. I opened it with shaky hands. I couldn't wait to read my first love letter and my pulses raced again. I wrote a reply on a torn-off page from an exercise book and tucked it into exactly the same little groove on hearing his return whistle.

I spent a sleepless night, lying on my back with my fingers clasped behind my head. How would our parents react when they found out? How long could we keep our secret? My eyes were wide open in the inky darkness. Charlie was snoring gently beside me. I hugged the comforter that divided our bed. A vision of my father's enraged face emerged close to mine. My father often sought my advice. What do you think *ma*, do you think it a good idea?

How could I possibly confess to Dad that I was in love with a boy three years younger than me? Even worse, he was the eldest son of a not too well-off Malayalee family, too poor to own their own house and who rented theirs from us. I was aware that Titus family practised a dowry system and not only would my Dad have to provide a dowry for me, but both Titus and I would be saddled with the responsibility of providing dowry's for his four younger sisters: me, my father's pride and joy, his clever, level headed daughter. Inevitably I would be faced with my mother's wrath too. I knew she would not rant and rave but withdraw in customary fashion into her shell. That would be unbearable.

I visualised the arguments. 'What future does he have? He is still at school. What profession could he go into to earn sufficient money to support not only you but his family as well? His family worship him. He is his mother's pride and joy.'

My head was reeling. Daylight was beginning to creep through the chinks in the window. I made out the outline of Charlie's tousled head on the pillow. His mouth was open slightly, the pillow damp with spittle from the side of his mouth, and he was blissfully unaware of my nightmare of a night. I succumbed to a deep exhausted sleep.

'Lily, aren't you well?'

I rubbed my swollen eyes with balled fists. 'What time is it, *ammah*?'

A dull headache was spreading to the right side of my head. It began to throb as I slowly awoke, massaging my temples with both hands. My eyes burnt from lack of sleep. The realisation that today was totally different from the previous day sank in. *I* was different. I was experiencing familiar sensations but in a new context: joy, shame, and betrayal.

That was the start of a beautiful love affair, mostly conducted through letters. Our religious prohibitions and our family and cultural values dictated strictly no encounters of a sexual nature. Every evening I waited with bated breath and pounding heart for Titus's familiar whistle, then crept into my bedroom and picked up his letter, so beautifully written, expressing his love. I never failed to slip my reply into the same nook. The crunch of his flip-flops never failed to quicken my heartbeat.

We were overwhelmed by the strength of the feelings that we had for one another. The difference in age was of no consequence. I was reckless and happy. Occasionally we managed to share a secret kiss at the bedroom window; I swooned inside, as I tasted the curry that he had had for supper and the saltiness from his upper lip.

At night I held my breath as I slid on to my feet, reassured by Charlie's gentle snores. From the trio of windows a rectangle of silver in the moonlight was my guide as I crossed the floor with half a dozen steps, aiming for the window on the far right. I held my breath whilst I tried to unlatch the window soundlessly, my heart pounding in my throat. I constantly anticipated the nights, the stolen kisses: the feel of his soft, insistent tongue, rough like the skin of an orange, the smell of the spices he had consumed that evening. The ache of his absence during the day was a constant reminder of the awakening of new feelings. I envied his family, his brothers and sisters, who had the right to brush past him, sit next to him, press their fingers into him, and hug him – acts that every fibre of my being yearned to perform. Only a few feet of air and wooden partitions separated us. We breathed the same air that circulated in the rafters above. We were young, in love for the first time, and mistakenly believed that love could conquer all.

Whenever Titus drew near my radar kicked in. I was acutely aware of his location. From his footfall I knew that he was close, scarcely needing to turn my head and betray my interest; his grip on me intensified even though he was beyond my reach. Coyness overtook me. My hand reached to twirl the tails of my plaits. My breasts rose and fell beneath my cotton blouse. I glanced at Charlie, striking a pose in his Terylene shirt, fashionably unbuttoned to show off his hairy chest as he leant against the doorway. I wondered if he could hear my heart beating. Had I given myself away? How long could I carry on before anyone became suspicious?

Once my feelings for Titus had been acknowledged I could no longer imagine how I had felt before that – my physical senses had been awakened and I had lost forever the safety that innocence had provided. This momentous event had changed the narrative of my life. I relived the poignancy of our mutual declaration over and over again. The consequences of it changed not only our lives but also those of both our families.

The future was a haze; I had no clear plans at all when my Dad unwittingly came to my rescue. 'Lily, you are just kicking your feet and there are no prospects of a job. All the proposals of marriage that have come you have refused. How about going back to school and sitting for your senior Cambridge exams? You can register in the private school. There is CYMA College in Ipoh Road. Go and sit for your exams; once you get that qualification you will have a better chance of getting a job.'

'But *appa*! Private education? It will cost you money. Since I failed my pre-u I don't feel like studying again. I have lost faith in my abilities *appa*. What if you spend all that money and I still fail? Wouldn't that be a waste?'

'I have faith in you. I am willing to take that gamble.'

'Well I don't. Don't tell me off if I fail.'

'I won't.'

'Sure, you promise?'

'Yes, I promise. Will you go then?'

'Okay. But I have warned you.'

Enrolling at CYMA College was a cinch. I could afford to pay their fees so that guaranteed me a place. The majority of the students hailed from rich backgrounds. Most were boys, biding their time prior to taking up partnerships in family-run businesses. I was one of only eight girls, one Malay three Chinese and four Indians.

Our English teacher, a Mrs Campos, had been a teacher at Convent Sentul. She had not changed much from my first memory of her. Her dark skin had leathered but her rounded stomach, her trademark, jutted out just as it did before. I recalled Geraldine's witty but somewhat cruel comment, 'you can rest a cup on Mrs Campos's stomach'. Our articulate teacher made her entrance in a well-starched *sari* with pleats that fell sharply in the middle, her ample bosom covered with a pinned back drape. Her salt-and-pepper wavy hair was pulled back from her rounded face and fixed into a neat bun. Her ever-roving eyes took in every movement in the class. She peered at us over the rims of her glasses, and a reproachful click followed if she caught sight of any untoward goings-on. Mrs Campos recognised me and we had a chat about my life in India and the return to my birth country.

'I know you are a bright girl, Lily,' she said. 'You will do well. You weren't meant to live in India – you would have been lost there, girl. I was married to a man from India and I know about the closed community they live in and the difficulties that girls face. Nice to have you back in Malaysia.' The friendly wink from behind her round-framed glasses was very welcoming.

The classroom atmosphere was full of suppressed sexual awareness, kept in control by college rules. Handsome Eurasian Alexander was courting a doe-eyed, lissom Chinese beauty. I became his confidante. 'I love her so much it hurts but she plays hard to get. What can I do?'

Playboy Ramlee, a Muslim and a member of an East Malaysian royal family, openly passed daily love letters to shy, dainty beauty Razia, who responded with embarrassed giggles. Could there be a future for them? At least they were both Muslims, which was a solid base to build on. Bold, brassy Indian beauty Padma, who claimed to have a string of admirers, was hotly pursued by the classroom character, larger than life, testosterone-filled Jayan. Meanwhile, I was riding my own emotional rollercoaster.

Volatile Chinese business tycoon's son Chin engaged in occasional fisticuffs with outwardly docile Catholic Indian boy Anthony. Level headed students pulled them apart. Desks and chairs squealed as they were straightened. Order was quickly restored before the teacher walked in. Shalin, with her mop of frizzy hair that needed daily taming into tightly woven plaits, was my shadow. I confided in her about my traumatic love life but she could only provide a sympathetic ear: there was no solution that she could offer. Parameswari was a quiet little beauty that almost faded into the background but she was a sage, always offering solutions to problems at the right moment.

One Chinese girl, a real beauty, aspired to be an opera singer. If I arrived early I would catch her standing on the balcony giving her voice full throttle, regardless of who was in the vicinity. She would invite us round to her rented one-bedroom flat next door. Blessed with an endless supply of money, courtesy of the tin-mining company that her father owned in Ipoh, she would entertain us with the sound of songs like 'Needles and Pins' by The Searchers on her very own gramophone.

Yoke Wah, glasses perched on the end of her nose, was the most studious of the bunch. She lived close to college in a large, detached brick-built house. The eldest of five, she loved her father, adored her grandmother but experienced a volatile relationship with her mother. We were often invited to partake of her tasty Chinese cuisine. No introductions were made to her mother but her grandmother had a smile and a wave for us as she swayed on the outdoor wrought-iron swing in the cool evening breeze.

The majority of the boys played truant. Classrooms were half empty at nine in the morning. Through open windows, textbooks tied to strings were lowered into the hands of waiting accomplices on the ground. After a nonchalant stroll out of the school gates, having collected their books, they either set off home or whiled away their time in coffee shops. 'Just going to the shop to buy an exercise book/an eraser/a bottle of ink' would be shouted out for the benefit of the seated, pot-bellied college caretaker who knowingly colluded with the rich students.

I cultivated a lasting friendship with Shalin. Shalin's widowed mother was courageously bringing up her seven children alone. She ruled with an iron fist, softened with the occasional show of love. I was a frequent visitor, spending weekends with them, and I was welcomed into the bosom of the family. Daily prayers were a must and religion played a large part in their lives. Regardless of the enticement of American and English series on the television, family prayers commenced at eight every night. Shalin's mother insisted that we kneel throughout prayers. Her only son, Rajan, manoeuvred himself to the back, resting his body on his heels. When his mum's disapproving eye searched him out he would lift himself upright on his knees and sway from side to side as he tried to maintain his balance. When he felt safe again he sank back on his heels whilst we struggled to suppress our giggles.

When prayers drew to a close, the youngest, Dolly, had usually succumbed to the gentle brush of sleep. Her yawns would lead to sleepy noises and a curled up pose on the cool cement floor. Her snores would set us off again and Shalin and I would exchange amused glances. The matriarch would stop in mid-recital of the prayers, aiming a sharp retort at Shalin but never at me. More shoulder shaking followed. We never completed a single evening's prayers without an incident. After the half-hour recital our knees clicked in unison as we rose, kicking our stiffened legs to re-start the circulation. Once we had settled in bed we would whisper together. A remark such as 'wasn't it funny to see Rajan trying to outwit my mother?' would result in further suppressed giggles. A sharp voice from the second room would reach our ears: 'Stop that chattering and go to sleep!'

Eventually Rajan's mother gave up and her snores grew louder, drowning out our whispering. We exchanged stories for hours before sleep finally claimed us. The following morning we were always subjected to her reproaches.

'And what time did you go to sleep? I could hear mutterings for a long time and now you are all going to be yawning in church. Come Lily,' she linked arms with me, 'walk with me,' as she claimed me as her walking companion. 'Oh look, Mum's got her favourite daughter in tow,' they laughed. No one minded.

Shalin's mother's curries, though tasty, were really fiery. I burnt the roof of my mouth the very first time I lunched with the family. The food set my fingers on fire. The family were highly amused by my attempts to cool my right hand under running water.

'I think you better eat with a spoon and fork,' they said, laughing. I adopted this habit from then on and continued to do so at home. Apart from anything else, it helped to maintain clear fingernails; no more curry stains to scrub after every meal.

Drawn by the presence of six beautiful girls, Charlie was often willing to give me a ride to the family's house on his motorbike. He was offered a warm welcome; tea and kuehs would be pressed on him, and a pleasant half-hour passed before he returned home. When his services were unavailable I took the half-hour walk along the very same railway track that the overfilled passenger train had followed when I attended my very first Thaipusam in gregarious Grace's company. I felt safe. The track was lined with family homes and terraced railway quarters. I was familiar with most of the householders; we were part of the local community and we all took pride in looking out for one another's safety. No adult was a stranger.

41

'Harsh lessons learnt…'

Betrayal

Titus and I met away from our house twice. The first date, during our early courting days, was at a dance at a mutual friend's house. I had been warmly welcomed as a fellow caroller by a group who visited Catholic houses in the area to serenade the occupants with Christmas carols. The evening culminated in a party at the house of one of Titus's friends. I was introduced to his friends and nods of approval were exchanged.

Our second meeting required a great deal of preparation and quite a lot of daring. Love made me break through my naturally cautious bonds. I engaged in a subterfuge that previously I would have shunned. Frustrated by the fact that physical contact between us was so limited, we planned meticulously. I announced to my family that a few friends from college and I were off to see a new, much talked about film, whilst Titus was supposedly meeting up with some of his school friends for a revision session. We met at Cathay Cinema, approaching our seats from opposite ends of the auditorium to avoid detection by family friends and left in similar fashion. *To Sir, with Love*, starring Sidney Poitier and Lulu amongst others, was being screened. Our hands touched tantalisingly as we ascended the steps of the central aisle and slid into the last-but-one row of seats. I slipped my arm through the crook of Titus's elbow but he unlatched it and cradled me so that my head rested on his shoulder. Nestled together, conscious of every breath we took, we stole kisses when the cinema screen darkened; his finger under my chin tilted my face towards his waiting lips.

We shared a bus journey another time, unplanned. I had to sit for an exam in town that day. We boarded the bus separately but I could feel him, sense him, one step behind me all the way. Titus allowed two passengers to board in front of him before following me to the back where we sat together. His right hand grasped my left and a jolt of electricity ran through me before I felt the most delicious euphoria for the length of the bus journey. I glanced at the muscle that jumped along the side of his jaw and noticed the sharp intake of his breath. The tremor in my voice accelerated when I answered his questions, as I glanced nervously round at our fellow passengers for familiar faces, people who could report us to our families. I heaved a sigh of relief at every bus stop when only strangers boarded the bus.

Our lovemaking was all in our minds; there was no close, body-to-body physical contact between us, which made the imagining of it all the more alluring. A most exquisite, refined pleasure was produced by its absence. My whole life up to that point, including my failure in the pre-university exams, seemed to have been a journey that led towards these moments of self-discovery. In combination with the ecstasy came sobering feelings of fear, guilt and helplessness, as well as a realisation of how hopeless our love was.

Our mothers played out their afternoon ritual as usual, the children raising dust around them with their skipping ropes. Titus would stroll up to the two mothers and engage them in ardent conversation, perhaps teasing them to invite a playful pat on his arm from his adoring mother. I leant against the doorway taking in the scene. Despite everyone else's presence, Titus held my eye with the boldness of youth, and an absolute sense of our private connection that made my heart flutter.

Inevitably, given the large size of our respective families and the crowded nature of our living arrangements, our secret was discovered. Charlie was working in a store in Petaling Jaya but spent weekends making improvements to our house. He acquired a gramophone from somewhere, and his vinyl singles of Engelbert Humperdinck's 'Please release me', 'Delilah' by Tom Jones, The Everly Brothers' 'All I Have To Do Is Dream' and Scott McKenzie's 'San Francisco' resonated round the garden while he repaired the wooden fence that had replaced our previous one of thorny and flower-decked bougainvillea. He often wore a pair of short brown shorts that made him look almost naked as the colour merged with his coffee brown torso. His muscles rippled and glistened with the sweat of his toil as he stopped to change the vinyls and crank up the gramophone. I kept him supplied with cups of orange squash and the occasional chat whilst Titus was roped in to hold the posts in place.

Charlie could afford some new clothes. On Sundays he poured himself into his latest tailored outfit – a Terylene shirt showed off his wide shoulders and firm midriff, narrowing to a trim waist. The sharp creases of his tight pale grey trousers hung just above a pair of highly polished black leather shoes. On festive days he sported a white cotton shirt with a Nehru collar, a gold stud slipped through the buttonhole. Titus, a year younger, could not compete with Charlie's wardrobe but there was a camaraderie between them and they enjoyed each other's company. However, Charlie's family ties overrode this friendship. Through mutual friends he had picked up an inkling of the relationship between his friend and his sister. To prevent a scandal from developing, he had confided in our mother. A particular incident confirmed Charlie's suspicions.

Titus and I sometimes met at the back of our house behind our kitchen door and exchanged stolen kisses there. Ironically, for the first and last time, locked in our embrace I felt a stirring, a hardening, beneath his cotton shorts. Suddenly the front gate creaked and we sprang apart; Titus made a quick getaway to the bathroom whilst I scuttled indoors, but I was not quick enough for the ever vigilant and protective Anna and Mariasoosai, who had arrived on an unexpected visit. On this particular day, Titus and I had managed to convince our respective families that we needed to stay at home to revise whilst they attended the usual church service. I felt a hot flush of shame as I opened our door with shaky hands, welcoming Anna and her husband. Mariasoosai's steely stare sent a sharp shiver through me from head to toe. My head reeled and my knees buckled. I drew Anna aside and tried in vain to convince her that our relationship was all above board. We were in love, and when the time was right we intended to get married. But she and her husband did not accept my explanation.

My brother-in-law had always nurtured a particularly fondness for me and had held me in high regard, so rightly he felt betrayed. He had trusted me. Inevitably, the whole family soon became acquainted with my so-called liaison. The truth was out. My love was tarnished and the magic destroyed by strong family opposition. The two mothers collaborated and decided that this was an impossible situation. We were duly reprimanded and humiliated – an innocent relationship, something that had brought us both so much happiness – was reduced to the seedy and the cheap. The age gap between us was unbridgeable. Neither my parents nor his would entertain the idea of a marriage outside their respective castes. Needling little digs punctuated the evening's conversation. Every sentence held a direct message.

'So far we have married off all our daughters respectably; why can't she be the same as the others? She is the most educated among them all, she should know better.'

'Stop torturing yourself Marie, it is not her education that is wrong. She will come to her senses, don't worry.'

My mother's sobs were interspersed with imploring speeches and cries of *Sesuvae, Sesuvae*, as she invoked the name of Christ in her calming mother tongue. Her pleas came straight from her heart, not from any taught English words. Eventually Mum did resort to English too, berating God, and asking what she had done to deserve this shame.

Most ominous of all was the silence from Dad. I could read his mind as he eyed me covertly, as though to gauge which part of me had been touched by that loathsome boy. I was his daughter, first and foremost: his beloved daughter, his pride and joy, who up until then had never failed him. He was not going to give up without a fight. His daughter's and the family's honour was at stake and no filthy Malayalee boy was going to take her away from him.

Dinner was eaten in silence; I had no appetite. My eyes were blurred with unshed tears. I crept into bed early that night. I took huge snorting breaths and my shoulders shook as at last the tears rolled down my cheeks, seeking refuge in my mouth. I tasted their saltiness. I forgot my night prayers; I forgot to entreat God to take my soul if I died during the night. I slept only intermittently that night. There were no customary footsteps leading to the outdoor bathroom that night. My eyelids stung the next morning. My cheeks felt like sponges, as if I had just returned from a visit to the dentist. A jab of my finger failed to raise any response.

I set off to college barely taking in the scenery. I was a zombie, both on my way to college and once I got there. I walked in relative safety to the bus stop, along the very same road that I used to tread fourteen years ago clutching my few pence to shop at Kitchi's. Now there was no danger from street thugs from the past to haunt me. I alighted a stop early to save on the fare and took the shortcut across the open field, the path well beaten by human feet. The scene didn't register. The figures of householders on the terraces that edged the field were shadows without form. The teachers' voices floated above my head.

My friend Rajeswari was sympathetic to my predicament. I was completely lost, guilty at having fallen in love and not knowing how to cope with the pressures piled on by both families. The desire to break loose and be free was unbearable but the bars of the cultural prison were firmly closed and padlocked and the key had been thrown away. Being in love was certainly an unreasonable feeling.

I was made to feel like a pariah, a watched animal that anyone could pounce on. Unhappiness was permanently etched on Mum's face. At first she refused to speak to me: then she laid down certain strict conditions. If I insisted on this shameful behaviour, carrying on with 'that boy', then I should not expect anyone in our family to support me. The emotional blackmail was the hardest to bear. I had always been close to my mother: I loved her deeply and the pain I was causing her was excruciating to me.

Mum prayed with her eyes firmly shut, apparently wanting to shut me out from her vision. She knelt on the hard cement floor in front of the altar swaying as though possessed, her face so fervent as she again questioned God as to what she had done to deserve this shame. Hot tears coursed down her velvet cheeks. She was too ashamed to acknowledge that her clever daughter could behave so stupidly when it came to matters of the heart. She hit her forehead repeatedly with the heel of her hand: 'my misfortune, my misfortune; God is punishing me for my past sins. I have to endure this!'

Unable to witness this picture of distress any more, I withdrew into my room. I was numb with shock, unable to feel anything. Was I really capable of causing so much grief? I fell into a fitful sleep and dreamt I was a young girl again, waking up after wetting my bed; yellow urine had accumulated in a puddle having seeped through the gaps of my doorframe bed. My Dad stood beside me, shaking his head. My body was aching from sleeping on the hard surface. Then a loud sob woke me and realisation came that I was still that young girl at heart, caught up in emotions that I could not comprehend.

Titus's mum presented me with a face like a closed cupboard whenever she passed me. I almost felt the slam of the door – don't look inside, you won't find anything here; there is nothing for sale here that you can afford to buy. Her eyes stared ahead, her steps quickened as she left a trail of dust in her wake. That was all I was worth, the dust under her feet. In her eyes I was a shameless hussy.

Titus was facing similar pressures from his relatives. We were both caught in a net of guilt and blackmail that our parents specialised in. The atmosphere suffocated us and filled every nook and cranny of our minds, dispelling all other thoughts. Gradually we were being ground down until we were exhausted. Weight was falling off me. What little I ate failed to nourish my frame and my face became thin and drawn. My blouse dropped over my shoulders and my *sarong* wound even further across my waist. The whole extended family was in full knowledge of my shame. I found my life unbearable. Our innocent love had become something sordid and horrid. Why couldn't the world be a simple place?

I should have realised immediately that the Indian cultural way of life would never have allowed me to marry Titus. My only recourse was to leave home and the awful atmosphere: to go away, to study and to play a waiting game.

One very harsh lesson I had learnt in the past about cultural expectations I should not have forgotten. It might have made me think twice before I embarked on such an unfortunate love affair. Would it have made me behave differently? I don't know the answer to that.

I was walking through the familiar rubber plantation one day, where the undergrowth was almost black as the sun did not reach it – but not as black as the story that I was about to discover. I was on my way to school at the time, in the company of the eldest daughter of an Indian family who had recently transferred to Sentul. Her father had been a colleague of my eldest brother-in-law, Arokiasamy, in Serdang. Having obtained a transfer the man was now working within Peter's office and enjoyed family friend status. Sheela was a year younger than me and had fallen in love with a much older boy.

We chatted in the usual fashion about school matters but she kept glancing at me sideways and then sighing.

'What's the matter, Sheela? Are you all right? Do you want to tell me something?'

'I want to tell you, but I am scared. If what I tell you comes out, I am dead. My father will kill me.'

'Oh my God, what is it? You can trust me. I won't tell anyone.'

'You must promise me, otherwise I cannot.'

My curiosity was aroused. 'Go on, I promise. Cross my heart and hope to die.'

Hesitantly, she started. 'I am happy but at the same time I am so scared. Lily, I have a boyfriend. I have fallen in love and I cannot keep it to myself. I cannot tell my family so I am trusting you.'

'But you are only fourteen! Are you sure you are in love?'

My heart skipped a beat; how exciting. How lucky she was, to have a boyfriend. However my face must have registered dismay when she told me his name. There was some unsavoury gossip about this boy. I was concerned for Sheela and warned her about the boy's reputation. Sheela was well aware that if the news came to light there would be hell to pay, as her father was a very strict man and renowned for his fierce temper. I was sick with worry, burdened with such potentially dangerous information and not knowing how to handle it. I wished she hadn't told me. What could I do? She was in danger, because the boy and his brothers were reputed to be local gangsters.

I decided to confide in my mother, hoping that she could provide guidance. Unfortunately Peter overheard part of our conversation. He demanded to know the whole story. I was cornered: I had no choice. I loathed having to betray my friend's confidence but I was too in awe of my brother to deny what had just been divulged. After I had reluctantly repeated my story, Mum and Peter's heads were bent close together, as they discussed in conspiratorial tones the best course of action to be taken. I was doomed whatever the outcome. I suffered a restless night but the next day's events made everything else, any other unpleasant experience I had ever had, pale into insignificance.

As was predictable, my brother, in his quest to stop this foolishness before anything serious happened, had spoken to Sheela's father. Two days later, Peter went to the front gate in response to a thunderous hammering. A distraught Sheela, flanked by her parents, was marched up the pathway, literally dragged along by her quivering dad, his nostrils flaring. Mother's and daughter's faces were streaked with tears and this big, dark man, closely resembling a gorilla in fight mode, looked completely menacing. My mother came and stood beside me as she had heard the commotion. A shocked silence descended. The atmosphere was charged with anger, pain and a feeling of helplessness. My knees felt as if they were going to buckle. The father swung a cane in his hand. His daughter's legs were already covered in ugly, red weals.

I was ordered to repeat what Sheela had said to me.

'Did my daughter tell you that she was in love with this fellow?' Her father spat out the question.

I nearly collapsed with fear. I willed myself to stand upright on heavy, reluctant legs; I could have fainted right there. I felt unable to breathe and as if I had swallowed broken glass. I glanced helplessly at my brother in a mute plea for help. What have you done? I thought. I had trusted him and he had betrayed that trust. Peter did not help me now, either instead, 'You had better tell him what you told me, Lily.'

My eyes were drawn to Sheela's; her terrified expression indicated the intensity of her fear and silently she pleaded with me, like an animal anticipating the trainer's whip. I stammered, my mouth open in shock and agony. The answer was wrung from my lips. I shuddered as I spoke.

'Yes, it is true. Sheela did tell me that she was in love with this guy.'

I wanted the ground to open up and swallow me; huge tears coursed freely down my cheeks. Deep, uncontrollable sobs overcame me and now I could not bring myself to look at Sheela's tear-stained face. I wished fervently that I had kept my mouth shut. Sheela realised that she would be in even more trouble if she admitted to the affair, so she tearfully denied everything. Her father's smothering and controlling nature ruled the family, allowing little room for personal freedom.

An icy look came into her father's eyes and again he began to swish his cane at his daughter's legs. We were all visibly distressed by now.

I hated myself for being the cause of this whole ghastly situation. Then at last my brother intervened to stop poor Sheela from being tortured any more. He prevailed on her father: 'Stop sir, you will kill your daughter. Take her home; you have caned her enough. Look at her legs – they are bleeding. I know you are angry but you are not achieving anything. I think you all need time to think. Look, the poor girl is exhausted; she can hardly stand. For pity's sake take her home, or you will be responsible for her murder.'

I learnt a very important lesson that day: never to interfere in anyone else's affairs.

42

'From dreams to reality...'

13 May

My own emotional problems were becoming too much to bear. My future was now under discussion and sagacious Rajeswari suggested one escape route that was worth considering.

'Lily, why don't you go to England and train to become a nurse?'

'What! A nurse? You mean wash people and give pills and things? Everybody looks down on them, they say nurses are cheap.'

'Who said so? I know lots of girls who have gone to England to be trained. If you come back here to work afterwards you will get a good salary. English-trained nurses are well-respected – sought-after, you know. I tell you, you could earn a lot of money.'

'My father always wanted me to be a doctor, so I don't know what he will say if I tell him I want to become a nurse now.'

'Ask him and see.'

'I cannot ask him for more money. He is already paying for my classes here and he is not a rich man. There are so many of us for him to look after.'

'You will only have to pay for your plane ticket. Once you get there they train you and pay you. You will get a salary, so your father wouldn't have to pay for your training. You can pay him back for the airfare.'

'Are you quite sure I wouldn't have to pay for the training?'

'Yes, I am very sure. Also, England is looking for nurses from Malaysia, and many girls have already gone. They had no problems. You just go to the British High Commission and fill out some forms and then they will tell you whether you can go or not.'

'Oh my God, that means I can escape for a few years and everything will be all right when I come back. Surely Titus's family won't mind welcoming me into their family then, because I will be able to earn a lot of money.'

'Yes, Lily, you are finding it so difficult at home at the moment and at least you will have a few years' break. Not that I want you to go; I will miss you.'

'Thanks Rajesh, you are such a good friend. I will talk to my father and see what he says.'

My mind flashed back to the times when my Dad had made promises to me of further studies either in England or Australia. My initial career choice had not materialised in India and with no great prospect of jobs in Malaysia, a spell overseas was looking pretty enticing. I had originally considered nursing in England to join my friend Alka but when Periavur had suggested I train in India, I had dropped the idea. Now it was once again on my horizon. I could escape from the emotional drain of the situation with Titus and his family, whilst the bonus of a guaranteed, well-paid job on my return was the clincher. My prayers were being answered. I had always wanted to travel to Europe. This dream would be realised and the time away would hopefully have cooled the fractious atmosphere between the two families. Titus could see no other way forward for us.

Of course all this depended on me getting good grades in my exams. I was thrown into panic mode. From the way the school year had progressed so far I had grave doubts about my ability to obtain the required grades but I knuckled down with hope in my heart and renewed vigour. I set about intensive studying for my finals. Textbooks whose virgin pages were still stuck together in their newness at last saw the light of day. Faithful Rajes engaged in some serious research to help me. She had connections. Past exam papers were scoured and the most likely questions circled; dear Rajes would rush over before specific exams, her little figure appearing at the gate. She walked up the path with her soft but quick steps, her head bowed and her hands clutching a sheaf of papers.

'Here Lily, study the questions I have circled in red. My cousin told me that these are the ones that are likely to crop up. He has sifted through the last ten years' exam papers and noticed a pattern in them. He is sure of his research.'

I hugged her. 'Thank you so much, Rajesh, for going to so much trouble for me. How can I ever repay you?'

'Just pass your exams and get to England, that will be payment enough for me.' Her gentle smile encouraged me; go on you can do it, it said.

The night before each exam I kept my head down. The gaslight hissed well into the night. Silence prevailed. Everyone, including boisterous Charlie, played their part as I bent over my books. He went to bed in the lighted room but made no protest. His gentle snores in the background were a pleasant distraction. Thankfully, the majority of the questions did match the marked ones that I had specifically revised. I sent silent thanks to Rajesh from the exam room. When the results were published, I had successfully obtained the armoury I needed to apply for a place in nursing. I failed just the one subject – my Malay paper. This had no bearing on an application for nursing training in England. I had obtained good grades in the required subjects.

I tentatively approached my Dad with the proposal; without any hesitation he agreed. His eyes lit up. I was offering him a practical solution to the Titus dilemma.

'Do what you have to do and tell me what help you need from me. I will keep the promise I made to you. I know, we will go and see Mr Dings. I know he sent his daughter to England for nursing last year. He will know what the next step is.'

There was no stopping Dad now. At the earliest opportunity we set off on his scooter to the home of my old school friend, Geraldine. Her father and mine were good friends as they were fellow members of the Indian National Congress. A welcome reunion with Geraldine followed and we left clutching the address of Lewisham Hospital in London where Geraldine's sister Linda was a trainee nurse.

Mr Dings promised to be a referee if I required one. A letter was drafted and sent off to the hospital. Months of waiting followed. I could not tolerate the atmosphere at home and needed to find work. Influential connections came into play again. For a token wage that just about covered my bus fare and lunch, I was employed as a trainee nurse in a dispensary in Brickfields. I weighed patients, tested urine samples, sterilised equipment for minor surgery, prepared injections for the doctor or senior nurse to administer and, under the senior nurse's supervision, counted and poured tablets and mixtures into bottles and labelled packages. I earned the staff's approval: 'you are a quick learner, I am sure you will do well in your training once you are accepted.'

My problems at home resulted in insomnia. I explained my predicament to the friendly Indian doctor. He dispensed a prescription for Soneryl, pink scored tablets, and told me to take two before I went to bed that night.

'Lily, *enderi*, wake up! It is time for you to get dressed and go to work.'

But I was a total zombie, unable to wake up. I managed to prize my eyelids open briefly but I had to let go again. My body was weightless. I grunted, turned over and fell back into a deep sleep. I slept all that day and all night as well. When I went back to work a day later, I shamefacedly had to confess that the two tablets had completely knocked me out. They were obviously too strong for me, and the doctor suggested I try taking a single tablet for the next time. But I decided to keep well away from any tablet in future. I had discovered the hard way that I must learn to live with the insomnia.

I served my apprenticeship at the dispensary for two months and took my leave. The dispensary no longer required my services: I had become an added expense. They wished me well, though, and hoped that I would hear from the hospital soon. I left clutching my letter of achievement, hoping that I would not have to wait too long for a letter of acceptance from England.

Meanwhile, the political situation in Malaysia was worsening. There was much jostling for the influential positions in the government; the old aristocratic class, groomed by the British, were deemed to be too pro-multicultural. The local Malay capitalist class was driven by aspirations for a strictly Malay state capital, in which non-Malays would have no representation. The Malays formed the largest ethnic community. When Islam was declared the country's official religion on 31 August 1957, Malaya lost its much-admired multi-religious status. The hunger for radicalism was impinging on the nation as a whole. Non-Malays had to convert to Islam before a marriage to a person of Malay origin could be considered. A class system was rapidly emerging in which the Indians were relegated to third-class status.

Factions and new political parties were emerging; alliances were being made amongst the wealthy to promote their own selfish interests. Malay replaced English as the official language, although English was still required for international trading. The Prime Minister, Tunku Abdul Rahman, was widely respected; but he had been in power since Independence in 1957 and he was of the old school, no longer in step with the radical views of the wealthy ruling class. The rural Malayan economy remained stagnant. The happy-go-lucky Malays who lived out in the country had been content in their traditional setting, eking out a living by working the paddy fields, netting fish and generally passing the time in their small communities at subsistence level. They produced enough food to eat and to sell to make a living for their families. But the trend now was towards migration from rural areas to urban ones, in search of better-paying occupations. Kampong Baru not too far from where Theresa lived was one such Malay Reserve gazetted during the colonial British rule so that urban Malays could practice their village lifestyle.

The industrious, astute and business-minded Chinese were thriving.

From their original backbreaking employment in the muddy tin mines they were branching out into the commercial field, making their mark and their fortune. The Indians, too, became active in commercial projects and began to climb up the professional ladder, migrating from the drudgery of the rubber plantations into urban areas. When the May 1969 elections came, only the third since Independence, the ruling Malay party lost a good proportion of their seats in what was widely perceived to be an anti-government demonstration: Many Chinese from the opposition party then went on a victory parade (although it was not a victory as such) against the police approved route through the Malay Reserve area. A Malay backlash followed. Rumours abounded of a gathering of young, trouble-seeking Malay youths who held a rally, wielding *parangs*, at the home of the Selangor Malay dignitary, Menteri Besar Dato' Harun, and the deputy Prime Minister, Tun Abdul Razak, with aspirations for an early takeover of leadership from the well-respected Prime Minister. A coup had been plotted, resulting in six thousand Chinese homes and businesses being burnt and 184 people killed.

These riots are etched in the memories of the whole community. On the 11th and 12th May the Chinese had been celebrating the failure of the ruling party to gain overall control. On the evening of 13th May the violence had erupted. Clashes between the *parang*-wielding Malays and the Chinese had occurred. The Chinese had been the initial targets. The destruction and the slaughter commenced at Kampung Baru and quickly spread to Batu Road, where mainly Chinese businesses flourished alongside some Indian ones. Chinese shops and houses were torched. Riot squads were brought in and curfews imposed but the killing continued.

Children were sent home from school for fear of the spread of violence. Malaysia had always been a country where all the races lived together in harmony but now peace had been destroyed and replaced with terror. Despite the curfew, vigilante groups formed to safeguard individual communities; merging into night's shadows, the men stood together in a close and trusting circle. Their voices were hushed, their urgent faces intently listening whilst at the same time being creased with fear. The women stood quietly in the shadow of their doorways, subdued and anxious. The interiors of our houses were lit dimly by flickering candlelight and the children lay inside, rigid with fear. It was ghostly silent everywhere; even the wind had dropped as though holding its breath so that every rustle of impending danger could be detected.

Our family was particularly worried about Charlie, working away in Petaling Jaya. I missed the familiar put putting of his Lambretta pulling up. The roadblocks had prevented him from returning home and the lack of a telephone in our house meant that he was unable to communicate with us.

'My God, it is Charlie again. Why does this always happen to him?'

I cried tears of frustration and fear, clutching my hands together in prayer, and praying that God would keep him safe. I joined Mum and Dad, who were kneeling in front of the altar. In the candlelight all my old fears of the darkness returned with a vengeance. There was little sleep for anyone that night.

Dad had volunteered with Titus and his father to join the vigilantes, which added to the stress on our already shattered nerves. Unable to attend their workplaces, the men gathered round a hastily dragged out table on the soft earth in front of our doorway. Games of gin rummy and rounds of whisky and water helped to pass the time and build bonds in times of crisis such as this, when personal and family safety was threatened.

The panic situation lasted for a few days. It was a harrowing time. We had no way of knowing whether the rest of the family was safe. To our immense relief, on the second day Charlie's motorbike returned during a brief lift of the curfew. My Dad and I hopped on the motorbike when it was safe to do so, as we were anxious for Theresa and her family's safety. On our way there we saw many signs of the uprising. Signboards were everywhere advertising the curfew times. The visible presence of the military, with guns on full display, fed our fears. I clung to Dad, my hands gripping his sides, and I drew strength from his calm stoicism. Nothing was going to stop him from checking on the safety of his family.

When we arrived at Theresa's we found them all safe and sound. My sister collapsed in a fainting heap when she saw us. We had to sprinkle water on her face to rouse her and when she did, she dissolved into fresh tears. After half an hour Dad decided that we ought to make our way back. Uncertainty still prevailed. A state of emergency was proclaimed on 15th May. The official estimate, announced on 21st May was 137 killed, 342 injured, 2912 persons arrested and numerous vehicles and buildings destroyed. Incidents were also reported involving ethnic Indians. Sporadic violence was occurring in a number of states. On 28th June a house in Sentul Pasar was set on fire by an unknown person or persons. In the interior of Sentul Pasar a row of dwelling houses was also set on fire. This was too close to home.

Censorship was implemented and so no one was any the wiser about fresh outbreaks of violence or unrest. We were living in a tinderbox.

Post-Independence, our forward-looking country was suddenly propelled into a totally precarious situation. The events of 13th May changed everything. There was tension in the air. Fear had been engendered amongst the different races; everyone was suspicious of everyone else. A period of uncertainty entered our lives once more. Juliet's family had also taken the decision to send their daughter to England to study nursing and my friend Yoke Wah applied to the same hospital as me. 'I need a break from my mother. Wouldn't it be good if we were both accepted?'

Eventually the life-changing letter, dated 13th June 1969, arrived.

'I have much pleasure in informing you that your application for student training at this hospital has been successful.'

I was offered a place for the January intake, as the August placements had already been filled. I was given the opportunity to arrive early so that I could work on the wards as a pre-student nurse. A detailed medical questionnaire was enclosed. More anxious moments followed. Would I pass my medical? Are my constant migraines going to prove an obstacle? I made an appointment at the Nathan Clinic in up-town Bungsar and thankfully all went well. The next stop was the Ministry of Education at the imposing Federal House: the hospital required a testimonial from a referee.

Dad was acquainted with a prominent lady whom he hoped would agree to be a second referee.

'Just in case there are any problems when you arrive in England, she is very famous and I am sure that a letter from her will carry a lot of weight,' he reassured me.

Mrs Ramachandran was in her middle fifties and a proud political figure with a string of letters after her name. Some were explained to me but about others I had no clue: JP, PJK, AMN, and an MBE bestowed on her by the Queen in England for services rendered during the process of Malay winning Independence. She and her husband had run a successful printing press and after his death Mrs Ramachandran continued to manage it on her own.

We set off on 21st June 1969 to visit her at her imposing white house in Pahang Road in Kuala Lumpur. The wind whipped my hair into my face as Dad pulled up at the traffic lights, balancing the scooter with one leg on the running board and the other firmly on the road.

'Mrs Ramachandran is the only Indian lady who can drive through red lights and the policeman will salute her instead of giving her a ticket. She is a well known figure in Kuala Lumpur. She will just wave to the policeman and continue speeding along. Everyone gives way to her car.'

My face butted his shoulder as I burst out laughing. When we arrived at her house she certainly appeared larger than life. She was well-endowed and wore a sleeveless white blouse – unheard-of attire on an Indian lady – 'Exposing her arms? Tut tut!' Over the blouse she wore a pristine, white, starched widow's *sari* with the folds draped on her shoulder and pinned in place by a brooch encrusted with a glistening white stone. Was it a diamond? I wondered. Her bosom heaved whenever she gave her throaty laugh. She was a tall woman, standing shoulder to shoulder with Dad. Her striking silver hair was pulled back severely and tied in a bun that sat high above the nape of her neck. The aura of a VIP oozed from her every pore, yet she was respectful of Dad and tapped his shoulder in camaraderie.

'Don't you worry, Mr Anthonysamy, I will type out a letter for you straight away. You are a good man. I am glad to be of help to you; you deserve it.' She winked at me as I stood next to Dad nervously.

'Vatsala, come here girl, make our guests a drink. You know Mr Anthony.' She nodded in the direction of Vatsala. 'My older daughter is doing very well with her *Bharata Natyam*.'

During my brief spell of fame on the stage I recalled a particular performance at the town hall when Mrs Ramachandran's daughter had performed a spectacular Indian dance routine. I vividly recalled the presence of a white-haired, majestic lady who had come backstage to collect her daughter. If she walked through that door now I was sure she would not recognise me.

My head jerked round as a beautiful, lissom figure dashed in, shouted out to her mother that she was going out, and nodded an acknowledgement to Dad. That is her, I thought, my heart racing. How uncanny. Sure enough, there had been no sign of recognition as her eyes slid past me. I searched for an excuse for her: perhaps there were so many visitors requesting her mother's benevolence, that she could not acknowledge them all.

'Young girls nowadays have no time, do they, Mr Anthonysamy?'

'She has certainly grown up into a remarkable young lady. You have done well by her, Mrs Ramachandran.'

She nodded, an indulgent smile fixed on her face.

The roar of an engine in the distance announced the quick getaway of the young lady. A maid walked in with the drinks. I was so nervous that I could barely swallow the refreshing, freshly squeezed lime juice. Dad continued to exchange political chitchat with Mrs Ramachandran as she finished tapping out her letter on headed paper. I clutched the important document tightly. This was going to change my future.

The remaining and most important obstacle now was to sort out the finances. My mother was willing to pawn all her jewellery, including her *thali*, the symbol of her wedding. With the addition of my own gold necklace, one that Mum had reserved for me as part of a future wedding gift, plus the loan that Dad had taken out at work, we raised the required sum. I was humbled by my parents' willing sacrifices. Not only were they ensuring my future employment prospects, they were also fulfilling a promise, but one that they could barely afford. Getting me away from the covert relationship with Titus must have given them an added incentive.

'Come Lily, get ready. We are going to Seremban. My friend has told me of a palm reader who is supposed to be very good. I have made an appointment for you with him.'

My family still had their doubts about my future and every avenue was being explored to break any future ties with Titus. I too was intrigued to learn anything about my future. Would Dad accept Titus if the stars foretold that he should do so?

'Your daughter has a great future overseas but you must not interfere in her future plans. She will make the right choices that will make for a bright future. I will go so far as to say that you don't have to worry about her at all. She will shine.'

Dad appeared satisfied with the man's predictions but I came away with mixed feelings. The old man had implied that my future lay overseas and that was not a part of my present plans. Where was Titus in all this? But at least Mum's fears seemed temporarily allayed by the palm reader's words and now she would even conduct a monosyllabic dialogue with me that I was grateful to accept.

Fears for my family's future safety meant that the excitement I felt at my impending departure was somewhat subdued. My younger cousin Josephine, Uncle James's only daughter, was anxious about our forthcoming separation and spent a couple of nights in Sentul. After dinner I walked up the path towards the rusty, squeaky front gate that had seen me grow up within its protection. Soon I would be walking out through it into the unknown. I linked arms with my sombre cousin. The sky was full of twinkling stars and the moon was silhouetted against it, shining brightly and deepening the shadows cast by the trees whilst lighting up the path along which we trod. Glow-worms glinted with a greenish hue amongst the hibiscus bushes. There was certain stillness in the balmy air, as though it was holding its breath – perhaps eavesdropping on the musings of two young girls as they discussed their dreams and aspirations. The air smelt fresh, as though nature was renewing its energy to cope with the commotion of the following day.

Josephine spoke first. 'You are so lucky, *akka*, to be going to England. Promise me you will write. You won't forget us, will you?'

I pressed her arm into my side. 'Of course not! I will be expecting replies from you, too. I will be lonely and will look forward to letters from home.'

I sensed her smile in the dark as she nodded her head. 'You might stay there and marry a white boy, eh?'

I ducked as a flutter of wings swiped past us: probably a bat I thought. Fruit bats often swooped through the grounds at great speed at night in their quest for food. They detached themselves from the nearby coconut trees, where they chewed on the palm fronds to construct simple shelters and, hanging upside-down, slept throughout the day.

I had a quick answer for my anxious cousin. 'Not me, I will be back after the three years of training.'

I was unaware of what fate had in store for me; as far as I knew I was leaving my heart behind and needed to collect it later. I hoped that three years was sufficient time for the two families to accept that Titus and I were serious about each other and that they would support us in our plans for the future. The alternative was too painful to contemplate.

A visit to the hair salon began the process of my Anglicisation. Twenty-two years of hair growth fell to the floor, snipped off with a few sickening flicks of the scissors. Thick black hair was piling up all around the chair in small hillocks.

'Would you like me to pack your hair for you?' asked the middle-aged Chinese hairdresser.

Her hopeful look indicated that she was banking on me saying no, so that she could turn my hair into a wig or hairpiece that she could sell to add to her profits. Having no personal use for my fallen mane, I shook my head, smiling as the lady's eyes lit up. Quick as a flash, the hair was secreted away into a brown paper bag and deposited out of reach on top of some wooden shelves.

'Is that okay for length?' asked the hairdresser, pointing to a mark on her whalebone comb. I nodded dumbly. A feeling of dread crept in as she shaped the layers; I was being transformed into a young man, apart from the soft curls that bounced on top of my head, reminiscent of my mother's natural waves. I walked home in silence. Mum's greeting was typically non-committal. 'Oh, you have had a lot taken off your hair, haven't you?'

Dad's reaction was a total contrast. As he walked into the sitting room after the day's work his smile froze when his gaze settled on my head.

'Who is that boy sitting in our front room?' he demanded.

He was furious that his little girl's appearance had been so drastically changed and he ignored me for a whole week. I felt more and more depressed as the week passed by. I grew even more impatient for my departure.

Dad's antagonism towards Titus was justified and I was well aware of that, but rational thoughts did not help. Although I was about to fulfil one of Dad's ambitions for me, it was partly because of the bleak situation at home that I was running away, and Dad could not forgive Titus for that. His beloved daughter was leaving and it was breaking his heart. Titus's reaction to my new haircut was in complete contrast; he thought that I looked cute and very young. But his encouraging words were totally eclipsed by my Dad's reaction.

A stream of well-wishers, including all my aunts and uncles, arrived to say good luck. Envelopes of ringgits were pushed into my hands. They marvelled at my bravery. Aunty Arul was particularly proud of her niece.

'I always knew Lily was the brains of the family. I have no doubt that she will pass all her exams.' She patted me affectionately on the head.

To them, I was an anomaly, a young girl of marriageable age setting off to an unknown foreign land on her own.

'It takes guts, girl, and you have plenty of that. Just don't forget to come home, eh Lily?' she said, pressing a ten ringgit note into the palm of my hand and curling my fingers around it. Then Aunty Arul planted kisses on both my cheeks as tears stung them.

England was eight thousand miles away from Malaysia. Most people perceived the country as having an air of mystery and prestige, a romanticised view that was confirmed by the fact that most ordinary folk would never be able to go there. The mastery exhibited by the English race was legendary.

Titus had accepted the inevitable. 'You won't forget me, will you? There will be hordes of white guys who will want to take you out. I am really torn. I know that if you stay on here our families will make our lives a misery, so I know you have to go.'

'Look, I promise I will come back home with qualifications that will provide me with a good job. We need that to convince our families that we can survive financially. Your mother might be persuaded to accept a well-educated girl who will also be bringing in a good wage to help the family.'

I drew his left hand forward and placed a gold ring on his finger. I had spent an afternoon at the jewellery shops in Foch Avenue selecting the ring, and parted with a few dollars more to have it engraved with the initial L.

'Here, this is for you to remember me by.'

At first he refused to accept it.

'I cannot take this. This must have cost you a lot of money. Besides, I haven't got anything of value for you, just this cheap bracelet.'

I was thrilled to receive the chrome bracelet though. The embossed, intertwined hearts were symbolic. We said our tearful farewells with promises of frequent letters.

'I will write to you first and give you an address to reply to. It will be my friend's address; I know I can trust her. I have already asked her permission and she is willing to pass on your letters to me.'

My tears flowed freely. How thoughtful of Titus; he had thought of everything. I packed my dreams and my despair into my grey suitcase, A LILY stencilled in large white lettering across the lid. My bundle of letters from Titus, secured with a rubber band, was wrapped in the folds of a dress and hidden at the bottom of my case. I said loudly, for all to hear, that I would pack my own case, that I did not need any help. When Irene stuck her nose in excitedly, I placed my hand protectively over the folded dresses. In the folds of my canary yellow one with a white border, especially sewn for the trip, nestled the precious bundle. My heart thumped guiltily every time someone made a move towards my suitcase. I took the precaution of keeping it locked, the key safely hidden in my purse, and did not let it out of my sight.

The heavens opened on the day of my departure. The rain was so heavy that it caused flooding, raising concerns as to whether we would reach the airport on time. Some roads were completely closed. We did make it in time, however, and the rains ceased. It was a Saturday and Titus was working a shift at the Turf Club. He had begged Charlie to pick him up from the club and give him a ride to the airport. 'I will try my best Li, but you know your brother. I am sure he won't bother to turn up. If I am not there I hope you will understand.' He was heartbroken. I nodded in acknowledgement. Fate was dealing us a very tough hand and we were powerless to do anything about it. My immediate family and some close friends, including Geraldine, braved the weather and the floods to wave goodbye. I scanned the milling crowd, vainly hoping that Titus would somehow manage to come.

Mum caught my anxious look; her face was set into grim lines. I had never before experienced a fall-out like this with my Mum. On the contrary, there had always been a closeness between us that none of my other sisters had; we were like yin and yang, good for one another. I had spent nearly all my life in her company. This was a major rift in our relationship. As far as she was concerned, I had gone against her wishes and foolishly listened to my heart instead of my head – the head that my parents had totally trusted. Mum's trust in me was broken irrevocably. I was paying dearly for those previous years of harmony. Up to the very last minute, Mum refused to talk to me, hug me or say goodbye. Her anger reached me in waves, stopping me in my tracks as I walked towards her. It was with a terribly heavy heart that I followed my friends Yoke Wah and Juliet Joseph to the waiting plane. Yoke Wah had been granted her wish to join me in England and she was lucky to have been allocated a place in the August intake too but Juliet was making her way to the Metropolitan Hospital in London.

The three of us left Malaysia for England on 30th August 1969. The emotional turmoil I had experienced had taken its toll. I was the skinniest I had ever been, my weight just tipping forty-one kilos. The hollows beneath my shoulders had deepened. My collarbones stood out. The passport photograph taken during that period shows a thin, elongated, barely recognisable face.

Titus and I had exchanged signed photographs; his was safely tucked into the sleeve of my diary. Finally a dream had come true, now that I was about to visit Europe and see places I had only read about. I was devastated at leaving my boyfriend behind and there was a deep sadness in me as I parted from my family. It was with mixed feelings that I waved goodbye from the tarmac and set foot in an aeroplane for the very first time. My life fitted into a square frame. The opposite sides both represented Malaysia, where I had spent the majority of my life so far; the lower frame was India and now the top end would be England. It held promises that I was eager to discover. Now I was actually flying to England, the island that I had been flying to in my dreams for the last twenty-two years.

Epilogue

We flew into Stansted airport and grouped together in the arrivals hall. I stepped timidly into my new life. The ache of missing my family made me weak; my legs almost refused to hold up my wasted body and I had to fight the urge to collapse on the ground and put my head down; perhaps I would wake up in Sentul. How on earth was I going to survive for three years? My throat throbbed with stress: I had lost my taste for adventure. Reality kicked in savagely as the unexpectedly cool air fanned the loneliness in my heart, raising goose pimples on my arms. Despite my melancholic state I was intrigued. Interspersed among the white faces were a number of black porters pushing trolleys laden with luggage – a new and unfamiliar race of people with tight, frizzy hair. 'Hey, these are the people Alka told me about.'

All three of us were enveloped in silence, lost in our own thoughts. The coach journey into Victoria Station began with promising green fields dotted with well-fattened black and white cows but this landscape soon gave way to grey façades of terraced buildings with concrete steps that led to shut doors, as we trundled along in the outskirts of London. My spirits dampened further. This journey was showing me a country that was a far cry from the breath-taking dreams back home. What had I done? Why did I leave the warmth and love of my family? I was trapped: I could not turn round and return home, as I did not possess the funds. My lips trembled; my family had invested all their hopes in me and I had burnt my bridges for the next few years.

Lewisham Hospital, a converted former poor house, looked equally daunting. As I entered the dining room, packed with groups of girls around Formica-topped tables, my eyes rounded with surprise; noting the sheer number of Malaysian girls. They reminded me of a regiment of army recruits in their mauve uniforms and starched white aprons; the stiff collars scratched their necks and the elaborate starched white caps nodded as the girls forked boiled vegetables and slices of meat coated in an unappetising muddy liquid into their mouths. Their Malaysian-ness seemed diluted and their foreignness increased. However, the din of Malaysian slang was balm to my aching heart. Inquisitive but friendly eyes peered at the latest Malaysian batch.

I hurried back to the nurses' home after my first day on a male surgical ward to pen a letter to my parents.

You will never guess what I had to do today. As the most junior nurse on the ward, I was on bedpan duties and not only was I expected to clean this bedridden old man's bottom, but had to carry the paper-covered stainless steel bedpan to the sluice and feed it into a bedpan washer. The smell was suffocating. It's not all bad though. I also administered my first injection today. There is a lot to learn but I'm ready for it.

Tears flowed freely as I double folded and licked the flaps of the pale blue aerogramme.

Nursing may not have been my career of choice, but I knuckled down to it.

Meanwhile, my relationship with Titus had come to an inevitable end, largely due to the continued opposition from both our families. They were unwilling to call a truce and both his mum and my dad had taken a firm stand. My first heartthrob and I came to a mutual understanding: but Titus made me promise that I would visit him when I returned to Malaysia after completing my training.

I met my future husband, Steve, at the hospital. He was filling in time as a porter. With his cheeky smile and ready wit he had both staff and patients eating out of his hands.

'You watch that porter, nurse, he has got his eye on you.'

Sure enough, his charms worked their magic and a few months after we began dating Steve became a bank employee and I felt settled enough to make my life in England: we married in 1973. Our wedding day was blessed with the presence of my wonderful Dad and my beloved brother Peter. I desperately missed my dear mother's presence.

After Steve and I became parents to daughters Rowena and Sarah, we made excited preparations for my return to Malaysia in 1980. My heart was in my mouth as I felt the wheels of the plane drop in preparation for landing. A forest of palm trees swayed on the edge of the runway. A sea of hands waved as we walked across the tarmac of the old Subang airport. Excitement buzzed all around as I recognised my siblings with their grown-up children and the many new additions to the family.

After eleven years' absence I was welcomed back into the bosom of Sentul Palace. Our imposing gate had disappeared, as had the impenetrable, fragrant bougainvillea hedges. The internal structure of the house had gone through a complete metamorphosis. Some welcome additions included an indoor bathroom with a squatting toilet and running taps. Electric light bulbs replaced the old kerosene oil lantern and lamps. But that familiar stink from the open drain curled into the sitting room, I was back home.

Enterprising Mum was now managing a general provisions shop. It faced the spot where our rusty old gate had once stood, occupying the first of the three terraced properties that had welcomed us back after our stay in India, and where my first love had been enacted. The bedroom façade had been opened up. The old well now filled in, had become the frontage of the shop. Glass-fronted fridge shelves were lined with cool bottles of Tiger Beer and a variety of fizzy drinks. The shop replaced the services of the long gone Kakka shop. Mum's familiar good morning towel was draped across her bosom and her serene smile filled my heart to bursting.

I fulfilled my promise when Steve and I visited the now happily married Titus. Titus had not changed a great deal and I was remarkably at ease. He was perched on the stool next to his pretty wife whilst we occupied the comfy visitors chairs. Titus's wife and his resident parents were taken with our girls and we parted amicably after exchanging news about our families and how long were we going to be around and when were we planning on a return trip.

I may have made England my home, but my adult life is peppered with childhood doctrines and traditions. Dad's post-meal family anecdotes still flow at our English dinner table.

'Mum, I love your stories, but I need you to write them down in black and white. They will be forgotten and the next generation will be none the wiser'.

'I am no writer, Rowena. How could I manage such an enormous task?'

My older daughter's remark winged me back to memories of my introverted, nine-year-old self, scribbling the start of numerous stories into my exercise book. Every adventure had been set in the land of my dreams, elusive, magical and seemingly unattainable England.

Two years after retiring from nursing I started tapping away on my laptop. Trapped memories spilled from tightly shut drawers at a rapid pace. It became apparent that I had packed a lot into those first twenty-two years. This book has become a labour of love.

I continue to live and enjoy my life in the land of my dreams. My sister's predictions had materialised. I became 'The *Vellakarachi*' 'The English Girl' who married for love and living in the land of my childhood dreams but a special part of me will forever be with my roots in the East.

Acknowledgements

The first seed sown of the idea to record my childhood in an era that will soon be forgotten was a suggestion from my daughter Rowena. Thank you Row, you have encouraged me all the way, giving me confidence in my ability in what has proved to be an enjoyable undertaking. My younger daughter Sarah was always in the background, providing me with endless cups of tea and snacks.

'How are you getting on with your book Mum? Nearly finished?'

When I replied that I hadn't, she would always say 'Don't worry, Mum. You will do it!'

I must acknowledge, too, how much my nursing career has enriched my life. Initially, I had doubts about my suitability to the job; I wondered whether I would ever be able to complete my training. I was a little girl lost, totally unprepared for the challenges and demands of the job, but that is exactly what built my self-confidence and self-assurance when I found that I could overcome them successfully. I came into contact with so many wonderful, inspiring people whom I held in great admiration. They shaped my life. From a naïve little student nurse in 1969, I retired in 2006 as a woman in a position of great responsibility, confident in my own abilities and able to pass on the knowledge that I had acquired to others less experienced than myself. Thank you, nursing profession: I owe you a huge amount.

My life has been made richer from knowing some wonderful friends. Emma Smith and Grace Palmer as a valuable friends who gave feedback and encouragement throughout, Paul and Mandy, Jim and Ann, Anne and Brendan, Dave and Dolly, Francis and Dave are some of our oldest friends, and there are so many other true, true friends, too numerous to mention by name. I am sure you know who you are. My siblings and my extended family, I thank you all for your faith and encouragement. A final thank you to my dear, devoted, wonderful husband Steve, my gorgeous daughters Rowena and Sarah, my son-in-law Mark, and my beautiful pride and joy, Madeleine, my precious granddaughter.

Bibliography

Malaysia: A Pictorial History 1400-2004 by Wendy Khadijah Moore, Archipelago Press Malaysia, 2004.

MAY 13. Declassified Documents on the Malaysian Riots of 1969 by Kua Kia Soong. SUARAM, 2011 New Edition, Malaysia.

Lightning Source UK Ltd.
Milton Keynes UK
UKOW03f2200200514

232030UK00001B/19/P